Succeeding in the

World of
Work

Succeeding in the
World of
Work

FIFTH EDITION

Grady Kimbrell
Educational Consultant
Santa Barbara, California

Ben S. Vineyard
Professor and Chairman Emeritus
Vocational and Technical Education
Pittsburg State University
Pittsburg, Kansas

GLENCOE
Macmillan/McGraw-Hill

New York, New York   Columbus, Ohio   Mission Hills, California   Peoria, Illinois

Teacher Reviewers and Consultants

Rita J. Britton
Marketing Education Co-op Coordinator
Northern High School
Detroit School District
Detroit, Michigan

Julia G. Ciarrocchi
Economics/Business Education Teacher
Laurel Highlands High School
Laurel Highlands School District
Uniontown, Pennsylvania

Jerry Wayne Harris
Co-operative Education Coordinator
Antioch Comprehensive High School
Metropolitan Nashville Public Schools
Antioch, Tennessee

Richard Howell
Diversified Occupations and
   Vocational Coordinator
Kelso High School
Kelso District 458
Kelso, Washington

Gary King
Southwestern College
Winfield, Kansas

Charlotte B. Little
Educational Consultant
Howard County Public Schools
Ellicott City, Maryland

Kenneth C. Munro
Industrial Cooperative
   Training Coordinator
Kokomo Area Career Center
Kokomo-Center Township Consolidated
   School Corporation
Kokomo, Indiana

Michael Wade Perry
Work Experience Coordinator
Southwest Miami High School
Dade County School District
Miami, Florida

David C. Ralston
Cooperative Education Coordinator
Smyrna High School
Rutherford County School District
Smyrna, Tennessee

Jack Sanders
Teacher/Coordinator,
   Industrial Cooperative Training
Seventy-First Senior High School
Fayetteville, North Carolina

Jane McEllhiney Stein
Educational Consultant
Soldotna, Alaska

Send all inquires to:
Glencoe/McGraw-Hill
15319 Chatsworth Street
P.O. Box 9609
Mission Hills, CA 91346-9609

ISBN 0-02-675582-3 (Student Text)
SBN 0-02-675583-1 (Teacher's Wraparound Edition)

7 8 9 10 11 12   AGH   99 98 97 96 95 94

About the Authors

Grady Kimbrell, nationally recognized author and consultant on career education, began his career in education teaching high school business in Kansas. After moving to California, Kimbrell taught business courses and coordinated students' in-class activities with their on-the-job experience. He later directed the work experience programs in three high schools in Santa Barbara, California.

Kimbrell has assisted school districts with a wide variety of research and evaluation activities. His research into on-the-job work activities led to the development of a career interest inventory now used in career guidance. In addition, he has served on numerous state instructional program committees and writing teams, designed educational computer programs, and produced educational films.

Kimbrell has degrees in business administration, educational psychology, and business education.

A nationally recognized author, vocational educator, and consultant, **Ben Vineyard** began his career in education teaching vocational technology shop in Mt. Vernon, Illinois. He later joined the faculty of Southern Illinois University where he taught industrial education courses, served as an academic advisor, and supervised work experience students.

After accepting a position at Pittsburg State University in Kansas, Vineyard directed the Kansas Vocational-Industrial Teacher Education Program and served as department chair. He also directed state and national research programs, developed curriculum materials for career and cooperative education programs, and served as a consultant for Kansas teachers and administrators.

Vineyard is a graduate of the Army Air Force Technical School. He holds a baccalaureate and a master's degree in industrial education and a doctorate in vocational education and industrial sociology.

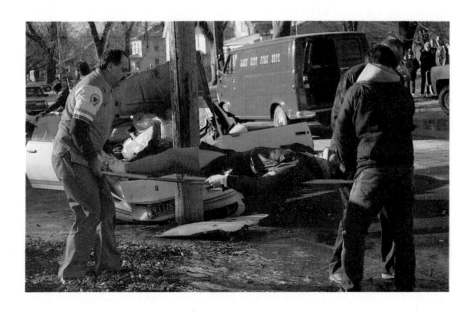

Welcome to
SUCCEEDING IN THE WORLD OF WORK

What do you want to do with your life? What do you *dream* of doing? What are you good at? What do you enjoy? Answering these questions is what this book is all about.

You may not know it, but you began your career search a long time ago. That's right! Think back to your earliest years, and see those things you surrounded yourself with. Perhaps you liked books—you read them, collected them, and wondered how they were put together. Perhaps mechanical things fascinated you, and you were forever taking them apart and putting them back together. You may have liked to spend time outside and enjoyed the changing seasons. You might have enjoyed cooking, helping around the house, or caring for children.

If you really think about it, there are probably one, two, or several things you have enjoyed throughout your life—things that made the time fly and made you feel good about yourself. Today, your challenge is to convert the things that make you happiest into a satisfying career. This book will help you do just that.

You will first take a look at your life-style—that is, the way you live—and the effect that your career will have on it. If you love the outdoors, for example, you may not like an office job. If you would rather deal with things instead of people, you may like working with computers more than you would like selling clothing.

You will then spend some time looking at your goals, values, skills, and aptitudes, or knacks for learning certain things. Once you discover how all of these things relate, you will explore 12 career interest areas and the skills you need to work in each.

From there, you'll plan for career success. You will look at the type of education you will need; how to find, apply, and interview for a job; and how to cope on the job. For those of you who think about opening a business or taking over the family firm, you will look at the rewards and risks of entrepreneurship.

Finally, you'll get a good overview of what you can expect once you're working and living on your own. You'll learn how to manage your money, make wise consumer purchases, and meet your adult responsibilities.

Throughout this course, you'll be getting to know the person you should know best—you! Get set, then, for one of the most exciting adventures of your life. Here are some things in the *Succeeding in the World of Work* program that will help you on your way.

Your Student Text

You'll enjoy reading *Succeeding in the World of Work*. The text gives you realistic examples to help you understand new concepts. Many of the features and activities will help you develop your skills and sharpen your ability to make decisions and solve problems. Several "extras" have been incorporated into the text to help you learn.

Unit Opening Pages   Each of the five units begins with a two-page unit opener that lists the chapters included in each unit. An inviting photo illustrates a major concept in the unit.

Chapter Opener   Each chapter begins with a page that prepares you for the terms and concepts you'll find in the chapter.

- An **opening color photo** shows a major concept in the chapter.
- The **Objectives** list the skills and knowledge you can expect to have mastered once you have completed the chapter.
- An **introduction** tells you what you will learn in the chapter.
- The **Terms to Know** list shows the words in boldface you will find throughout the chapter.

Illustrations with Teaching Captions   You'll enjoy looking at the full-color photographs and illustrations throughout the text. As you do, spend some time imagining yourself in the many situations pictured. Try answering all of the questions posed in the captions, too. They'll help you remember chapter material and relate it to your own life.

End-of-Chapter Activities   The end-of-chapter activities, called ''Review Your Learning,'' will help you review and remember chapter content.

- The **Chapter Summary** summarizes the major points covered in the chapter.
- The **Terms to Know** section relists the Terms to Know from the chapter's opening page and asks you to do an activity with the chapter vocabulary.
- The **Study Questions** will help you remember chapter content.
- The **Critical Thinking** questions will help you sharpen your reasoning and judgment skills.
- The questions entitled **Discussion Starters** are for class discussion.
- The section entitled **Building Basic Skills** helps you improve your skills in Mathematics, Communication, Human Relations, Citizenship, Computer Literacy, Leadership, Problem Solving, and Decision Making.
- With the **Suggested Activities** you will apply chapter concepts to real-life situations.

Additional Text Features

Several text features will get you thinking about situations you will encounter in the world of work.

Case Studies   Each case study, color-screened in mauve, gives you a real-life application of the chapter content. One to four case studies, each running from a quarter to a half page, appear in each chapter.

Situation/Solution   Color-screened in light blue, each quarter- to half-page Situation/Solution feature presents a hypothetical situation you might encounter in the work world. It then poses some critical thinking questions to get you thinking about how you would deal with the situation.

Make a Decision   These features are color-screened in lavender; there are one or two in each chapter. They will have you making decisions on such wide-ranging content-related themes as how you would spend an inheritance to enhance your life-style, to whether you would take a lower-paying job to get more job satisfaction.

There are no right or wrong answers. Rather, how you arrive at your decisions are the important aspects of these features. They show you that a decision-making strategy, such as the one presented on pages 13–14 of the text, can help you make the best decisions possible.

Strive for Success   These personality profiles, color-screened in light teal, run one full page per chapter. Each features someone who has achieved in an unusual career, works in a nontraditional career for his or her gender, or who has achieved despite great personal odds such as a handicap. These features will help you see that achievement in any area is possible when there is desire and initiative.

Checking Up   These short features, color-screened in tan, come at the end of each lesson. They contain three questions you can use to help you remember the material you just read.

Glossary and Index   Both the Glossary and Index are easy to understand and use. The Glossary contains nearly 200 defined terms. Following each definition in parentheses is the number of the page on which the term is explained. All key terms included in the lists at the beginning and end of each chapter are defined in the Glossary. When reading this text, if you encounter a word you've seen before but whose meaning you can't remember, check the Glossary and page reference for further explanation. The Index lists key terms and concepts along with important graphs, charts, and other illustrations relating to the chapter content.

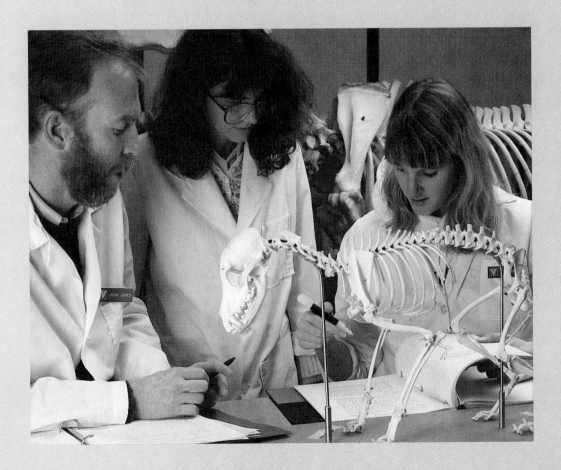

Succeeding in the
World of
Work

UNIT
One

Planning Your Future

CHAPTERS

The World of Work: Choices and Challenges

OBJECTIVES

After studying this chapter and doing the activities, you will be able to:

- discuss how your career will affect your overall life-style;
- describe how women's place in the working world has changed since the 1950s;
- explain why people work, other than for money; and
- use a strategy for making career decisions.

TERMS TO KNOW

work
job
career
life-style
identity
esteem
self-realization

*W*hen you were growing up, did you ever pretend that you were an astronaut? Did you ever think about being a movie star or a truck driver or a doctor? Most of us have daydreams in which we look and act like a real-life hero or a character in a favorite TV show. While our daydreams may not have been realistic, they started us thinking about the world of work.

Your place in the world of work will influence every aspect of your life. Your job will also probably be the main activity in your life. This is why choosing the kind of work you will do is one of the most important decisions you will ever make.

In this chapter you will learn about work—why it is important and how it affects your life. You will also learn about the decision-making skills that everyone needs to choose a satisfying career.

1 Life-styles and Careers

A survey put this question to high school seniors: "Soon you'll be graduating. Each of you will be going in a different direction, making your own life. What, more than anything else, do you want out of life?" Do you know how you would have answered that question? Here are some answers the survey takers received:

- "To be able to travel and live wherever I want."
- "To make a better life for me and my family than my parents had."
- "To become rich and famous."
- "Just to enjoy life, wherever I am."

Although their answers differed, most of the seniors surveyed shared a common idea about the future. They all wanted, each in his or her own way, a happy, satisfying life-style.

You've probably heard the word *life-style* many times. Have you ever thought about what it means? Do you have any idea what it has to do with the world of work?

Before you can answer these questions, you must be able to use a few key terms correctly. These terms include *job, work,* and *career.* They are terms that are often confused—that is, one term is used when another is meant.

For most people, for example, *work* means having a job and getting paid for doing it. In this text, however, we will define **work** as any productive activity that results in something useful. People who do work are usually paid for it—but not always.

To a working person, *job* may mean one particular task. Usually, though, people use the word **job** to mean the collection of tasks or duties that a person does to earn a living. This is what we mean when we talk about jobs such as truck driver, housekeeper, and teacher.

The work a person does over a period of years is known as a **career.** Most people have many different jobs in their careers. We usually think of a career as a sequence of jobs in the same field of work.

Work, job, and career are all part of our life-style. In simple terms, **life-style** is the way we live. It includes where we live, the kind of food we eat, the way we spend our free time, and what we do to support ourselves.

In sum, a life-style is something we each create for ourselves by the way we choose to use our time and resources. This means, of course, that each person's life-style is unique.

Life-style Patterns

If you were to try to diagram your life-style including all of its different elements, the result might look something like Figure 1-1. The pattern of people, places, and activities would be very complex. It would be hard for you to describe in words, let alone discuss or evaluate.

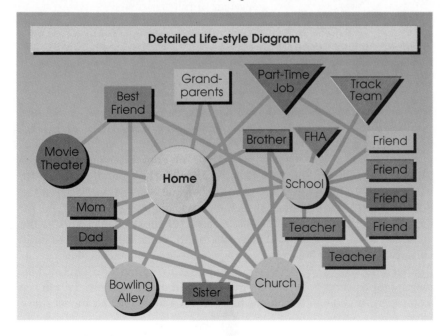

Detailed Life-style Diagram

Figure 1-1 This life-style diagram details all the significant relationships in a particular high school student's life. Which relationships are most important? How do you know?

Simplified Life-Style Diagram

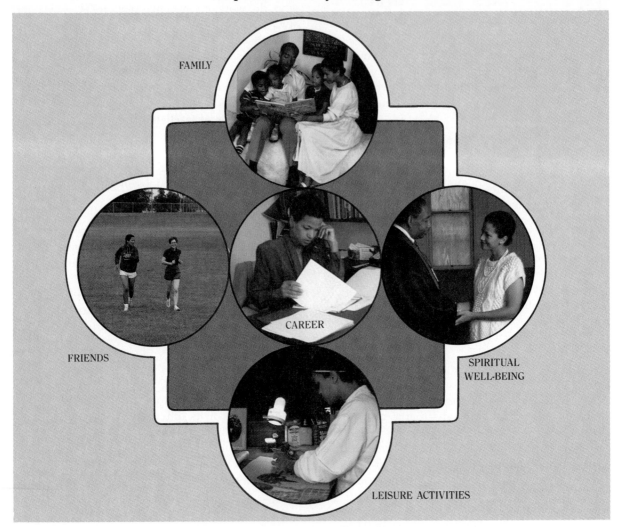

FAMILY

FRIENDS

CAREER

SPIRITUAL
WELL-BEING

LEISURE ACTIVITIES

Figure 1-2   This diagram offers a clearer, simpler way to describe an individual's life-style. Is there any person, place, or activity shown in Figure 1-1 that would not fall within one of the diagram's five principal categories? Explain.

To use this text effectively, however, you must be able to discuss and evaluate your life-style—the one you have now and the one you want in the future. To make this possible, you will need another, simpler way to depict the pattern of your life. The method shown in Figure 1-2 will help. It groups the various aspects of your life into five major categories—family, friends, career, leisure, and spiritual well-being.

Notice that each circle in the life-style diagram is the same size. This particular pattern depicts a life-style in which each of the five categories is of equal importance. In reality, of course, most people consider certain parts of their lives more impor-

tant than others. In cases like these, a diagram would show circles of various sizes, as in Figure 1-3.

Each major part of your life-style affects the others. This is particularly true of your work. Perhaps you noticed that career was placed at the center of each life-style diagram. This was done for a very good reason: for most people work *is* the central activity around which they plan their daily lives.

Are you beginning to understand what a life-style pattern is? Even more important, do you see the connection between life-style and the world of work?

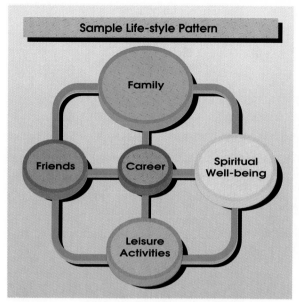

Sample Life-style Pattern

Figure 1-3 This diagram shows the life-style pattern of someone for whom family is most important. How would the diagram look if this person's job came first in his or her life?

Other things will help make up your total identity, but you will be known mainly by the work you do. Your work becomes your identity. We don't say, "Jim works as a teacher." We say, "Jim *is* a teacher." Sara doesn't work as a plumber. She *is* a plumber. Even the work you *plan* to do is used to identify you. For example, college students are sometimes identified as pre-law or pre-med students because they plan to work as lawyers or doctors.

As you start turning your dreams into reality, keep in mind the impact that your work will have on your overall life-style. The work you do to earn a living will probably

- determine your circle of friends,
- determine how much time you'll have to spend with your family,
- determine your standard of living (as a result of how much you earn from your job), and
- influence your political views.

Your Work—Your Identity

Your life-style is determined mainly by your role as a student. Being a student is probably the main activity in your life. Your **identity**—the personal quality or activity by which you are best known—is that of a student. When you are introduced to another person, you may be asked, "Where do you go to school?" or "What grade are you in?"

As an adult, you will have a new identity. It will be determined by the kind of work you do to earn a living. When you are introduced to another person, you may be asked, "What do you do?" or "Where do you work?"

MAKE A DECISION

Suppose you just inherited $250,000 from a rich uncle whom you never met. In your uncle's will, he suggested that you use the money to make your life-style happier and more satisfying. Think about the ways in which you could use the money. What's your decision—how will you spend your inheritance to improve your life-style? Give the reasons for your decision.

Case Study 1

Neil was a mechanic in the service department of a Chevrolet dealership. While he worked in the service department, Neil became close friends with several of the other mechanics. He joined the company bowling team because George, another mechanic, was on the team. Since Neil was single and had no family, he spent most of his free time with his buddies in the service department.

Neil was not as interested in repairing cars as he was in selling them. As soon as he got the chance, he moved out to the showroom as one of the dealership's regular salespeople. He made friends with the salespeople quickly. Before long he was spending most of his time away from work with two or three of them. He still talked to his old friends in the service department when he got the chance. However, there just didn't seem to be enough time. Neil even gave up his bowling nights so that he could work out with his new friends at the health club he joined.

Your job, as your main daily activity, will probably determine your identity. What does their identity as young professionals suggest about the life-style of the people shown here?

It follows that other people, just by knowing the kind of work you do, will be able to guess a great deal about you. They'll probably know who some of your friends are, where you live, where you work, how much you earn, how much education you have, and how you spend your leisure time.

Women in the Workplace

How long will your work have such a powerful impact on your overall life-style? Consider this: after completion of high school, you can expect to live for another 50 to 60 years. The average man entering the labor market today will work for 40 years. This hasn't changed much since the turn of the century. What has changed, though, is the amount of time women spend working outside the home.

During World War II, many women went to work in America's factories to replace men who had gone overseas to fight. These women proved themselves capable workers, but most gave up their factory jobs and resumed their roles as homemakers after the war.

Throughout the 1950s, men outnumbered women in the work force, but several factors combined to change that. For one, the cost of living (especially housing) began rising sharply. By the mid-1970s, many families needed two incomes just to support a comfortable life-style.

Another factor promoting change was the feminist movement. As women entered the work force for economic reasons, they often found their possibilities limited. Many wanted and needed jobs that paid well. The best-paying positions, however, especially in management and the professions, were traditionally filled by men. Jobs traditionally filled by women—such as nursing, teaching, and secretarial work—were poorly paid by comparison. Feminism made people more aware of this kind of discrimination.

With the help of such legislation as the Equal Employment Opportunity Act (which you will read about in Chapter 6), women soon began to gain access to largely male fields. As their prospects improved, record numbers of women began to pursue education and training leading to full-time careers. With overt prejudice against them declining, women have become more visible in higher-level positions in both government and private industry.

Today half of all U.S. workers are women, and they continue to enter the paid work force at a rate of 1.5 million a year. If current trends continue, women can expect to pursue careers for as long as men.

Case Study 2

Phillip and Kathy met at work. She was a secretary, and he was a salesman. They dated for a year and then decided to get married.

Phillip had a good income, but it was hardly enough to cover all their expenses. They decided that Kathy should continue working so they could afford a nice apartment and car. With Kathy working, they were also able to save some money each month toward a down payment on a house.

A month before their first child was born, Kathy quit her job. She did not begin working again until after their second child was in the first grade. By then the family had moved to another city, and Kathy had found a part-time job as a secretary at the local high school. She had also begun taking night classes in data processing.

Soon Kathy was offered a full-time job as a computer operator with a large insurance firm. Through the years, she changed jobs two more times to accept better positions. She continued to work until her son had completed two years of college, moved to his own apartment, and begun his first full-time job. At this point Kathy decided to quit her job and go to school full time. In a few years, she hopes to begin a new career —as a computer programmer/analyst.

Why People Work

You probably have a good idea about why most people work—to earn money, right? However, many people with more money than they could ever spend continue to work. Why? To understand, it will help to look briefly at the ideas of a famous psychologist.

Dr. A. H. Maslow studied the basic needs of human beings. He categorized these needs and arranged them in five levels (Figure 1-4). According to Maslow's theories, each level of needs had to be satisfied for the next level to become important.

Survival and Safety Needs   Maslow's list begins with the most basic needs—the needs for food, water, and good health. These are survival needs. We all must satisfy these needs if we are to continue living.

After our survival needs are met, we become concerned about safety. We need protection from physical danger. We need to know that we are safe at home, at work, and wherever we travel.

How do we satisfy our survival and safety needs? Most of us satisfy these needs by working. We work to earn money so that we can buy food, clothing, and shelter. Many people must work long and hard for the money they need to buy groceries and pay bills that come due regularly. For millions of people this is the main purpose of work—to earn enough money for survival and safety needs.

Of course, if you are like most people, you will want more money than you need to buy just the essentials. You will also want to buy some of the

Women are increasingly entering fields that used to be thought of as exclusively male. Name three such fields not specifically mentioned in your text.

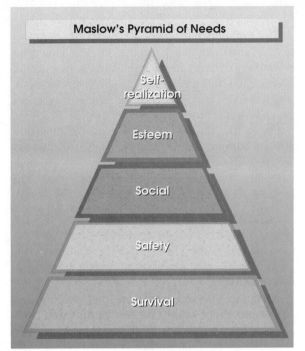

Maslow's Pyramid of Needs

Self-realization

Esteem

Social

Safety

Survival

Figure 1-4 According to Maslow, all human beings have certain needs, ranging from basic survival to the ultimate need, self-realization. How can a career satisfy all of these needs?

extras that make life enjoyable—vacations, automobiles, movie tickets. The more extras you want, the more money you will need to earn.

Social Needs After our safety needs are met, we look for companionship and affection. Sometimes this need is called a "sense of belonging." It means that someone cares about us, that we've been accepted by people we respect.

Our social needs are often met by our family and close friends. Companionship and meeting people may seem like strange reasons for working, but isn't social contact one of the things you enjoy most about going to school? You probably like to be with other people. Work, like school, gives you a chance to meet and be with people.

The people you spend your workday with will be important in your life. You will socialize with them on the job and sometimes after hours. Thus, your place of work will be a source of social contacts and possibly one or two close friends.

Esteem Needs After social needs are met, we seek **esteem**—both self-esteem and esteem from others. What is esteem? It is your worth or value as

seen by others. Self-esteem is your worth or value as seen by you. It is the credit you give yourself for being a good, worthwhile person.

The esteem that others feel for you determines how they will treat you. When others hold you in high esteem, it bolsters your self-esteem. This self-esteem is a special feeling, rather like the one you get when the team you're on wins a game. Self-esteem doesn't come and go, though, like the feeling you get with games won and lost. Self-esteem stays with you as long as you feel good about yourself.

Case Study 3

In 1985 Buddy Ebsen was added to ABC's weekly "Matt Houston" series. Ebsen, who was 76 years old at the time, had been in show business most of his life. He had appeared in dozens of movies and starred in two long-running television series, "The Beverly Hillbillies" and "Barnaby Jones."

As a result of his acting success, Ebsen was financially secure. It wasn't necessary for him ever to work again. Why, then, did he return to the daily grind of a weekly TV series? "I'm used to getting up at dawn and going to the studio to be with my pals on the set," he explained. "It's my life-style, and I wouldn't trade it for any other."

Self-esteem is an important reason for working. If you do your work well, others respect you for it. When this happens, you feel proud and respect yourself. For most people the chief source of both esteem from others and self-esteem is success in the world of work.

Self-realization Needs According to Maslow, **self-realization** is the highest level of needs you are capable of reaching. If you reach all the important goals in your life, you will have achieved self-realization. Very few people ever reach this level. Of those who do, however, more than 90 percent credit their career as being responsible. It is through their work that they achieve self-realization.

Strive for Success

Hail to the Chief

American history is filled with stories of police officers that use such phrases as "the boys in blue" or "the man behind the badge." The introduction of women into law enforcement has done away with these clichés. In fact, if you were to walk into the police chief's office in Houston, Texas, you would find that "the man behind the badge" is a woman.

When she was named police chief in 1990, Elizabeth M. Watson became the first woman to head the police force of one of the nation's 20 largest cities. When you consider that only 20 years earlier there were not even any female patrol officers, Watson's achievement is all the more remarkable. In 1970, according to Dr. Susan Martin, who has studied the role of women in police work for the Police Foundation of New York, "Women were limited to working with women, children, and typewriters."

In 1971, however, the federal Equal Employment Opportunity Act made it illegal for governmental bodies or agencies (such as police departments) to discriminate in hiring on the basis of sex. It was this law that gave Watson the opportunity to become a police officer in 1972. In 1976 (on her wedding day), she was promoted from beat officer to detective and five years later, to lieutenant.

A female lieutenant was a milestone in 1981, but Watson didn't stop there. She moved on to become a captain in 1984—the first woman ever to hold that post in Houston. In 1987 she was named deputy chief and took over the West Side Command Station.

Watson comes from a family of police officers—her grandfather was a police officer, as were several uncles and cousins. Her husband, Robert, is also on the Houston police force.

Like all successful people, Watson places a high priority on doing her job well. She is also aware of her status as a trailblazer for women in

law enforcement. "I am deeply committed to policing," explains Watson. "If in the course of doing that I serve as a role model to other women, I am doubly honored."

Jobs can fulfill a whole range of needs. What needs are the people in each of these photographs working to supply?

When Someone Toots His Horn—at Your Expense

You have been co-workers with your friend Matt for several years. Often now when you see him on the job, however, you come away feeling bad. He seems to be going out of his way to put you down in front of your fellow employees. He belittles your suggestions and minimizes your accomplishments. He repeatedly brings up the few embarrassing moments you have had on the job.

Because it's all done with Matt's customary humor, you have a difficult time responding. You're afraid you might seem overly sensitive. Everyone else thinks Matt has a wonderful way with people—something he's very proud of and refers to frequently. Indeed, when you and he are together outside of work, he *is* fun to be with. The put-downs disappear, and he's the friend you used to know.

1. Your co-workers, who laugh when Matt makes his jokes at your expense, are probably not aware of how hurt you are. How should you respond to them?

2. You learn that in his most recent salary review, Matt was compared unfavorably to you and a number of other quieter and more diligent employees. How would you react to this information?

3. How do you plan to get through your difficulties with Matt? What personal resources can you draw on or develop?

✓ CHECKING UP

1. What is your life-style, and how is it affected by your choice of career?

2. Why has the number of women in the work force increased sharply since the 1950s?

3. In Maslow's pyramid of needs, survival needs are at the bottom. Does this mean they are least important? Explain.

2 Decision Making

You have seen that the work you do will

- influence every part of your life-style,
- provide your identity as a person,
- continue for most of your adult life, and
- help satisfy your basic human needs.

By now it should be obvious that your career choice is one of the most important decisions you will ever make. Not just a job, but your entire life-style for many years to come is at stake.

Knowing this, you would think that most people would choose their careers very carefully. It is estimated, however, that half of all employed people do *not* choose the jobs they want. Most people simply "fall" into one job or another, depending on what's available at the time they're looking. Some people get lucky, but many end up with careers—and life-styles—they don't really enjoy.

Why does this happen? There are two reasons. First, people often lack decision-making and planning skills. Second, even when they have the skills, they don't see the future as something to which those skills can be applied. People will spend a great deal of time making decisions about a six-week trip to Europe or even a single evening's entertainment. If they're driving from Chicago to Los Angeles, they'll look at a road map and call ahead for motel reservations. It just doesn't seem to occur to them that they can do much the same thing with their lives. As a result, half of all Americans are not very satisfied with their life-styles.

A Seven-Step Process

None of us remembers our earliest decisions in life. They may have been choices between orange juice and milk or who should rock us to sleep. We had only to cry to make our choices known.

As young children we made decisions about which games to play. As we grew older we began deciding which clothes to wear. Those were simple decisions, however. If we made bad choices, we probably didn't have too many regrets the next day.

When we began to spend money, our choices seemed more important. If we bought a sweater that didn't match our other clothes or a record that we didn't care for, we felt bad. We felt as though we had made a big mistake.

Decisions that will affect your life for many years should be made carefully and logically. The seven-step decision-making process shown in Figure 1-5 can help. It will increase your chances of making the right choice.

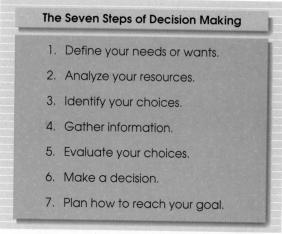

The Seven Steps of Decision Making

1. Define your needs or wants.
2. Analyze your resources.
3. Identify your choices.
4. Gather information.
5. Evaluate your choices.
6. Make a decision.
7. Plan how to reach your goal.

Figure 1-5 A systematic approach to decision making increases the likelihood that you will be satisfied with your eventual choice. Can you see why? Explain.

For example, suppose you wanted to buy a car. Here's how the process would work.

- *Step 1—Define your needs or wants.* That's simple: you *want* a car.
- *Step 2—Analyze your resources.* This means studying your finances to see how you'll pay for the car. If you'll need a loan, for example, you'll have to check financial institutions for the best interest rate and payment terms.
- *Step 3—Identify your choices.* To do this, you'll need to check all the available sources of cars. These might include new-car dealers, used-car dealers, and owner-advertised cars in the classified ads. The result will be a list of all the cars you can choose from.
- *Step 4—Gather information.* For each car on your list, you will need to know such things as cost, condition, insurance, and warranty.
- *Step 5—Evaluate your choices.* Review the information you have gathered to determine which factors are the most important to you. You might use a system of pluses and minuses to rate your choices.
- *Step 6—Make a decision.* Decide which car best meets your needs for the price you are willing to pay.

- *Step 7—Plan how to reach your goal.* Finalize your plans to buy the car. List all the things you need to do, such as arrange for a loan, inform the car dealer, and buy insurance. This kind of forethought will ensure that nothing keeps you from getting your car as quickly as possible.

You still make simple, routine decisions every day. In the months and years just ahead, however, you will be making some major decisions. Some, such as which car to buy, will affect you for several years. Others—such as whom you marry, whether or not to continue your education, and which career to choose—will affect you for your whole life.

Choosing a Career

The decision-making process is a little more complex when you choose a career. The steps are the same, but some will have several parts.

Your Needs and Wants   The first step is to define your future needs and wants. Where will you want to live? How much of your time will you want to spend at your job? Will you want to do much traveling, or will you prefer to stay close to home? How much money will you need?

These are just a few of the questions you'll need to answer in determining your needs and wants. How do you go about answering these questions?

A good place to begin is with your daydreams and your life-style goals. In Chapter 2 you will read about how you can use your dreams and goals to identify your future needs and wants.

Your Resources   The second step, analyzing your resources, involves much more than it did in the car-buying example. Your "resources" for choosing a career are the things that make you who you are. Such things as your values, interests, skills, and personality together make up your personal resources.

You can study your resources through observation, testing, and experience. A thorough study will provide a good understanding of yourself. In Chapter 2 you will also learn a great deal about how to study and analyze yourself.

Your Choices   The third step in the decision-making process is to identify your choices. In career decision making this means picking several careers that you think might fulfill your needs and wants. If you're like many teenagers, you are probably not sure what you want to do when you graduate from high school. You may not even know what sorts of careers there are to choose from.

This is why it's so important to spend some time exploring careers. The more careers you are aware of, the better your chances of finding one that's right for you. Reading the first part of Chapter 3 will increase your awareness of available careers.

Whether you're choosing a life-style or making a major consumer purchase, the decision-making process is the same. What step would you say the young people shown here have reached?

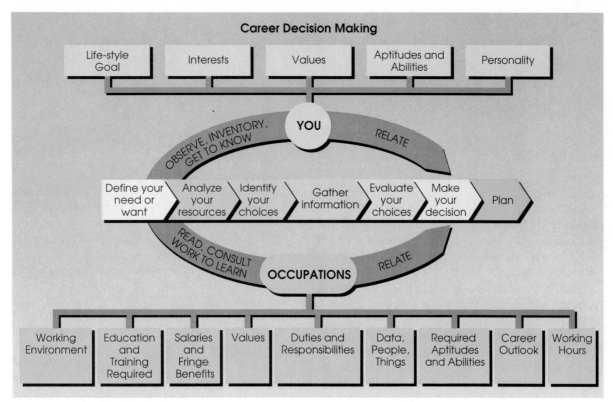

Career Decision Making

Figure 1-6 Over the next few chapters, you will be proceeding through the seven-step decision-making process, trying to choose a career for yourself. This diagram previews your course. What two general areas will you be exploring before you actually make a career decision and begin to plan for it?

Career Research After you have identified several interesting careers, you are ready for the fourth step in the decision-making process. In this step you will gather information on each possible career. You will need to find out about such things as job duties and responsibilities, work relationships, required skills, and much, much more. The last part of Chapter 3 explains how to go about doing your career research.

The Evaluation Process In the fifth step you will evaluate your career choices. At this point you will understand yourself, and you will have all the information you need about your chosen careers. You will now be able to match your values, interests, and skills with the career information you've gathered. This evaluation process should prepare you for making a decision. Chapter 4 has suggestions that will help you evaluate your choices.

Your Decision and Plan of Action In the last two steps of the decision-making process, you will actually make your career choice and plan

how to reach your career goal. You may change your goal several times, but it's still important to make a decision and plan. You need something to work toward while you are learning more about yourself and the world of work. If your decision becomes unrealistic or undesirable, you can repeat the decision-making process to arrive at a new goal. Chapter 4 will help you make a decision and a plan of action.

✓ CHECKING UP

1. What are the seven steps of the decision-making process?
2. When you are making a decision about a career, what sorts of things qualify as your wants and needs?
3. What is the difference between making a decision and planning (the last two steps of the decision-making process)?

1 *Review Your Learning*

CHAPTER SUMMARY

Like everyone else, you will want to live the life-style that will make you happy. Of all the things that will make up your life-style, your career will probably be the most important. As an adult you will probably be identified by the kind of work you do. Your work will determine, at least in part, your circle of friends, where you live, and how you spend your leisure time.

People work for several reasons. They work for money to pay for necessities such as food, clothing, and housing. They also work to satisfy their needs for social contact, esteem, and self-realization. In many families, both husband and wife must work to support their chosen life-style. Career opportunities for women are improving, even in traditionally male areas such as corporate management and the professions.

Your career choice is one of the most important decisions you will ever make. Using the seven-step decision-making process will increase your chances of making the right choice for you. The seven steps are (1) define your needs and wants, (2) analyze your resources, (3) identify your choices, (4) gather information, (5) evaluate your choices, (6) make a decision, and (7) plan how to reach your goal.

TERMS TO KNOW

On a separate sheet of paper, write a paragraph using all of the following terms:

career
esteem
identity
job
life-style
self-realization
work

STUDY QUESTIONS

1. What are the five major aspects of a person's life-style?
2. What are the five basic needs in Maslow's pyramid of needs?
3. What is the main reason most people work?
4. What is the identity of most teenagers? of most adults?
5. What is the difference between a job and a career?
6. Name four things that you can often guess about a person by knowing the kind of work he or she does.
7. How has the position of women in the workplace changed since World War II?
8. Why are half of all Americans not very well satisfied with their lives?
9. What is the first step in achieving a life-style that will be satisfying in 5, 10, or 20 years?
10. What are the seven steps in the decision-making process?

CRITICAL THINKING

1. In a few sentences, profile a person (real or fictional) who works mainly to meet each of the following needs:

   • Survival needs
   • Social needs
   • Esteem needs
   • Self-realization needs

2. Your Aunt Carol is making dinner reservations for your family at a fashionable local restaurant. When asked for a name, she responds, "Dr. Armstrong." You know she is a doctor (she has a Ph.D. in education), but she almost never uses the title. What concept that you learned about in this chapter is she

using to her advantage? Explain her probable reasoning.

3. Think of a decision you made recently. (It can even be a small decision, such as whether to go to a movie.) Thinking back, which of the steps in the decision-making process outlined in this chapter did you use, even without knowing it at the time? Would the outcome have been different if you had gone through more of the steps? What does this imply about the decision-making process?

DISCUSSION STARTERS

1. What would you put at the center of your life-style diagram now? How do you expect that to change over the next ten years?
2. Your brother has his own unique style of career planning. "I'm just going to try everything that comes along," he says, "until I find something I like." He is definitely not using the seven-step process introduced in this chapter, but is his method totally without merit? Why or why not?
3. How do you think the career you choose will affect the decisions you make about *political* issues? Why?
4. Think of an adult you know who really seems to enjoy his or her work. What basic needs do you think this person's job is filling in his or her life? Explain.

BUILDING BASIC SKILLS

Math

1. You believe your desired life-style will require a high-paying job. You've heard that auto mechanics make $23 an hour. How much is that per year if you work 40 hours a week for 50 weeks?

Decision Making

2. You have a choice of two jobs in your chosen field. One is a well-paid, high status position in a big industrial city. The other is a less well-paid position in a small town close to some high mountains with plenty of recreational possibilities. Which would you choose and why?

Communication

3. You are feeling unappreciated by one of the following:

   • Your parents
   • Your teammates
   • Your boss

   How would you let them know?

SUGGESTED ACTIVITIES

1. Pretend that the date is ten years from today. Describe, in 500 words or less, your life-style. Include the city and state where you are living. Also include descriptions of the following:

   • The area where you live
   • Both the outside and inside of the building in which you live
   • The person or persons who live with you
   • The car(s) and any other vehicles that you own

   Tell about your favorite leisure activities, your relationships with family and friends, and anything else that will be important to you ten years from now. Then describe the place where you work and the kind of work you do to provide this life-style.

2. Interview a woman who has been successful in a predominantly male field. In addition to questioning her about what she does and how she chose her career, ask specifically about any difficulties she may have encountered because of her gender. Present your findings to the class in an oral report.

Getting to Know Yourself

As you know from reading Chapter 1, a satisfying life-style depends greatly on a satisfying career. For that reason, you've probably decided not to be among the 50 percent who "fall" into a career. Instead, you will use the seven-step decision-making process to choose a career that's right for you. In doing this, you will take a big step toward controlling your own life-style.

Before you start exploring careers, get to know yourself a little better. You should have a good understanding of your own values, abilities, and personality. Then you can match yourself with a realistic, satisfying career. This chapter will help you get to know yourself better.

1 *Setting a Life-style Goal*

Your life-style goal is the way you see yourself living in the future. Thinking about your life-style goal is like daydreaming. This kind of daydreaming can tell you a great deal about yourself. As you read in Chapter 1, it can help you identify your strongest needs and wants.

Daydreaming how you want to live will help you decide certain things about your career goal. Will you want a comfortable life-style that requires a good income? Will you be satisfied with a simpler, less expensive life-style?

Some of your daydreams are probably pure fantasy, not likely ever to come true. A tall, heavy-set person dreams of becoming a professional jockey. An extremely awkward, uncoordinated person dreams of becoming a ballet dancer.

Many of your daydreams, though, are good indications of realistic life-style goals. A character in the play *South Pacific* sings, "You've got to have a dream. If you don't have a dream, how you gonna have a dream come true?" The point is that if you have no idea about where you want to go, how will you ever get there?

Many of your daydreams will give you clues about what sort of life-style you will want 5, 10, or 20 years from now, so start paying attention to your daydreams. When you realize that you've just dreamed about a life-style goal, get a pencil and paper. Write down the life-style that you've just imagined for yourself. Later, when you identify and research careers, you can look for careers that will make this life-style dream come true.

What Are Your Values?

The ideas, relationships, and other things that are important to you are your **values.** If you believe money is important, then money is one of your values. If your family and friends come first in your life, then you value them above all else.

While you were growing up, you probably shared most of your parents' values. For example, if your parents placed a great deal of importance on education, chances are you did, too. If their religion was very important to them, you most likely shared many of their religious beliefs.

As you got older, you began to question many of the values you grew up with. You may have hung onto the values that made sense to you and forgot about those that did not. You probably placed less emphasis on some and more emphasis on others. You may have even added some values of your own.

It is important to know what your values are when you make career decisions. For example, if you place a high value on helping others, you won't want a job that seems socially useless or harmful, no matter how big the salary. If spending time with your family is important to you, you won't want a career that requires a great deal of travel.

Ten general values are listed below. Think about which of these values are most important to you.

- *Fame.* Do you want a career that will make you famous? If you don't expect to be famous throughout the country, do you want at least to be well known in your state or town?

- *Money.* Is it important to you to earn a great deal of money?

- *Power.* Do you like having power over other people? Would you rather be a boss than someone who takes orders?

- *Religion.* Will your religion come before all other areas in your life-style? Will the demands of your job take second place to your religious activities?

- *Humanitarianism.* Is helping other people one of the most satisfying things you do? Will you insist on a career in which you do something for people and society?

- *Family.* Do you want to stay close to your family members? Would you turn down career opportunities that take you away from your family?

- *Health.* Is your physical and mental health more important than anything else? Must you work only in the most healthful environments?

- *Aesthetics.* Do you value art, music, and drama? Would you prefer a career in which you can appreciate and add to the beauty in the world?

- *Creativity.* Do you feel the need to create new things? Would you sacrifice security for a chance to create?

- *Social contact.* Is it important to you that you work with other people? Do you always try to avoid situations in which you will be working alone?

Your values are evident in everything you do. What do these activities suggest about the values of the young people participating in them?

Give some thought to what your values are before you choose a career. As you read and learn about a career, think about how that career would match your values. Don't choose a career that would cause you to go against your values.

What Are Your Interests?

You can get to know and understand yourself better by looking at your **interests.** Your interests are the things that you enjoy doing the most. You will want to consider your interests carefully when choosing a career.

Your Favorite Activities Think for a moment—what activities do you like doing most? What, for example, are your hobbies? They are probably things that you do well and that give you satisfaction. Did you know that many successful photographers first took pictures only as a hobby? Many people earn a living doing something that they used to do only as a hobby.

MAKE A DECISION

You are driving home from a party late one night. Several of your closest friends are in the car with you. You start to slow down when you see someone with car trouble waving for you to stop. Your friends begin to laugh and kid around as you all notice the person in trouble is someone whom everyone makes fun of at school. Your friends are saying things like, "You're not going to stop for *him*, are you?" You think maybe you should stop, however. What do you do— stop or keep going? You must make a quick decision. Give the reasons for your decision.

Which classes in school have been your favorites? Your favorite subjects are good indications of your interests. Do you like math? Have you taken any vocational classes? Perhaps you have developed a strong interest from one of these classes. If you really enjoy one of your classes, there is a good chance you could be successful pursuing a career in that area.

If you have taken part in school and social activities, you probably have many interests. If you haven't been involved in such activities, you may want to start getting involved. It's impossible to know if you'll be interested in something until you try it. The more interests you develop, the better your chances of finding a career that will satisfy you.

Preferences for Data, People, or Things
Would you enjoy working with **data** (facts, such as numbers, words, and symbols)? How would you feel about doing most of your work with people? Are you a person who likes to work with things— putting parts together, sewing clothes, or repairing machines? To find a career you will enjoy, you will need to know if you are most interested in data, people, or things.

Of course, very few jobs are limited to just one of these three categories. Most jobs involve combinations of the three. It is possible, though, to identify jobs as being *primarily* involved with one or two of these. For example, accountants, secretaries, and counselors work primarily with people and data. Salespeople deal mostly with people and things. Graphic designers and computer operators work mainly with data and things.

As you research a career to see which of the three categories is primarily involved, look beyond the surface. To a patient, for example, it may seem that nurses work primarily with people, but much of their time is spent working with data and things. A mechanic, who appears to deal solely with things, may spend a great deal of time keeping records, ordering parts, and figuring charges.

Many hobbies have the potential for being turned into full-time careers. If this hobbyist wanted to turn professional, what special factors might she have going in her favor?

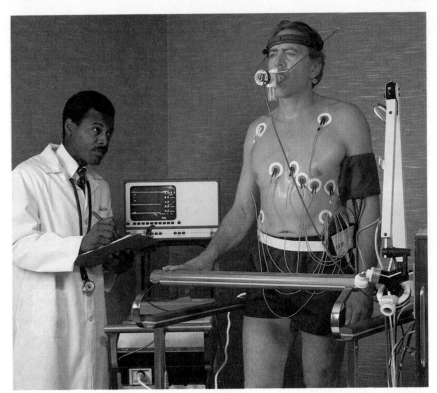

Most jobs involve data, people, *and* things. Is this true of the work done by the medical technician shown here? Explain.

Another important factor is the difficulty of the work in each of the three areas. For example, waiters and ministers both work with people. The waiter probably works with more people, but the "people" part of the waiter's job is less difficult. It requires fewer people skills. The people skills the waiter uses are serving food efficiently and making people feel welcome. The minister counsels and guides people, often when they are distressed and troubled. This means that the level of people skills required for the minister's job is much higher than that required for the waiter's job.

Here's another example. Cashiers and math professors both work with data. The cashier probably deals with data more times in a given day than does the math professor, but consider the difficulty of the two data jobs. The cashier simply adds numbers on a machine or piece of paper and makes change. The math professor works with complex math formulas and equations. A much higher level of data skills is required for the math professor's job.

The U.S. Department of Labor, in a book called the *Dictionary of Occupational Titles,* has rated every job according to its difficulty in each of the three categories—data, people, and things. With this book you can find out the various difficulty levels for any career you wish to research.

Interest Surveys   If you need help in finding out what your interests are, you should take an interest survey. There are many different surveys available. One of these, the *World of Work Career Interest Survey,* is similar to a test—but there are no right or wrong answers. You are given a long list of work activities, and you decide how much you would like to do each one. Your choices indicate which career groups, or jobs, you might enjoy. Your teacher, counselor, or work-experience coordinator can arrange for you to take one of these surveys.

✓ CHECKING UP

1. What are values, and how are they likely to affect your choice of career?
2. How can you determine what your major interests are?
3. Suggest three jobs not mentioned in your text that deal primarily with data, people, and things, respectively.

2 *Is Your Goal Realistic?*

It takes more than interest in a particular career to be successful. Many jobs require specialized skills. These can be learned, but learning them quickly and well often requires a certain amount of natural talent. Personality traits, too, play a role. Without factors like these working for you, you may have a difficult time making a particular career choice a reality.

Your Aptitudes and Abilities

To be successful in some careers, you must have the necessary aptitude or ability. An **aptitude** is a knack, or potential, for learning certain skills. An **ability** is a skill that has already been developed.

In many careers (especially those such as music, art, and sports) a great deal of aptitude or natural ability is needed. This does not mean, however, that ability alone is enough to be successful. Hard work in the form of practice, training, and experience is also necessary.

To choose a career in which you can be successful, you must know your aptitudes and abilities. You don't want to choose a career only to find that you cannot perform the tasks you'll be expected to perform. How do you find out what your aptitudes and abilities are? You can do several different things.

A good place to begin is with yourself. What do *you* think your strongest abilities are? Are you good at expressing ideas? Are you a skilled mechanic? Do you paint pictures that people praise and admire? Can you do math problems faster than anyone in your class?

Your grades usually give a good indication of your mental aptitudes and abilities. Your overall grade point average should tell a great deal about whether or not you have the ability to do well in college. Your grades in individual courses should suggest your strongest mental abilities.

Of course, if you don't try very hard in school, you may have more aptitude for certain kinds of work than your grades indicate. Developing your aptitudes into useful abilities will be difficult unless you make the effort.

Usually your teachers can let you know whether or not you have the aptitude for certain kinds of

work. For example, suppose you're taking shorthand this semester. Your shorthand teacher can probably tell whether or not you have the aptitude to develop good shorthand skills. The same is true for other skills courses, such as auto mechanics, electronics, drafting, typing, and bookkeeping.

Your school counselor can also help you learn about your strengths and weaknesses. Just as there are tests to determine your interests, there are tests to measure your abilities and aptitudes. Some tests show how easy or difficult it would be for you to develop skills in a special field. The tests predict your potential for learning such things as clerical skills, radio code, and playing a musical instrument. If you have not taken an aptitude test, ask your counselor to give you one.

Figure 2-1 lists some of the aptitudes measured by aptitude tests. Such tests can tell you if you have the abilities needed to succeed in different kinds of work.

If you are considering a career that requires special ability, be sure you have an aptitude for it. Many young people, for example, dream of becoming professional athletes. Very few, however, have the necessary natural talent for this career. You should try to be realistic. A goal is worthwhile only if there is a possibility of reaching it.

Case Study 1

David began playing baseball when he was only four years old. His father, a semiprofessional player who loved the game, practiced with him. David could run fast and was well coordinated.

In grade school David was always the first person selected when it came time to choose gym teams. In high school David played center field on the varsity baseball team. He batted .390 during his three years in high school and was also an outstanding fielder. When he graduated, he signed with a major-league team.

Learning to play baseball was easy for David because of his aptitude. He was born with the natural talent to become a great baseball player. As a professional player, he had several years of training to develop his aptitude into outstanding ability.

Types of Aptitudes	
Aptitude	**Description**
General	Good understanding of facts, opinions, concepts, and reasoning; related to school achievement.
Verbal	Good understanding of words and ideas and their meanings; able to use words and ideas easily and clearly.
Numerical	Good at doing arithmetic and math problems; can work quickly and accurately.
Spatial	Good at visualizing shapes, heights, widths, and depths mentally; can visualize in three dimensions.
Form perception	Good at observing detail in objects and drawings; can distinguish between shapes.
Clerical perception	Good at observing all details and noticing errors in spelling, punctuation, etc.; accurate in recording details.
Motor coordination	Good at moving eyes and hands or fingers together to do a job rapidly and smoothly.
Finger dexterity	Good at moving the fingers quickly and accurately to work with small objects.
Manual dexterity	Good at working with the hands.
Eye-hand-foot coordination	Good at moving the hands and feet together as needed, quickly and accurately.
Color discrimination	Good at noticing differences and similarities between colors and shapes of colors.

Figure 2-1　Aptitude tests indicate your strengths and weaknesses in areas such as those listed here. Name one career you think would require each type of aptitude.

Make a list of what you believe are your strongest abilities. Don't be modest—give yourself credit for the things you do well. Also acknowledge your weaknesses—we all have them. Then plan to do the best you can with what you have. You will be a happier worker and a more satisfied human being if you choose a career that does not ask too much—or too little.

Your Personality

How would you describe your own personality? What words would you think of if someone asked you to talk about your personality? Do words like *friendly, shy, outgoing, happy,* and *quiet* come to mind? Can you think of any others?

It is important that you try to understand your personality better than you probably do now. The more you know about your personality, the better your chances of finding a career you will enjoy. Understanding your personality can help you find jobs with co-workers who have similar personalities. It can also help you find jobs that are done in environments that suit your personality. Things like these will make your work more enjoyable and you happier.

Your school counselor can help you identify aptitudes and abilities you might not even realize you have. How?

Strive for Success

Sweet Sounds of Success

Although people don't often think of a career in music as being especially athletic, conducting an orchestra is hard physical work. By the intermission of a concert, the conductor is often as winded and covered with sweat as a professional basketball player at halftime.

The principal conductor of England's Royal Opera in London is no different. What makes Jeffrey Tate's effort so impressive, however, is the fact that he is severely physically disabled—his spine twisted and one leg much shorter than the other, almost useless.

As a small child, Tate seemed perfectly normal —except for his flat feet. When his mother consulted a specialist about this condition, however, she learned that the problem was far more grave. Tate's spine was seriously deformed.

Tate underwent two operations to combat the crippling effects and nerve damage caused by the unnatural curvature of his spine. The first surgery helped keep his left leg from becoming completely paralyzed. The second straightened his spine enough so that he would not lose his ability to walk.

Both operations were successful. Tate can walk, although he needs the assistance of a cane. However, his spine looks like an *S* from the back and a *C* from the side. One shoulder is hunched up to his ear, and he has to wear a special metal brace with an artificial foot attached to his real left foot so his legs will be the same length. He uses as much energy walking a city block as an athlete does running a 400-meter dash, and (because of the way his body is twisted) he can't breathe very deeply.

Tate felt so grateful to the doctors who had worked with such dedication on his body that he decided to become a physician himself. After a year's surgical internship, however, he turned to his first love—music. Although he had no formal training as a conductor, Tate wound up conducting rehearsals at the Royal Opera.

Tate was sure he would never have the strength to stand for an entire opera. When he

was given a chance to conduct an actual performance, however, he felt he had to give it a try. Though the first rehearsal was a "nightmare," he kept on. When the performance finally came, he received a standing ovation. In 1987 he was named principal conductor of the Royal Opera. In spite of the huge odds against him, Jeffrey Tate had reached the heights of the opera world— and he's not finished yet.

Employers are very concerned about personality. When they call schools to discuss the kinds of student workers they want, they often say, "Send me someone with a nice personality." When they explain why they hired one person rather than another, personality also enters into it. Employers make comments like these:

- "I hired Antonio because he's so personable —he has such a nice smile."
- "I chose Lorna because she's so pleasant. I thought she was just the kind of person my customers would like."
- "Brad's the best. He really knows how to put people at ease."

Personable, pleasant, putting people at ease— their words are a little different, but all of these employers are describing personality.

Before you can examine your own personality more closely, you must know what personality is. There are many different ways to define it. Here we will say that **personality** is the combination of all the attitudes, interests, values, behaviors, and characteristics that make you the person you are. Your personality is that combination of things that makes you unique, or different from every other person on earth.

Many psychologists have developed complex theories to explain personality. They use words like *self-concept, extrovert, introvert, dominant, submissive, impulsive,* and *secure.* Looking more closely at a few of the ways in which psychologists talk about personality may help you understand your own personality better.

Self-concept

Your **self-concept** is the way you see yourself—your feelings about your own worth and value. Your self-concept changes from day to day. When you do something really well or when someone pays you a compliment, your self-concept improves. You tend to think of yourself as a good, worthwhile person. When you fail at something, however, or someone points out a fault, your self-concept goes down. At this point you might have a very low opinion of your worth.

Although you experience highs and lows, you do have a consistent, ongoing self-concept. In general, you either like yourself, dislike yourself, or feel something in between. You have ideas about what you can and cannot do. You have a picture in your mind of the kind of person you are.

This person would clearly have "personality" to most potential employers. In the sense that most employers use the term, what does it mean? (*Note:* Once you have completed this lesson, come back to this question and decide whether or not such employers are right.)

How you see yourself provides important clues to your personality. This, in turn, suggests careers you would probably enjoy and in which you would be successful. If you see yourself as a very attractive person, perhaps you should consider careers in modeling or entertainment. If you see yourself as a friendly person who can communicate easily, you may be successful selling products or providing people with a service.

Take some time to examine your own feelings about yourself. Do you have a realistic opinion of yourself? Do you give yourself the credit you deserve without exaggerating your good points? You may want to compare your own ideas about yourself with the opinions other people have of you. If it looks as though you see yourself clearly, use your self-concept to guide you in your career decision making.

Personality Types

Some of the most respected ideas about personalities and how they relate to career choices were developed by Dr. John Holland, a psychologist. A quick look at Holland's ideas may help you to learn more about your own personality.

Holland says that there are six basic personality types and that all people resemble one of these types more or less. The six types are listed and described below.

- *Realistic.* Realistic people like to work with objects, tools, and machines. They avoid educational activities and social situations. They value money, power, and status.
- *Investigative.* Investigative people like to examine physical, biological, and cultural situations so that they can understand and control them. Investigative people do not like persuasive, social activities. They usually develop strong mathematical and scientific skills.
- *Artistic.* Artistic people like to be involved in free, unregulated activities so that they can create new art forms and products. Artistic people avoid rigid, unchanging systems and activities. Artistic people develop skills in languages, art, music, drama, and writing.

- *Social.* Social people like to help, teach, train, cure, and enlighten other people. Social people avoid working with materials, tools, and machines. They are usually skilled at getting along with others, and they value social and ethical activities.
- *Enterprising.* Enterprising people like to manipulate other people in order to achieve their goals and make money. Enterprising people avoid scientific and investigative activities. They value political and economic achievement and prefer to be leaders rather than followers.
- *Conventional.* Conventional people like to keep records, file materials, and organize information, often with the aid of business machines. Conventional people avoid free, unregulated activities. They value business and economic achievement and have clerical and numerical abilities.

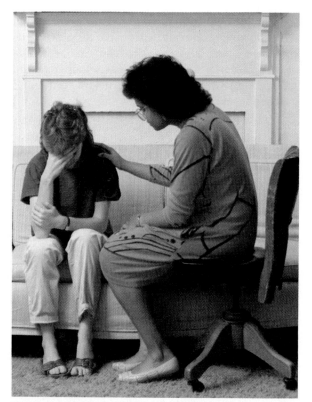

Holland's work suggests that most people are actually combinations of personality types. What mixture of types does the work done by each of these individuals suggest?

SITUATION
SOLUTION

When Aptitudes and Abilities Lead Nowhere

You are a product manager for a large computer firm. In addition to overseeing the writing of promotional and training materials for a line of personal computers, you make presentations to salespeople and occasionally customers. Oral presentations are not something you enjoy or do particularly well. (You're a nervous speaker with a devotion to detail that often overwhelms your listeners.) Still, you persevere because presentations are part of your job.

If your presentations aren't great, however, your training manuals are. Thorough, organized, and clearly written, they're the best in the company. In fact, your boss has suggested a shift in your job duties. It would relieve you of your responsibility for doing presentations and let you specialize in doing printed materials.

Others in your position might be grateful, but you are not. Presentations, however personally difficult, give you visibility within the company. They offer you a chance to travel, talk with salespeople, make new contacts, and keep abreast of what's happening in the field. Editing manuals offers you none of these things. It is, in your opinion, a one-way ticket to nowhere. You're afraid if you accept your boss's suggestion that your career will be derailed, that you'll be off the fast promotion track to the top of the company.

1. How would you respond to your boss's offer to change your responsibilities?

2. Given the obvious mismatch between some of your job duties and your personality and abilities, wouldn't you be happier without the added burden and pressure of doing presentations? Explain why or why not.

3. Assuming you do not wish to give up your responsibility for doing presentations, what alternatives could you recommend to your boss?

In Holland's book, *Making Vocational Choices: A Theory of Careers,* you can read more about the six personality types. You can also take a test that Holland developed to help people find out what unique mixture of personality types they happen to be. The scores from this test can help you match your personality to appropriate occupations.

Many other psychologists have developed personality tests and inventories. If you would like to find out more about your personality, talk to your counselor. He or she can describe the various personality tests available.

Of course, you may not need to take a test to find out about your own personality and how it relates to careers. You may already have a good idea of what your personality is and what sort of career would be compatible with it. For example, you may know that you are a nervous person who would not like a career making high-risk decisions in business management. You may be a highly social person who needs to be around people and could not spend long hours working alone. Another possibility is that you are the independent type who will need to be your own boss rather than someone who takes orders.

It might help to make a long list of words that describe you. (You could also make a list of words that describe all the things that you are not.) Then, as you research careers, find out whether or not people with your characteristics usually enter and succeed in each career.

✔ CHECKING UP

1. What is the difference between an aptitude and an ability?

2. Characterize each of Holland's six basic personality types in a half dozen words or less.

3. Why is it important to consider your personality type in selecting a career?

Review Your Learning

CHAPTER SUMMARY

You should not explore any occupations until you have a good understanding of yourself—your dreams, values, interests, aptitudes, abilities, and personality. Only when you know all these things about yourself can you be reasonably sure of finding a career that you will enjoy and in which you will be successful.

You should consider your daydreams to find out what kind of life-style you would like to have in the years to come. Your main interests and your preferences for working with data, people, or things are indicators of what kinds of job duties you would most likely enjoy. Your aptitudes and abilities suggest what things you can learn to do most easily. Finally, your values and your personality, if compatible with the career you select, should ensure satisfaction on the job and a sense of genuine accomplishment.

TERMS TO KNOW

On a separate sheet of paper, write sentences for each of the following terms:

values
interests
data
aptitude
ability
personality
self-concept

STUDY QUESTIONS

1. How can dreaming help you in your career decision-making process?
2. Name at least five things that many people value.
3. In making a career decision, why is it good to have many interests rather than just a few?
4. What book rates jobs in terms of their data-people-things difficulty?
5. Why are your aptitudes and abilities important considerations in your choice of a career?
6. How can your school counselor help you identify your aptitudes and abilities?
7. What are Holland's six basic personality types?
8. Which of Holland's personality types would you expect a high school English teacher to be?

CRITICAL THINKING

1. Mira wants to be a nurse. What sorts of values would you expect her to have? What sorts of things would she be unlikely to value?
2. Joel enjoys working with people. He also does extremely well in his science courses (biology is his favorite). Suggest at least three careers that would combine Joel's interests.
3. Think of an adult you know whose personality is a mismatch for his or her career. Describe the nature of the incompatibility. Then suggest a better job for this person.

DISCUSSION STARTERS

1. How could having strong religious values affect your career choice?
2. What hobbies or interests that you have now could be turned into a career? How?
3. How can a negative self-concept affect your success in finding a satisfactory career?
4. Do you think Holland's personality types really are "basic"? Can you think of anyone you know who doesn't fit into one of Holland's categories? If so, describe this person. Can you think of any personality types you would add to Holland's list? If so, name and describe these types.

Review Your Learning

BUILDING BASIC SKILLS

Math

1. A survey of your class yields the following results: 16 prefer working with people, 9 with data, and 6 with things. If the class has 31 students, what percentage of the class do each of these numbers represent?

Human Relations

2. Your friend Roger is sure he'll be a professional baseball player when he gets out of school. He's so sure that he's started cutting classes, saying they're a waste of time. You know Roger probably *is* good enough to be a professional ball player, but you also know he needs to have a good education no matter what he does. How do you convince him to take school more seriously?

Communication

3. Write a personal statement of your values for inclusion in a community college application. Of the ten values described in this chapter, select the two or three that are most important to you and concentrate on them.

SUGGESTED ACTIVITIES

1. In this activity, you and each person in the class will make a collage. (A collage is made by pasting a variety of materials on a flat surface, such as a sheet of cardboard.) This will be done in steps:

   • *Preparation.* Collect the materials you will need for your collage—old magazines (at least a dozen); scissors; colored pens, crayons, or poster paint (with brushes); and a piece of cardboard or poster board.

   • *Assembly.* Make a collage that represents you. Try to show some of your values, interests, relationships with others, personality, and/or life-style goals through your selection of illustrations. Make your collage at home. Then give it directly to your teacher *without* letting other students see it.

   • *Evaluation.* Your teacher will place all the collages around the room to give everyone a chance to see them and try to guess who created each. Speculation about each artist should be accompanied by reasons supporting the views expressed. In this way, each student will gain an appreciation of how others see him or her.

   • *Follow-up Discussion.* Following the evaluation session, claim your collage. Join with the class to discuss the significance of the images you and others used in creating your works.

2. Compare Holland's personality categories with any other similar system you can find in professional or popular literature. Do a written analysis of how the systems differ, which you think is better (the more accurate or more helpful), and why.

Researching Careers

You learned in Chapter 1 how the decision-making process can be used to reach a career decision. The first step was to begin dreaming about how you would like to live in 5, 10, or even 20 years. The next step was to analyze your resources, which meant getting to know more about your own values, interests, abilities, and personality. After reading Chapter 2 you should have a good idea of who you are.

This chapter will help you with the third and fourth steps in the career decision-making process. You will identify several careers that you believe will fulfill your needs and wants. Then you will research these careers to see if they match your life-style goals and personal resources.

OBJECTIVES

After studying this chapter and doing the activities, you will be able to:

- discuss how exploring career areas can help you identify careers you want to research;
- describe what to look for when researching careers;
- determine whether the values associated with a particular career are compatible with your own;
- find information on careers; and
- explain how work experience can help you learn about careers.

TERMS TO KNOW

career interest areas
work environment
fringe benefits
audiovisuals
career consultation
cooperative programs

1 Exploring Careers

Maybe you already have some ideas about careers you would enjoy. If so, make a list of these careers and start your research. The second part of this chapter will show you how to do a thorough job.

On the other hand, you may have no idea which careers would interest you the most. Like many people, you may not even be aware of the many different kinds of jobs that are available. In this case, you would need to explore the various career possibilities before making a list and starting your research.

In fact, even if you already have several careers in mind, you might want to do some exploring. Perhaps you'll find one or two careers that you didn't know about. You may want to add these to your list. Remember, the more careers you research, the better your chances of finding one that's right for you.

Informal Research

Where do you get ideas about careers you might like? You can talk to friends and family members. You can start noticing the jobs people are doing as you go about your daily routine. While you read, do your school work, and watch television, you can be thinking of possible careers.

You can also get some career ideas in the next few pages of this book. Spend some time reading through the general career information that follows. Don't rush through this material. Take your time and imagine yourself in many of these ca-

reers. As you explore and daydream about yourself in all kinds of jobs, list the careers that you want to learn more about.

Career Interest Areas

One way of grouping jobs for easier career exploration is to organize them by **career interest areas.** Each interest area is a category of jobs that are similar in terms of the interests they involve. This means that a person interested in one job in a particular area will probably be interested in other jobs in that area. By learning about the general interest areas, you may get a better idea of the *kinds* of jobs you would enjoy.

On each of the twelve pages beginning with page 33, you will read a brief description of one of the career interest areas. The aptitudes and abilities most needed for jobs in that area are listed, along with some questions. The questions will help you decide whether or not you would be interested in that area of work.

MAKE A DECISION

After you read about the 12 career interest areas, you will probably be more interested in some than in others. Narrow the choices to your three favorites. Then use the decision-making process to choose the one area that sounds most appealing to you. What's your decision—which career interest area would you most like to explore further? Give the reasons for your decision.

If you are on the lookout for career possibilities, you will notice people working at jobs you never knew existed. Describe an unusual job you have heard about or seen someone performing.

Artistic

Careers in the artistic interest area would give you a chance to express your creativity. The artistic area includes the literary arts; the visual arts; the performing arts (drama, music, and dance); crafts; and modeling.

People who work in the literary arts like to write and edit (correct and improve). Some write plays, movie scripts, short stories, and novels. Others edit the work of writers to make their books and articles more interesting and easier to read.

Workers in the visual arts may paint portraits or landscapes, design scenery for plays, or sculpt statues. Others work as photographers, taking pictures for magazines, newspapers, and books.

People in the performing arts like to perform in front of others. They may act in plays, in movies, or on television. Others sing, play musical instruments, or dance.

Aptitudes and Abilities Needed

Writers must be able to express themselves well with words. A good imagination is helpful for almost any kind of writing. Some writers must also be skilled at gathering and organizing information. Others must have a sense of humor or a great deal of knowledge about a certain subject.

Artists, photographers, and sculptors must understand and apply artistic techniques. They need to "see" how the final product will look from rough sketches. Of course, they must be able to use their brushes, pens, or sculpturing tools with skill.

Actors and actresses must be able to express ideas and emotions through facial expression, voice inflection, and body motion. They also must be able to memorize lines, speak clearly, and perform with poise.

Most musicians must be able to read music. They also must be able to sing or play an instrument with skill. Dancers must move with grace and rhythm, coordinating body movements to the music and to the movements of other dancers. Singing, dancing, playing instruments—all of these occupations require a natural talent and usually many years of training.

Many people who work in performing arts are talented in all three areas: they act, sing or play a musical instrument, and dance. Modeling requires poise similar to that needed by an actor.

Is This Work for You?

- Have you written an original story, poem, or newspaper article?
- Can you create original characters and situations in stories and plays?
- Have you taken courses in drawing or sketching? Was your work selected for display?
- Have you taken photographs of your family and friends, activities, or landscapes? Were they of good quality?
- Have you performed in a play? Do you enjoy performing before an audience?
- Have you memorized long passages of poetry? Can you recite them before an audience?
- Have you spoken on radio or television? Can you control your voice, and is it pleasing?
- Have you sung or played a musical instrument in school programs? Have you had lessons in singing or playing a musical instrument?
- Can you read music? Have you ever written a song?
- Have you taken dancing lessons? Have you performed as a dancer before an audience?
- Have you modeled for an artist or photographer?

Mechanical

People who work in the mechanical career area apply mechanical principles to practical situations through the use of machines and hand tools. There are several thousand different jobs in the mechanical area. People in engineering careers plan, design, and direct the construction of buildings, bridges, roads, airports, and dams. Workers in management careers manage industrial plants where technical work is done. Engineering technology workers collect and record technical information. Other workers operate vehicles such as airplanes, ships, trucks, vans, locomotives, or ambulances.

Craft technology workers do highly skilled hand or machine work. Systems operation workers operate and maintain equipment. Quality control workers inspect or test materials and products, while materials control workers receive, store, or ship them.

Crafts workers use their hands and hand tools to make or repair products. Equipment operation workers operate heavy machines or equipment.

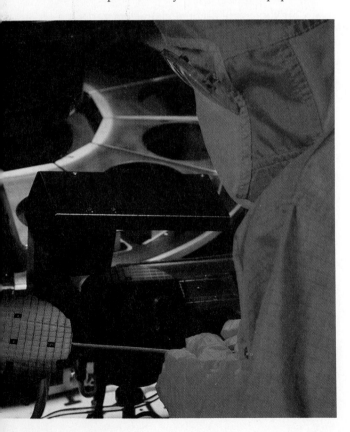

Aptitudes and Abilities Needed

Engineers must understand the principles of chemistry, geology, physics, and related sciences. They must also be able to use higher-level math to solve complicated problems.

Management workers must plan and direct the work of others, either directly or through lower-level supervisors. They must react quickly in emergency situations to make important decisions. These decisions often involve the safety of others and great amounts of money.

Engineering technology workers must use math to solve problems and clear language to write technical reports. Pilots must coordinate the use of their hands, feet, and eyes to control a ship or airplane. They must react quickly in emergencies and use judgment to make decisions that affect the lives of passengers.

Craft and craft technology workers must read blueprints or sketches and picture how a finished product will look. They must also be able to use their eyes, hands, and fingers to operate or adjust equipment.

Is This Work for You?

- Have you taken algebra, geometry, and advanced math? Can you solve practical problems using math?

- Have you taken physics courses? Do you like to study energy and matter?

- Have you built or repaired a radio, a television, or an amplifier? Do you understand electrical or electronic terms or drawings?

- Have you served as a leader in school activities? Have you directed the work of other students?

- Have you taken courses in mechanical drawing? Do you like this kind of activity?

- Do you like to read airplane or boat magazines? Do you like and understand technical articles?

- Have you made minor repairs around the house? Do you like working with your hands?

- Have you repaired or installed parts on an automobile? Do you like this work?

Industrial

Industrial careers include production technology, production work, and quality control. Some industrial workers do skilled machine work to make products. Some set up machines and teach others to operate them. Others check the quality of products. Most industrial work is done in factories.

Production technology workers set up production machinery and make sure it is operating correctly. They may use precision measuring devices to find defects in the production process. Production workers also set up machines. The workers then use these machines to make paper, plastic, or metal products. Other workers use power screwdrivers or riveting machines to fasten the parts of a product together. Quality control workers check products for defects.

Aptitudes and Abilities Needed

Most industrial workers need basic math skills for measuring, planning schedules, and keeping production records. Production technology workers must be able to read and understand blueprints. (This is required for setting up and adjusting machines and equipment.) Production workers must be able to read and follow instructions, both to set up and to operate the machines they use.

An important skill in many factories is detecting differences in the shape, size, and texture of materials. Many industrial workers must also adjust to doing the same thing over and over according to a set procedure.

Is This Work for You?

- Have you taken industrial arts or machine shop courses? Did you learn to use measuring devices, such as gauges and micrometers? Do you like to set up machines according to written standards?
- Have you taken general or applied math courses? Do you like activities that use math skills, such as measuring?
- Have you assembled a bicycle or toy by following drawings or written instructions? Did you have a fairly easy time doing this?
- Have you held a part-time job where mechanical equipment was used? Do you like working around mechanical equipment?
- Have you sorted paper, metal, or glass for recycling? Were you able to tell the difference between similar types of materials?
- Would you like to work in a factory?

Scientific

The scientific area can be divided into four groups: physical sciences, life sciences, medical science, and laboratory technology. Workers in these careers discover, collect, and analyze information about the natural world. They solve problems in medicine, life sciences, and natural sciences.

People who work in the physical sciences may help solve pollution problems or study the causes of earthquakes. Some conduct experiments to develop new metals. Many use advanced math to solve complex problems.

Workers in the life sciences may do research to find better ways of processing food. Others experiment with growing bacteria to learn about diseases.

People in the medical sciences are involved in the prevention, diagnosis, and treatment of disease. Laboratory technology workers perform tests in chemistry, biology, or physics.

Aptitudes and Abilities Needed

Workers in the physical and life sciences must use logic and the scientific method to investigate many kinds of problems. They must be able to make decisions based on their own judgments or information that can be measured. Most need highly developed math skills.

People in the medical sciences must also use a great deal of logic and scientific reasoning to diagnose and treat injuries and illnesses. They must be able to deal with people or animals who are in pain or under stress. Great skill and accuracy in the use of eyes, hands, and fingers are all important.

Laboratory technology workers must understand and use scientific and technical language and symbols. This work requires great accuracy in conducting scientific tests.

Is This Work for You?

- Have you taken and enjoyed courses in earth science or astronomy?

- Have you collected rocks or minerals as a hobby? Can you recognize differences in ores and minerals?

- Can you skillfully handle small instruments, such as tweezers?

- Have you taken algebra or geometry? Can you read and understand charts and graphs?

- Have you owned a chemistry set or microscope? Do you like testing new ideas with this equipment?

- Have you taken courses in biology or zoology? Do you like working with plants or animals?

- Have you studied plants in a garden, forest, or laboratory? Can you identify different kinds of plants?

- Have you had any first aid training?

- Do you enjoy watching medical shows on television? Can you understand the technical terms used?

Plants and Animals

Workers in the plants and animal area are involved primarily in farming, forestry, and fishing. The types of jobs included are management, supervision, planting and harvesting of crops, and the care and training of animals.

The people in management may plan and oversee the sale and shipment of farm crops or animals. Some study market trends to plan the type and quality of crops to plant. Others plan and direct projects for cutting timber and replanting forests.

Supervisors oversee workers who plant and harvest crops. The supervisors often work right alongside the workers they're supervising. Many of these workers live and work in rural areas on farms, ranches, or forest preserves.

Among those who care for and train animals, some train horses for racing. Others feed, exercise, and groom pets. Some train and care for animals used in entertainment.

Aptitudes and Abilities Needed

Managers must understand and apply procedures related to the kinds of work they are managing. For example, farm managers must understand the necessity of rotating crops so that the farm soil will stay fertile. Managers of cattle ranches must know how to feed cattle so that they can produce beef of prime quality. All managers must know how to keep accurate financial and production records.

Supervisors must understand and give directions well. They must get a clear picture of the work to be done from their managers and then pass this information along clearly to the workers they supervise. Many supervisors must demonstrate the use of tools and equipment to workers. Basic math skills are needed to keep records for workers.

Those involved in the care and training of animals must understand the habits and physical needs of the animals under their care. The ability to work quickly and skillfully with one's hands is necessary for many jobs. Typical tasks include trimming the nails of dogs and cats, fastening shoes to horses' hooves, or helping a veterinarian give shots to sick animals.

Is This Work for You?

- Have you raised or cared for an animal? Do you like the responsibility of caring for animals?

- Have you taken care of a sick or injured animal? Can you tell if an animal is getting sick or better by the way it looks or acts?

- Have you raised plants? Would you like to take a course to learn more about how plants grow?

- Have you been a member of the FFA or 4-H? Did you complete any projects that required planning, budgeting, and record keeping?

- Have you worked all day mowing lawns, planting or trimming trees, or picking fruit? Are you interested in supervising this kind of work?

- Do you like to camp, fish, or hunt? Would you like a full-time job doing these things?

Leading-Influencing

People who work in leading-influencing careers influence others with their high-level verbal or numerical abilities. These careers include jobs in education, law, business administration, finance, and social research. There are also jobs in math and statistics, communication, promotion, and many related careers.

Workers may use advanced math and statistics to solve problems or conduct research. Some design or write computer programs. Others teach in public or private schools.

Social research workers study human behavior. They may analyze information on jobs or interpret information on economic conditions. Others research the mental development of people.

Those in law careers advise and represent persons in legal matters. They may represent clients who are suing or being sued. Some prepare wills, deeds, and other legal documents. Lawyers are often elected to public office.

Business administrators direct activities in private companies or government agencies. Those in services administration manage programs and projects in health, education, welfare, and recreation.

Communication workers write, edit, and report facts. Most of these jobs are with radio or television stations, newspapers, and publishing firms. Promotion workers raise funds, advertise goods and services, and influence people in their actions.

Aptitudes and Abilities Needed

All workers in the leading-influencing area must be able to speak and write clearly. Good language and math skills are needed to analyze and interpret information. Those dealing with math and statistics must be able to use advanced logic and scientific thinking to solve complex problems. More and more, they must also be able to use computer technology.

People in education must understand and use basic principles of effective teaching. Social research workers must know how to apply various theories and methods of research so that the data they collect will be regarded as valid. Those in law careers must understand, interpret, and know how to apply statutes and legal principles.

Those in business and finance must interpret statistics and financial reports. Many need to understand and use computers. Administrators must think logically to make good decisions.

Communication workers must use words that give readers and listeners a clear picture. The ability to speak clearly and easily is especially important.

Is This Work for You?

- Have you taken courses in advanced math? Do you like solving difficult problems?
- Have you had experience using a calculator? Can you use many of the functions?
- Have you helped friends or relatives with homework? Can you explain things well?
- Have you done research projects or surveys? Do you enjoy these activities?
- Have you taken debate or speech courses? Do you feel at ease presenting a point of view in front of a group?
- Have you supervised activities of others? Were their jobs done well?
- Have you been a treasurer of a school or community group? Can you keep accurate financial records?
- Have you worked on a school newspaper? Can you report events accurately?
- Have you worked for a political campaign? Can you understand and influence the public?

Physical Performing

Workers in the physical performing area either participate in sports or perform physical feats. Those in sports may play on professional teams, coach players, or officiate at games. Some instruct or recruit players. Others regulate sporting events. Most of these jobs are in football, baseball, basketball, hockey, golf, tennis, or horse racing. Most players practice five or six days a week for about six to nine months a year. Football games are played once a week during a season of about five months. Baseball and basketball games are played several times each week. Golf and tennis events take place on a less regular basis. Horse racing occurs daily, four to six days a week during the season. Jockeys may ride in several races each day.

Workers who perform physical feats often work in circuses, carnivals, theaters, and amusement parks. Some show their gymnastic skill on a high wire or trapeze. Some juggle and balance things, such as balls, knives, or plates. Others perform acrobatic stunts on horseback. Stunt performers are also used in movies and television shows.

Aptitudes and Abilities Needed

Professional athletes and those performing physical feats need exceptional eye, hand, and body coordination. In most sports, superior speed and strength are needed. The ability to judge distance, speed, and movement of objects or people is important, too. Of course, all athletes must have the highly developed skills needed for the particular game they play. Coaches and umpires must understand the rules of the game. Some jobs in this career area, such as those involved with regulating sports events, do not require athletic skills.

Is This Work for You?

- Have you competed in sports? Do you know the rules of any sport well enough to be a referee, judge, or umpire?
- Have you been an umpire or official in informal games? Can you make decisions quickly and firmly?
- Have you coached a team or individual in athletic events? Were you effective?
- Have you competed against others in athletic events? Do you remain calm and alert during competition?
- Have you won any special sports events? Do you excel in any athletic skill?
- Have you performed stunts that required daring and skill? Do you perform them without great fear?
- Have you had a hobby or specialty act such as juggling, acrobatics, or wire walking? Do you perform well before an audience?

Accommodating

Workers in the accommodating group attend to the wishes of others, usually on a one-to-one basis. Everyone in this group provides a service. Some provide hospitality, barber, and beauty services. Others provide passenger, customer, and attendant services.

Hospitality workers may greet guests and answer questions about social and recreational activities in a hotel. Some greet and seat customers in a restaurant. Others provide personal services to airplane passengers, such as answering questions or serving meals. Still others serve meals to customers in restaurants, work as chauffeurs, or carry baggage.

Those in barber and beauty services may cut, trim, shampoo, curl, or style hair. Some give hair- and scalp-conditioning treatments or facials. Some clean, shape, and polish fingernails.

Aptitudes and Abilities Needed

Everyone who works in this cluster must be able to get along well with all kinds of people. Those in hospitality need to speak clearly and put others at ease. Workers in barber and beauty services must understand written instructions for applying hair coloring and permanent waving solutions. They must use a variety of tools, such as scissors, tweezers, combs, curlers, and hair dryers.

Those in passenger services must read maps to locate addresses and select the best routes. They must judge distances and speeds to avoid accidents. Customer service workers must talk with different kinds of people to find out what services they desire or to provide them with the information they want.

The ability to move fingers and hands easily and quickly to handle dishes, money, and merchandise is important in many jobs. Some attendant services require lifting and carrying things such as luggage, trays of dishes, and bags of golf clubs. Many of these jobs require one to do the same task over and over, often in the same way.

Is This Work for You?

- Have you taken courses in speech? Do you like to speak to groups?
- Have you planned or organized a party? Can you lead others in games and group activities?
- Have you cut someone's hair? Do you style your own hair? Do you like to try new and different hair styles?
- Have you applied theatrical make-up? Do you enjoy changing the appearance of others?
- Have you worked at a health spa or athletic club? Do you enjoy helping others?
- Have you driven a vehicle in heavy traffic? Did you stay calm?
- Have you given directions to anyone who was lost? Did you make the directions clear?
- Have you served food or beverages at a party? Can you do this without spilling or dropping things?
- Have you collected tickets or ushered at a play? Do you remain courteous when others are rude to you?
- Have you had a part-time job as a waiter or waitress in a local restaurant? Did you enjoy waiting on people?

Humanitarian

Workers in the humanitarian career area help people with mental, spiritual, social, physical, or vocational concerns. They provide social services, nursing care, and therapy. Some do specialized teaching, while others attend to the needs of children and adults who require special care.

Social service workers help people deal with their personal problems. Some counsel individuals to help them overcome emotional or social difficulties. Others help parolees find jobs and adjust to life after prison. Still others help parents with child-rearing problems and students with educational and career plans. Many social service jobs are in schools, mental health clinics, guidance centers, welfare offices, and churches.

People in nursing may provide general nursing care to patients in a hospital. They may give medications to patients as prescribed by a doctor. Some plan and carry out school health programs. Therapy workers may direct and help patients in physical therapy exercises. Others train the physically handicapped in daily routines, such as grooming, dressing, and using the telephone. Many of these jobs are in hospitals, nursing homes, and rehabilitation centers.

Child and adult care workers help the elderly, the very young, and the handicapped. These workers may help elderly persons bathe, feed, or dress themselves. Some use electronic equipment to collect medical data. Others entertain and supervise children in nurseries. Many of these jobs are in hospitals, clinics, schools, day care centers, and private homes.

Aptitudes and Abilities Needed

Social service workers must care a great deal about people, their needs, and their welfare. These workers must be sincere and honest enough to gain the confidence of those they are trying to help. Counselors must use logical thinking to help others define and solve personal problems.

People in nursing careers must follow instructions exactly and record information accurately. Many need special medical skills to care for or treat sick or handicapped people. Those in nursing and therapy, and those who care for children

and adults, must stay calm and work quickly in emergencies.

Is This Work for You?

- Have friends come to you for advice or help with personal problems? Did you help them?
- Have you taken courses in psychology, sociology, or other social sciences? Do you like to study human behavior?
- Have you worked as an aide in a hospital, day care center, or nursing home? Do you like helping people who are ill or injured?
- Have you taken a first aid course? Do you remember actions you should take in an emergency?

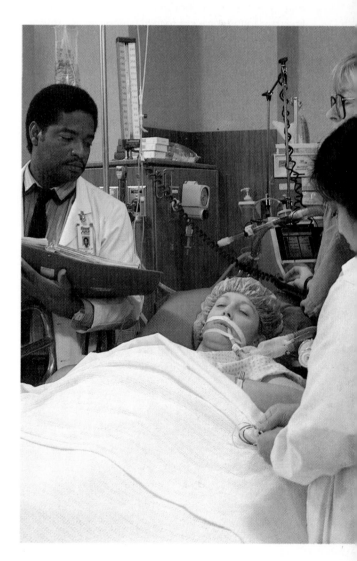

Business Detail

Workers in the business detail area perform clearly defined activities requiring accuracy and attention to detail. Most work is done in an office setting.

Administrative workers may prepare correspondence and keep records for a company. Some organize and oversee clerical operations. Jobs in this group are found in offices of businesses, industries, doctors, lawyers, and other professionals.

Workers dealing with mathematical detail often use a calculator to compute answers and keep records. Some compute wages for payroll records, while others compute the cost of labor and materials for production records. Jobs in this group are found wherever record keeping is important. Many of the jobs are in banks, finance companies, accounting firms, or the payroll and inventory control departments of businesses and government.

Those in financial detail may compute payments and interest on loans. Some operate cash registers in grocery stores. Others record bids for items and collect deposits at auctions. Jobs in this group are found wherever money is paid to or received from the public.

Workers in oral communications may operate a telephone switchboard or register guests in a hotel. Others receive callers at an office and direct them to the proper area. Some interview people and compile information for surveys. Other business detail workers sort and deliver mail, take dictation, and type letters and reports. Some workers operate check-writing or billing machines. These jobs are found in private businesses, schools, hospitals, and government agencies.

Aptitudes and Abilities Needed

Business detail workers must get along well with all kinds of people. They must be able to change work activities often but also be able to keep doing the same thing for hours at a time. The ability to speak clearly is important in most jobs involving business detail.

Administrative detail workers must follow instructions without close supervision. Those in mathematical detail work must be able to use a calculator, record numbers correctly, and follow procedures for keeping records. Financial detail workers must use math to figure the cost of things and make change. Workers in oral communications must speak clearly and listen carefully.

Is This Work for You?

- Have you taken courses in business math and typing? Is your work accurate?
- Have you taken courses in bookkeeping or accounting? Do you like working with numbers?
- Have you balanced a checking account or figured interest rates? Are you able to spot errors quickly?
- Have you been in charge of records for a club or social group? Do you like organizing files?
- Have you worked part-time in an office? Did you enjoy this work?
- Have you sold tickets, candy, or other items? Can you make change rapidly and accurately?
- Have you ever used spreadsheet software to help you make and follow a personal budget? Were you able to follow the software manual? Did you enjoy experimenting with the program?
- Have you ever served as the secretary of an organization? Did you find it easy to keep the group's minutes and prepare any necessary correspondence?

Selling

Workers in the selling career area sell goods or services. Some spend all of their time in a single location, such as a department store or an automobile dealership. Others travel regularly, calling on businesses or individuals in many different locations. Some workers in this group are known as vendors. They work at stadiums, street fairs, restaurants, or wherever crowds gather for entertainment or recreation.

People in sales technology may call on businesses to sell radio or television advertising time. Others sell computers or professional supplies to dentists, doctors, or engineers.

Those in general sales may call people on the telephone to sell goods. Most of the people in this area, however, work in retail stores selling clothing, sporting goods, jewelry, furniture, and household appliances. An auctioneer sells goods to the highest bidder at an auction. Vendors may sell popcorn, peanuts, sandwiches, and drinks.

Aptitudes and Abilities Needed

People involved in selling must be able to express themselves well. Salespersons must keep up their enthusiasm in all meetings with buyers. They must persuade others to make decisions to buy, and this often means helping customers make up their minds. While doing this, they must treat customers with courtesy and respect, even in difficult situations. Salespeople must also be able to keep up their confidence when potential customers decide not to buy.

Those involved in selling must also have a thorough understanding of the good or service that they are selling. Customers won't buy from a salesperson who doesn't seem to know much about the good or service being offered.

Basic math skills are needed to compute markup on prices, the cost of installing equipment, or discounts on sales. Accurate records must be kept on contracts, sales, and purchases.

Those in vending jobs may need to be able to speak clearly and loudly, perhaps singing or calling out to attract attention. They may need to stand or walk for long periods at a time. They must often climb stairs or push through crowds while carrying heavy containers or pushing a cart.

Is This Work for You?

- Have you taken sales-related courses? Did you enjoy them?
- Have you sold things to raise money for a school or civic project? Do you enjoy this sort of activity?
- Have you attended auctions? Can you guess, in advance, the selling prices of items?
- Have you made speeches or been in debates? Do you like presenting ideas to people?
- Have you worked as a salesperson in a store? Do you enjoy sales work?
- Have you taken basic math courses? Can you compute percentages in your head?

Protective

The protective career area includes workers in safety and law enforcement and those in security services. Workers in these careers protect people and property. Most workers are employees of the federal, state, or local governments. Most work in departments such as the police department or fire department.

Careers in safety and law enforcement involve making sure that people obey laws and regulations. Some workers patrol certain areas, issue tickets, investigate disturbances, provide first aid, and arrest suspects. Others patrol an area to observe fishing or hunting activities and to warn or arrest persons violating fish and game laws. Some manage or supervise the work of others.

Those in security services protect people and animals from injury or danger. They may guard money and valuables being transported by an armored car. Some guard inmates and direct their activities in prison. Others respond to alarms to fight fires, give first aid, and protect property.

Aptitudes and Abilities Needed

Safety and law enforcement workers must work well under pressure and in the face of danger. They must use guns, fire-fighting equipment, or safety devices. Investigators must be able to use practical thinking to conduct or supervise investigations.

Security workers must use reason and judgment in dealing with all kinds of people. They must think clearly and react quickly in emergencies. They must be willing to work in physically demanding and dangerous situations.

Is This Work for You?

- Do you enjoy watching TV detective shows? When you read detective stories, do you try to solve the mysteries?

- Have you taken courses in government, civics, or criminology? Did you find these subjects interesting?

- Have you worked as a camp counselor or other group leader? Do you like helping people?

- Have you been a member of a volunteer fire or rescue squad? Can you stay calm in emergencies?

- Have you taken a first aid course? Can you treat injuries quickly and skillfully?

✓ CHECKING UP

1. What is a career interest area?
2. Why is it important to explore various career areas before doing any in-depth career research?
3. Name six career interest areas that might be of interest to someone with an aptitude for math.

2 *What To Research*

You should now have a list of careers you think you might enjoy, and you should be ready to research them thoroughly. Before you start, however, think about what you'll be looking for.

There are nine factors you ought to consider as you do your research:

- Values required
- Duties and responsibilities
- Work environment
- Working hours
- Aptitudes and abilities required
- Education and training required
- Data-people-things relationships
- Salary and fringe benefits
- Career outlook

Try to gather information on each of these factors for each career you investigate. This will enable you to compare careers directly and make a wise career decision.

Values Required

Some careers require the people entering them to hold certain values. For example, the pastor of a church would need to place religion high on a list of personal values. An artist would have to rank creativity high, while a politician would probably need to feel that power is an important value. Unless you have certain values, success in some careers is unlikely.

In Chapter 2 you considered your own values. When you research a career, think about whether or not that career requires certain values. Then decide how well the values related to the career match up with your own.

Duties and Responsibilities

Duties and responsibilities are different for every job. One job may involve a great deal of hard, physical work but no responsibility for supervising others. Another job might involve continual supervision and management of lower-level workers but almost no physical activity. The number of different duties and responsibilities is almost limitless.

You will find that some work activities would actually be fun. Others would be okay, some would be boring, and some you would dislike very much. If you're going to spend 2,000 hours a year at work, it's worth the time it takes to choose carefully and pick a job you will enjoy doing.

| SITUATION |
| SOLUTION |

Asking for More Responsibility

You have been working at the local Radio Shack for more than a year, stocking shelves and occasionally running the cash register. Your boss, Mr. Brown, is very pleased with your work, but he's never suggested you do anything more around the store. You, however, have been thinking a great deal about careers; and you've decided that you would like a job in accounting. You've been offered a position keeping records at a printer's shop, but you really like the people you work with at Radio Shack.

1. How could you convince Mr. Brown that he should allow you to help with the store bookkeeping?
2. Mr. Brown is reluctant to let you, a relatively inexperienced student, take over any of this work. He explains that he already has a very good bookkeeping service. What can you say to make him reconsider?
3. If Mr. Brown remains steadfast in his opposition, what will you do?

Work Environment

Closely related to work activities is the work environment. The **work environment** is made up of working conditions, such as the sounds, smells, sights, and temperature surrounding the worker. It also includes the physical demands placed on the worker.

A major factor in determining work environment is whether a job is done indoors or outdoors. Some people do not like to be confined indoors during their working hours. They prefer to be in the sun and fresh air. Others like to work indoors, where the temperature can be controlled. This is especially true of people who live where it is very hot in the summer and very cold in the winter.

There are several questions to keep in mind about work environment. Is the work done mainly indoors or outdoors? Is it done sitting down or standing up? Will you have to endure extremes of heat and cold? Perhaps most important, is the work environment dangerous in any way? If so, you must decide whether or not extra pay would make working there worthwhile to you.

Strive for Success

The Dancer Who Came in from the Cold

It is the stuff of great spy novels. His skills and knowledge make him invaluable to the government of the Soviet Union. He is important to them yet dissatisfied with them. The secret police watch him at all times for fear he will defect to the United States.

In Canada on official business, he gets his chance. A Canadian journalist secretly slips him a note with a New York telephone number on it. He understands—it's an offer to help him defect. If he places the call and is successful, he can take his skills and knowledge and put them to better use in the West. If he places the call and is caught, however, it means the end of his career —and 15 years in a labor camp. It's a difficult and dangerous decision. Finally, his heart racing, he dials the number.

Who is this man so important to his government and yet so desperate to escape—an important physicist, a powerful general? Hardly—he is a ballet dancer, the best ballet dancer in the Soviet Union and perhaps the world. He is Mikhail Baryshnikov.

For Baryshnikov, the road to success began in the city of Riga in the Soviet republic of Latvia, where he was born in 1948. When he was a child, his mother often took him to see the ballet. There he was impressed by the strength of the dancers, by their huge leaps and dazzling turns. He also loved the stories the dance told.

When he was 12, Baryshnikov was admitted to Riga's School of Opera and Ballet Theater. Three years later, he entered Leningrad's Kirov Ballet School, where most of the Soviet Union's best dancers train. To succeed at the Kirov school took great skill as well as great determination.

At 17, Baryshnikov joined the world-famous Kirov Ballet. Before long he was a lead dancer, making a good living and enjoying many more privileges than the average Soviet citizen. He loved the dancing and was loved by audiences and critics alike.

However, there was something missing for Baryshnikov—he lacked the creative freedom to

explore many different styles of dancing. The Soviet government, which controlled almost every aspect of Soviet life, had forbidden such experimentation.

Baryshnikov defected to the United States in 1974. His love of ballet and drive for excellence led him to the top of the ballet world, and his need for artistic and personal freedom led him to the United States. Once here, he became the most popular ballet dancer in American history— the director of the American Ballet Theater, the toast of Broadway, and even a movie star.

Working conditions are often critical to an employee's success on the job. What kinds of difficulties would the workers shown here encounter if their work environments were suddenly exchanged?

Working Hours

The average work week is about 40 hours. The most common working hours are from 8 a.m. to 5 p.m., Monday through Friday. Some jobs, though, require less than eight hours of work a day. A short workday is sometimes referred to as "banker's hours" because banks used to close early in the afternoon. (Actually, most bank employees work several hours after closing time.)

Other jobs require more than eight hours of work in a day, and many require working on weekends. For example, most retail stores are open on Saturday, and many are open on Sunday. This means that salespeople must often work on weekends. These people usually get a day off during the week, but in some cases they may work more than 40 hours.

Some jobs require working nights. For example, hospitals must be staffed through the night, so some nurses work from 3 p.m. to 11 p.m. When they leave, the next shift comes on duty and works until 7 a.m. Many factories also employ people to work night shifts.

Do you have a preference for particular working hours? If so, as you research each career, you should note the usual hours of work.

Aptitudes and Abilities Required

You already know that it takes more than an interest to succeed in a career. Each career has its own set of required skills.

Some skills are easy to learn, but others take a long time to develop. It takes years to learn the diagnostic skills needed to be a medical doctor. The math skills required of an engineer also take years to develop.

As you know, skills for any kind of work are more easily learned if you have an aptitude for learning them. In Chapter 2 you analyzed your own aptitudes and abilities. As you do your research, find out which aptitudes and abilities are needed for each career. You can then match your natural talents with careers that require those same abilities.

Education and Training Required

Different careers require different kinds and levels of education and training. You will need to know the minimum requirements for each career. This could mean a grade school, high school, or college education. It could also mean two years of training at a business or technical school or a community college.

Further career education does not always mean four or more years taking notes in a college classroom. What are some other alternatives?

You may have already decided that you do not want to continue schooling of any kind after you leave high school. If so, you need to find out the educational requirements for each career you research so that you can eliminate those careers that require additional education.

If you haven't made any educational decisions, your research will help you. You may find a career you think would be just right for you. If that career requires a college education, you will know what you need to do about further schooling. You will read more about the importance of education and training in the next chapter.

Data-People-Things Relationships

You have thought about whether you would prefer working with data, people, or things. Of course, almost every job requires that you get along with people. Some jobs, such as those in sales, require working with large numbers of people—most of them complete strangers. For such careers, you would need a strong people preference. Other careers require more interest in working with data or things.

As you read in Chapter 2, the *Dictionary of Occupational Titles* is a good source of information on data-people-things functions for thousands of jobs. Your teacher or librarian can help you find the data-people-things ratings in this reference.

Salary and Fringe Benefits

One of the main reasons for working is to support your chosen life-style. Do you like to do things that cost a great deal of money? If so, you will want to check the average salary for each career that seems interesting to you. Eventually, you will want to choose a career that pays well.

Don't make the mistake of looking at just the beginning salary. Find out how much the people earn who have been working in that career for 5, 10, or 15 years. Are they earning much more than beginning workers? It is important to find out what kind of salary increases you can expect. In a few years you may have a family to support. Would you be able to support a family with the income from this career? Since most beginning workers don't have to support a family, they sometimes forget to look at the earnings of those who do.

Case Study 1

Both Paula and Bob continued working after they were married. They both had good jobs, and together they earned enough for a very comfortable life-style.

After Paula and Bob had been married for two years, Paula learned that she was pregnant. Six months later she quit her job. Bob and Paula soon realized that it would be very hard to live on just one salary. By watching their money very carefully, though, they were able to get by for a while.

Paula knew she would have to go back to work soon after the baby was born. She wanted to stay home with her child, but she had no choice. Bob's salary alone would not be enough for the three of them.

Fringe benefits are the "extras" provided by many employers. They include such things as paid vacations, health and life insurance, bonuses, and retirement plans. Some careers offer more fringe benefits than others.

Fast-growing Occupations 1988–2000		
Occupation	**Growth Rate (%)**	**New Jobs**
Paralegals	75	62,000
Medical assistants	70	104,000
Home health aides	68	160,000
Radiologic technologists and technicians	66	87,000
Data processing equipment repairers	61	44,000
Medical record technicians	60	28,000
Medical secretaries	58	120,000
Physical therapists	57	39,000
Surgical technologists	56	20,000
Operations research analysts	55	30,000
Securities and financial services sales representatives	55	109,000
Travel agents	54	77,000
Computer systems analysts	53	214,000
Physical and corrective therapy assistants	53	21,000
Social welfare service aides	52	47,000
Occupational therapists	49	16,000
Computer programmers	48	250,000
Human services workers	45	53,000
Respiratory therapists	41	23,000
Correction officers and jailers	41	76,000

Source: *Occupational Outlook Quarterly* (Fall 1989)

Figure 3-1 In the 1990s, these 20 occupations will grow much faster than average. Find two occupations that are expected to have the same growth rate but produce very different new-job totals. Explain how this is possible.

As with pay increases, fringe benefits will become more and more important to you as you get older. A retirement plan may be the furthest thing from your mind now, but you will one day be very interested in such plans. Health insurance is also an extremely important concern, given the high cost of medical care. A company that offers many fringe benefits is often preferable to one that offers a high starting salary and no benefits.

Career Outlook

Suppose you find a career you think you would enjoy. This career pays well and fits with your data-people-things preferences. There's only one problem with it—there aren't many jobs available.

The long-term outlook for a career is very important. If the outlook is poor, there probably won't be many jobs available. You certainly don't want to spend a great deal of time and money on education for a career that may not exist.

Check the outlook for each career you research. You probably won't want to choose a career if the outlook for jobs is too limited.

✓ CHECKING UP

1. What types of information should you look for when researching careers?
2. Jobs don't have values—people do. Is this statement true or false? Explain.
3. What is the difference between a salary and a fringe benefit?

3 *How To Research*

Researching careers means carefully gathering and studying information about several different careers. There are three main sources of career information. To do the best job of career research, you will need to use all of them.

- *Libraries.* Check all books, pamphlets, magazines, directories, films, computerized guidance systems, and video cassettes in your school and public libraries.

- *Career consultations.* Talk directly with workers in various careers.

- *Work.* Work at jobs in the career areas that appeal to you.

Libraries

It is easier to research careers now than ever before. More information on careers has been printed in the last decade than in the previous three centuries!

Your school and public libraries are both excellent sources of career information. Some school libraries have a special section devoted entirely to career information. These sections are often called career information centers.

If your school has a career information center, that is the place to start your research. If there is no career center, start with the library's card catalog (your library may have a microfilm reader or data bank in place of a card catalog).

Books   Looking up the subject *careers* in the card catalog will give you a list of all the available books on careers. If you want information on a particular career area (such as business, science, or engineering) look up that topic in the catalog.

The U.S. Department of Labor publishes three books that will be especially helpful to you in your career research—the *Dictionary of Occupational Titles,* the *Occupational Outlook Handbook,* and the *Guide for Occupational Exploration.* Most school and public libraries will have these references.

The *Dictionary of Occupational Titles (DOT)* describes the work activities of more than 20,000 jobs. Although it contains a great deal of information, the *DOT* is well organized and easy to use. Simply look up the name of the job you want to research in the alphabetical index of occupational titles. There you will find a nine-digit code number for that job. You can then turn to the front section of the book, which is arranged by code numbers, and find the job description you want.

It's a good idea to write down the *DOT* numbers for the jobs you are researching. The reason for this

Figure 3-2   The *Dictionary of Occupational Titles* is organized by code numbers. You look up the job title in the index at the back of the book and then use the code number to locate the discussion in the front. What is the code number for the job *customer engineering specialist (office machines)*?

and dispatches workers to job. Keeps records of repairs, installation, removal of equipment or appliances, and hours required on each job. May be designated according to utility as TELEGRAPHIC-SERVICE DISPATCHER (tel. & tel.).

959.361-010   CUSTOMER SERVICE REPRESENTATIVE (light, heat, & power) field inspector; special-gas-and-electric service investigator.
   Investigates customer complaints concerning gas leakage or low pressure, and abnormal consumption of gas or electricity by gas and electric appliances: Ascertains number and type of appliances used on premises to determine rate of utility consumption. Turns off appliances and observes gas or electric meter to detect power leakage. Examines meter for defects, such as shorts, grounds, and power loss or gas leakage. Covers gas watches for bubble formation to determines repairs and adjustments, such as cleanjets, and replacing defective meters and ls. Shuts off service and notifies repair ed, such as replacement of underground perform emergency repairs to gas service uilding. May collect delinquent accounts. ecifications for distribution changes, such n of poles or service lines, utilizing necesinvestigate illegal use of gas or electricity ght, heat, & power); UTILITIES SERVICE INVESTIGATOR (light, heat, & power)].

959.367-010   ELECTRIC POWERLINE EXAMINER (light, heat, &

AL INDEX OF OCCUPATIONAL TITLES

CUSTOMER-COMPLAINT CLERK (clerical) 241.367-014
customer engineer (any ind.) 633.281-030
CUSTOMER-ENGINEERING SPECIALIST (office mach.) 828.281-010
CUSTOMER-EQUIPMENT ENGINEER (tel. & tel.) 003.187-018
CUSTOMER-FACILITIES SUPERVISOR (tel. & tel.) 822.131-014
customer-order clerk (clerical) 249.367-054
customer-return inspector (fabric. plastics prod.; plastics mat.) 559.381-010
customer security clerk (air trans.) 372.667-010
customer service agent (air trans.) 248.367-018
customer-service clerk (insurance) 249.262-010
CUSTOMER-SERVICE CLERK (ret. tr.) 299.367-010
customer servicer (any ind.) 637.261-018
CUSTOMER-SERVICE REPRESENTATIVE (light, heat, & power; tel. & tel.; waterworks) 239.367-010
CUSTOMER SERVICE REPRESENTATIVE (light, heat, & power) 959.361-010
customer-service representative (light, heat, & power) 241.267-034
CUSTOMER-SERVICE-REPRESENTATIVE INSTRUCTOR (light, heat, & power; tel. & tel.; waterworks) 239.227-010
CUSTOMER-SERVICE REPRESENTATIVE SUPERVISOR (light,

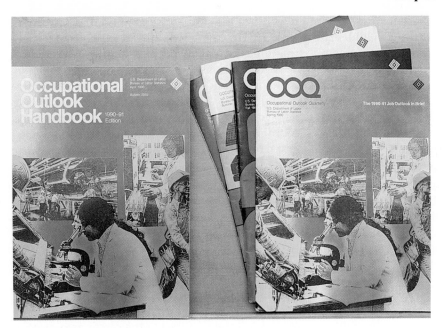

The *Occupational Outlook Handbook* is a good starting point for most career research. How is it related to the *Occupational Outlook Quarterly*?

is that many other sources of information use the *DOT* numbers to organize their information.

The *Occupational Outlook Handbook (OOH)* is one of the most helpful resources available for career research. Updated every two years, the *OOH* discusses more than 200 occupations. It provides detailed information about the following:

- How much education and training a job requires
- Usual hours of work
- Working conditions
- Expected earnings
- Job outlook
- Sources of additional information

One caution, however—such things as salaries and job outlooks change from time to time. When you use the *OOH*, try to get the most recent edition. Don't waste your time gathering old information.

A supplement to the *OOH*, the *Occupational Outlook Quarterly*, is published four times a year. The *Quarterly* is probably the most up-to-date source of information on employment trends.

The *Guide for Occupational Exploration (GOE)* is organized by interest groups. There are 12 of these groups, each divided into subcategories called worker trait groups. Each worker trait group (there are 66 in all) has descriptive information, a listing of jobs within the group, and answers to questions about the following:

- Kind of work done
- Skills needed
- Interests and aptitudes
- Preparation (education and training)

The 12 career areas described on pages 33–44 are the areas used to organize the *GOE*.

Magazines   Since most magazines are published weekly or monthly, magazine articles provide the most up-to-date information on careers. Use the *Reader's Guide to Periodical Literature* to find articles on careers you want to research. The *Reader's Guide* is an index of major magazines and journal articles. It is available in either book form or on microfilm. Articles are listed alphabetically by subject.

Files   Many libraries and career information centers also have pamphlet files. These files store pieces of information other than books and magazines. Occupational briefs, short summaries of specific jobs, are examples of the kind of information you can find on file.

The information in pamphlet files is usually indexed in the card catalog. If you are not sure where the files are located or how to use them, ask your librarian for help.

Audiovisuals   Most libraries and career centers also have a collection of audiovisual materials. **Audiovisuals** are all the things you watch and listen to, such as films, slide presentations, tape cassettes, and videotapes. Chances are your library has some filmstrips and films that tell and show you what it's like to work in certain careers.

Check with your librarian to find out what audiovisuals are available. Once you know where the materials are located and how to operate the equipment, you will be able to follow up your reading with audiovisual presentations.

Computerized Guidance Systems Your school library may have a computerized career guidance system. Most computerized systems help you determine your career interests and provide you with lists of suitable careers. Many systems also provide up-to-date information on such topics as salaries, duties, job outlook, and educational institutions.

Career Consultations

You can learn a great deal about a career by talking with someone who has worked in that area for many years. Such a meeting, held with the express purpose of obtaining information about a career, is called a **career consultation.**

After you have researched several careers, you should arrange career consultations for the two or three that interest you most. If possible, meet at the workplace. This will help you get a feel for the work environment and may even give you a chance to see people doing the kind of work you think you would like to do.

What should you ask during a career consultation? Learn all you can about the demands and

rewards of the career. Ask about duties (most and least liked), hours, working conditions, the best training, and the job outlook locally.

Next to actually working, a career consultation is the best way to learn about careers. Most successful people are happy to talk about their work. Ask your teacher, counselor, or work experience coordinator to help you. They can probably suggest names of successful people who will talk with you about their careers.

Part-Time Work

By far, the best way to learn about a career is by working at a part-time job in the field. You can work during the summer, after school, or on weekends. Your job should be one that you can do well and that you find interesting. Most important, however, it should give you an opportunity to observe a variety of jobs in the career area of your choice.

Part-time work provides the following benefits:

- An opportunity to explore careers and decide whether or not they are right for you
- A chance to broaden your understanding of the working world
- A time to develop work habits that will help you succeed in a full-time job
- A way to ease the transition from student to full-time worker

Working at a *variety* of part-time jobs enhances these benefits by giving you a chance to compare. In addition, the knowledge that you can adjust to

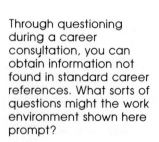

Through questioning during a career consultation, you can obtain information not found in standard career references. What sorts of questions might the work environment shown here prompt?

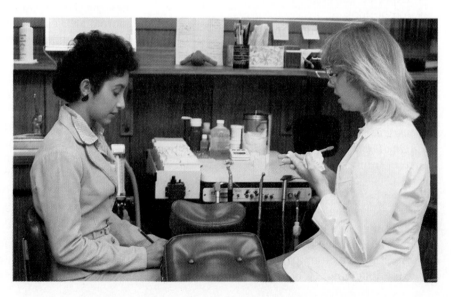

Case Study 2

Between their junior and senior years in high school, Alan and Lisa began working at Charter Motor Company, a local garage and service station. They were hired as service station attendants and worked full-time until school began in the fall. They pumped gas, cleaned windshields, and checked tire pressure. They made change for cash customers and wrote out credit slips for credit customers. When there were no gasoline customers, they helped the shop mechanics. Alan and Lisa made minor repairs, installed fan belts and batteries, and sometimes helped with oil changes and tune-ups.

At the end of the summer, Alan and Lisa went back to school. A full-time worker replaced them during school hours, but they continued working part-time after school.

By this time Alan knew that he didn't care much for direct contact with customers. He preferred helping the mechanics, and he mentioned this to his boss. Because there was an increase in the station's repair business, Alan became an assistant to one of the shop mechanics.

Lisa, on the other hand, liked contact with customers more than any other part of her job. Soon she was selling them tires, batteries, and other accessories.

After graduating, Alan stayed with Charter Motor Company as a full-time mechanic. Lisa began a sales training program. She worked for the oil company that supplied Charter.

different work situations and different job demands is a big confidence builder.

Work Experience Programs Does your school have a work experience or career development program? Such a program can help you select realistic career goals and find part-time work related to these goals. Work experience programs are known by several names—cooperative education, cooperative work experience, work study, and diversified occupations, to name a few.

Many of the vocational work experience programs are called **cooperative programs** because of

the cooperation that goes on between the school and employers. A teacher-coordinator teaches a class related to the work the students are doing and supervises them on their jobs. Employers pay students at least the minimum wage, and the school usually grants credits for time spent on the job.

Probably the most common type of work experience program you will encounter is the vocational program. Vocational work experience provides specific career preparation. Students in vocational programs get jobs related to the careers they are preparing for in school.

Another common type of work experience program is general work experience. General work experience provides useful experiences for young people through school-supervised, part-time employment. This work does not need to be related to a specific career goal. It is part of the total school program.

Students successfully completing a general work experience program receive school credits. They, too, are paid the minimum wage. The program's goals are to develop desirable attitudes and to help students see the relationship between their schooling and job success.

A third type of work experience program is the exploratory program. Exploratory programs provide students with an opportunity to try several different kinds of jobs. In most such programs students receive credits but no pay.

While the lack of pay is a disadvantage, there are some advantages to jobs in exploratory programs. The main advantage is the variety of work experiences available in such programs. You can try jobs that would not ordinarily be available to you on a paid basis. Employer attitude is another advantage. When employers are not paying you, they are often more willing to take the time to show you around. As a result, you get more opportunities to talk to different kinds of workers and to explore the work environment.

Volunteer Work If you can't get a part-time job through a school program, you might try volunteer work. You can volunteer at hospitals, the American Red Cross, schools, the YMCA/YWCA, and humane societies. Your counselor or work experience coordinator can probably refer you to organizations that need volunteers.

Many schools give credits for volunteer work done through a work experience program. Most

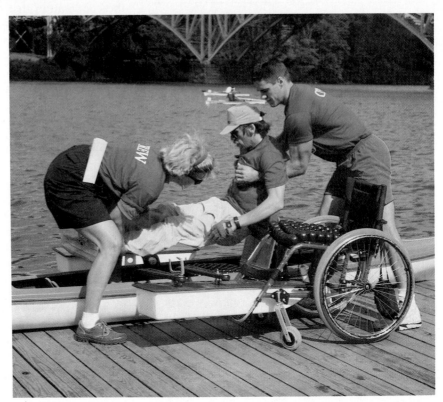

A wide variety of public, social, and charitable organizations depend on volunteer help to maintain their programs. How can such unpaid work help you make a career decision?

volunteer work falls into these categories:

- Office jobs (bookkeeper, receptionist, typist, and switchboard operator)
- Health career jobs (animal caretaker, blood-pressure screener, candy striper, first-aid instructor, laboratory aide, and X-ray aide)
- Recreation jobs (camp counselor, crafts instructor, dance teacher, and referee/umpire)

- Education jobs (teacher's aide and tutor)

Working on Your Own   Even without a work experience program or the possibility of volunteer work, you may still find part-time work. You could go into business for yourself. Many people are willing to pay students to wash cars, paint walls, or weed lawns.

If you are interested in working for yourself, be sure to read Chapter 14. It explains many of the things you need to know about starting a business.

---

*M*AKE A DECISIO*N*

Suppose you work after school and on Saturdays in a fast-food restaurant. You earn a few cents more than the minimum wage. One day your work experience coordinator comes to you and asks if you would like to "explore" (on an unpaid basis) exactly the kind of work you've been wanting to try. Unfortunately, the working hours of the exploratory job are the same as the hours you've been working at the restaurant. What's your decision—will you keep your paying job or take the exploratory work experience? Give the reasons for your decision.

✓ CHECKING UP

1. Name three basic career references you are likely to find in the public library. Then describe one feature that makes each reference different from the other.
2. What can a career consultation tell you about a job that library research cannot?
3. What special benefits does a part-time job have for someone doing career research?

Review Your Learning

CHAPTER SUMMARY

The third and fourth steps in the career decision-making process are to identify some careers that interest you and then to explore them. If you don't have any career ideas of your own, exploring the U.S. Department of Labor's career interest areas is a good way to find some possibilities.

In doing your research, you must find out many things about each career. You must learn how much education and training are required; what aptitudes and abilities are needed; and whether the work is primarily with data, people, or things.

There are several effective ways to research careers. You can learn a great deal by reading the many career books, magazines, and pamphlets at your school and local public library. You can also learn about specific careers by conducting career consultations with people who have been successful in areas that interest you. The best way to research a career, though, is to get a part-time job in that field.

TERMS TO KNOW

Write a short letter requesting an interview with someone who works in a career that interests you. Use all of the following terms:

career interest area
work environment
fringe benefits
audiovisuals
career consultation
cooperative program

STUDY QUESTIONS

1. Why should you research several careers?
2. Where are at least two places you can get career ideas in your day-to-day living?
3. If you place a high value on having a great deal of leisure time, is a career in sales a good choice for you? Why or why not?
4. How are all the jobs in a career interest area related to each other?
5. If creativity is one of your values and one of your abilities, what career interest area might you want to explore?
6. If you enjoy watching TV detective shows, what career area might you be interested in?
7. Name at least three things a person must be able to do to be successful at selling.
8. If you value helping other people more than any other activity, which career area should you be sure to explore?
9. What nine factors should you consider for each career that you research?
10. What are four types of fringe benefits?
11. What are the three major sources of career information?
12. Name four types of work experience programs.

CRITICAL THINKING

1. Assume you have a choice of two jobs you think you might enjoy. The first job has a high starting salary, but those who have been with the company for five years earn just about the same amount. The second job has a lower starting salary, but those who have been with the company five years earn much more than experienced workers at the first company. Which of the jobs would you take? Explain your answer.
2. Speculate about what might be a good career choice for someone who has both artistic talent and an aptitude for science.
3. Assume that you place the highest value on spending time with your family. You also like detailed work that you can do at your own pace and have an aptitude for math. What are some careers that are compatible with your aptitudes, skills, and values?

Review Your Learning

DISCUSSION STARTERS

1. It will probably not be possible for you to find a career in which all of the nine factors you should consider in your career research match what you would most prefer. Given this probability, in which areas (job values, duties and responsibilities, work environment, etc.) would you be most willing to compromise? least willing?
2. Describe how a person might be able to combine interests from two or more interest areas into one career. Give several examples of jobs that cross interest boundaries.
3. Describe your ideal work environment. To what extent and how does it differ from your classmates' descriptions? What do you think accounts for these differences?
4. What, if any, special personality traits do you think might be necessary for a woman who chooses a traditionally male career, such as fire fighting or truck driving?

BUILDING BASIC SKILLS

Math

1. In comparing two jobs in the sales field, you see that one offers a starting salary of $19,000, with a health insurance policy worth $200 a month and an auto expense allowance of $.20 a mile up to 500 miles a month. The other job offers a salary of $22,000 a year but no fringe benefits. Which job pays more overall (assuming you drive an average of 400 miles per month)? How much more?

Leadership

2. You've been working in the research division of Super Chemco Industries for six months now. The decision to take the job with the company was a hard one for you. You had intended to use your scientific skills to teach high school chemistry. You liked working with young people, and you felt that you wanted to return something to the school system that had made you the first person in your family to graduate from college. What changed your mind was financial reality—you could earn twice as much in industry. Still, your unmet values are nagging you. How can you communicate your social concerns (and even possibly satisfy them) within the corporate structure of Super Chemco?

Decision Making

3. After working at the Yogurt Palace for six months, you've been offered a promotion to assistant manager. With the promotion comes a 15 percent raise—and the satisfaction of knowing you'll be the youngest assistant manager the store has ever had. You'll also have to increase your work load from 16 to 24 hours a week. Should you accept the promotion or not? (*Note:* It's your last semester of high school, and you'll be going away to college in the fall.)

SUGGESTED ACTIVITIES

1. Select two careers you would like to learn about. Then find one successful person working in each of these areas and interview them about the kind of work they do.
2. Prepare a collage illustrating one career interest area that you think you would enjoy. Show some of the different workers in that area. Include pictures of the various work environments.

Planning for Success

*D*id you follow through on the suggestions in the first three chapters? If so, you have completed the first four steps in the career decision-making process. If not, you may need more time to define your needs and wants, analyze your resources, identify your choices, and gather information on each choice.

When you have done all of these things, you are ready for the last steps in the decision-making process. These steps involve evaluating your choices, making a decision, and planning how you will reach your ultimate career goal. This chapter will help you with each of these important steps.

1 *Making a Career Decision*

As you approach the final stages of the career decision-making process, you may feel you're not ready to make such an important choice. You may feel you need more time, that you just don't know what you want to do.

It's only natural for you to hesitate at this point. If you choose a career now, you may work in that career for years—even a lifetime. You want to be sure you're making the right choice. You may think that you should take several more months (or even several more years) to make such an important decision.

Career decisions *are* important—perhaps the most important decisions you'll ever make. This does not mean, however, that you should wait until you're absolutely sure what you want to do before you decide. You may know some recent high school graduates who have not yet made any career decisions. What are these people doing? Are they making any progress toward achieving their life-style goals, or are they wasting time, waiting until they "find themselves"? Some of these people may be using "I need more time" as an excuse to avoid making a difficult decision. Such people may reach their thirtieth birthdays and still have not made their first career decisions. Don't you be among them. Try to decide—now.

Evaluating Your Choices

The fifth step in the decision-making process is to evaluate your choices. In this step you will compare what you've learned about yourself with the career information you've gathered. You will do this to find the best possible match between yourself and a career.

A good tool to use in evaluating your choices is a **personal career profile** (Figure 4-1). It allows you to arrange side-by-side what you have learned about yourself and what you have learned about your career choices. You should prepare a profile for each of the careers in which you are interested. The most efficient way to do this is to write the personal information just once and then duplicate as many copies of the form as you will need.

After completing all of your profiles, go back and reread them very carefully. Then ask yourself these questions:

- Does this career match up well with my values?
- Will I find the duties and responsibilities of this career interesting?
- Will I be happy with the work environment?
- Will the working hours be compatible with my desired life-style?
- Do I have the skills needed in this career—or the aptitudes to develop them?
- Am I willing to continue my education as long as necessary to work in this career? Can I afford to do so?
- Do the data-people-things requirements in this career match up well with my own preferences?
- Will this career pay well enough for me to live the life-style I want to live in 5, 10, or 20 years? Will it provide the fringe benefits I'll need?
- What is the career outlook? Will there be jobs available in this career when I am ready to begin work? Is the long-term outlook good?

Staying Flexible

You are now ready for the sixth step in the career decision-making process. It's time to make your choice. Which career do you want to pursue?

Making this decision will have a positive influence on your life. It will give you a sense of direction, something to work toward. For perhaps the first time in your life, you will know where you are going.

Still, as noted earlier, making such a decision can be scary. It may help to keep in mind that your choice now is not—and should not—be carved in stone. It's a *flexible* decision—even as you make it, you know you may change your mind. Six months or a year from now, you may find that your choice was not a good one for you. Maybe you overlooked some important information or misjudged your willingness to continue your education. What will you do? You will simply go through the decision-making process again. This time, however, you'll be more informed about yourself and your career aspirations.

Personal Career Profile

Name _Lucinda Martinez_   Date _May 12, 1991_   Career _Teacher_

Personal Information	**Career Information**	**Match** (1–5, with 5 being the best match)
Your Values: The value scales I took showed that I like to help other people (humanitarianism). I like having "power" over others—I like to be a leader. Doing creative things is fun, too.	**Career Values:** As a teacher, I would have a chance to help others—that's what it's all about. Teachers certainly have plenty of opportunities to be leaders, too. Teachers also need to be creative.	4
Your Interests: My hobby interests have always been photography, reading, tennis, and most outdoor sports. After flying with Dan last summer, I'd dearly love to take flying lessons. My career interest survey showed that I might like a career in leading/influencing, science, or maybe a "humanitarian" career.	**Career Duties and Responsibilities:** As a teacher, I would present information, direct student discussions and activities in class. I would help each student individually, too. (Maybe I could teach PE, sports, or science in a high school.) A teacher's working conditions would be good in most schools. (Summers off!)	4
Your Personality: I like people, and I have a good attitude toward learning. I have an "open" mind. I'm enthusiastic, too; but I don't have the energy and drive that some people have. I don't know if I could work night after night.	**Personality Type Needed:** A teacher must like kids—even when they aren't very likable! I would have to prepare my lessons every day—couldn't just forget about it. Teachers need to be organized, too—not like Mr. Jackson! They also need to treat all their students alike.	4
Data-People-Things Preferences: I think I like working with people most of all. I wouldn't want to be stuck in an office all day with only "data" to talk to. I also wouldn't like working only with things. Some data would be okay, though.	**Data-People-Things Relationships:** Teachers work mostly with people— their students, other teachers, the principal, parents. They work with data (information), too, though. I don't think they work much with things.	4
Skills and Aptitudes: I may have some "natural" teaching skills—the kids at the YMCA always come to me for help. I helped several kids in Miss Moore's class. Math and science are easy for me. I'm also the best softball player in 4th period PE!	**Skills and Aptitudes Required:** Being able to present information so students can understand it is a very important skill. Of course, you must know your subject. An appetite for learning new approaches to teaching is important, too.	4
Education/Training Acceptable: I sure never thought I would go to college—I never even liked doing the homework in high school! Here I am, though, a senior with no real prospects of a good job. Maybe college is the answer.	**Education/Training Required:** Four years (it sounds like forever, but I guess it does go fast)—four years of college is required before you can begin teaching in most states. Some states require course work beyond that.	2

Figure 4-1   To make it easier to use several career profiles at once, the form has a third column that allows you to express in number form how closely your personal and career traits match. The higher the number, the closer the match. Is teaching a good career choice for the person who filled out this sample form? Explain.

Career planning can be the difference between drifting and moving purposefully toward the life-style you want. What role does a personal career profile play in this process?

Changing a career decision is not necessarily a bad thing, especially if you make the change before you begin working or early in your career. Changes made after you've been working for a few years can be more costly in terms of both time and money. Many people do, however, change their careers later in life. Government studies show that the average American changes careers five times.

The thing to remember is that changing a decision is better than never having made a decision at all. If you make a decision, you will find out whether you like a certain career. If it turns out that you don't, you'll at least have eliminated one possibility. You will also be that much closer to the right career for you.

✓ CHECKING UP

1. Why is it *not* a good idea to put off making a career decision for a few years until you "find yourself"?

2. How does a personal career profile help you decide on a career?

3. Refer to the data-people-things entries in the sample career profile (Figure 4-1). In what respects might some of the student author's comments be inaccurate?

2 *Drawing Up a Plan of Action*

Have you made a career decision? Did you decide which of your career choices is the best match for your particular interests and abilities? If so, you should now begin planning how you will reach your goal.

There is no substitute for planning if you want to be successful and happy. Having a plan doesn't guarantee success, but it greatly improves your chances.

In planning to reach your ultimate career goal, you will first need to establish some intermediate planning goals. In establishing these goals, you will make decisions about the kind and amount of education and training you will need. This lesson will help you frame your planning goals in the most helpful form. It will also help you learn more about the importance of education and training. You will then be ready to draw up a plan of action for achieving your ultimate career goal.

Setting Planning Goals

Planning goals are all the steps you must take to get from where you are now to where you want to be. As you achieve these goals, you gain confidence. Your life seems to have a sense of direction. You move steadily toward your ultimate career goal.

Be Specific To know whether or not you are making progress toward your ultimate career goal, you must make your planning goals specific. A statement such as "I want to be a success" is too general. It doesn't really give you anything to aim for. "I want to be accepted by a college with a good journalism program" is much more specific. It is a planning goal that will help you. It is a goal that makes it much easier for you to figure out what you need to do to succeed.

Try writing out statements of all your planning goals. Then see if you can make them more specific. The more specific the statements, the faster you will progress toward your ultimate career goal.

Be Realistic Besides being specific, your planning goals should be realistic. Not everyone can be a rock star or a professional athlete. If you're 5'3", you will probably never play basketball for the Lakers. If you're color blind, you probably won't be a famous painter. If you have looked closely at your aptitudes and abilities, you should be able to set realistic planning goals.

Planning Goals	
General	**Specific**
I want to be involved in publishing.	I want to edit science magazines and journals for high school and college students.
I want to drive a truck.	I want a steady job driving a delivery truck for a large department store.
I want to have something to do with food.	I want to be a cook in a hotel restaurant.
I want to work with computers.	I want to be an electronics technician specializing in the repair of business computer systems.
I want to work with tools and machines.	I want to be a tool and die maker for an automobile manufacturer.

Figure 4-2 Having a general idea of what you want to do in career terms is not good enough. You must go back and rewrite any general planning goals to make them as specific as possible. Study the goals shown here. Which do you think would be more helpful? Why?

Do not confuse the term *realistic* with *traditional,* however. Most truck drivers, carpenters, airline pilots, doctors, lawyers, and politicians have traditionally been men; but in recent years these traditions have been changing. Today women have many more choices. It is very realistic for teenaged girls to consider the careers listed here—or any others, for that matter.

Consider Short-, Medium-, and Long-Range Goals When you set your planning goals, think in terms of short-, medium-, and long-range goals. They will be your stepping stones on the way to achieving your ultimate career goal and desired life-style. In other words, they will help you know that you are on the right track and on schedule.

Let's say your ultimate goal is to operate a chain of successful restaurants. A long-range goal might be to open your own restaurant by the time you are 40. A medium-range goal might be to become the chef at a good restaurant by the time you are 30. A short-range goal might be to attend cooking school.

Your short-, medium-, and long-range goals will also help you determine whether or not you need to change your ultimate goal. Suppose you want to be a surgical nurse. You may set a short-range goal to work as a candy striper. Working as a candy striper will help you decide if you really like nursing. If you discover that you don't, your short-range goal will have prevented you from wasting years of hard work and training.

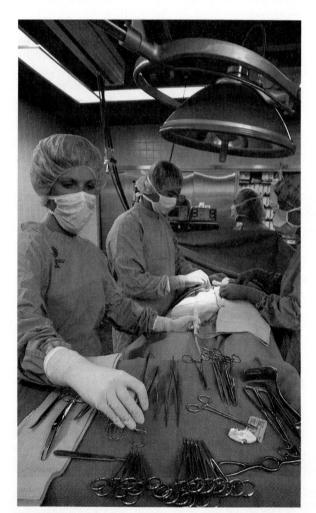
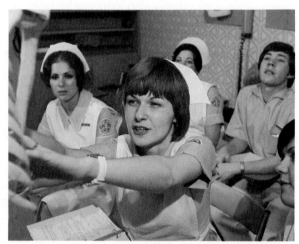
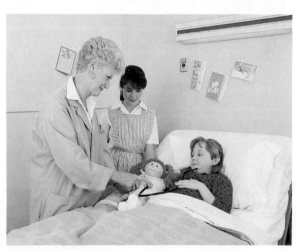

Planning goals define the steps you must take to reach your ultimate career goal. Which types of planning goals are illustrated here?

Strive for Success

His Best Foot Forward

Born in Dublin in 1933, Christy Brown was the tenth among 12 children of a poor Irish bricklayer and his wife. Born so severely crippled by cerebral palsy that the only part of his body he could control was his left foot, Brown spent the first four years of his life scooting around the floor of his house on his back. The rest of the family thought Brown was too severely retarded to understand them and never talked directly to him. His mother was convinced, however, that inside his twisted and uncontrollable body was a sensitive little boy.

Two things happened to show other people that Mrs. Brown was right. The first incident occurred when Brown was five, alone in the house with his mother. She fainted and fell down the stairs, seriously hurting herself. Brown scooted himself down the staircase, across the room, and banged his head on the front door until a neighbor came. He saved his mother's life.

Sometime later, the family was sitting around the dining table. Brown was on the floor close to one of his sisters, who was writing with chalk on a slate. Brown grabbed the chalk from his sister's hand with his foot, got it between his toes, and tried to draw or write something on the floor. After a few minutes, the family read in messy, uneven, letters the word *Mother*.

There was a party in the Brown house that night, and soon afterward Mrs. Brown applied to government social service agencies to have Brown tested. Before long, he had a government-supplied speech therapist and began to talk. The Browns were told he was a very bright boy.

As he used his left foot more and more, it became as good as a hand for drawing and writing. Brown began to spend much of his time drawing pictures and, later, painting. In painting he could express the frustration he felt at being locked in a body that wouldn't do what he wanted it to do. After his speech therapist showed Brown's paintings to other people, Brown was on his way to making his living as an artist. When he was 27, he had his own show at a Dublin art gallery, and critics praised him.

Brown also became a writer. When he was 21, his autobiography, *My Left Foot,* was published. It took him years to pick out the letters on a typewriter with the toes of his left foot. It was a painful and slow way to write, and he often felt frustrated and angry, but he never gave up. His persistence paid off, and the book sold very well in many countries.

Deciding on Education and Training

As you set your goals, you probably began to realize the importance of education and training. Almost all jobs in any career require some special training. The amount of training can vary from a few days of on-the-job experience to several years of college work. This means that at least one of your goals should involve getting the education and training that you will need in your chosen career.

Graduation from high school has become the minimum requirement for most jobs. Although you can get a job without a high school diploma, your opportunities are likely to be very limited. The jobs available for people without high school diplomas are usually the jobs no one else wants.

Labor Department surveys show a close relationship between job security and education. It is also true that most careers requiring more education and training pay higher salaries in the long run.

Education and training do not guarantee success in the world of work. They do, however, greatly improve your chances for success. The more education and training you have, the more career opportunities you'll have to choose from. This is why it is so important for you to select the program you need and get started learning.

On-the-Job-Training   Many companies offer workers on-the-job training. This training can last from a few days to two or three years. The starting pay for on-the-job training is low, but it increases gradually. Some industries offer in-plant training programs that include formal classroom instruction. Other companies send workers to junior colleges and other schools.

To find the type of on-the-job training you want, apply to the local job service office of the state employment service. You may also apply directly to company personnel offices and private employment agencies.

Apprenticeship   An **apprentice** is someone who learns how to do a certain job through hands-on experience under the guidance of a skilled worker. There are apprenticeship programs for more than 400 occupations.

The most popular apprenticeship programs are in the trades. A **trade** is an occupation that requires

---

SITUATION
SOLUTION

Sharing Work Space

Your work experience teacher tells you that your employer has complained that you leave the desk you share with another employee in a mess. You know that each time this has happened it has been because the other employee arrived early and insisted that you give up the desk before you had a chance to tidy up. The other employee has worked for the company for ten years, and you don't want to get on his bad side.

1. What can you say to the other employee the next time he arrives early and wants you to move?
2. How will you convince your work experience teacher that the situation will not hurt the work experience program?
3. What can you do to show the other employee that you appreciate being able to use his desk?

---

manual or mechanical skill. Trade occupations are those such as machining, plumbing, carpentry, painting, and sheet metal work.

An apprenticeship offers several advantages to young workers entering the world of work. First, training through experience is an excellent way to learn trade skills and job-related information. Another advantage is that your training does not cost much. In fact, you can earn money while you are an apprentice. You would be paid less than skilled workers, but as your skills increased, so would your pay.

The length of time required to complete an apprenticeship program varies. It can take up to six years. The average, though, is about four years.

Most apprenticeship programs are registered with the federal or state government. Apprentices who complete these programs receive certificates from the U.S. Department of Labor or the state apprenticeship agency. For more information on apprenticeship programs in your area, contact your local state employment office or write to the Department of Labor. Your teacher may have addresses and telephone numbers.

An apprenticeship allows you to learn under the personal guidance of someone who is an expert in the trade you have chosen. What other advantage does this form of training offer?

Vocational Schools The work that a person does to earn a living is said to be that person's **vocation.** The Vocational Education Act of 1963 established a system of schools to help people learn vocations.

Vocational schools offer work-related programs for high school students and young adults just out of school. Most vocational schools also offer evening programs for adults.

Vocational-technical schools have two purposes. First, they try to provide programs in which people can learn skills that will meet the labor needs of the community. Second, they give students a chance to learn the skills they need to get a job.

Vocational schools are not expensive to attend. Some charge as little as $16 per year for basic fees. Class fees for tools and materials depend on the course but are low in most schools.

You can take a variety of courses in a vocational school. Business, health, industry, and agriculture are just a few of the career areas covered. Some of the larger schools offer training for more than 40 industrial occupations.

The vocational school in your area may have a program that will help you reach one of your career goals. How much longer will you be in high school? You may still have time to complete the program you need. If not, you can attend the area vocational school after graduation. See your counselor for more information.

Trade Schools Private trade schools teach students how to solve real work problems in joblike settings. These schools often have programs that are not available in public vocational schools. Trade schools, however, are more expensive than vocational schools. The costs range from a few hundred to several thousand dollars for a complete program.

The length of time needed to complete a trade school program depends on the skills you want to learn. Since you would take only courses in your chosen field, you can complete most programs in less than two years.

Have you chosen a career in the trades? Do you want to begin work as soon as possible? If so, you should ask your school counselor about trade schools.

Community Colleges   Community colleges are sometimes called junior or city colleges. Such schools offer two years of college-level work in vocational and academic areas.

Many of the same vocational and technical courses offered in trade schools are available in community colleges. In fact, community colleges offer instruction in more than 60 occupational areas. These include agriculture, restaurant management, business, health, industry, and service occupations. The credit you earn in many of these courses can be transferred to a four-year college.

Many community colleges offer courses at night. This makes it possible for you to work during the day and go to school in the evening. In this way you can acquire needed education and training while earning some money.

Community colleges are much less expensive to attend than private trade schools and four-year colleges. If you attend a local junior college, you may not pay any **tuition** (the cost of attending a school) at all. Your only expenses would probably be for books and perhaps a small student activity fee. If you live at home, you won't have to pay room and board costs either.

You probably have a community college near you. Talk to your school counselor. He or she probably knows what programs are available. If the community college offers the courses you want, you may want to enroll.

Colleges and Universities   A **profession** is a career that requires specialized training and a long period of academic preparation. Some examples of professions are law, medicine, and teaching. If you plan to enter a profession, you will probably need a college degree.

Most professions require a bachelor's degree, which usually means four years of college. Other professions require six to eight years of college. Over 2,000 colleges and universities offer professional and technical training to qualified high school graduates.

Every college will require you to take a certain number of general education courses. You will also be required to take a certain number of courses in your area of specialization. Beyond these requirements, you may choose the courses you like.

Selecting a college is much like making a career decision. There are a great many factors to consider. To pick the best school for you, you will want to

Large private and state universities usually offer students the broadest range of study areas. For what kinds of students would this be an advantage?

go through all seven steps of the decision-making process.

Not all colleges offer the same programs. Some colleges are especially good for one kind of program but not as strong in others. To start, then, you will want to find several colleges with strong programs in your area of interest. You should compare these schools on the basis of size, location, cost, overall quality, and entrance and graduation requirements.

Location and size will probably be important considerations in your choice. You may want to stay close to home, or you may not. You may want to attend a very large state university, or perhaps you would be more comfortable in a small private school.

The cost of a college education varies greatly, depending on the type of school you choose. State schools are usually less expensive than private schools. However, to take advantage of the lower costs you must usually be a state resident. For example, if you live in Iowa you would pay much more to attend the University of Michigan than a student from Michigan.

You may be able to get some help in paying your college expenses. You can apply for scholarships and grants, some of which may pay for almost all your costs. You can borrow money, sometimes without interest, to pay for your education. Many students work part-time while attending college to help pay their expenses.

Like costs, entrance and graduation requirements vary greatly from school to school. Some colleges accept only those students who were in the top 10 or 15 percent of their graduating classes. Many colleges reject students who haven't had certain high school courses. You'll also find that once you are admitted, the number and variety of courses required for graduation will be greater at some schools than at others.

There are many sources of information on colleges and universities. The best place to start is usually your school guidance office. There you will find college catalogs, directories, and many other helpful references.

Talk to your counselor. He or she knows a great deal about most of the schools in your local area and state. Your counselor also knows how to get more detailed information about any school in which you are interested.

Case Study 1

Christine and George grew up as next-door neighbors in a Chicago suburb. They were good friends and attended the same schools from kindergarten through high school.

During their senior year, both George and Christine discussed their career goals with their counselor, Mr. Johnson. He helped them work through the decision-making process, and both chose career goals.

George decided he wanted to become an engineer. He knew it would be a difficult program because it would require a great deal of math. What's more, many of the colleges Mr. Johnson recommended had *five-year* programs for engineering, which sounded like an enormous amount of work to George. Still, George had a vision of his future life-style, and it required the good income an engineering job would provide.

Christine chose accounting as her career goal. She had always enjoyed working with numbers.

Both Christine and George applied to the University of Illinois, and both were accepted. One of the key choices Christine and George had to make early in their college careers was whether to study or to socialize. Christine kept a good balance of study and social activities and graduated with an A- average in the spring of 1995. George's college life took a different turn. There were parties almost every weekend, and George went to most of them. After two years, George had a C-average, which was not good enough to continue in engineering.

George switched his career goal to science teacher. (He thought that education courses might be a little easier.) As a result, it would take him five years to graduate with a four-year degree. When someone asked him how changing career goals would affect him, George was philosophical. "Oh, I won't have as luxurious a life-style as I had planned—teachers don't make as much as engineers—but not too many people really get what they want out of life anyway."

Adult Education   College is not the only road to a successful career. Another avenue is called adult, or continuing, education. This route may take longer, but the satisfaction is just as great.

Today much attention is being given to adult education. Most city high schools offer evening courses in business and industrial education. Some private schools have evening programs for people who work during the day. In many subjects, correspondence courses are also offered.

Colleges and universities also encourage older people to return to school. They do this by offering evening courses of special interest to adults. Anyone who wants to learn has many opportunities.

Military-Service Training   The military service is the largest employer in the United States, hiring 330,000 new recruits each year. The four services (the Army, Navy, Air Force, and Marine Corps) offer training in over 200 different occupations, ranging from health care to computer programming and photography. In fact, there is a military training program for almost any technical career you can think of and some professional careers (such as engineering or accountancy) as well.

Depending on the type of training you choose, you must enlist for up to six years of active duty. Check with an armed services recruiting office to see how long of an enlistment is required for your chosen career.

The services require that all applicants take the Armed Services Vocational Aptitude Battery (ASVAB). Like most aptitude tests, this one is designed to help people discover which careers they are most suited for. If the test shows that you have an aptitude for your chosen career, the military service can usually guarantee that you will receive appropriate training during your enlistment. Most high schools offer the ASVAB. Check with your counselor.

Many of the job skills taught in the military can be readily—and profitably—transferred to civilian life. Name at least three careers like the one shown here for which you can begin your preparation in the military.

During the time you are receiving your in-service training, you will be paid. Indeed, if you choose a career in which there is a shortage of qualified people, you may even be eligible for a bonus of up to $8,000. Once you have finished serving the enlistment period you signed up for, you can take your new skills into the civilian world.

The military services also offer grants for college, technical education, or apprenticeship programs after you finish your enlistment obligation. The GI Bill is a program in which the service enlistee has an amount deducted from his or her pay each month up to a total of $1,200. In return, the government pays $10,800 towards the participant's education costs. This program is available to all people who join the services.

The individual services also offer other grants of up to $25,000. These require that you enlist for at least four years of active duty, with another four years in the reserves. Such programs help educate many young men and women who could not otherwise afford college or technical school.

There are also military programs for people who are in college, including scholarship programs that pay the total cost of a four-year college education. Students on these scholarships are considered to be in training for the service while they are in school. They take some military training courses in addition to their regular classwork. After graduation, they must serve four years' active duty as officers in the service.

Many people like military life; others do not. If you think you might like serving in the military, see your counselor or an armed services recruiter.

MAKE A DECISION

You have already made your flexible career decision. You know what you want to do, but you are not yet sure how you are going to go about reaching your goal. You could go to school full-time for two years, four years, or even six years and then enter your career field. You could also get an entry-level job, save some money, and go to school later. You could even combine these two approaches. What's your decision—full-time school now, work later; work now, school later; or one of the combinations in between? Give the reasons for your decision.

Case Study 2

After doing a great deal of career exploration and research, Joe wasn't entirely sure what he wanted to do, but he made the best decision he could at the time. He decided that he wanted to own his own airplane and have his own crop-dusting business. He had grown up working on farms and loved outdoor life. He also liked machines, speed, and excitement—and he had always dreamed of flying an airplane.

The first thing Joe did after making his decision was to talk with his school counselor. She answered most of Joe's questions and told him where he could find more information. Joe left the counselor's office ready to write his plan of action.

Luckily, Joe had already taken several agriculture courses, and he belonged to the Future Farmers of America. During his last semester of high school, he would take all the math courses he could (it would help with navigation problems). He would also see about getting a part-time job at the local fertilizer dealership. (An airport job would have been great, but there were no airports nearby.)

Joe did not have enough money to buy a plane. He didn't even have money for the training program he would need to get his pilot's license. Since well-paid jobs were scarce locally, Joe knew he would have a difficult time saving any money. He decided the best plan for him would be to join the Air Force. He didn't think he could handle the officer-pilot program, but airplane maintenance was a possibility. (It was also something he would need to know for his own business.) While he was in the service, he would save money for his pilot training.

After leaving the Air Force, Joe planned to take flying lessons at the flying school affiliated with the local community college. He would also take some business courses. These would help him manage his own business.

With this general plan in mind, Joe wrote down the short-, medium-, and long-range goals that would lead to his ultimate career goal—crop duster. His final career plan is shown in Figure 4-3.

Career Plan

Short-Range Goals		Long-Range Goals	
	Complete by		Complete by
Take algebra	December 1991	Take pilot training course	August 1998
Talk to Air Force recruiter	October 15, 1991	Take business administration courses at Valley Community College	August 1998
Get part-time job with fertilizer distributor (substitute other ag-related job if not available)	November 1, 1991	Work part-time at Municipal Airport as airplane mechanic	October 1998
Take geometry	May 25, 1992		
Graduate from high school	June 1, 1992	Graduate from pilot training course	July 1999
Join Air Force	July 1, 1992	Obtain associate's degree	May 2000

Medium-Range Goals		Full-time job as airplane mechanic	Fall 2000
Acquire general experience and knowledge of airplane maintenance	1992–1998	Save more money and shop for plane	Winter 2000–2001
Save 15–20 percent of pay	1992–1998	Buy plane	Spring 2001
Use free time to read and study about airplanes and business management	1992–1998		

Ultimate Career Goal

	Complete by
Begin doing business as crop duster	Summer 2001

Figure 4-3   A career plan should include specific goals arranged in chronological order. Does Joe, the author of this sample plan, intend to get a college degree? When, where, and how?

Writing down your plan of action is an important part of career decision making. Why?

Committing Yourself on Paper

You have just read about many different ways you can get the education and training you need to reach your ultimate career goal. You now need to choose the program or school that will help you the most. If you will be in high school another semester or so, you can take some high school courses that will help you. If you will graduate soon, begin now to select the educational and training programs you'll need after high school.

Answering the following questions will give you most of the information you need to prepare your career plan.

- What is my ultimate career goal?
- What high school courses can I still take to help me reach my career goal?
- What education and training must I acquire if I am to attain my career goal?
- Of the necessary education and training, how much must I get before I enter the career field in which I am interested?
- What kinds of schools offer the education and training I need?
- How much money will I need to pay for my education and training? Where will this money come from?
- How much of the education and training I need can I get on the job?
- What part-time jobs will help me develop the knowledge and skills I need to reach my career goal?

After answering these questions (and any others that occur to you), start preparing your plan. Set it up in terms of short-, medium-, and long-range goals.

It is important that you write these down. The writing process will force you to develop specific plans. Fill in dates by which you will have begun or accomplished each planning goal. This will help you check from time to time whether you are making progress toward your ultimate goal.

Remember that your decisions and plans are flexible. You can always change them—in fact, you probably will. The advantage to having a plan, though, is that you will be moving ahead. Even as you change your goals, you will be getting closer to a career that is right for you.

✓ CHECKING UP

1. How do you develop a plan of action for achieving a career goal?
2. Assume that you need two years of technical training after high school to pursue your chosen career, but you have little money to pay for it. What are your educational options?
3. What will most likely be the first goals you enter in your own career plan?

CHAPTER SUMMARY

In this chapter you continued with the career decision-making process you started in Chapter 1. First you evaluated your career choices by matching your knowledge about yourself with your career information. You then learned the importance of making a flexible choice—one that would give you something to work toward and prevent you from wasting time.

After making your career decision, you learned about the need to plan your career. This meant establishing planning goals and choosing the kind and amount of education and training you would need. The education and training options included on-the-job training, apprenticeships, vocational and trade schools, community colleges, four-year colleges and universities, military service, and adult education.

Finally, you wrote out your career plan. You set planning goals for yourself and assigned time limits to these goals so that you could check your progress. You developed a plan of action that should take you to your ultimate career goal.

TERMS TO KNOW

On a separate sheet of paper, write sentences for each of the following terms:

personal career profile
planning goals
apprentice
trade
vocation
tuition
profession

STUDY QUESTIONS

1. What is the main purpose of evaluating the career choices that you have researched?
2. What is a personal career profile, and how is it used?
3. What often happens to high school graduates who have no idea what career they want to pursue?
4. How often does the average American change careers?
5. What are two words that describe the kinds of career goals you need to set for yourself?
6. What are the three kinds of goals around which you should organize your career plan?
7. What is the minimum educational requirement for most jobs?
8. How long does it take to complete an average apprenticeship?
9. What are the two purposes served by vocational schools?
10. What is one advantage of attending a community college instead of a four-year college?
11. What is the minimum educational requirement for most professions?
12. Where is the best place to start looking for information on colleges?

CRITICAL THINKING

1. A friend of yours wants to drop out. What reasons would you give him or her for staying in school?
2. You have decided that your ultimate career goal is to own a fast-food restaurant. What short-, medium-, and long-range goals should you set for yourself?
3. Two careers appeal to you—recording engineer and electrician. The local community college has a two-year training course for recording engineers, and your counselor seems sure you could qualify for admission. However, you've also been offered an apprenticeship as part of a program run by the local electricians' union. You know such

openings are rare and that at the end of your training you will be assured of a job. Which of these two options should you choose and why?

4. At present, what career do you plan to enter? Why did you choose it?

DISCUSSION STARTERS

1. Think of someone you know who never made a career decision but just "fell" into a job. How satisfied is this person with his or her work and life-style? Describe how you think a personal career profile for this person would read for his or her current job. If it's not a particularly good match, recommend some other occupations you feel might be better.
2. You have set your sights on a career in banking but discover that the career outlook is poor at this time. What alternate choices might you consider that would allow you to switch easily to banking sometime in the future should the outlook improve?
3. How long ago did you take the first steps in choosing a career? What were they?

BUILDING BASIC SKILLS

Math
1. The total cost of going to the state university is $5,000 per semester, including tuition, books, and living expenses. If you are able to work 15 hours per week at $6 per hour and there are 18 weeks in a semester, how much of your costs will you be able to earn? How much will have to come from other sources?
2. As part of your career plan, you want to have an after-tax income of $21,000. If your gross salary is $2,400 per month and all your payroll deductions (including taxes) come to 30 percent of that amount, what is your after-tax income for the year? Have you reached your goal?

Problem Solving
3. Everything seems to be going Ted's way. A good student and an outstanding athlete

(he's captain of the swim team), he has decided to combine his interests and study to be an oceanographer. He has no financial worries about attending college because he's been offered a full athletic scholarship to State University. One day after an awards assembly, however, a teacher remarks, "Gee, I didn't know State had an oceanography program." In fact, it doesn't. It's clear that Ted has a problem, one he could have avoided with better research and career planning. Now that he recognizes his mistake, what can Ted do to salvage the situation?

Communication
4. Your parents are not happy about your decision to join the police force because they know it's a dangerous career. What can you say to convince them that it's the best choice for you?

SUGGESTED ACTIVITIES

1. Ask your counselor to let you look through several catalogs of colleges that offer majors in areas related to your career goal. Choose three of these colleges, and estimate the cost of attending for one year. Include tuition, fees, books, transportation, and (if you would be living away from home) room and board. Summarize your data in a chart. Select one of the colleges as your first choice, and be ready to explain your decision to the class.
2. Make a report on the adult education programs in your community. Focus on the courses that would relate to your chosen career. (If you decide not to attend college full-time, you may be interested in taking some of these classes after graduation.) Sources for this information are public and private high schools, vocational schools, two- or four-year colleges, and social service organizations. Use a telephone book to obtain addresses and telephone numbers for these agencies.

UNIT
Two

No Sale
Is Ever Final!

74

Entering the World of Work

CHAPTERS

Finding and Applying for a Job

*I*f you have made your career decision, you should have some short-term planning goals. One of those goals is probably getting a part-time job in your chosen career area. You now need to find and successfully apply for such a job.

Even if you haven't decided on your career goal, you may want a part-time job. You may want to buy a car or some new clothes. Maybe you need to save money for further education. Whatever your reasons for wanting to work, there are some proven ways to find and get jobs.

1 *Exploring Sources of Job Leads*

Finding even a part-time job that you can do well and enjoy takes some planning. Some people don't bother with a plan at all. For example, you may have heard friends talk about their luck in getting a job: "Boy, did I luck out! Summer vacation starts Friday, and my uncle offered me a job starting next Monday. I don't really know what it is, but at least I won't have to go out job hunting."

If it turns out to be the right job, then such people really are lucky. Taking the first job that's offered is like trying to hit a target with your eyes closed—you've got a chance, but the odds are against you. Some people spend months, even years, doing a job they don't like. Then they hear of another job and try their "luck" again. With a little planning, however, they could find a job they like—one they could really do well and in which they could take some genuine pride.

A **job lead** is information about a possible job opening. In looking for a job, you want to find as many leads as possible. The more leads you have, the better your chances are of finding the job you want.

Where do you go to find job leads? Some of the best sources are described in this lesson. From these sources you can build a long list of possibilities.

School Counselors and Teachers

Your school probably has at least one counselor or teacher who helps students find jobs. Large high schools often have a work experience or placement office with several counselors. These counselors are excellent sources of job leads.

The school personnel can be very helpful because they know a great deal about you. They know your abilities, aptitudes, grades, and attendance record. They also have information on your attitudes and personality. With this information they have a chance of finding a good job for you.

The fact that your school refers you to a job, however, does not mean that you will be hired. Schools often refer several students for the same job. If this happens, you will have to compete for the job with other students from your school. You should therefore try to make the best possible impression when you apply—and continue to pursue other sources of job leads.

Family and Friends

Among your best sources of job leads are members of your own family. Friends of your family and your personal friends are also very good sources.

Family members and friends who have jobs are involved in the business world daily. They may know of job opportunities for which you are qualified. Perhaps you have a friend who recently began working. This friend may have heard about a job lead that's just right for you.

Make a list of family members and friends who might help you with job leads. Begin with members of your own family. Then add the names of friends of your family. It's especially important to include those people who are in business for themselves. They might be able to hire you. Even if they can't, they may know other business people who are looking for workers like you.

Add to your list any friends who work for companies where you think you might like to work. Then add the names of your own school friends and neighbors who might be connected with a business in which you are interested. A classmate's parent may work for a company that's looking for someone with your qualifications.

Friends, neighbors, and acquaintances are a good place to start looking for job leads. Why?

Some young people hesitate to ask their influential friends about job possibilities. These young people do not want to get a job by using "pull." However, there's nothing wrong with having a friend or family member help you get a job—if you are qualified for it. The only kind of "pull" to be avoided is the kind that gets you a job for which you are *not* qualified. When this happens, both you and the company that hired you suffer.

Many jobs are never advertised in the paper or listed with a placement agency. These jobs are filled by friends and acquaintances of company employees. For this reason, you shouldn't limit your job search to answering ads. Ask family members and friends for job leads.

Employment Agencies

Employment agencies help people find jobs. Those who are looking for jobs submit their names to the agency. Businesses call the agency when they have job openings. The employment agency then serves as a sort of go-between, matching qualified job-hunters with available jobs.

There are two basic kinds of employment agencies—public and private. Public agencies are operated by either the federal or the state government. Their services are free. Private agencies are managed by people who are trying to make a profit. This means that private agencies must charge a fee for their services.

Most large cities have both public and private employment agencies. The public agencies are identified by the names of the states in which they are located—for example, the Minnesota State Employment Service.

Fill out an application form with the public employment agency nearest you. You will then be interviewed to determine your interests and qualifications. If and when a job is listed that seems right for you, someone from that office will notify you. If you are interested in the job, the employment office will refer you to the company.

Do not overlook the help that a private employment agency might give you. Private agencies often know about jobs that are not listed with the state employment service. Just remember—these agencies charge a fee for their services.

When you register with a private agency, you will have to sign an agreement. This agreement will say that if the agency helps you find a job, you will pay the agency a fee. The fee is usually a certain amount or a percentage of your first year's salary. You do not have to pay the fee unless the agency finds you a job that you accept. In some cases the employer will pay this fee for you.

Public employment agencies provide help and information to all job seekers free of charge. Why, however, do you think that private agencies often know about jobs not listed with public agencies?

Strive for Success

From the Playing Field to the Bench

Have you ever heard someone call a student a "jock" and known that what was really meant was "dummy"? Have you ever laughed at the image of a good student as a nerd with no athletic ability? These ideas are stereotypes, and they are unfair. Byron White is a man who turns this kind of stereotype on its head.

White is an Associate Justice of the United States Supreme Court, the highest court in the country. He has served since 1962, when he was appointed to a life term by President John Kennedy.

Although he is a fairly skinny guy who wears glasses, Byron White has never been one to trip over his shoelaces. At the University of Colorado, he was an all-American running back on the football team. While on the team, he rushed for 290 yards in one game in 1937, a record that would last 50 years. No wonder they call him Whizzer!

While at Colorado, White earned a prestigious Rhodes Scholarship to Oxford University in England. These scholarships are given to college graduates who are both outstanding students and great athletes. Before he went to Oxford, though, White decided to take a break from the academic life—he played a season of professional football with the Pittsburgh Steelers. Then he went to England. However, when World War II broke out the following year, all Rhodes Scholars were sent home to the United States.

White entered Yale University Law School that fall. As if that were not enough to keep him busy, he also played professional football for the Detroit Lions! He graduated from Yale with high honors.

White ended his football career the year America entered the war. He joined the Navy and served alongside John F. Kennedy in a PT boat squadron. The two became friends during their tour of duty—a friendship that was to last until Kennedy's assassination in 1963.

After the war, White returned to Colorado to practice law. Two years later he went to Washington to clerk for the Chief Justice of the Supreme Court. He remained physically active, playing football and basketball with friends and other people in government, keeping his body as sharp as his mind.

When Kennedy was elected President in 1960, he named White Deputy Attorney General. When an opening occurred on the Supreme Court in 1962, the football star was asked to fill it. That was the signal for people to start thinking in stereotypes!

The newspapers criticized Kennedy for selecting a man who had never even served as a judge to be a Justice on the nation's highest court. They called White a jock and spoke about his incredible college football records as if they proved he couldn't possibly be intelligent enough to sit on the Supreme Court. Nonetheless, White was confirmed by Congress and has served on the Court ever since.

Sensitive to being judged not for himself but as a great athlete, White has always empathized with other people who were the victims of prejudice. He has stood against discrimination in his decisions on the Court. In his seventies now, Whizzer White still knows that there is no conflict between a strong body and a strong mind. On the contrary, the two go together very well.

Newspaper Advertisements

Read the help-wanted advertisements in the newspaper. These ads will help you learn a great deal about the job market. You will get an idea of the salaries being offered for different kinds of work and the qualifications needed for the kind of work that interests you. Follow up every newspaper ad that looks promising.

Be careful, though, when you respond to newspaper ads. Don't apply for jobs that require deposits of money. These "jobs" are often nothing more than attempts to sell you something. Other ads may require that you enroll in a course—for a fee—before you are hired. The people who place ads like these generally take your money, but they have no jobs to offer.

Government Offices

The U.S. government is the largest employer in the country. The federal government hires thousands of new employees each year for many kinds of jobs. City, county, and state governments also hire many workers.

There are a number of advantages to government jobs. Most are under a civil service or merit system. These systems protect workers from unfair dismissal. The pay and working conditions for government jobs are also usually quite good.

Find out where the government offices are located in your area. Then call or visit these offices to find out about job openings.

Schools

In most cities the local school district is an important source of jobs. In addition to teachers, schools hire many kinds of workers. Among them are secretaries, file clerks, switchboard operators, library clerks, gardeners, custodians, cooks, and maintenance workers. Working conditions are usually very good. If you are interested in working in one of your local schools, check with the school district's personnel office.

Colleges, too, hire many workers besides teachers and professors. Many people enjoy working on a college campus. There they can associate with people who are interested in education and self-improvement. If there is a college in your city and the work sounds interesting to you, apply at the college personnel office.

Direct calling is a way to uncover job leads entirely on your own. What are the disadvantages of this procedure, however?

Direct Calls

In addition to following up leads from sources already mentioned, you may want to make some direct calls on your own. Making direct calls means either telephoning or visiting potential employers. You will not be responding to an ad or following up a referral.

It takes a great deal of work to find a job through direct calls. You don't know which companies have openings, and you don't know the people who work for companies that interest you. You will probably make many phone calls and visits before you succeed. If you contact enough businesses, though, you will probably find some that are looking for workers with your skills.

Go through the Yellow Pages of your telephone book looking for companies that interest you. Make a list of these, including their addresses and telephone numbers. Then call or visit each company, and ask if there are any job vacancies.

✓ CHECKING UP

1. What is a job lead?
2. How does an employment agency operate?
3. List six sources of job leads.

2 *Applying for a Job*

Once you have a list of job leads, you can begin applying for some jobs. The process of applying for a job is an important part of getting the job you want. Do not take it lightly.

Employers are looking for the best person to fill the job. They want to know whether or not you have the ability to do the work. They will be influenced by the way you dress and whether or not you are well-groomed. They will also notice if you use slang or any other language that is not standard English. In fact, they will want to know everything about you that relates to the job.

Employers have several ways of getting the information they need to choose the best person for the job. Most employers will have you fill out an application form. Some will have you write a letter of application and prepare a resume. For some jobs you will be asked to take performance or other tests. Almost all employers will want to interview you before they decide to hire you.

How you go about providing employers with the information they want often determines whether or not you get the job. Following the suggestions on the next few pages will increase your chances of being successful.

Obtaining Necessary Documents

If you are hired, you will need certain documents. You should apply for these now, *before* you go job hunting. Given the choice between someone who has the necessary paperwork and someone who doesn't, if all other factors are equal, an employer would probably prefer the person who knew enough to think ahead.

The first document you will need is a social security card. You probably already have one of these because your parents need it to fill out their federal income tax return. While you need not carry the card with you, you should know where it is. You should write down or memorize your social security number so that you can supply it easily to a potential or actual employer. Without a number, you cannot be paid.

If you are under 16, you will also probably need a work permit before you can start a job. Some states require work permits for all workers under the age of 18.

State and federal labor laws list jobs that are considered too dangerous for young workers. These laws also limit the hours that young people can work. A work permit shows that a young worker has been advised of these laws. In some states, work permits must specify the exact job duties and hours of work.

Work permits are usually issued by schools. Ask your counselor or work experience coordinator if you will need a work permit. Doing so now may save you time as well as help you get the job you want.

If you don't carry your social security card with you, you should memorize the number so that you can enter it quickly and easily on job applications. In what other situations might you need to know your social security number?

Using Standard English

In Chapter 10 you will learn about the importance of communication in the world of work. You will find out why employers always try to hire workers who can communicate effectively. You will also learn how you can improve your communication skills.

Before you can demonstrate your communication skills on the job, you must get the job. You can increase your chances of getting hired by using standard English when you apply. **Standard English** is the formal style of writing and speaking you have learned in school. It is "standard" because it means the same thing to everyone.

Potential employers have several opportunities to notice your ability (or inability) to use standard English. When they read your application form, they will see whether or not you can write grammatically and spell properly. If you write a letter of application, employers will have another chance to evaluate your language skills. Finally, in the interview, employers will listen carefully to the way you speak to make sure your vocabulary and grammar are acceptable.

To understand the importance of using standard English, imagine for a moment that your application form or letter contained poor grammar or misspelled words. What would happen? Many employers wouldn't even bother to interview you. They receive so many applications that they don't need to give anyone a second chance.

Suppose you do use good grammar and spell words correctly on your application form and in your letter. You will probably be asked in for an interview. Using standard English in the interview will help you in two ways. First, the employer will take your proper use of the language as a sign that you are a well-educated person. Second, using standard English will show the employer that you can communicate clearly. Both of these things can improve your chances of being hired.

On the other hand, if you do not use standard English in the interview, the employer may think that you are not very intelligent. He or she will probably assume you've done poorly in school. If your English is very bad, the employer may not even be able to understand you. If this happens, you will certainly not be offered the job. This is especially true if you are applying for a position, such as salesclerk or receptionist, that involves dealing directly with customers.

Using standard English means more than using accepted vocabulary and grammar. It also means not using phrases such as *you know, like,* and *okay* over and over. These phrases and others may slip into your speech without your noticing. They can be irritating to those listening to you—and the last thing you want to do is irritate a potential employer.

Think of it this way—you can use casual expressions in casual situations. Applying for a job, however, is not a casual situation, no matter how comfortable you feel about it. Your purpose—in your application and in your interview—is to show the employer that you are a competent person. Being a competent person involves communicating well with others. It also involves projecting an image that others will respect.

Filling Out Application Forms

The employer's main purpose in having you fill out an application form is to obtain information about you. Employers may also use the application to determine how neat you are and whether or not you can use standard English. If you remember this, you can gain an advantage over the many applicants who fill out their forms quickly and carelessly.

Follow the suggestions below for filling out an application form. They will help you sell yourself to the employer.

- *Complete the application form as neatly as possible.* The employer will regard it as an example of your best work. If you fill out the form in the employer's office, use a pen. If you fill it out at home and can type, use a typewriter.
- *Answer every question that applies to you.* If a question does not apply, write, "NA" (for Not Applicable) or place a dash in the space. This shows that you did not overlook the item.
- *Use your correct name (not a nickname) on the application form.* Study the form carefully before you begin writing. Specific places are usually provided for your first name, middle initial, and last name.
- *Spell all words correctly.* If you are not sure of a spelling, use another word (one you can spell) with the same meaning.

On occasion, you might have to fill out a job application in an employer's office just before an interview. What steps could you take to help you do a better job under these circumstances?

- *Give your complete address.* Include your zip code—five or nine digits, whichever form is indicated.
- *Supply only the information requested, in its simplest and most useful form.* If there is a question about your place of birth, for example, indicate the city and state—not the name of the hospital.
- *Be specific about your job preference.* If the application form asks what job you are applying for, answer with a job title or type of work. Do not write, "Anything." Employers expect you to state clearly the kind of work you can and want to do.
- *Prepare any lengthy lists of information in advance.* Most application forms, for example, include a section on education. If you have attended several schools, for your own reference you should write down their names and the years you attended. This procedure will help you enter the information quickly and accurately.
- *Be prepared to list several references.* **References** are people who will speak on your behalf, who will tell the employer you would be a good employee.

You should ask permission of any people you plan to list as references. Certain people are con-

sidered especially good references. The pastor of your church, a former employer, a teacher who knows you well, and friends who are established in business are some examples. Try to include some of these people as references.

Some applications contain questions you don't have to answer. You have the legal right to withhold information that does not relate to your ability to perform the job in question. Employers are not supposed to ask your race, religion, sex, or marital status. They may not ask if you have ever been arrested. They do not need to know if you have children, who takes care of your children, or if you are planning to have children. You are not required to provide information about your military or financial status.

If you are asked a question that you feel is illegal, you must decide what to do. If you are sure your answer won't hurt your chances of getting the job, you may simply answer the question. Otherwise, you can point out that the question is illegal. You should realize, however, that this may reduce your chances of getting the job. Your third option is to ignore the question entirely.

An example of a correctly completed application form is shown in Figure 5-1. Study it carefully.

Continued on page 86

Kmart. Corporation

APPLICATION FOR EMPLOYMENT

A K mart Corporation Store is truly a pleasant place to work. An expression of Customer Appreciation is expected from all employees by promoting the feeling of friendliness and warmth to each customer who visits our store. Details of the "TYFSOK" program will be explained during indoctrination.

DATE September 18, 19 91   **PERSONAL (Please print using ball point pen)**

FULL NAME	First Rebecca	Middle Sue	Last Carson	Social Security Number 987	65	4321

| PRESENT ADDRESS | Street 21 West Third St. | City Houston, | State TX | Zip 77048 | How long 8 yrs. | Telephone No. (713) 868-9931 |

If no phone, how may we contact you? —

Are you 18 years of age or older? ☐ Yes ☑ No

List activities or commitments that may interfere with attendance requirements.
High School Classes (8:30 a.m. – 2:30 p.m.)

List handicaps or health problems that should be considered in job placement.

Have you ever applied for employment to the K mart Corporation or a subsidiary before? ☐ Yes ☑ No   If "yes," where? —   Approximate Date Mo. — Yr. —   How referred to us? By work experience coordinator

Have you ever been convicted of a felony? ☐ Yes ☑ No   If "yes," when? Mo. — Yr. —   Explain: —

IDENTITY AND EMPLOYMENT ELIGIBILITY VERIFICATION

When requested, can you provide genuine documentation establishing your identity and eligibility to be legally employed in the United States? ☑ Yes ☐ No

Will Visa or immigration status prevent lawful employment? ☐ Yes ☑ No

EMPLOYMENT INTERESTS AND SKILLS

SCHEDULE DESIRED: ☑ DAY ☑ EVENING ☐ ANY HOURS   FULL TIME ☐   PART TIME ☑   SEASONAL ☐

AVAILABLE HOURS:		Sunday	Monday	Tuesday	Wednesday	Thursday	Friday	Saturday
	DAY	—	3–5	3–5	3–5	3–5	3–5	8–5
	EVENING	—	5–9	5–9	5–9	5–9	5–9	—

DATE AVAILABLE FOR WORK – 9-23-91   TOTAL HOURS PER WEEK DESIRED – 18 hours   SALARY EXPECTED – $5.50/hr.

TYPE OF WORK PREFERRED	EXAMPLES: Service Employee Checkout Service Employee Food Dept. Apparel (Women's-Mens-Children) Camera/Jewelry Sporting Goods Mechanic Stockroom, etc.	1. Position desired Apparel sales	Years experience in this work —
		2. Sporting goods sales	—
		3. Stockroom	—

EDUCATION

SCHOOLS	NAME AND ADDRESS OF SCHOOL OR COLLEGE	Dates Attended From	To	MAJOR STUDIES	Last Grade Completed	Graduation Date
HIGH SCHOOL	Central High School, Houston, TX	9-88	Present	Business education	11	—
COLLEGE TRADE OR BUSINESS SCHOOL	—	—	—	—	—	—

THE CIVIL RIGHTS ACT OF 1964 PROHIBITS DISCRIMINATION IN EMPLOYMENT PRACTICE BECAUSE OF RACE, COLOR, RELIGION, SEX OR NATIONAL ORIGIN.
(An Equal Opportunity Employer)

Figure 5-1 Most employment application forms ask for similar information—the kind of work you want, your education, your employment history, and the names of any references. In this form, the jobs the applicant has held in the past are listed in reverse chronological order. What, judging from the application, does this term mean?

U.S. MILITARY

Branch of Service	Date of Entry	Date Released	ACTIVE DUTY DATE		Type of Duty
			From Mo. — Yr. —	To Mo. — Yr. —	
—	—	—			—

What specialized training did you receive?
—

EMPLOYMENT EXPERIENCE

GIVE PAST EMPLOYMENT AS COMPLETELY AS POSSIBLE, STARTING WITH YOUR PRESENT OR LATEST EMPLOYER, INCLUDE SUMMER EMPLOYMENT.

	MO.	DAY	YR.	EMPLOYER'S NAME & ADDRESS — CITY — STATE — ZIP	Name & Title of Immediate Superior	Last Position You Held & Salary	Reason for Leaving
From	3	2	91	Present or Last Employer Bidwell's Department Store	Carl Taylor	Cashier	—
To	Present			Address 801 Rice Boulevard Houston, TX 77036 Telephone (713) 662-4593	Store Manager	$5.00 per hour	
From	11	26	90	Employer Sandbox Children's Toys	Nettie Fillmore	Sales-person	Not enough work (could
To	2	15	91	Address 1111 Villanova Street Houston, TX 77051 Telephone (713) 383-5541	Owner	$4.65 per hour	only give me 10 hrs. per week)
From	6	25	90	Employer Industrial Systems, Inc.	Delores Salazar	File clerk	To take a job related to my
To	11	16	90	Address 17 Greyburn Place Houston, TX 77048 Telephone (713) 711-1821	Office Manager	$4.40 per hour	career interest (sales)
From	6	19	89	Employer Star Stationery and Office Supplies	Sam Warren	Stock-person	Return to school — end
To	9	1	89	Address 334 Conroy Street Houston, TX 77051 Telephone (713) 777-8998	Stock Supervisor	$4.25 per hour	of summer job

REFERENCES

GIVE NAME OF THREE PERSONS YOU ARE NOT RELATED TO AND BY WHOM YOU HAVE NOT BEEN EMPLOYED. THESE PEOPLE SHOULD HAVE KNOWN YOU FOR SEVERAL YEARS.

NAME	ADDRESS STREET, CITY, STATE, ZIP	OCCUPATION	YEARS OF ACQUAINTANCE
Cindy Lopez	2241 Highpoint Road Houston, TX 77042 Telephone (713) 622-2313	Work Experience Coordinator Central High School	2
Mildred Boyagian	897 University Avenue Crystal City, TX 78839 Telephone (512) 383-2121	Owner, Happy Child Day Care Center	10
Ralph Masterson	6178 Lawrence Way Houston, TX 77051 Telephone (713) 868-8282	Pastor, Union Circle Church	8

GIVE NAME OF ANY RELATIVES, AND/OR ACQUAINTANCES, EMPLOYED BY K MART CORPORATION OR A SUBSIDIARY:

NAME	POSITION	LOCATION	RELATIONSHIP
—	—	—	—

ADDITIONAL INFORMATION FOR PLACEMENT CONSIDERATION

Among the business education courses I have taken are marketing and business math — both of which, I believe, will help me be an effective salesperson. I have also studied speech, with a special emphasis on persuasive speaking.

APPLICANT SIGNATURE *Rebecca Sue Carson*	DATE SIGNED 9-18-91

CODE (28) 0-944510-114 – Pads 100 – (Rev. 4/89) – FS – MS – Litho in U.S.A.

RETENTION: 8 years from date of separation
(2 years for applicants not hired)

Typing gives a letter of application a professional look. What other advantages do you think it has over writing a letter in longhand?

Writing Letters of Application

A potential employer does not usually interview everyone who applies for a job. You must convince the employer that you are one of the applicants who should be interviewed. This is why your application form and letter of application are so important. They are the means by which you sell yourself to an employer.

There are times when writing a letter of application is the only way to get a personal interview. You write a letter of application in the following situations.

- When you wish to apply for an out-of-town job, especially if the job is a business or professional position
- When you answer a newspaper advertisement that asks you to apply by mail
- When you wish to be interviewed by business friends of your family
- When an employer asks you to write a letter of application

In many cases an employer gets his or her first impression of you from your letter of application. You want that impression to be a good one. Therefore, unless you are specifically asked to write your letter in longhand, you should type it. A typed letter is easier to read. In addition—if it is neat, organized, and grammatically correct—it suggests that you are a careful and capable person.

If you can't type, ask a friend to type your letter for you. If you do not know anyone who types, you can have a local typing service type your letter for a small fee.

Content   Here are some suggestions for writing an effective letter of application. They will help you organize your thoughts.

- *Write a first copy, and then revise and develop it.* Keep working on your letter until it says what you want to say in the way you want to say it.
- *Concentrate on the contributions you could make to the company.* Do not tell the employer how badly you need a job.
- *In your first sentence, establish a point of contact.* This sentence should tell where or from whom you learned about the job. You might say, "At the suggestion of Mr. Oxford (a mutual friend), I am writing regarding the job as messenger in your office." If you are writing in answer to a newspaper ad, you might begin, "Your advertisement in today's *News Press* for a typist-clerk describes the work that I think I do best."
- *In the second sentence, state that you are applying for the job.* You might say, "Please consider me an applicant for the position" or "I should like to be considered an applicant for this job."

- *In your second paragraph, begin describing the education and experience you have that qualify you for the job.* If you have a great deal to say about both your education and experience, use a separate paragraph for each. If you have little to say, describe both in the same paragraph. If you have no experience, don't make excuses. Instead, tell how your education in subjects related to the work (typing, bookkeeping, or auto shop, for example) will help you in this job.
- *In your last paragraph, ask for an interview at the employer's convenience.* Be sure to include your telephone number so the employer can contact you.
- *Ask a teacher or a friend in business to help you polish your letter.* When you have it the way you want, type it neatly.

Some businesses receive dozens of application letters for each job. If they advertise in the newspaper, they may receive hundreds. They usually interview only those applicants who are qualified for the job and whose letters are neat and well written. This means that if you are very careful about how you write your letter, you will have a big advantage. Figure 5-2 shows an example of a well-written letter of application.

After you have written one good letter, you can make it the model for other letters of application. Of course, you will have to change the first paragraph. (Information about the specific job and how you learned about it will vary from letter to letter.) The paragraphs about your education and experience and the last paragraph, however, will need little change.

Format　Before you type the final version of your letter, look again at Figure 5-2. This time pay special attention to the labels. They point out the main parts of a business letter. Also study the spacing notations. They will help you format, or arrange, your letter so that it looks businesslike and professional.

The main parts of a business letter are formatted in the following manner:

- *Heading.* The heading should include your address and the date you are writing the letter. You can place the heading at either the left or the center of the page. Type your street address about two inches (or 12 lines) from the top of the sheet. On the next line,

type your city, state, and zip code. On the third line, type the date.
- *Inside address.* The inside address consists of the name and address of the person or company to whom you are writing. It must start at the left margin. The first line of the inside address should be about four or five lines down from the bottom of the heading. (If your letter is very short, leave more space between the heading and the inside address. This will allow you to center your letter on the page.)
- *Salutation.* If you are addressing your letter to an individual, use the salutation *Dear Mr. (Ms., Mrs.),* followed by the person's last name and a colon. If you are writing to a company or personnel office and do not know the name of the person who will read your letter, use the salutation *Dear Sir or Madam,* also followed by a colon.
- *Body.* This is the main part of your letter. It should consist of at least three paragraphs —the first explaining why you are writing, the second giving your background, and the third requesting an interview.
- *Closing.* Use the closing *Yours truly, Very truly yours,* or *Respectfully yours,* followed by a comma. Only the first word should be capitalized. The closing should be placed two lines down from the body and aligned with the heading. If, for example, the heading was placed at the center of the page, the closing should begin at that point, too.
- *Signature block.* After the closing, space down four lines and type your name. This will create a "block" in which you can place your signature.

Before you remove your letter from the typewriter, read it carefully to see if there are any mistakes. (This precaution will help you make neater corrections. Overtyping is easier if the paper has not been repositioned in the machine.) Take special care in rereading the inside address. It would not make a very good impression to misspell the name of the company or person with whom you wish to interview. Also, be sure the address is correct. A mistake here could delay your letter or even make it undeliverable. Once you are sure everything is correct, sign your name in ink above the typewritten signature.

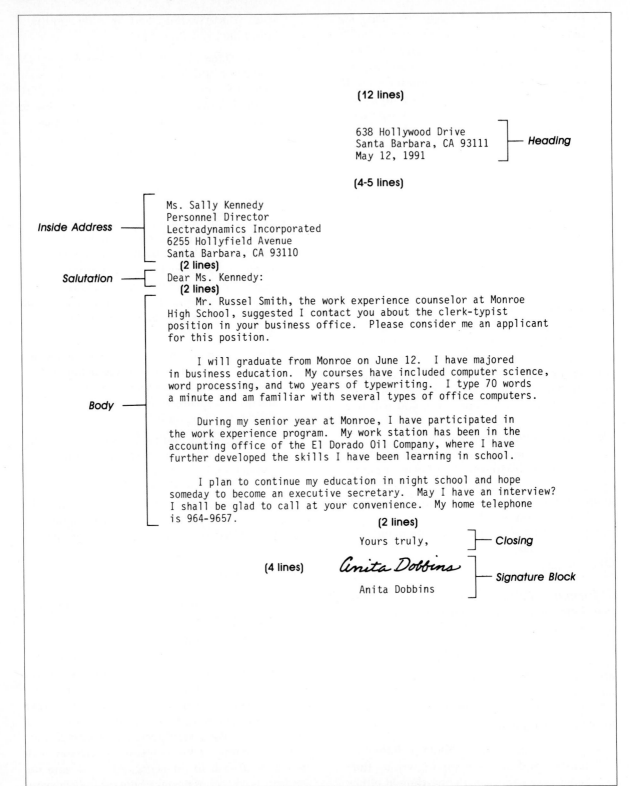

(12 lines)

638 Hollywood Drive
Santa Barbara, CA 93111   —— *Heading*
May 12, 1991

(4-5 lines)

Inside Address ——
Ms. Sally Kennedy
Personnel Director
Lectradynamics Incorporated
6255 Hollyfield Avenue
Santa Barbara, CA 93110
(2 lines)
Salutation —— Dear Ms. Kennedy:
(2 lines)

Body ——
    Mr. Russel Smith, the work experience counselor at Monroe High School, suggested I contact you about the clerk-typist position in your business office. Please consider me an applicant for this position.

    I will graduate from Monroe on June 12. I have majored in business education. My courses have included computer science, word processing, and two years of typewriting. I type 70 words a minute and am familiar with several types of office computers.

    During my senior year at Monroe, I have participated in the work experience program. My work station has been in the accounting office of the El Dorado Oil Company, where I have further developed the skills I have been learning in school.

    I plan to continue my education in night school and hope someday to become an executive secretary. May I have an interview? I shall be glad to call at your convenience. My home telephone is 964-9657.

(2 lines)

Yours truly,   —— *Closing*

(4 lines)   *Anita Dobbins*
Anita Dobbins   —— *Signature Block*

Figure 5-2 A neat, well-formatted, and carefully written letter can give a potential employer a good impression of you before you even set foot in the door. Analyze the body of this letter. What purpose does each paragraph serve?

A well-written resume can be used again and again to apply for many different jobs. Under what circumstances, however, might a resume change as frequently, say, as a letter of application?

Preparing Resumes

A good letter of application will probably convince an employer to call you in for an interview. You can, however, increase your chances of getting an interview by including a resume with your letter. A **resume** is a brief summary of personal information, education, skills, work experience, activities, and interests. It is more detailed than a letter of application and presents its information in a format that is easier for an employer to use—especially in an interview.

You can model your own resume on the one in Figure 5-3. In addition to the information shown there, you can include relevant courses you have taken in school and hobbies or interests that relate to the job for which you are applying. If you have no work experience, don't mention it. Simply omit the section and concentrate on the qualities and abilities you do have. If you feel your resume is too short, you can lengthen it by including the names of your references.

Be as careful and neat in preparing your resume as you were in preparing your letter of application. Limit the document to a single page. When it is complete, make enough copies to use throughout

your job search. Then you can easily include one with each letter of application you send.

Taking Tests

It is increasingly common for job seekers to be tested in some way as part of the job application process. Where there are large numbers of applicants, such tests can serve to narrow the field. They can also give employers a more objective basis for making a decision.

Performance Tests The kind of test you are asked to take will depend on the kind of job you are seeking. For example, if you are applying for a job as a secretary, you will probably be given a typing test. If you are applying for a job as a welder, you will probably be asked to do some welds. If you are applying for a job as a retail sales clerk, you will probably be given a test of your math skills.

The employer's main purpose in giving a test is to find out if you can do the job adequately. The employer may also use the test results to compare your skills with those of other applicants. Thus, how well you do on the test could determine whether or not you get the job.

Daniel Brophy
510 W. Gibson Street
Towanda, IL 61702
(309) 442-1798

CAREER OBJECTIVES

Immediate: Junior Production Editor
Long-range: Managing Editor

WORK EXPERIENCE

July 1990-present   Production Assistant, Williams Publishing Company,
                           Bloomington, Illinois. Responsible for a variety
                           of tasks involved in textbook production, including
                           photo acquisition and paste-up of dummy layouts.

August 1988-June 1990   Sales Associate (part-time), P.A. Bergner and
                           Company, Peoria, Illinois. Responsible for
                           customer service, some record keeping, and the
                           taking of inventory.

Summers, 1987 and 1988   Swimming Instructor, Limestone High School,
                           Bartonville, Illinois. Taught diving and life-
                           saving techniques to intermediate- and upper-level
                           students.

EDUCATION

High School Diploma (College Preparatory Program), Limestone High School,
Bartonville, Illinois

Grade Point Average--3.8 (on a 4.0 scale)

HONORS AND ACTIVITIES

Dean's Honor List
Student Council Member
Student Career Day Leader
Yearbook, Sports Editor
Swimming Team

REFERENCES

Available on request

Figure 5-3 A resume arranges information about a job applicant in a
way that can be grasped quickly. Compare the resume shown here with
the application letter in Figure 5-2. Which would be easier to use in an
interview? Why?

If you believe you will have to take a test, ask someone who has taken a similar test what it is like. Practice your skills beforehand, but don't let the thought of the test worry you. People score much better on tests when they are relaxed.

Be sure you understand the instructions about how to take the test before you begin, and then work calmly. If the test is timed, be aware of how much time you have left. However, don't panic if time is running short. Be methodical, and you will do your best. Answer those questions you are sure of, and then go back to ones you are unclear about. If the test covers any math, find out in advance if you will be able to use a calculator, and have one with you. If you finish before the time is up, go over your answers again, checking for mistakes.

Polygraph Tests   Until the late 1980s, many employers required prospective employees to take polygraph, or lie detector, tests if they were going to be working in a job handling money or expensive merchandise. A polygraph is a machine that has wires attached to it with electrodes at the ends.

The electrodes, which are placed on the test subject's skin, measure the chemical changes in the skin that usually accompany nervousness or fear. Such feelings can indicate that someone is lying. The examiner asks the subject questions and reads the graph on the machine that measures the person's response. If a person is naturally nervous or just frightened by the prospect of the test, the test results may not be accurate.

There has been a great deal of controversy over whether polygraph tests actually can determine if a person is lying or likely to steal. Because of this controversy, in 1988 Congress passed a law making it illegal for most employers to require such tests of job applicants. However, if you apply for a job in law enforcement or government or if you wish to work in a pharmacy or hospital where narcotics are handled, you may still be required to take such a test. Employers can also require that employees they suspect of stealing or other dishonesty take the tests. They must have reason to suspect the employee, though—they can't just give the tests without cause.

Some form of testing is a major part of the application process for many jobs. How might you prepare for a performance test like the one shown here?

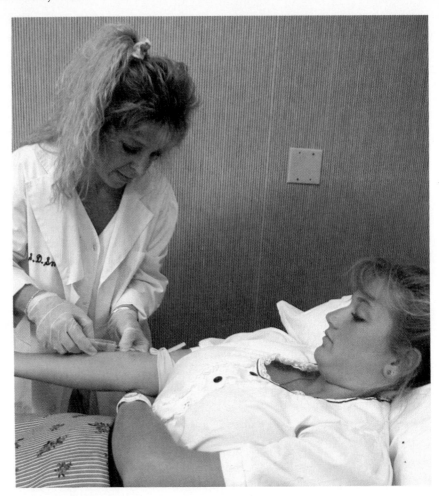

Today many preemployment physicals include drug testing. Can you suggest some jobs not listed in this lesson that might require such testing?

Drug Tests   Drug testing is another area that is controversial. The laws covering drug testing are similar to those regarding lie detector tests—with one exception. Employers *are* allowed to test employees' blood or urine for illegal drugs as a condition of employment. Once employees have been hired, however, they cannot be randomly tested for drugs unless the employer proves it is necessary because of the nature of the job. People who work with explosives, for example, or those who handle drugs in their work can be tested. It is also permitted to give drug tests after an accident to learn whether drug abuse was a cause. Drug testing is mandatory for everyone joining the military.

Testing is required by any private company or state or local government agency that receives more than $25,000 in federal grant money to develop a drug abuse prevention program. Beyond this, the federal government neither requires nor forbids drug testing. Local governments can pass laws that make it illegal, and some, such as San Francisco, have outlawed random drug testing in the workplace.

✓ CHECKING UP

1. Why is it important to use standard English throughout the job application process?
2. What are the six main parts of a well-formatted job application letter?
3. What is a resume, and how does it differ from a job application letter?

3 *Interviewing for a Job*

Application forms, letters of application, resumes, and tests are all important parts of getting the job you want. You will probably not be hired, though, until you have had an interview. An **interview** is a formal meeting between an employer and a job applicant. For the employer, the interview is a way to find out whether or not the applicant is the best person for the job. For you, the applicant, the interview is a way to find out whether or not you would like the job.

An employment interview can be one of the most important experiences of your life. What happens in this 20- or 30-minute period may influence your whole career, yet some job applicants give the impression that they are at the interview simply because they have nothing better to do. A personnel manager for a large corporation on the West Coast told about a young woman who came to an interview wearing a bathing suit. She was on her way home from the beach! Of course, she didn't get the job.

The purpose of an interview is to allow the employer to learn several things about you.

- Your attitude toward people and work
- Your education
- Your work experience
- Your career plans

The interview also gives you a chance to learn more about the job and the company.

Preparing for an Interview

You should prepare for an interview. The better prepared you are, the greater your chances for success once the interview begins.

If you call for an appointment, state your name clearly. Then tell how you learned of the job opening. Write down the exact time and place of the interview. Get the correct spelling of the interviewer's name and make sure you can pronounce the name correctly. Most often you will be interviewed by either the employer or the personnel manager.

Things to Know Before the interview, study your resume. Be prepared to answer any questions you might be asked about the information in it.

Learn all you can about the company. What products or services does it offer? How many people does it employ?

Some companies publish brochures and annual reports that are good sources of information. Others print catalogs that describe their products. You can even learn about a company from reading about it in the Yellow Pages. You may also ask your family or teacher what they know about the firm.

This information will give you something besides yourself to talk about during the interview. It will also show the interviewer that you are interested in the company—something that is sure to make a good impression on the interviewer.

Things to Do You should take several things with you to the interview—a pen and pencil, your social security card or number, and a copy of your resume. The resume is necessary even if you have already mailed one to the employer. He or she may have misplaced it or perhaps never received it.

Go to the interview alone. Do not take anyone with you. One teenaged job seeker took a friend along to an interview as a confidence booster. The friend was also looking for work. As it happened, the employer liked the friend's qualifications better than those of the person he was interviewing, and so the employer hired the friend. Employers seldom hire applicants who bring other people with them to an interview.

Arrive five minutes early. If you drive to the interview, allow some extra time for the possibility of heavy traffic. If you are even one minute late—or rush in at the last minute—you will appear to be a careless person. It's not a good idea to arrive too early either. Arriving five minutes before the time set for the interview is about right.

Usually the first person you speak to when you arrive is a receptionist or the interviewer's secretary. Be very polite to this person. The employer may ask his or her opinion of you after you have left.

How to Dress Your appearance is an extremely important part of any interview. When you arrive, the employer's first impression of you will be based on how you look. Obviously you want to make a good first impression.

You should, of course, take a bath or shower before dressing for the interview. (This may seem obvious, but some people fail to do it.) Beware of using too much perfume or cologne. Strong smells, even pleasing ones, can be extremely distracting, even oppressive. It goes without saying that smells many people find unpleasant should be avoided as well. The strong smell of cigarettes, for example, is very offensive to those who do not smoke.

Your hair should be freshly shampooed and neatly combed in a conservative hair style. Young men should be clean shaven. Young women should use makeup sparingly.

Many interviewers say they always notice an applicant's hands. Therefore, you should be sure that your hands and nails are clean and that your nails and cuticles are neatly trimmed.

When you select your clothes for the interview, remember that you are looking for a job, not going to a party. The type of clothes you wear should depend on the type of job you are applying for. If you are applying for a factory or construction job, neat, clean work clothes are appropriate. Young men looking for a sales or office job should wear a dress shirt and tie with a suit or sport coat. Young women should wear a dress, a suit, or a conservative blouse and skirt. In terms of style, your clothes should be classic, not faddish. They need not be expensive, but they should be clean and unwrinkled.

Finally, pay attention to the details—to your accessories. People who take the time to shine their shoes, for example, make a better impression than those who do not. Leather shoes are more impressive than tennis or canvas shoes. Matching dress socks should be worn to the interview, not white athletic socks. Hose and dress shoes are appropriate for young women. Jewelry should be kept to a minimum and large or jangly pieces avoided entirely.

An employer will look at you as a potential representative of the company. When two applicants have about the same qualifications, the employer will hire the one who makes the better appearance.

Your attire for an interview should be as carefully prepared as your resume and for the same reason—it's an important way to impress an employer. What do pressed clothes and shined shoes say about you as an applicant? What other elements of personal attire do you think might require similar attention? What sort of attention? When would be the best time to start thinking about such preparations, and why?

Conducting Yourself Properly During an Interview

You may be introduced to the interviewer by the receptionist or secretary. If not, the interviewer may introduce himself or herself to you. If this happens, say something such as "Hello, I'm John Jones, and I'm interested in the job as trainee in your bank." Speak clearly and loudly enough to be heard—and smile.

Do not offer to shake hands unless the interviewer offers first. When shaking hands, always grasp the person's hand firmly.

Stand until the interviewer asks you to sit. If you are not asked to sit down, then stand during the interview. If you do sit, sit alertly. Don't slouch!

Although you will feel nervous at first, you will become more relaxed as the interview progresses. It is normal to be a little nervous, but there is nothing to be afraid of.

Your eyes should meet the interviewer's eyes often. Some people do not trust a person who cannot look them in the eye.

Don't make the mistake of placing your purse, notepad, or any other possession on the edge of the interviewer's desk. The interviewer might think you are being disrespectful or too casual about the interview. If you are carrying something, keep it beside you.

Try to keep your hands still. Usually it is best to keep them in your lap. Don't lean on the interviewer's desk or try to read papers on the desk. Never chew gum or smoke during an interview.

There are two basic ways of interviewing. One method is for the interviewer simply to ask you to talk about yourself. If this happens, you must do most of the talking. Be sure to discuss all of your

A firm, confident handshake is a part of your "body language" that an interviewer will be using to evaluate you. What do you think a limp, weak handshake says about an applicant? a bone-crushing grab? vigorous up-and-down pumping?

qualifications for the job. It is also a good idea to show that you are interested in the company. Give some specific reasons for wanting to work for the firm. (This is why it's important to learn as much as possible about the company before you go to the interview.)

In the other type of interview, the interviewer finds out about your qualifications by asking specific questions. This is probably the most common type of interview. The questions in Figure 5-4 are some of the ones most frequently asked. Be prepared to answer such questions completely and honestly. If you do not know the answer to a question, say so. If you try to fake it, the interviewer will probably know. This makes a poor impression, and you will probably not be hired, even if your qualifications are good.

Two questions that are usually asked deserve special attention.

- "What kind of work would you like to do?"
- "What salary do you expect?"

Too many young people answer the first question by saying, "Anything." This irritates many interviewers. They want to put you in the job for which you are best qualified. There is no job titled "Anything."

Common Interview Questions

- Why would you like to work for our company?
- What kind of work would you like to do?
- Are you looking for permanent or temporary work?
- What makes you think that you can do this job?
- What jobs have you had? Why did you leave?
- What school subjects did you like best? least? Why?
- What extra-curricular activities did you participate in at school?
- What do you want to be doing in five years? in ten years?
- Do you prefer working alone or with others?
- What is your main strength? your main weakness?
- How do you spend your spare time?
- What salary do you expect?
- Have you had any serious illnesses?
- Do you smoke?
- How do you feel about working overtime?
- What grades have you received in your schoolwork?
- When can you begin work?
- How did you become interested in this company?
- What questions do you want to ask?

Figure 5-4 In the course of an interview, you will probably be asked several of these questions. Which would you find easiest to answer? Which would give you the most difficulty?

SITUATION

SOLUTION

When All the Other Applicants Are Men

Your sister Jo, who's 24, arrives for a job interview with Harris Trucking. Jo has been driving the delivery van for your family's florist shop for the past two years and has a perfect driving record. There are five other people waiting for interviews, however, and they are all men. They're discussing their past jobs, and it's clear that most of them have had some experience as professional drivers. Your sister is afraid she'll be at a disadvantage because she isn't a man.

1. How can Jo show the interviewer that she's as good a driver as the men?

2. What should Jo do if the interviewer offers her an office job that pays less, telling her they may give her a chance to drive at some future date?

3. The receptionist tells your sister that there's a company policy against hiring women as drivers. Jo knows that this is illegal. What should she do?

If you are asked what salary you expect, do not mention a specific amount—it may be too low. If you give a low amount and are hired, you may be paid less than other people doing the same work. If you mention an amount that's too high, you may not be hired at all. The interviewer may feel that you would not be satisfied with a lower salary. In answer to the salary question, say, "I'm sure you know better than I do what a fair salary would be. What do you usually pay for this kind of work?" If the interviewer presses you for a specific answer, mention an amount that you believe others get for this kind of work.

Sometimes interviewers don't mention salary at all. In these cases, wait until the interview is almost over. Then ask what you would be paid if you were hired. Don't ask this question early in the interview. The interviewer might think you are interested only in what you will get out of the job.

If you are applying for a permanent, full-time position, it is all right to ask whether or not you will get a vacation. Again, wait until the end of the interview to ask this question. Part-time and temporary workers usually do not get paid vacations.

You may be asked to talk with someone in the company besides the interviewer. This person might be a department head or someone you would be working with if hired. Being asked to talk to a second person usually means that the interviewer is impressed with you. Should this occur, your chances of being hired are very good.

When the interview is over—go! You know it's over when you have described your qualifications and the interviewer has no more questions. Failing to leave immediately may cost you your chance to be hired.

If you have not been offered a job, you have two alternatives. You can ask whether or not you will be called, or you can ask if you may call back in a few days to find out the interviewer's decision. Thank the interviewer for his or her time, and leave. If you pass the receptionist or the secretary on your way out, thank that person, too.

Following Up an Interview

After each job interview, take a few minutes to evaluate your performance. Which questions did you answer particularly well? Which could you have answered better? Did the interviewer ask any questions you weren't expecting? If so, you might want to jot them down so that you'll be ready if they're asked in another interview.

Can you think of any additional information about yourself that you should have provided? Evaluate your appearance and how well you presented yourself verbally. Did you use standard English?

If you evaluate yourself after each interview, you will learn from each experience. You will get better and better at making a good impression in an interview situation.

If the interviewer neither offered nor refused you the job, there's still time to make a favorable impression. Follow up the interview with a thank-you letter. Since few people do this, it will make the interviewer remember you.

Your thank-you letter need not be long. Just thank the interviewer for his or her time. Mention again that you are interested in the job. If you forgot to say something that you feel you should have said, include it in your letter.

Prepare your thank-you letter carefully. (See the suggestions for preparing business letters on pages 86–88.) After you have completed your letter, mail it promptly.

Case Study 1

When Mizuko turned 16, she started looking for her first part-time job. (Her goal was to earn money for a summer trip to Hawaii.) Mizuko had excellent skills—she typed 80 words a minute—and was interested in a law career. She was therefore excited to learn through a friend of her parents that there was an opening for a part-time typist at a local law firm.

Mizuko knew that there would be other applicants for the job and that some would have better qualifications, so she followed up on leads for other positions as well. She also purposely scheduled her interview at the law firm to follow two other interviews. They would provide some practice in interviewing and, hopefully, give her confidence. Finally, she read about the law firm and prepared some questions to ask her interviewer.

On the day of the law firm interview, Mizuko reviewed the information she had collected. She selected a conservative suit to wear, took time to get dressed, and wore only one item of jewelry—her birthstone ring. When she arrived at the law firm, she shook the interviewer's hand firmly and maintained eye contact throughout the interview.

Mizuko's preparation paid off. She was offered two jobs—and accepted the one at the law firm. She's now doing something that she enjoys and that will provide her with valuable work experience related to her career goal.

✓ CHECKING UP

1. Why is it important to learn something about a company before you interview there?
2. List three things you should do in the course of an interview. List three things you should not do.
3. What is the best way to follow up an interview, and why is it so effective?

CHAPTER SUMMARY

There are proven ways to find and get the job that you want. You begin by locating as many job leads as possible. Some good sources of job leads are school counselors and teachers, family and friends, employment agencies, newspaper ads, government offices, schools, and direct calls. By making use of all these job-lead sources, you will increase your chances of finding the best job for you.

As soon as you have a complete list of leads, you can begin applying for jobs. It is very important that you put a great deal of serious effort into this process. How you go about applying may determine whether or not you get the job.

To apply successfully for a job, use standard English in all of your written and spoken communications with the employer. Prepare all application forms, letters, and resumes as neatly as possible. When you are granted an interview, take some time to prepare for it and make sure your appearance is just right. Finally, you will want to practice and put to use all of the interviewing tips provided in this chapter. By doing all of these things you will increase your chances of being offered a job.

TERMS TO KNOW

On a separate sheet of paper, write a single sentence using all of the following terms:

job lead
standard English
references
resume
interview

STUDY QUESTIONS

1. Why is accepting the first job offered often not a good idea?

2. What are five good sources of job leads?

3. Why is it important to have as many job leads as possible?

4. Why is it important to use standard English in a letter of application and during an interview?

5. There will be questions on most application forms that will not apply to you. How will you show that you did not overlook these items?

6. Why is it a bad idea to answer a question about your job preference with the word *anything?*

7. What four situations call for writing a letter of application?

8. What is the purpose of the first paragraph of a letter of application? the last paragraph?

9. What kind of information should be included on a resume?

10. List three things you should do when setting up an appointment for an interview.

11. List three things you should take with you to an interview.

12. Why is it important to go alone to a job interview?

13. What are the two types of job interviews?

14. What should you do after an interview if you are still being considered for the job?

CRITICAL THINKING

1. There are 16 other applicants for a job you're seeking with a local radio station. You know that only 5 of the applicants will be interviewed. What can you do to ensure that you'll be among them?

2. Lois calls to tell you about a great job lead she's found. She must pay a sales company $300, and in return they'll guarantee her a list of customers for their products. She says they're sure she can make $2,000 the first month working only 20 hours a week. What do you tell her?

3. Assume you're the receptionist in the cartoon below. If your employer later asks what you thought of this particular job applicant, what would you say? Give the reasons for your evaluation.

HEY YOU - QUICK! I GOTTA MAKE A COPY OF MY RESUME FOR YOUR BOSS, AN' THIS HERE MACHINE'S BROKE!

DISCUSSION STARTERS

1. Suppose you were offered two jobs. One is a paying job in a fast-food restaurant. The other is an unpaid job in a career you think you might like as an adult. You cannot take both positions. Which would you choose and why?

2. Explain some of your experiences with first impressions. How do first impressions change as you get to know a person? Can an employer usually get a true impression of an applicant in half an hour?

BUILDING BASIC SKILLS

Math

1. You've been offered two jobs. One pays $5.15 an hour; the other, $4.85 an hour. You'd like to take the higher-paying position. However, if you do, you will have to take a bus to work which will cost you $1.50 each day. You can walk to the other job. If you plan to work four days a week and five hours a day, how much would you make at each job? If you subtract your bus fare from the higher-paying job, does it still pay more?

Human Relations

2. Tracy asks you for advice about her upcoming interview for a job as a receptionist in a doctor's office. You're sure that on the basis of her skills she could be hired, but she also wears heavy makeup and an abundance of costume jewelry, which gives her an unprofessional look. How can you talk to Tracy about her appearance without hurting her feelings?

Citizenship

3. You have been offered a job with Cooper Industries, which operates a toxic waste dump in your area. The job pays well, and you will be on a management track. As a condition of employment, however, the company asks you to sign a statement agreeing to report any problems you see on the site to company officials, not government agencies. What will you do?

SUGGESTED ACTIVITIES

1. Select one job lead from the Help Wanted ads in your local newspaper. Write a letter of application.

2. Divide into groups of three or four. Each group should then select one person to be the interviewer. The other students should take turns interviewing as job applicants. After the interviews, discuss with the entire class the correct and incorrect behavior shown in the interviews.

You, Your Employer, and Your Co-Workers

OBJECTIVES
After studying this chapter and doing the activities, you will be able to:

- identify the single most important factor in achieving job success;
- describe what an employer will expect from you;
- describe what you can expect from an employer;
- list the steps to take should you lose your job; and
- explain how to get along with your co-workers.

TERMS TO KNOW
attitude
initiative
wages
salary
commission
discrimination
termination notice
layoff notice
severance pay
unemployment
   compensation

*O*nce you get a job, you will want to keep it. More than that, you will want to be successful.

In this chapter you will learn how to increase your chances of being successful on the job. You will learn what your employer will expect from you and what you can rightfully expect from your employer. You will also learn what you can do to get along with your co-workers. After reading this chapter, you will be on your way to a successful job experience.

100

1 *What Your Employer Expects of You*

Your employer will pay you regularly. In exchange, your employer will expect certain things from you. Your success on the job will depend on how well you meet your employer's expectations.

There is an old saying—"A day's work for a day's pay." At the very least, your employer will expect a good day's work from you. In addition, your employer will expect you to display the following qualities:

- Positive attitude
- Cooperativeness
- Honesty
- Initiative
- Willingness to learn
- Willingness to follow directions
- Dependability
- Enthusiasm
- Ability to accept criticism
- Loyalty

Positive Attitude

Perhaps the most important factor in your job success is your own attitude. Your **attitude** is your basic outlook on life. It is your way of looking at the world and the people in it.

Attitudes are often classified into two general types—positive and negative. People with positive attitudes tend to be optimistic, cheerful, and outgoing. They see life as exciting, worthwhile, and enjoyable. They usually get along well with other people and are happy most of the time.

People with negative attitudes complain a great deal. They are often angry and withdrawn. They are unhappy much of the time, and they do not seem to like other people. They usually have difficulty getting along with others.

How well you get along with your employer and your co-workers will depend on your attitude. If you have a negative attitude, your employer and your co-workers will respond negatively to you. If you have a positive attitude, they will respond positively. Some characteristics of people with positive and negative attitudes are listed in Figure 6-1.

The main reason young workers lose their jobs is because they don't get along well with others. In fact, one study of beginning workers who had been fired showed that 82 percent lost their jobs because they did not get along with their fellow workers.

If you have a positive attitude, you are already on your way to success on the job. If you think you

Positive and Negative Attitudes Compared

Positive Attitude	Negative Attitude
■ Smiles easily	■ Rarely smiles
■ Willing to change ideas and behavior	■ Unwilling to change
■ Can see another person's point of view	■ Can't see another person's point of view
■ Rarely complains	■ Complains about nearly everything
■ Accepts responsibility for mistakes	■ Blames others for own mistakes
■ Seldom criticizes others	■ Very critical of others
■ Is considerate of others	■ Thinks only of self
■ Looks other people in the eyes when talking with them	■ Does not look other people in the eyes
■ Respects the opinions of others	■ Forces own opinions on others
■ Never makes excuses	■ Often makes excuses
■ Has a variety of interests	■ Has few interests

Figure 6-1 A positive attitude is an ideal toward which you should work throughout your career. Which characteristics of such an attitude do you think are easiest to cultivate? Which are most difficult?

may have a negative attitude, you'll be happy to know you can change it. You can work at becoming the kind of person who likes other people. The younger you are when you start, the sooner you can develop a positive attitude—and the sooner you will be successful and happy on the job.

Cooperativeness

The employer who pays your salary has a right to expect your full cooperation. Full cooperation means working well with everyone on the job to reach a common goal.

You can show your willingness to cooperate in many ways. One way is to do the tasks you don't like to do without complaining or trying to get someone else to do them for you. Another way to cooperate is to do your fair share of the work when you work with others. You can also cooperate by respecting your co-workers' ideas, even if they differ from your own.

Too many people have the attitude that each worker is responsible for only his or her own job. These people resent being asked to help others do their jobs. Don't make this mistake. Instead, pitch in willingly when a co-worker is behind or needs help. You may even want to volunteer your help when you see that a co-worker is having trouble.

Case Study 1

Sara is 19 and has a full-time job as a waitress in a restaurant known for its fine food and excellent service. Sara dresses neatly and is always well-groomed. She has a good memory and never makes mistakes on orders. Her arithmetic is always correct on customers' checks. However, Sara doesn't smile easily and is often irritable. This makes the customers uncomfortable. As a result, Sara's tips are usually smaller than those of the other waitresses.

The busiest day of the year for the restaurant is Mother's Day. Every worker is expected to work on that day. Sara, however, wanted to visit her own mother in Chicago on Mother's Day, so she begged the restaurant manager to give her the day off without pay. Although the manager agreed, he and the other waitresses felt that Sara had let them down. Everyone else had to work that much harder. For this reason, and because Sara finds it so difficult to get along with other employees and the customers, the manager has decided to fire her.

Cooperative effort often yields a bonus—it can make a tedious or unpleasant task go faster. Why do you think this is so?

Honesty

Employers expect their workers to be honest with them and with the company, but some workers are not. Probably the most common type of dishonesty on the job is stealing time. Your time during working hours does not belong to you. It belongs to your employer. Still, some people arrive at work a few minutes late every day. Others steal time from their employers by taking long breaks or by stopping work before the end of the workday.

If your hours of work are eight to five, arrive a few minutes before eight. Then you can actually start working at eight. You should continue working, except for breaks and lunch, until five.

Stealing time costs companies a great deal of money. This type of stealing is probably the most costly form of dishonesty in business. Think of it this way—the money lost is money that might have been used to increase your salary or benefits.

Another type of dishonesty on the job is stealing company property. Many workers have been fired for stealing materials and tools that belonged to their employers. In one case a young man regularly used the office postage stamps for personal letters. He was not fired, but when it came time to select a new office manager, he was passed over. His dishonesty cost him a chance to advance in the company.

Be honest with your employer and your company. Don't steal company time or property. As an honest worker you will have a much better chance of being successful in your work.

Initiative

Suppose you have completed your job and no one has told you what to do next. What would you do? Would you sit and wait for instructions from your boss, or would you find something that needed to be done and do it?

Most employers expect their employees to take some **initiative.** Taking initiative means doing what needs to be done without being told to do it. After you have been on the job awhile, your employer will probably expect you to find things to do without your being told.

You must use good judgment when taking initiative. Do not attempt to do work that you are not qualified to do.

Remember—if you never do any more than you get paid for, you will never get paid for any more than you do. Showing initiative will help you be successful on your job.

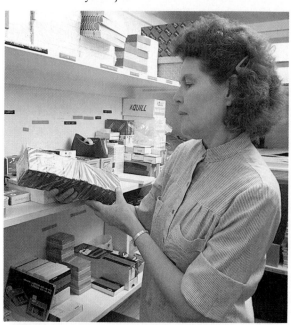

Open stocks of supplies are convenient for workers but may tempt some to take advantage or even steal. To avoid problems, what procedures might a company suggest its employees follow?

Case Study 2

Michael had just graduated from high school when he was hired as a secretary. Michael was a very pleasant person and a good typist. As soon as he completed any work he had to do, however, he always pulled out a magazine and read. There was other work to do, but Michael never did it. He only worked when he was told exactly what job to do.

Because Michael never took the initiative to find something to do, his boss, Mrs. Wilson, had to supervise him constantly. This took so much of Mrs. Wilson's time that she could not get her own work done. She discussed the problem with Michael on two separate occasions, but he was either unable or unwilling to change. Finally Mrs. Wilson had to let him go. Michael's replacement kept busy and required little supervision, and Mrs. Wilson was able to do her own work.

MAKE A DECISION

Suppose you have just finished everything your boss told you to do, and there are still two hours left until quitting time. Your boss left a few minutes ago, saying she wouldn't be back for the rest of the day. You know there are several work-related things you could do during the remaining two hours, but there's also your homework for English tomorrow. It's an important assignment, and you won't have much time after work. What's your decision—will you do your job, your English assignment, or some of each? Give the reasons for your decision.

Willingness to Learn

Employers expect their workers to learn the way things are done in the company. Learning a company's methods is usually not much of a problem for new workers.

You should make a special effort to learn everything you can about your job and your company. The more skills and knowledge you acquire, the better. Most workers who are promoted are workers who have taken the trouble to learn more than just their own daily tasks.

Willingness to Follow Directions

When you are given directions about how to do your work, you are expected to follow them exactly. That is why directions are given. You may not understand the reason for doing things in a certain way, but your employer or supervisor has a reason. Do the work as you are told.

After you have worked on the job awhile, you may make suggestions if you think your ideas will be well received. Be careful about this. Some people resent suggestions, even if they are good ones.

Dependability

Employers expect their workers to be on the job every day and to be there on time. Employees who come to work late can be fired. Even if they aren't fired, they are resented by the workers who do come to work on time. As a result, undependable workers will have problems working cooperatively with fellow workers.

If you are ill and can't go to work, call your employer or the person in charge. Say that you will be absent and explain why. Call as soon as you know that you can't go to work. Many workers have lost their jobs because they did not call their employers to report an absence.

Don't miss work unless you must. Be at work on time and work your full shift. Your employer will soon learn that you are a dependable worker, someone who can be counted on.

Enthusiasm

Employers know that the most productive employees are those who like their work and show enthusiasm for it. Your employer will expect you to be enthusiastic about your work. If you enjoy your work, this will be easy.

However, you may not like some parts of your work. You would be fortunate if you found everything about your job interesting. If there are certain things you don't like doing, don't dwell on how much you dislike these tasks. Instead, focus on the positive parts of the job. When other people ask how you like your job, tell them about the good things. This will help make the job more interesting and enjoyable. Your enthusiasm will grow, and you'll be a much happier person. You will also be a more productive and successful employee.

Ability to Accept Criticism

Constructive criticism is necessary on every job. Criticism is the employer's way of letting you know how the job is supposed to be done. Your employer will expect you to accept criticism without snapping back or sulking.

Regardless of how you may feel when you are criticized, try to take it good-naturedly. Listen carefully and politely to your critic. Then thank him or her for trying to help you.

Accepting criticism means more than just listening politely and thanking the person. It means making use of the criticism. Think about your critic's comments, and try to see how they can help you become a better worker.

Of course, there are employers and supervisors who are unfairly critical, and some lose their tempers. Short of quitting, however, there is nothing you can do about such things. You must listen politely without losing your temper. Regardless of how criticism is delivered, it can be constructive or destructive, depending on how you use it.

An employer has the right to demand that a job be done the way he or she wants it done. Which of the two employee responses shown here would be better for all parties concerned? Explain why.

Case Study 3

Nancy was a bookkeeper in a bank. She was a good worker. She almost never missed a day of work, and she was always on time. Nancy's problem was that she could not accept criticism and benefit from it. On several occasions she made incorrect entries in her records. Each time this happened, her supervisor told her she must give more attention to certain details of her job. Nancy's response was to sulk. She wouldn't speak or smile for the rest of the day.

Nancy's sulking put a great strain on her supervisor because he could see the effect his criticism had on her. Still, he felt the criticism was necessary. Finally he had to let Nancy go because it took so much of his time to figure out how to approach her without hurting her feelings.

Loyalty

You have probably heard the expression "Don't bite the hand that feeds you." This is certainly true in your relationship with your employer. You must be for your employer and the company, not against them. Always show company loyalty.

No person is perfect, and neither is any company. You may not agree with everything your employer does. You may object to some of the company policies, but you should not complain to your friends or "run down" the company. Employers expect their workers to keep to themselves those things that pertain to the business.

You will never be happy working for an employer if you have only negative things to say about him or her. If for some reason you cannot be loyal, look for another job. If you must look for another job, resist the temptation to be critical of your present employer, especially when talking to other employers. No one wants to hire a disloyal employee.

✓ CHECKING UP

1. Of all the qualities employers expect their employees to have, which is the most important? Why do you think this is so?

2. On the job, what does it mean to "take initiative"?

3. If you are too ill to go to work, what should you do?

2 *What You Can Expect of Your Employer*

After reading about what your employer can expect of you, you may feel that you are expected to give a great deal without getting much in return. This is not so. You have a right to expect certain things from your employer. Some employers are more considerate than others, but in general you can expect your employer to provide the following things:

- Payments
- Safe working conditions
- Training
- Introductions to co-workers
- Explanations of policies, rules, regulations, and changes in your duties
- Evaluations of your work
- Honesty
- Fairness
- Fringe benefits
- Standard separation procedures

Payments

You can expect your employer to pay you for the work you do. You can also expect your employer to take care of various payments on your behalf. Your employer should deduct income taxes from your pay and set aside money for your social security and worker's compensation benefits. You will read more about these benefits in Chapter 23.

Your employer can figure your pay in several different ways. You will probably agree on the type of payment when you are hired. In most cases your pay will be calculated in the same manner as the pay for people doing similar jobs. In a few cases (usually where sales jobs are involved), workers are given choices in how their pay will be figured.

Wages   Most beginning workers are paid a certain amount for each hour they work. Pay received for hourly work is usually referred to as **wages.** For example, your wage might be $4 an hour, $5.35 an hour, or (if you're highly skilled) $20 an hour.

As a wage earner, you will probably receive paychecks of varying amounts from one payday to the next. The reason for this is that you will probably not work the same number of hours every pay period. Even if you work the same

number of hours every day, there may be more workdays in some pay periods than in others.

If you work more than 40 hours a week, you can expect your employer to pay you overtime. Overtime, also called time and a half, is a wage 50 percent higher than what you are normally paid. You can figure how much your overtime rate is by dividing your regular rate by two and then adding that amount to your regular rate. For example, if you are making $4 an hour, your overtime rate would be $6 an hour ($4 ÷ 2 = $2; $4 + $2 = $6).

State and federal laws require that employers pay workers overtime for every hour they work in excess of 40 hours a week. There are, however, some exceptions to this rule. For example, employers with fewer than four employees and employers whose businesses make less than a certain amount of money do not have to pay workers overtime.

If you have questions about whether or not you should receive overtime pay, first ask your employer. If you are still uncertain, call the nearest

Companies that pay wages often use time clocks to keep track of the hours their employees work. Assume this employee normally works a 7-hour day. If she works 40 hours this week, how many hours of overtime is that?

office of the Wage and Hour Division of the Labor Department. The number will be listed under U.S. Labor Department in the White Pages of the telephone book.

Salary   Instead of paying you by the hour, your employer may pay you a salary. A **salary** is a fixed amount of pay for a certain period of time, usually a year or a month. Salaried workers receive the same amount each paycheck, whether they work the same number of hours or not.

Most managers, supervisors, and company executives receive a yearly salary rather than hourly wages. Whether they average 80 hours or 30 hours of work a week, they receive the amount agreed upon at the beginning of the year. They do *not* receive overtime pay.

Commissions   Most salespeople are paid a commission. A **commission** is a payment that is a percentage of the total amount sold by a salesperson. For example, suppose you have a job selling vacuum cleaners and are paid a 50 percent commission. If one week you sell $1,000 worth of vacuum cleaners, your employer will pay you $500. If the next week you sell no vacuum cleaners, your employer will not pay you anything.

Most employers pay their beginning salespeople a wage or salary while they are learning how to sell the company's product. As these new salespeople gain experience, more of their pay is based on commissions and less on the wage or salary.

Safe Working Conditions

Your employer should provide safe working conditions for all workers. You should not be asked to use a machine that could be dangerous unless you have been taught how to operate it safely. You should not be asked to work in an unsafe environment. You have the right to expect your employer to fix faulty equipment and do anything else necessary to eliminate hazards on the job.

Training

Your employer should provide whatever training you need to learn the job. The way employers do this will differ from company to company. The amount and type of training you receive usually depend on the difficulty of the job.

You may simply be asked to watch an experienced worker do the job you will be doing, or a worker may be assigned to teach you how to do the job. In some cases your employer may even send you to school for training.

Introductions

Your employer should introduce you to all of your co-workers. This common courtesy is one you can expect, but it is not always observed. If your employer does not show you this consideration, perhaps other workers will make the introductions. If not, you will have to introduce yourself to your co-workers.

You can usually expect an employer to teach you what you need to know to do a job. In the situation shown here, however, what skills might the employer expect the employee to have already?

Explanations

Your employer should explain company policies, rules, and regulations so that you understand them. If you do not understand exactly how they affect you, ask for further explanation.

Your employer should also explain any changes that will affect you and your work. Your duties, working relationships, salary, and vacation schedules are some of the things that could change.

Your employer is probably very busy and may assume that you already understand such changes. If for some reason your employer does not explain the changes, ask him or her to explain them. You have a right to know why the changes have been made.

Evaluations

Your employer should evaluate your work and tell you how you are doing. He or she will probably watch you work and will notice how you get along with other workers. Your employer may then prepare a work evaluation, a written report on your job performance. In many cases these evaluations are used to decide whether or not you will be promoted, given a raise, kept in the same position with the same pay, or fired.

After evaluating you, your employer will probably discuss the evaluation with you. This is up to your employer, though. Some employers choose not to discuss the evaluations.

If you do discuss the evaluation with your employer, you will probably discuss it in private to avoid any possible embarrassment. Your employer should discuss both your strengths and weaknesses. Some employers try to save time by discussing weaknesses only. This is not a good way to conduct evaluation interviews. Still, if your boss does it this way, try to profit from the criticism.

The employer's purpose in pointing out your weaknesses is to make you a better worker. It is to your advantage as well as to the company's that you improve in your job. If you follow your employer's recommendations, you will increase your chances of receiving better pay raises. Even more important, you will be able to take greater pride in your work.

If your boss points out your weaknesses but does not suggest how you can improve, ask for suggestions. Your boss should be able to help you. By asking questions you will also show your employer that you are genuinely interested in improving your work.

Study the employee evaluation form given to you by your teacher to get an idea of the kinds of things your employer will expect. When you know your employer's expectations, you can make sure you meet them. This will help you advance faster in the world of work.

The trend today is to put work evaluations in writing and have both employer and employee sign them. What are the advantages of this procedure?

MAKE A DECISION

You've been working at your new job for six months now, and you think you're doing pretty well. You'd like to know what your supervisor thinks, however, and what you can do to move up in the company. The problem is that your supervisor has never commented on your performance—or anyone else's. Whenever anyone tries to talk with him, he gets upset because he's so busy. You want a work evaluation, but you don't want to anger your supervisor. What do you do—speak up and ask for an evaluation or keep quiet and wait? Give the reasons for your decision.

ty Act, part of the 1964 Civil Rights Act. It forbids discrimination by employers, employment agencies, and unions on the basis of race, color, religion, sex, or national origin. The Age Discrimination Act of 1967 makes it illegal to discriminate against people over 40 in hiring or on the job. In 1973, Congress passed the Rehabilitation Act to protect people with physical or mental disabilities from discrimination as well. The purpose of all these laws is to be certain that people are judged on the basis of their ability to do the job. Because of these laws, minorities and women have made great progress in the past 25 years.

Fair Employment Practices The term *fair employment practice* means just what you'd expect. The Fair Labor Standards Act sets the standards for fair treatment in three main areas—child labor, wages and hours, and equal pay.

Honesty

Just as your employer expects you to be honest, you can expect your employer to be honest with you. Your employer should pay you what he or she promised to pay you when you took the job. Your employer should not try to deny you any benefits or privileges to which you are entitled.

Fairness

If you think you are being treated unfairly on the job, you may want to discuss the problem with your employer. Whether or not you do depends on your personality, your employer's personality, and your relationship with your employer.

If you do decide to talk about the problem with your employer, don't simply lay the blame on someone else. Be cooperative and understanding. This will help persuade your employer to see things your way.

Freedom from Discrimination The word *discrimination* can mean the ability to distinguish one thing or person from another. As it's used in the workplace, however, **discrimination** means treating someone unfairly because of prejudice. Racial, sexual, religious, or age-related discrimination are the most common. Disabled people are also often the victims of discrimination.

There are several federal laws to protect people from discrimination on the job. The most important of these is the Equal Employment Opportuni-

SITUATION
SOLUTION

When Someone Else Takes the Credit

You've been working with your supervisor on a new advertising layout for the store. Most of the new ideas have been yours, and your supervisor has praised them highly. When he makes the final presentation to the department head, though, he doesn't mention you. He takes all the credit for the layout himself. You need to get along with your supervisor, since your promotions depend on his evaluations. However, the situation is really bothering you.

1. The day after the presentation, your supervisor doesn't discuss it with you (although you have heard that the department head loved it). What do you say to your supervisor?

2. You have not received a raise or promotion in six months. Your supervisor asks you to help him with another ad layout, mentioning how successful the last one was. How do you respond?

3. Your co-workers encourage you to complain to the department head about the situation. What do you do?

Federal law prohibits discrimination in the workplace against physically challenged individuals. From a business viewpoint, why does such discrimination *not* make sense?

If you are working now, you have probably come in contact with someone enforcing child labor laws. They are the reason minors must have a work permit before beginning work. These laws also protect young people from work in dangerous or fatiguing jobs, such as those in factories and mines; and they prohibit people aged 15 or younger from working during school hours. States have also passed their own child labor laws. If there is a conflict between state and federal laws, the one that is more protective of the child is enforced.

The minimum wage, which most employers must pay their workers, is set by Congress in the Fair Labor Standards Act. In April 1990 the minimum wage was raised to $3.80 an hour. Some states have passed their own minimum wage laws that require employers to pay a higher wage than the federal standard. Employers are allowed to pay some people (usually young people) less than the minimum wage for some jobs. Usually these are jobs in which the employee receives training that counts as part of his or her wages, or they might be seasonal jobs such as wrapping Christmas presents. Some jobs, such as babysitting or gardening, are not covered by minimum wage laws.

The Fair Labor Standards Act deals with other areas as well. It defines the standard work week in the United States—40 hours, after which you must be paid overtime. It also makes it illegal to pay one person more than another for the same work.

Affirmative Action   Another way people are attempting to make employment more fair is through affirmative action programs. These are designed to help people who may have suffered discrimination in the past catch up. Affirmative action programs encourage employers to give special consideration to racial minorities, women, and disabled people. There is controversy about such programs. Critics think they give an unfair advantage to the people who benefit from them. It is certain, however, that they have helped many people to compete more effectively in the workplace.

Fringe Benefits

Most companies that hire full-time employees provide at least some fringe benefits. The most common of these is paid vacation. Paid vacations are usually available to new employees once they have completed six months to a year of service.

Health insurance is another common benefit, mainly for employees of large companies. (With the high cost of medical care, it is often beyond the reach of small companies.) The cost of such coverage is usually shared by employer and employee. However, the trend today is to shift more of the burden to employees.

There are other, less common benefits. These include retirement plans, bonuses, and life insurance. In addition, the 1990s are likely to see increased pressure for firms to add family-oriented benefits like unpaid leave for family emergencies and child care assistance.

In the past, working parents had to make their own arrangements for child care. As more and more women have entered the workplace, however, employers have begun to realize that if they want to attract and keep good employees they will have to offer help in this area. As a result, large companies are now beginning to set up on-site child care centers. Employees bring their children to work and leave them at a facility located right in the factory, hospital, or office building where they do their jobs. Other companies are helping their employees pay for child care at private centers. Because more than half of working women are mothers, it is easy to see why child care has been called the benefit of the nineties.

Standard Separation Procedures

You will probably be successful in the world of work. Nonetheless, you should be aware of the possibility of losing your job. It can happen for reasons that are totally beyond your control. Most companies have standard procedures for dealing with such situations.

Termination   If for some reason your employer is not satisfied with your performance, he or she may give you a **termination notice.** In more common terms, this means you have been fired. A termination notice is a statement from your employer that you have been dismissed from your job with the company.

If you lose your job, don't place all the blame on your employer. Instead, think about what happened and how you could have prevented it. Try to learn from your mistakes. If you can see what you did wrong, the experience can be a constructive one. Then there will be less chance of your being fired from your next job.

Begin immediately to look for the job that you think will be right for you. The places to go and the methods to use are the same as when you were looking for your first job. These were discussed in Chapter 5.

For an increasing number of two-income families in the United States, findng adequate day care for children is a major problem. Why does it make sense for businesses to start getting involved by providing financial support or on-site facilities?

Strive for Success

The Dollar-a-Year Executive

Everyone in business dreams of making it to the top and enjoying the power, prestige, and money —especially the money—that comes with success. When Lee Iacocca made it to the top as president of the Chrysler Corporation, he enjoyed the power and prestige of his position. The money was a different story, though—Iacocca's salary was only one dollar a year!

Iacocca was born in 1924 in Allentown, Pennsylvania, the son of working-class Italian immigrants. After graduation from college, he was chosen as one of 50 students from across the country to join a new student engineer program at Ford Motor Company. Before his training was finished, however, Iacocca decided that engineering was not for him. He wanted to be "where the action was," in sales and marketing, so he started over selling Ford trucks. He advanced rapidly and in 1956 was promoted into top management at the age of 32.

By 1960 Iacocca was head of the Ford car division, where he was the driving force behind the development of the Ford Mustang. Incredibly, the car sold 418,812 units in its first year (1964)— an unbeaten record in the auto industry. The next year Iacocca was made a vice-president of the company and five years later, president.

By 1973 dwindling oil reserves and rising gas prices were causing American consumers to look for more fuel-efficient cars. Iacocca wanted Ford to enter this new market with a line of small cars, but the board of directors at Ford was against the idea. This disagreement grew increasingly bitter, and finally in 1978 Iacocca was fired.

Three months later, though, he was right back on top in the car business—this time as president of Chrysler Corporation, the third of America's "Big Three" auto makers. It was a less-than-glorious start, however. The day he was hired, Chrysler reported it had lost more money in the previous three months than ever before in its history. The company was nearly bankrupt.

Iacocca needed to do something drastic, so he went to the federal government and asked for $1.5 billion in loan guarantees. He spent weeks testifying before Congressional committees. Finally, to get the guarantee approved, he promised that Chrysler would pay back all of its loans by 1983. It was a promise that no one really

believed, not even the rest of Chrysler's top management.

In the following three years, though, the company that had been losing half a billion dollars every three months earned enough to make good Iacocca's word. To do it, Iacocca cut expenses to the bone—starting with his own salary, which he reduced to one dollar a year! He made other extraordinary changes, giving workers stock in the company and appointing the president of the United Auto Workers to the board of directors. His style of management, based on the recognition that *all* employees (not just managers) are important to a company's success, worked wonders. Chrysler began making smaller, more fuel-efficient cars and completely reversed its poor reputation for service. Led by Iacocca, the company went from being the laughing stock of the American auto industry to one of its biggest success stories.

Layoff Suppose your company is not doing well and you were one of the last employees hired. In this case, you may be given a layoff notice. A **layoff notice** is a statement from your employer that your period of employment is over, usually temporarily.

Being laid off is not the same as being fired. People are not laid off because of unsatisfactory work. They are usually laid off because there isn't enough work to do. In some cases they are laid off because their employers cannot afford to pay their wages.

It is customary for employers to notify you if you are to be laid off. Although they are not legally required to do so, some employers may give you **severance pay** when you are laid off. This means that because you are "severed" (or cut off) from your job, you will receive a check. Depending on your situation and pay period, your check could be equal to one, two, or several weeks' pay.

Unemployment Compensation If you are laid off or fired, you may be eligible for unemployment compensation. **Unemployment compensation** is money given to people who have recently become unemployed. Unemployment checks are provided for a limited time to those who are able to work and who are actively seeking jobs.

To qualify for unemployment compensation, you must have earned a certain amount of money prior to losing your job. Students working part-time do not usually qualify because their yearly earnings do not meet the minimum requirements. Your state unemployment office can tell you what the minimum is. You can read more about unemployment compensation in Chapter 23.

If your company is not doing well and you were one of the last employees hired, your employer may give you a layoff notice stating that your period of employment is temporarily over. What else might an employer give you if you are laid off?

✓ CHECKING UP

1. Describe three ways in which an employer could pay you.
2. What sorts of fair employment practices can you expect an employer to observe?
3. What should you do if you receive a termination notice?

3 How to Get Along with Your Co-Workers

Very few jobs are done by one person working alone. In your job you will probably have to work with several people. This means that in addition to meeting your boss's expectations, you must get along with your co-workers. You cannot become truly successful in your work all by yourself. To be successful you must have the friendly cooperation of your co-workers.

The reasons why you should try to get along with your co-workers are obvious. First, you will be much happier and enjoy your work more if you are on good terms with your co-workers. Second, if you and your co-workers enjoy working together, you will all get more done. This will make your employer happy, which could result in pay raises and promotions.

Accept Differences

Getting along well with your co-workers is not always easy. No two people are exactly alike. People see things differently and react in different ways to the same situation. Different attitudes and beliefs can lead to conflicts.

To get along well with your co-workers, you must accept them as worthy individuals. You must accept them even if they are very different from you. Nobody is perfect, but everyone has some good qualities. Try to understand your co-workers'

attitudes and behaviors. If you do this, you will be doing your part to encourage good working relationships.

If one of your co-workers is extremely difficult to get along with, do not judge him or her too harshly. There may be good reasons for that person's behavior. Perhaps a bad experience has had a negative effect on your co-worker. Maybe this person has serious problems at home. Whatever the cause, try to do *more* than your share in bringing about a good working relationship. You never know—someday you may be the one in need of some extra understanding, tolerance, and cooperation.

Remember You're a Beginner

As a beginning worker, you should keep your eyes and ears open. Don't spend a great deal of time talking—just be friendly and ask questions about your work. You will probably find that your more experienced co-workers will be happy to help you get started. Some of them may point out your mistakes. If so, they are probably trying to do you a favor. Accept it as a favor, and thank them.

Some of your co-workers may offer suggestions for better ways of doing things. If their suggestions seem like good ones and if they don't conflict with your boss's instructions, try them out. If they work well, use them.

Once you understand your job, do it yourself. Do not depend too much on others. Your co-workers have their own work to do.

As a beginning worker, look to more experienced co-workers for guidance and advice. How does this receptive attitude help new employees get along in a new work environment?

A sense of humor can help an employee get along with co-workers. From an employer's viewpoint, what benefits does it offer?

Maintain Proper Formality

At first, you may be uncertain about how formal or informal you should be with your employer and your co-workers. It is better to be too formal than too informal. Of course, you should smile and be pleasant to everyone, but don't get too chummy too soon.

If you are too eager, you may become close friends with a co-worker who is not really someone you want as a close friend. If this happens, it could put a strain on your working relationship with that person. It is better to go slowly, getting to know everyone before you develop any close relationships.

On your job, employees may call each other by their first names. If so, it would be only natural for you to call your co-workers by their first names. In many companies, though, beginning workers are expected to call older co-workers—and the boss— by their last names. Again, if you are not sure, it's better to be too formal than too chummy.

Stay Neutral in Disputes

One of the best ways to keep up a good working relationship with all of your co-workers is to mind your own business. No matter where you work,

there will probably be disputes between people. If you get involved in such disagreements, you will lose every time. You may strengthen your friendship with one person for the moment, but you may well damage your working relationships with other workers for a long time. The best thing to do is to remain neutral.

Keep Your Sense of Humor

If you don't already have a good sense of humor, try to develop one. Try to laugh when the joke is on you. People tend to like people who can laugh at themselves.

✓ CHECKING UP

1. Why is it *essential* that you learn how to get along with people on the job?
2. Why should you make a special effort to improve your relationship with a difficult co-worker?
3. In what sense is taking sides in a job dispute between two co-workers a lose-lose proposition for you?

CHAPTER SUMMARY

The most important factor in your job success is usually your own attitude. The main reason young workers lose their jobs is because they don't get along with other people. If you have a positive attitude, you are on your way to success. If you have a negative attitude, you can and should change it.

Your employer will expect certain things from you in addition to a positive attitude: cooperation, honesty, initiative, a willingness to learn, a willingness to follow directions, dependability, enthusiasm, the ability to accept criticism, and loyalty. Your success on the job will depend on how well you meet your employer's expectations.

As an employee you have the right to expect certain things from your employer. These things include payments, safe working conditions, training, introductions, explanations, and evaluations. Most employers also provide at least some fringe benefits and standard procedures for ending the employer/employee relationship.

You cannot be truly successful in your work unless you get along with your co-workers. You can encourage good co-worker relationships by accepting differences, remembering that you are a beginner, maintaining the proper formality, staying neutral in disputes, and having a sense of humor.

TERMS TO KNOW

On a separate sheet of paper, write definitions for each of the following terms:

attitude
initiative
wages
salary
commission
discrimination
termination notice
layoff notice
severance pay
unemployment compensation

STUDY QUESTIONS

1. How can you tell if someone has a positive attitude?
2. What is the main reason that young workers lose their jobs?
3. Besides a day's work for a day's pay, name five things that an employer usually expects of workers.
4. Why is it a good idea for a worker to do some of the tasks that he or she finds unpleasant?
5. What are two types of dishonesty on the job?
6. How should an employee deal with criticism of his or her work?
7. List five things that a worker can reasonably expect from an employer.
8. Give two reasons why workers are laid off.
9. How do you go about getting a new job after you have been laid off or fired?
10. Name two reasons why it is important to get along well with co-workers.
11. Why isn't it a good idea to become close friends with a co-worker during the first week or two on the job?

CRITICAL THINKING

1. Suggest some ways you can change a negative attitude into a positive one.
2. Your employer never seems satisfied with your work. What should you do?
3. Your friend Maureen works weekends and evenings for a mortgage company. She always has a purseful of specialty items—pens, pencils, markers, key rings, and memo pads with the company's name and logo on

them. She hands them around at school, freely admitting how she's come by them. "Hey, the company gives this stuff away all the time. It's publicity, and that's what I'm doing—giving them free publicity." Do you agree? Why or why not?

4. You work closely with someone who arrives late every day and doesn't do much after getting there. You feel you're doing much more than your share of the work. Your undependable co-worker and your supervisor, however, are close friends. Which course of action would you take and why?

- Talk with your co-worker about the situation.
- Talk with your supervisor about the situation.
- Talk to no one, and continue to do more than your share.
- Quit your job.

5. Of the things an employer expects of workers, which do you feel are most important? Rank them in order, and compare your list with those of your classmates.

6. Of the things you can reasonably expect of an employer, which do you feel are most important? Rank them in order, and compare your list with those of your classmates.

DISCUSSION STARTERS

1. Which do you think has a greater influence on attitudes—heredity or environment? Explain.

2. How do you respond to criticism? Would your usual response tend to help or hurt you if your employer were the one doing the criticizing?

3. Have you personally experienced discrimination? What sort of discrimination was it? How did you deal with it? How would you deal with a similar situation on the job?

BUILDING BASIC SKILLS

Math

1. You work ten hours of overtime. If your base wage is $4.80 an hour, how much will your gross pay be this week?

2. The minimum wage is $3.80 per hour, but your work experience teacher tells you that you will make only two-thirds of that amount in the program because your training counts as part of your wage. If you work 15 hours this week, how much will you earn?

Communication

3. A new co-worker, Trudy, never seems to listen when you explain things to her. As a result, she keeps making mistakes. You are responsible for training her, and you are afraid your employer is going to think you're not doing a good job if Trudy doesn't catch on soon. What steps can you take to get and hold Trudy's attention?

Human Relations

4. A new employee in your office, Phil, is constantly encouraging people to take long coffee breaks and lunches. When the department manager is gone, Phil doesn't work at all. He goes from desk to desk, talking to anyone who will listen. Everyone feels uncomfortable about the situation—some are even irritated—but no one has said anything to either Phil or the manager. You finally decide to act. What do you do?

SUGGESTED ACTIVITIES

1. Pick a characteristic of a negative attitude that you sometimes see in yourself. For one week concentrate on acting in the opposite manner. At the end of the week, write a short report describing your attempts to change and evaluating your success. Note especially if people reacted any differently to you.

2. Interview a local employer about the problems of young workers. Ask this person to explain what his or her firm expects of first-time employees. Ask if the company has a program to help such people adjust to their new environment and responsibilities, and, if so, find out how it operates.

Progressing Toward Your Career Goal

OBJECTIVES

After studying this chapter and doing the activities, you will be able to:

- discuss the factors that determine whether a worker receives a raise;
- describe what employers look for when making promotions;
- explain how appearance can increase a worker's chances for success;
- list the qualities that make a good supervisor; and
- summarize the proper procedure for quitting a job.

TERMS TO KNOW

merit raise
promotion
seniority
perseverance
supervisor
delegate

*B*efore you read this chapter, answer these questions:

- Are you now working?
- Are you meeting your employer's expectations?
- Are you getting along with your employer and your co-workers?

If you answered yes to each of these questions, you are already on your way to success in the world of work. If you want to advance further, read this chapter carefully. It will help you learn how to get a raise, a promotion, or both—and it will help you move closer to your ultimate career goal.

1 *Raises*

You may not have ambitious goals. You may be happy for many years doing the work you are doing right now. One thing is almost certain, however—you will want to make more money. Even if you stay on the same job, you will want to be given raises.

What do you have to do to get a raise? Several factors are involved. In most cases your performance on the job is the most important factor. The company you work for and the type of job you do are also important.

Your Performance

You cannot expect a raise unless you are doing your job adequately. This means meeting your employer's expectations as described in Chapter 6. It also means getting along well with your co-workers.

You may get a raise by simply doing an adequate job—or you may not. Don't take this chance. If you want a raise, do more than what is expected of you. This is where the initiative and enthusiasm discussed in Chapter 6 become important. The harder you work and the more you do, the better your chances for a raise. Remember, you can't expect to be paid more for doing less!

If you have had a work evaluation, you probably have a good idea of how well you are doing in your job. If your employer pointed out weaknesses, you should already be working to improve in these areas. If you haven't had an evaluation, ask for one. Let your employer know that you are interested in doing well and eventually earning a raise.

Company Policy

The company you work for probably has its own policy regarding raises. You may have asked about this policy during your interview. If not, schedule a meeting with your employer to discuss the company's policy.

Don't be afraid to ask for this explanation. You will not be asking for a raise, simply an explanation. As you learned in Chapter 6, all workers are entitled to an explanation of company policy.

Some companies have a policy of giving their employees automatic raises. These are raises given to employees after they have worked for the company for a certain period of time—usually six months or a year. In almost all cases workers must be doing at least adequate work to receive such raises.

Some companies that give automatic raises to all workers also provide bonuses for especially outstanding work. These bonuses are often called **merit raises** to distinguish them from automatic raises. A merit raise may consist of slightly more or a great deal more than an automatic raise, depending on the quality of work being rewarded.

In still other companies there may be no plan for automatic raises at regular intervals. In most of these companies the employer simply gives raises on the basis of merit. If at any time the employer feels that someone deserves an increase, he or she simply raises that worker's pay. In these companies the best workers are usually given raises fairly often. Less productive workers may not receive raises for long periods of time, perhaps for years.

In many companies, supervisors regularly evaluate each worker's performance (including the person's initiative and enthusiasm) to help determine annual raises. What is your company's policy regarding raises?

The low skills level of some jobs limits their ability to command greatly increased wages. To earn more, what would this worker have to do?

You can see that your company's policy plays a big part in determining whether or not you get a raise. In some companies, for example, no one gets a raise during the first year. In such a company, even the most outstanding workers must wait until their second year to get a raise.

Your Job

Whether or not you get a raise will often depend on the type of job you do. For most jobs there is a "going rate." This means that most of the workers who do a certain job receive about the same pay. There is usually a limit on how much employers will pay someone to do that type of job.

If you are working at an unskilled job, for example, the employer may not be willing to pay more than minimum wage. As noted in Chapter 6, the minimum wage is set by law. It is the lowest amount per hour that employers are allowed to pay. Check with the state employment office in your area to find out what the minimum wage is at the present time.

An employer may not be able to afford to pay more than minimum wage, even to outstanding workers. If you are working at such a job and want a raise, you will probably have to earn a promotion to make more money.

Some jobs are union jobs. This means that the pay for all workers doing a certain type of work is determined by union contract. The contract states when raises will be given and specifies their amount. In these cases the employer cannot give raises to certain workers even if he or she wants to.

If you have a union job, your pay scale is set for you. You cannot change it. If you want to know when you are supposed to get a raise, ask your union representative. You will read more about unions and union contracts in Chapter 13.

✓ CHECKING UP

1. Describe the minimum performance standards for getting a raise.
2. What is the difference between an automatic raise and a merit raise?
3. How can the type of job you have limit your ability to command a raise?

2 *Promotions*

Regardless of how well you perform in your present job, you may never receive enough in raises to earn as much as you would like. You will therefore probably want to work for a **promotion,** or advancement to a higher-level job. Indeed, you may be able to achieve your ultimate career goal in no other way.

Almost everyone likes promotions. Promotions make people feel important and appreciated. These feelings contribute to a person's sense of worth and self-esteem. In almost all cases, promotions also mean more money.

The best time to find out about opportunities for promotion within a company is during the job interview. You should ask your interviewer what your chances are for advancement if you do well. After you have begun work, don't bother your employer by constantly asking questions about promotions.

Who Gets Promoted?

If you want a promotion, you must earn it. How? First, you must increase your knowledge and skills in your present job. Second, you must do your work in the best possible way. These are the minimum requirements for you to be considered for a promotion.

In deciding who will be promoted, employers consider several other factors. These are described on the next few pages.

Seniority　**Seniority** is the privileged status that results from continuous service with one company. Those who have worked for a company the longest have the greatest seniority.

Employees who have achieved seniority have proven themselves to be steady, dependable workers. This is why most companies consider seniority when making promotions. Most companies do not, however, give employees promotions on the basis of seniority alone.

Knowledge of Job　Your knowledge of your present job is an important factor in determining whether or not you get a promotion. Are you very knowledgeable about your work? Are you always trying to learn as much as you can to improve your skills? Most employers feel that if you are both knowledgeable and open to learning more, you can probably do a more difficult job.

Quality of Work　The quality of your work is also considered by your employer. If you do your work well, you will probably perform well in a job with more responsibility.

Quantity of Work　Some employees do their work well, but they do it slowly. Employers are looking for workers who do their work well and do it quickly. Your employer will probably notice how much work you get done. From these observations your employer will determine how much work you would probably accomplish on a more responsible job.

Initiative　As you know, employers expect their workers to take some initiative. Your employer will watch to see how often you look for tasks that need doing and do them without being told. If you do your own work without much supervision and then do whatever else needs doing, your employer may think you would make a good supervisor. This could mean a promotion for you.

Perseverance　Once you begin a task, do you always carry it through to completion? If you are a person with **perseverance,** you finish what you start.

Not everyone has perseverance. You probably know people who begin projects but never finish them. Being able to finish a job, even if it becomes tiresome and boring, is important to your career success. No employer will promote a worker with a history of uncompleted jobs.

Ability to Cooperate　The importance of being able to cooperate with others was discussed in Chapter 6. As you will remember, most beginning workers who lose their jobs lose them because they are unable to cooperate with their employers and co-workers.

Cooperation is necessary simply to keep your job, but it's even more important if you want a promotion. A promotion usually means greater responsibility, which often means getting along with more people. Some of these people may be difficult to work with. This is why employers want to promote only those people who have the ability to cooperate.

Ability to Think　A promotion often means taking a job that involves decision making. For such a job, employers want someone who can think for himself or herself.

Employers are always looking for someone who can analyze problems. They want someone who can figure out the best way of doing a particular task. Always try to think for yourself. You will then have a better chance for promotion than the employee who must always ask someone what to do.

Ability to Adapt

Do you have the ability to adapt to new situations? Can you learn to do things other than those for which you were originally hired?

Your employer probably expects you to do whatever needs to be done. This could mean doing some tasks that were not mentioned when you were hired. Jobs and duties change. If you can adapt to changes, you are a more valuable employee than one who cannot. Again, this makes you a more likely candidate for promotion.

Education and Training

In considering you for promotion, your employer will want to know whether or not you have adequate education and training for the new job. Of course, the more training you have had, the greater your chances for being promoted.

It's up to you to see that you get the education and training you need for the job you want. If you haven't done so already, you need to find out what education and training you will need to reach your ultimate career goal. You may find that you will need several levels of education.

If you read Chapter 3, you know that the *Occupational Outlook Handbook* can help you decide what education and training you need. Your school's work experience and counseling offices probably have copies of the *OOH*. Your public library may also have a copy.

In every job there are recurring tasks that employees can tackle when their own personal work loads are lighter. Speculate about what these tasks might be for some other occupations.

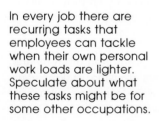

Strive for Success

Baseball's Amazing Leftie

Left-handed people face certain hardships in a world that is mostly right-handed. For example, mechanical things like can openers, doors, and American cars are built for right-handed people and are therefore more difficult for lefties to handle.

This is not the case with baseball, however. In baseball being left-handed can be an advantage, especially for a pitcher. This is because most hitters are right-handed, and it is more difficult for a right-handed person to hit left-handed pitching.

Some players have tried switching from right-handed to left-handed in the hope that they would become better pitchers. Jim Abbott did not have to switch, however. In fact, he never had a choice. He was born without a right hand.

Though he was fitted as a child with an artificial hand made of metal and plastic, Abbott felt it was clumsy and soon stopped wearing it. A sports nut as a child, he spent hours every day pitching against the wall of the family home. To catch the ball, he would quickly move his glove from the nub at the end of his right arm to his left hand. He was able to make the switch very quickly and rarely let a ball get by him.

Abbott began playing Little League baseball as a 10-year-old and pitched his first no-hitter when he was 11. He says that in those days he was encouraged to believe he could do anything he chose to do. He admits that if people had told him he couldn't play because of his disability, he "would have been crushed and never gone on."

In high school in Flint, Michigan, Abbott played three years of varsity baseball. During his senior year he struck out an average of two batters each inning and only allowed two hits per game. He also batted .427 and played left field, first base, and shortstop in addition to pitching.

Baseball, however, wasn't Abbott's only sport. He also went out for football and basketball. He played quarterback on the football team and led it to the semifinals of the state championship in his senior year. Even in basketball he was the highest scorer in the school.

It's no wonder that the Toronto Blue Jays wanted to sign Abbott right out of high school. He decided, however, to go to college first. His career at the University of Michigan was a continuation of the success he had enjoyed in high school. He led the Wolverines to the NCAA tournament each year he played in college and was a starter on the 1988 U.S. Olympic team. Following his graduation, he was drafted by the California Angels and today is the team's starting pitcher.

You can also learn what education and training you need to reach your goals by asking your employer. A company organization chart can help you identify some medium-range goals. Once you know the specific positions you want to attain, you can better determine what education and training you need.

The more education and training you have, the sooner you will reach your career goal. If two employees have identical qualifications except for educational background, the promotion will go to the one with more education and training.

How do you get education and training if you're working full time? Some companies provide their own courses for employees. These companies believe that money for education is well spent. Both the company and the employee benefit. If there is a college or university in your city, night classes are probably available. Also, many public schools offer evening classes for adults. If such formal training is not available in your area, you can take correspondence courses and read trade magazines and books.

Appearance In deciding who will be promoted, most employers consider appearance. They know that people who look successful have a better chance of being successful.

Appearance is as important as any other factor in determining who gets promoted. If you and another employee are about equal in other areas, the employer may base the final decision on who makes the better appearance.

We are all strongly influenced by how people look—it may not be fair, but it's true. For example, suppose you entered a restaurant and were approached by one of these individuals wearing a manager's nametag. How would you feel about the establishment?

Look at others in your workplace. Do some wear shined leather shoes while others wear dirty tennis shoes? Do some wear slacks or dresses while others wear jeans? Do some of the men wear jackets and ties while others wear open-collar shirts? If you notice these differences, ask yourself which of the workers have greater authority. You will probably find that those who dress in a neat, nonfaddish way have greater authority. They are probably paid more, too.

Of course, the kind of work you do will affect your style of dress. For some jobs, such as construction and farm work, jeans are the accepted dress. Other jobs require uniforms. Even so, there is usually some small way in which you can make a better impression in your manner of dress.

On the job, dressing for success means dressing a little neater than the average employee. It means wearing what the person in charge believes is the look of success. For example, employers and supervisors expect their employees to have accepta-

ble hairstyles. It doesn't matter how you like to wear your hair. If your hairstyle is offensive to the person in charge, that person will be much less likely to promote you or give you a raise.

Why Seek a Promotion?

In almost all cases, promotions mean more responsibility. This often includes greater authority over other workers. Many people like authority and responsibility; many do not.

You don't have to accept a promotion just because it's offered. You may not think that you're ready to handle the added responsibility. Perhaps you feel that you'd be unhappy telling other people what to do. In either case, it might be better to turn down the promotion. This is not often done, but you may want to wait until you feel more comfortable about accepting greater responsibility.

Suppose that accepting a certain promotion would mean supervising other employees. In deciding whether or not you are ready for this promotion, consider both the advantages and disadvantages of being a **supervisor** (someone in charge of other workers).

Advantages of Being a Supervisor One advantage of being a supervisor is higher pay. Most supervisors are paid more money than the workers they supervise. This is the way it should be since supervisors have more responsibility.

Another advantage is prestige. Good supervisors are usually looked up to and respected by workers.

A third advantage of being a supervisor is that the work is usually more interesting. Supervisors are not normally required to do dull or routine work. Instead, they usually do a variety of more challenging and rewarding jobs. This means that there is a greater chance to be creative and to try new things.

Perhaps the most important advantage of being a supervisor is the chance to be a leader. The supervisor has greater influence in determining how the company will be run. By handling the extra responsibility and demonstrating leadership ability, the supervisor shows that he or she is worthy of further advancement.

Disadvantages of Being a Supervisor Usually supervisors have a different kind of relationship with their employees than the employees have among themselves. The supervisor is the boss. People act and talk differently with the boss

---

Case Study 1

A person who has carefully studied the reactions of people to clothing is John T. Molloy. Molloy has been described by *Time* magazine as a "wardrobe engineer." In his book, *Dress for Success,* Molloy describes how people react to various kinds of clothing. Here's one of his experiments.

"To determine how people feel about tie-wearers in strictly economic terms, I took twin pictures of the same man. In one, he was wearing a gray suit and tie. In the other, he wore a similar suit but with no tie and an open-collar shirt. Over 100 people picked at random were asked to estimate the yearly income of each of the . . . 'twins.' . . . the 'twin' wearing the tie was generally awarded $3,000 to $4,000 more per year than his 'brother.'

"Using the same set of photos but questioning only women, I asked which of the men the women would trust enough to let into their homes, provided they didn't know him. Sixty percent of the women trusted neither, but of the 40 percent who trusted one of them, they chose the man with the tie almost without exception."

MAKE A DECISION

You have just been offered a promotion. If you accept, you will receive about $100 more each month in salary. Your new duties will include supervising 25 other workers and attending 2-hour management meetings after work once a week. In your present position you are responsible for only your own work, and you are never asked to work more than the regular 40 hours. What's your decision—accept the promotion or decline it? Give the reasons for your decision.

than the mistakes made by other workers. Many of the supervisor's mistakes are multiplied by the number of workers under his or her direction. This means added pressure to do everything right. Most supervisors see this pressure as a disadvantage.

How to Be an Effective Supervisor

If you do accept a promotion that includes supervising the work of others, then learn to be a good supervisor. This is easy for some people but difficult for others.

If you have no supervisory experience, you will probably not be placed in charge of a large number of workers. Your first promotion to a supervisory position may place you in charge of only one or two workers. If so, you will have a better chance to learn how to be a good supervisor.

If being a supervisor seems difficult at first, don't be discouraged. You can improve if you work at it. The next few pages offer some guidelines for becoming an effective supervisor.

Give Clear Directions Communication is often the biggest problem a supervisor has. Even the hardest workers will be unproductive if they don't understand what they are supposed to do. If they don't know what to do, it may be the supervisor's fault. He or she may have given too little direction or failed to make the directions clear.

than they do with their co-workers. They usually are not quite so free in what they say. Many supervisors think of this as a disadvantage.

Another disadvantage is that a supervisor is often a target for criticism. Because the supervisor's paycheck is bigger, employees often feel that the supervisor should do more than they do. If the employees don't feel that the supervisor is doing enough work, they will probably be critical.

A third disadvantage of being a supervisor is the increased pressure to do a good job. A supervisor's mistakes are usually more costly to the company

How well employees perform often depends on the ability of their superiors to communicate clearly. If the manager shown here fails to impress her salespeople with the importance of presenting merchandise well or carefully maintaining displays, what might be the cost?

Treating employees fairly involves making reasonable demands and letting the employees know clearly what those demands are. What technique is this supervisor using to ensure that these things are communicated to his people?

As a supervisor, you should give all the direction needed for each job. In some cases you may not be sure that the workers have understood your directions. If you're not sure, ask them some questions about what you've said. You will be able to tell from their answers whether or not they understood you. You can also improve communication by making the workers feel comfortable about asking you questions. If they know they can ask questions without being made to feel ignorant, they will ask when they are uncertain. This will make your job of giving clear directions much easier.

Train New Workers   If you are a supervisor, you may need to break in new workers. To make these workers as productive as possible, you will need to train them properly. You may do the actual training, or you may assign this task to one of your experienced workers. If you assign the training to someone else, choose a person who knows the work and has a flair for teaching. New workers trained by productive, enthusiastic workers are more likely to become productive, enthusiastic workers themselves.

Be Consistent   Be consistent in handling your supervisory duties. If you say that a certain job must be done in a certain way, make sure that it is always done in that way by every worker.

Another way of being consistent is to follow through on what you say. If, for example, you tell an employee that you will deduct part of his or her salary for being late, do it! If you do not follow through, your workers will not respect you and will tend to do as they please.

Treat Workers Fairly   If you expect the workers you are supervising to do their best work for you, you must treat them fairly. Do not let one worker come to work late or get by with sloppy work if you make everyone else arrive on time and do a good job.

Another part of being fair with your workers is being reasonable. Do not make demands that your workers can't meet.

If a worker tells you that you are being unfair, listen to the complaint calmly. Give the complaint careful consideration. If the employee is right, you may want to change your mind about the matter. If you think this person is wrong, explain your reasoning. You may not convince the worker that you are right, but he or she will appreciate your efforts to be fair.

Be Firm When Necessary   As a supervisor you must sometimes be firm with your workers. Do not let employees take unfair advantage of you, the company, or other workers. This doesn't mean that you should yell or lose your temper.

Case Study 2

After attending college for one year, Ellen began working for the Maddox Company as a typist. One year later she was promoted to stenographer. Three years after this promotion, she became secretary to one of the vice-presidents of the company. She was an excellent worker, and everyone liked her very much.

When the office manager left, Ellen asked for the job. Company officials thought she would make a good office manager, even though she had no experience supervising other workers.

Ellen was placed in charge of an office staff of 16 employees. When several of these people started coming to work late and leaving early, Ellen knew she should do something; but she was afraid she might make them angry with her. When some of the workers started taking half-hour coffee breaks, Ellen didn't know what to do; so she did nothing (and worried about doing that). It wasn't long before some of the workers began talking back to Ellen when she gave them work to do. Finally, in frustration, Ellen went to the vice-president and asked to be relieved of her responsibilities as office manager.

Every situation requiring discipline is different from every other. With some workers a friendly suggestion is all that's needed. With others you may have to be more firm and direct.

Sometimes problems result from the behavior of one employee toward another. Again, be firm when necessary. If the problem is a severe one, you may need to move an employee to another office or department.

Consider the Welfare of Your Workers   If possible, do what is best for your workers. This does not mean you should do whatever the employees ask, but you should be concerned about whether or not they are being treated fairly. Do whatever you can to help them in their work without sacrificing the amount or quality of work done. If necessary, be willing to go to your boss and request changes that will benefit your workers.

Set a Good Example   Always try to set a good example for your workers. One supervisor was a bright young man who always came to work 20 or 30 minutes late. He dressed well and had a good appearance, but his work was sloppy. He seemed to have his mind on other things. This set a bad example that was followed by some of his workers. They began showing up late for work and the quality of their work dropped off. Finally, the young supervisor was replaced.

The new supervisor was always on time and the quality of his work was top-notch. Soon the employees' work improved. One worker who had regularly come to work 15 minutes late—just in time to beat the previous supervisor—started showing up 5 minutes early. The new supervisor hadn't said anything to this worker. He had simply set a good example.

SITUATION
SOLUTION

When a Supervisor Won't Let Go

You have been working at Palmer Graphics for 18 months and have been very productive, receiving three raises in that time. Two months ago a new supervisor was appointed in your section who doesn't seem able to delegate responsibility. He is doing half the section work, won't let anyone else work on the most important projects, and continually rechecks your work. You and others are beginning to be bored and resentful, and overall production in the section is off.

1. The section receives a memo from top management saying that production has to increase or there may be layoffs. Will you approach your supervisor about his inability to delegate or go directly to the top?

2. The supervisor's response is to take on even more of the work, leaving you with almost nothing to do. How can you show the management that you are still eager to produce?

3. The supervisor complains to the owner that you and others are the ones not producing as much as previously. He has the figures that prove this is so. What do you tell the owner?

Delegating some responsibilities is often the only way a busy manager can get his or her job done well or efficiently. It's also good for employee morale. Explain why.

Delegate Responsibility Some supervisors try to do too much. You may know people who take work home every night. In some cases this is necessary. In many cases, though, the supervisors are simply not managing their time and employees efficiently. They are not **delegating,** or giving jobs and responsibilities to others. These supervisors probably have workers with light work schedules who are capable of doing more.

Why do some supervisors try to handle everything themselves? Some are just poor organizers. Others may feel that no one else is able to handle the job. Still others want to feel important. They don't delegate responsibility because they want everyone else to depend on them.

If you are a supervisor, don't try to do everything yourself. Organize your responsibilities and decide which ones you can delegate to your workers. Decide who can best handle each job. In some cases you may even want to take the time to teach some workers how to do new tasks.

When you delegate responsibility, distribute the work fairly, according to each person's strengths and potential. Don't give away all of your work and

responsibility, however. This would cause you to lose the respect of your workers—and perhaps your job.

Once you have turned over some responsibilities, you will be better able to handle those that remain. In addition, your workers will appreciate the opportunity to show that they can be counted on to handle important work. You, your workers, and the company will all benefit from your ability to delegate.

✓ CHECKING UP

1. Of the nearly dozen factors that employers consider in making promotions, which do you feel are the most important and why?

2. What does it mean to "dress for success"?

3. What is delegating, and why is it important to a supervisor?

3 *Changing Companies*

Suppose there are no opportunities for promotion in your present company, or suppose a new company offers you a job that you feel is a step up. In either case, you may decide to change companies in order to advance toward your career goal.

Before you decide to leave your present company, though, consider how the change might affect you. Would the new job really increase your chances for promotion? Does the new company usually give the more responsible jobs to its employees, or does it hire outsiders to fill the best jobs? How well do you think you would fit in with the new group of co-workers? Answer these questions before making your decision. You will also want to be sure that the new job is related to your ultimate career goal. Don't leave your present company unless it is.

Sometimes taking a new job with another company is the best thing to do. Sometimes it's not. It's always best to have the new job before you quit the old one, however. People who quit their jobs to look for something better seldom find it. To make

Sometimes changing companies is the best thing you can do to advance toward your career goal. Before you leave your present company, however, what things should you consider before making your decision?

matters worse, they are without a paycheck all the time they are looking.

If you decide to quit your present job, you should observe certain courtesies in the way you do it. Unless company policy states otherwise, notify your immediate supervisor of your intent to leave the company. In large companies it is often necessary to notify the personnel office, too. You may be asked to put your notice in writing. If this is the policy, follow it.

Don't wait until your last day on the job to tell your employer you are quitting. Give your notice far enough in advance so that your employer can find a replacement before you leave. Courtesy requires that you give your notice at least two weeks in advance. If you are paid once a month, it is customary to give at least a month's notice.

When you apply for new jobs, your next potential employers may get in touch with your former employer. If you failed to give proper notice, you may get a bad recommendation. This could cost you the job you want.

✓ CHECKING UP

1. Suggest two reasons why someone satisfied with his or her present job might still decide to go to work for another company.
2. Why is it not a good idea to quit a job in order to look for another one?
3. What courtesies should you observe in leaving a job?

Review Your Learning

CHAPTER SUMMARY

As you progress in your career, you will want—and expect—some raises. Whether or not you receive them will depend primarily on your performance on the job. Company policy and the job you have will also play a role, however.

To earn more money and move closer to your ultimate career goal, you will probably need to be promoted. Many factors, such as seniority, initiative, education, and appearance determine who gets promoted. Before you accept a promotion, you should consider both the advantages and disadvantages. A promotion usually means more money and prestige, but it also means more responsibility and longer hours. If you do accept a promotion and become a supervisor, you can increase your effectiveness by doing such things as giving clear directions, treating workers fairly, and setting a good example.

Advancing toward your career goal may require changing companies. A decision to change companies should be made very carefully. Never leave your present job until you have a new one.

TERMS TO KNOW

On a separate sheet of paper, write a paragraph using all of the following terms:

merit raises
promotion
seniority
perseverance
supervisor
delegate

STUDY QUESTIONS

1. What are three factors in determining whether or not workers receive raises?

2. How can an employer evaluation help you get a raise?

3. When is the best time to find out about opportunities for a promotion?

4. What are 11 factors that employers consider in deciding who will be promoted?

5. Name at least two ways you can get education and training while working full time.

6. What can your appearance tell your employer about you?

7. What are four advantages of being a supervisor?

8. What are three disadvantages to being a supervisor?

9. List eight things a person can do to become a more effective supervisor.

10. Why is it important to be courteous when quitting a job?

CRITICAL THINKING

1. If you were a supervisor in a factory that made electronic circuit boards, would you be more interested in the quality or the quantity of work performed by the people you supervised? Why?

2. Think of someone you know who has a great deal of initiative. What are some specific actions that show a person has this quality?

3. If you were counting on going to a baseball game and the friends you were going with decided that a movie would be more fun instead, how would you respond? What does this say about your ability to adapt easily to change?

4. What do you consider to be the most important traits of a supervisor? Explain the reasoning behind your choices.

5. Based on the cartoon below, rate the employee's potential for promotion and explain your

evaluation. Then suggest the best way for the supervisor to respond.

CLEANING UP ISN'T MY JOB!

DISCUSSION STARTERS

1. Are the qualities that are important for success in the working world the same as those you need to do well in school?
2. What do you think the term *dead-end job* means? What circumstances might result in a person's ending up in this kind of job?

BUILDING BASIC SKILLS

Math

1. Your manager offers you a promotion that includes a salary increase of $50 per week. It also means taking home some work, however—about an hour's worth every day, five days a week.

- If your present salary is $520 per week for a 40-hour week, how much are you making per hour now?
- How much will you make if you accept the promotion?

Human Relations

2. The supervisor at Freddie's Burger Shoppe, Freddie's son Doug, spends a great deal of time talking to one of the cashiers, your friend Molly. While this is going on, the other cashier is doing most of the work and customers are becoming impatient at having to wait. Molly has confessed to you that she feels very uncomfortable about the situation. What would you advise her to do?

Problem Solving

3. Eddie, a bagger at the local supermarket, is a guy who just can't say no. Every time the manager asks him to work overtime, he agrees, even though his schoolwork is suffering. Eddie says he wants a career in the grocery business. You know, however, that if he wants to get into a management training program he'll need good grades. What advice would you give him?

SUGGESTED ACTIVITY

Read John Molloy's book, *The New Dress for Success*, and write a three- or four-page report on it. Include the following:

- Examples from your own experience that support or refute the author's ideas
- Your opinion as to whether the book's recommendations put any group or gender at a disadvantage

Your Personal Effectiveness

OBJECTIVES
After studying this chapter and doing the activities, you will be able to:

- list the qualities that personally effective people have;
- take the steps you must to improve yourself;
- increase your understanding of other people by watching and analyzing their body language; and
- identify and practice the skills that will help you influence people.

TERMS TO KNOW
personal effectiveness
tact
body language
empathize
assertive

*Y*ou can divide all the people in the world into two groups. One group consists of people who *let* things happen. The other group is made up of people who *make* things happen. Which group do you think you are in?

You read earlier that people who plan and choose their careers are the happiest and most satisfied. These people are the ones who make things happen their way. The ability to do this is called **personal effectiveness.** Personally effective people progress quickly toward their career goals.

Personal effectiveness includes the ability to influence people. To be personally effective, you must be good at getting other people to see things your way. Improving your own personal traits and learning some persuasive techniques are two ways you can increase your effectiveness with others. This chapter gives you several suggestions for doing both.

1 *Improving Yourself*

You are not as effective in human relationships as you could be—no one is. We all have room for improvement. Most people don't make the effort to become more personally effective, but it can be done. If you want to, you can learn to make things happen in your life.

Important Personal Traits

Many different traits go together to make up your personality. Which traits you have and the amount of each determine what your personality is like. You need to be aware of your traits before you can begin any efforts at self-improvement.

Below are brief descriptions of some common personal traits and qualities. You read about several of these in Chapters 6 and 7 because these traits are important to success in the world of work. The qualities described here are important in all human relationships—on the job and off.

- *Motivation—the desire to achieve and succeed.* This is often the most important factor in success. To be successful, you must want to be successful.

- *Attitude—your basic outlook on life.* Your attitude can be generally positive or generally negative. You want it to be positive.

- *Self-control—being able to control your emotions.* You cannot be personally effective without controlling negative feelings, such as anger. Learn to express these feelings in ways that do not hurt others.

- *Loyalty—supporting family, friends, and employers in all situations, especially difficult ones.* Loyalty will make you someone to be trusted. In addition, if you are loyal to others, they will be loyal to you.

- *Sense of humor—the quality that enables you to see the funny side of things.* Having a sense of humor contributes to both your physical and mental well-being. It also tends to make people like you.

- *Common sense—the ability to recognize and do what is reasonable.* Common sense also means using good judgment and learning from experience.

- *Foresight—the ability to look ahead.* People with foresight make plans. They are always prepared.

- *Dependability—the quality that makes you someone who can be counted on.* Dependable people get the job done on time, every time.

- *Honesty—the determination not to lie, steal, or cheat.* In the end you will be happier and more successful taking the honest route rather than the dishonest one.

- *Initiative—doing what needs to be done without being told.* Don't wait for someone else to do it; do it yourself—now.

- *Open-mindedness—trying to see both sides of a question or argument.* Open-minded people are usually intelligent and happy because they keep their minds open to new, fresh ideas.

- *Tact—saying and doing things in a way that will not offend others.* Successful people know how to use **tact.** They know how to point out mistakes and problems without making people angry or unhappy.

- *Enthusiasm—happiness, excitement, and energy.* Good things seem to happen to enthusiastic people. Everyone enjoys being around them.

- *Courtesy—good manners and a true concern for other people.* Courtesy will do more than anything else to make others like you. Nothing so valuable costs so little.

- *Good health—being physically fit and mentally sound.* Take care of yourself. Poor health makes everything just that much more difficult, if not impossible.

- *Friendliness—openly displaying good feelings toward others.* People will be friendly to you if you are friendly to them.

- *Punctuality—being on time.* Your employer and your friends will not be able to depend on you if you get into the habit of being late.

- *Neatness—being clean and well groomed.* Most people are bothered by dirtiness and sloppiness. A neat, clean appearance is essential to success.

- *Voice tone and quality—the way you sound when you speak.* The tone and quality of your voice often affects people just as much as what you say. Chapter 10 has more on how to make good use of your voice.

You have just read a brief description of 19 personal qualities important to success. How well do you rate in each? To find out, make yourself a chart. Fold a sheet of paper in half lengthwise. On the left side of the paper list the 19 traits. Divide the right side into three columns marked Good, Fair, and Poor. For each listed trait place a check mark in one of the three rating columns. Try to be honest with yourself. When your evaluation chart is complete, pay special attention to any items having check marks in the Poor column. These are the areas in which you will most likely want to improve. In the next section you'll learn how.

Four Steps to Self-improvement

Your personal traits have been developing since you were born. They have become habits, and they can be difficult to change. However, it will be easier to change these habits this year than next year—or five years from now.

It will also be easier to change if you have a good reason for making the effort—a reason that is important to you. If you do not have such a reason, you will probably go on being your same old self, bad habits and all.

Successful self-improvement is not a hit-or-miss proposition. It follows a series of clearly defined steps.

Work on One Trait at a Time   Start with the trait you feel is most in need of improvement. Concentrate on this one to the exclusion of all others. If you try to work on several traits at once, you will probably not be able to follow through on any of them. The task will seem overwhelming.

Make a Plan   Not only make a plan, but stick to it—no excuses! You might, for example, concentrate on developing the opposite habit from the one you want to break. Suppose you never have any enthusiasm. To correct this bad habit you might make a special point of noticing things that get you excited. You could concentrate on expressing your feelings about the things you like. Every day you would go out of your way to find some things and express your enthusiasm for them. You would gradually find yourself getting enthusiastic about more things—and with less effort.

Check Your Progress   At first you will need to check your progress often—possibly every day. After you have followed your plan for several weeks, you may find that you have indeed made progress. Keep checking yourself for weeks, even months, however. This will prevent you from slipping back into your old habits.

If you feel your friends will be honest, ask them if they think you are progressing. Knowing that others are checking on us from time to time helps us change our habits. This is one of the main reasons why many people who go to clubs such as Weight Watchers can lose weight and stay slim. The people in the club keep tabs on each other.

Move On   Once you feel you have made real progress on one trait, begin working on another. At this point you will probably be feeling good about yourself. You will have confidence in your ability to improve. You will feel that you can change lifelong habits.

Other people will also probably notice your progress. They will encourage you to keep up the good work. This will provide a further incentive for you to tackle another trait.

MAKE A DECISION

You know of several ways in which you can improve yourself. You realize that the best strategy for self-improvement is to concentrate on improving one bad habit or weakness at a time. The only thing that's preventing you from getting started is deciding which weakness or habit you should work on first. What's your decision—which personality trait will you concentrate on first? Give the reasons for your choice.

✓ CHECKING UP

1. How does a personally effective individual behave?
2. How does courtesy differ from tact? punctuality from dependability?
3. List the four steps to self-improvement?

2 *Influencing Others*

There are times when being personally effective means convincing other people to see things your way. This is more important in some careers than others. Managers and salespeople, for example, must be skilled at influencing others.

How good are you at getting others to see things your way? Would you like to improve your persuasive skills? In this section you will read about several things you can do to get your point across effectively.

Understanding Others

If you want someone to accept your way of thinking, you need to understand that person. You need to know what he or she thinks and feels. The more you know about the person, the better able you will be to pick the approach that will work most effectively.

Since everyone is different, the right approach with one person may be the wrong approach with another. What makes one person like you may make another person dislike you. When you're trying to persuade someone, you want to say and do the things that appeal to that person.

Of course, you can't make an in-depth study of every person you deal with. How then do you find out whether or not you are communicating with that person in the most effective way? There are several things you can do.

When you have the chance, get to know the person better. Consider his or her personality traits. Knowing more about these can help you understand other people as well as yourself.

You can also notice a person's interests. What does that person do during his or her leisure time? These interests often provide clues to a person's values. Knowing someone's values can be a big help in finding the best way to persuade that person.

Another way to learn more about people is to observe their body language. **Body language** refers to the things people say through their physical actions. For example, picture in your mind someone with stooped shoulders, walking head down and eyes to the ground. What is this person saying with body language? He or she may be showing sadness or lack of confidence. On the other hand, a person who walks with shoulders back, head up, and arms swinging conveys a carefree, happy image.

Facial expressions are often the best indications of a person's emotions and feelings. Eyes especially tell a great deal about a person. If you are close enough to see a person's eyes clearly, you can learn a great deal. You can tell whether the person has a positive or negative feeling about what you are saying. If the pupils enlarge, the feeling is positive. If they become smaller, the feeling is negative. These changes occur quickly, though, so you have to watch closely. This is usually not a problem since looking the other person in the eye shows attentiveness.

Tightly closed lips usually mean disapproval. When people fidget (or move restlessly) in their chairs, you can tell that they are bored with what you are saying.

There are many other ways people show their feelings through body language. In fact, several books have been written on the subject. You might want to consult one of these for additional pointers.

Showing Interest

In 1936 Dale Carnegie wrote a book called *How to Win Friends and Influence People*. This book has now sold more than 10 million copies. It has been so popular because it explains Carnegie's techniques for getting people to react in a certain way.

In his book Carnegie says, "You can win more friends in two months by becoming interested in other people than you can in two years by trying to get other people interested in you." His point is that the most effective way to influence people is to be interested in them. The interest must, however, be genuine. Most people can spot a phony a mile away.

Smiling

An old song includes the words "When you're smilin', the whole world smiles with you." The writer of that song must have known something about human relationships. Other people react to you more favorably when you smile than when you don't.

The expression on your face says more about you than the clothes you wear or the company you keep. When you smile at a person, it's like saying, "I like you." Your smile attracts others to you, and smooths the way if you are trying to influence others to do something.

Whether you realize it or not, you use body language to negotiate your way through numerous situations daily. Consider these three people. If the restaurant were crowded and you had to share a table, with whom would you choose to sit and why?

Making Others Feel Important

In Chapter 1 you learned about Maslow's theory of basic human needs. You may remember that one need is the need for esteem. Some people meet all of their lower-level needs but do not have enough self-esteem. These people don't feel good about themselves—they don't feel important.

Everyone wants to feel important. You can win people over to your side by making them feel this way. Think about your own feelings. When someone says something that makes you feel important, you probably have a good feeling toward that person.

One simple way to make a person feel important is to know and use the correct pronunciation of his or her name. Remembering the name shows that you care about the person. Pronouncing the name correctly shows how much you respect him or her. Take advantage of this knowledge. Use the other person's name in your conversations.

Another way to make people feel important is to give them your sincere, undivided attention. Ask them questions to show that you are interested in their ideas. Be a good listener, and concentrate on everything they say. When you think someone has made an especially intelligent remark, tell that person so.

Empathizing

Influencing other people does not mean that you must be a fast, convincing talker. In fact, you can earn someone's trust and respect much faster by listening rather than talking.

A good listener gets along well with most people, especially if the listener empathizes with the speaker. To **empathize** means to see someone else's point of view, to sympathize with their situation. You can't really be a good listener unless you are empathetic.

Henry Ford, the founder of Ford Motor Company, was asked the secret of his success. He said, "If there is any one secret to success, it lies in the ability to get the other person's point of view and see things from his angle as well as your own."

Giving Away Credit

Sometimes you should give up some of the things that make you feel important. In certain cases, for example, it is a good idea to let others take credit for your ideas. Doing this will help you achieve your human relationship goals.

Let's say you have an idea for a better way to do something at work. If you try to push the new procedure on your own, you may be successful— or you may not be. If you enlist the aid of your supervisor or a more experienced employee, however, success is more likely to follow.

Remember, your supervisor is another human being. He or she needs attention and needs to feel important. If your supervisor has high self-esteem, he or she may help you with your idea; but what should you do if your supervisor is insecure? Then you should give away your idea—or at least the credit for it. Let your supervisor "discover" your plan.

You could work for months, even years, trying to convince people of the value of your own idea. If you give the credit to someone else, though, your goal may be achieved very quickly. You will probably gain a friend by making the other person feel important.

Of course, there is a limit to the kinds of ideas you should give away. If you come up with a new invention that might make you rich, don't give that idea away!

It is often said that you cannot really know someone until "you've walked a mile in his shoes." What techniques for influencing people might fit this description?

Strive for Success

Ride Makes History with Trek

"Space, the final frontier. . . . The mission—to boldly go where no *woman* has gone before."

An episode of "Star Trek," right? Wrong—it's something more exciting, more challenging—and more heartbreaking. It's a real-life adventure, the real life of Sally Ride.

The first American woman in space, Ride has experienced both the best and the worst of our quest for the stars. From the triumph of her first trip into space in the space shuttle *Challenger* to the investigation of that vessel's tragic loss two years later, Ride was an important part of the space shuttle program and a model of achievement for the country.

Born in Los Angeles in 1951, Ride quickly earned notice as both a scholar and an athlete. One year after she graduated from high school with honors, she was ranked in the top 20 for all 18-year-old tennis players in the country. Following high school, she attended Stanford University where she earned degrees in both English and astrophysics. She continued her work in astrophysics, receiving her Ph.D. from Stanford in 1978. That same year she entered the NASA training program for astronauts.

The program was academically challenging as well as physically grueling. It lasted a full year and included classroom work, flight training, survival training, and mission training. Ride successfully completed the program and, at the age of 32, became the youngest astronaut to circle the earth in a spacecraft.

On her six-day mission in June 1984, Ride and four other astronauts traveled 2.5 million miles. They launched communications satellites for the Canadian and Indonesian governments, conducted experiments involving the production of pharmaceuticals in space, and completed important tests of the shuttle's remote manipulator arm.

Less than two years later, Ride watched as *Challenger* lifted off again. This time, however, the mission ended in tragedy when the shuttle

exploded. Ride was appointed to the presidential commission that investigated the accident. With other commission members, she worked not only to find out what went wrong with *Challenger* but also to ensure that such a thing would never happen again. In 1987, Ride resigned from the astronaut program to accept a fellowship at Stanford.

Avoiding Arguments

Have you ever tried to convince someone to see things your way? Did you end up in an argument? If so, you probably didn't really convince the other person of anything. Even when you win arguments, they often cause other people to have bad feelings about you. You may have trouble dealing with these people for a long time thereafter.

Have you ever known people who like to argue? You may have noticed that nobody really wins. The more people argue, the more difficult it will be for them to work well with others. The only way to "win" an argument is to avoid it.

Letting People Save Face

When people are wrong about something and know it, they have a temporary loss of self-esteem. After a while, they may admit their error and even take pride in doing so. This won't happen, though, if someone else tries to force them to admit the mistake.

To refer to the error—to say, "You were wrong" or "I told you so"—makes people uncomfortable. When you do this, you back people into a corner. You can guess how these people will feel about you after you point out their mistake.

It never pays to tell others about their mistakes (unless, of course, you are their supervisor). Let them save face. Ignore the situation and talk about something else. You will keep an old friend—or possibly win a new one.

Case Study 1

Jane Chen sells recording equipment for a large company. She is a very successful salesperson who never gets trapped into an argument.

One day she walked into an insurance firm in Los Angeles. She hoped to sell several different pieces of recording equipment. As she walked into the office of the vice-president to make her sales presentation, she was greeted with, "Oh yes, I should have canceled our appointment. I've decided to buy the equipment from the Brand-X Company."

Of course, the vice-president was expecting an argument—or at least some negative comment about the other firm's equipment. However, Jane simply said, "Brand X is an excellent product. I'm sure you'll be happy with it." The vice-president didn't know what to say. He was expecting an argument, and instead Jane complimented him and the competitor's product.

Jane smiled often. She showed a sincere interest in the insurance firm. She complimented the vice-president on the leadership of the company executives. After 20 minutes the vice-president asked for a demonstration of her equipment. The sale was made the same day.

Even when you win a workplace argument, you lose. Why?

SITUATION
SOLUTION

Dealing with Rumors

Some of your co-workers have been giving you the cold shoulder lately. They've avoided asking you to lunch and haven't acknowledged your hellos. You can't imagine what the problem might be. Then you overhear someone who works in your department identifying you as the person who complained and got smoking banned from the office. You did indeed complain. You're asthmatic, and your health has suffered as a result of the smoke-filled work environment. However, you asked only for a location shift for yourself and some additional air filtration devices.

1. What, if anything, would you say to the person you overheard spreading the rumor?

2. Your complaint was made in a private conversation with the office manager, a conversation that apparently did not remain private. Would you mention this to the office manager? to the co-workers you overheard? Why or why not? If you were to discuss the matter, what would you say?

3. How might you influence those who are cold-shouldering you to see things your way?

Admitting Your Mistakes

Never mention mistakes other people make, but always admit your own. In the long run, you gain nothing by making excuses when you are wrong. On the other hand, there is something noble about quickly admitting your errors.

When you admit your mistakes, no one else has a chance to prove you wrong. In fact, other people are usually very understanding. They may even gain respect for you. This, in turn, makes it easier for you to influence them.

Giving Sincere Praise

Do you want to influence others? Do you want to change their behavior? If so, never begin with criticism. Criticism puts most people on the defensive.

Instead of criticizing, begin by looking for the things you sincerely feel are worthy of praise. Tell people what you like about them. Compliment them when they do or say something deserving of a compliment. Most people will respond to your praise by trying to do all they can to please you.

Being Positive

Have you ever known someone who complained constantly or who had nothing good to say about anyone or anything? Some people are constant complainers. They can talk for hours about nothing but the bad things. These people have a negative attitude toward life.

People with a negative outlook are not very convincing. Happy people are much more persuasive. If you want to influence someone, be optimistic. Look on the bright side. Emphasize the positive.

A little praise goes a long way. In the workplace, what does this mean?

Let's listen to three different salespeople. Try to decide which one will make the sale.

- Salesperson 1—"You don't want to buy this broom, do you?"
- Salesperson 2—"I'd like to interest you in the unusual features of this broom."
- Salesperson 3—"I have two unusual brooms here. Broom A is designed for heavy-duty work. Broom B is for sweeping up small particles such as sugar and sand. Which broom would best meet your needs?"

Did you notice that the first salesperson makes it easy for the customer to say no? The second salesperson invites the customer to listen, and the answer could be yes or no. The third salesperson doesn't ask for a yes or no but rather for a choice between Broom A and Broom B. The third salesperson assumes that the customer's answer will be yes to one of the brooms. That salesperson emphasized the positive.

You've probably heard the old question about whether the glass is half full or half empty. You can often say what you think in either positive or negative terms. You will be much more effective with others if you choose the positive way.

Catching the Mood

Another important factor in influencing others is catching people in the right mood. People are much more agreeable if they are in a good mood.

How can you tell if someone is in a good mood? Sometimes you can tell by an answer to a greeting. Listen to the person's voice. Say, "Good morning. How are you?" The reply will likely be something like, "Fine, thank you." If the "Fine, thank you" is said with a rising pitch, that person is probably in a good mood. If it is said with a falling pitch, the person is probably not in a good mood. In the latter case, it might be wise to wait to discuss an important issue.

Do more than just listen to what someone says. Listen to how they say it. Listen for enthusiasm, anxiety, hesitation—any clues to how the person feels.

Executives and the most successful salespeople know that the best time to talk anybody into anything is during a meal. We are all more open to influence from others while eating something we like, but this period lasts only a short time. It starts with the first bite and ends shortly after the meal has been eaten.

Talking business over a meal is an extremely common practice. Why do you think people are more easily influenced in this situation?

Case Study *2*

Marty is a computer programmer for a large school district. She writes programs that tell the computer what it must do to print hundreds of different kinds of reports. After each program is written in a special computer language, Marty prints a practice report and checks it for errors. This is called debugging.

On Friday afternoon Marty was discussing the need for a new kind of report with the business manager and assistant superintendent. Her supervisor, Mrs. Caroll, broke into the meeting and began scolding. "Marty, I just ran the new attendance report, and it's full of errors! Now I'll have to come in this weekend and do it myself!"

Marty resisted the urge to give Mrs. Caroll an argument right then and there. Instead, she waited until the business manager and assistant superintendent had left and then took a few minutes to collect her thoughts. She briefly considered saying nothing about the incident but then realized if she didn't it would bother her for weeks. Besides, she felt that Mrs. Caroll was wrong in the way she had handled the matter.

Marty requested a meeting with Mrs. Caroll. Once inside the supervisor's office with the door closed, she explained her view of the situation. "Mrs. Caroll, I'm sure there were errors in the attendance report. I only completed that program this morning and haven't had a chance to debug it. I'll make the corrections this afternoon, but I want you to know that your remarks in front of the business manager and assistant superintendent embarrassed me. Also, I'm afraid they'll think this department isn't very efficient. If you have criticisms of my work in the future, I hope you'll be kind enough to tell me in private."

Being Assertive

People respect other people who are assertive without being too assertive. Being **assertive** means standing up for your rights, beliefs, and ideas. To be personally effective, you must be assertive without being aggressive, or pushy.

Do you relate to others in a confident manner? To be assertive you must show confidence. One way to do this is to speak with authority. This does not mean you should talk like a know-it-all. It just means that you should know what you are talking about. Then you will feel comfortable in your discussions with others.

It isn't easy to be assertive without being aggressive. It is especially difficult for beginning workers who have had little experience in human relationships on the job. You can improve your self-confidence and become more assertive by spending some time visiting with co-workers. Let them get to know you. Talk about your likes and dislikes. Talk about your hobbies. Also, show your interest in their likes and dislikes. As you get to know your co-workers better, you will feel more comfortable asserting yourself.

If you follow the suggestions in this chapter for influencing others, people will probably like you. If you do your job well, people will respect you. This will give you the confidence you need to speak up and assert yourself when necessary.

✓ CHECKING UP

1. During a presentation on retirement benefits, you observe your co-workers. What is the body language of each of these people saying?
   - Rochelle spends most of the presentation picking or biting her cuticles.
   - Albert sighs often, periodically glances at his watch, and occasionally fixes the speaker with a hard gaze—after which he goes back to skimming the computer printout on his lap.
   - Vivian nods her agreement with a point and makes a notation on her pad.

2. One way to influence people is to make them feel important. How would you rate Rochelle, Albert, and Vivian in terms of their use of this technique?

3. How can giving sincere praise influence someone to see things your way?

Review Your Learning

CHAPTER SUMMARY

You have a choice. You can be a person who lets things happen or one who makes things happen. When you make things happen you are being personally effective. You are making decisions and planning to ensure a happy, satisfying career.

An important part of being personally effective is getting rid of bad habits and improving good ones. It's not easy, but if you want to you can improve yourself. By working on one habit at a time, planning your improvement, and doing honest self-checks, you can eliminate negative traits. You can also improve yourself in areas such as motivation, friendliness, courtesy, and neatness.

Being personally effective also means influencing people. The most successful people in the world of work have learned to make other people see things their way. They've learned the importance of understanding and observing people so that they can tailor their approach to the person. They've also mastered tactics like making others feel important, being positive, empathizing, and giving away credit. By using these tactics, you too can win friends and influence people.

TERMS TO KNOW

On a separate sheet of paper, write a brief description of a situation that illustrates each of the following terms:

personal effectiveness
tact
body language
empathize
assertive

STUDY QUESTIONS

1. List at least a dozen personal traits you should examine to determine if they represent areas in which you need to improve.

2. Which personality trait, more than any other, will make people like you?

3. Which trait is often the first and most important in achieving success?

4. What quality are successful people using when they point out errors without angering those who made them?

5. Why is it important in carrying out a self-improvement plan to concentrate on one bad habit at a time?

6. What is the most important thing for you to do when trying to influence people?

7. Which method of influencing people did Henry Ford believe to be the most important for success?

8. What is the only situation in which it is to your advantage to point out someone's mistakes?

9. List at least six things you can do to be more effective at influencing people.

10. What is the difference between being assertive and arguing?

CRITICAL THINKING

1. Tad and Tasha have been dating for several months, but now Tasha says she wants to break it off. She says Tad is always late for dates and seems bored to be with her. Tad says he wants to change. Which traits would you advise him to work on? What do you think will determine his success?

2. Gracie knows she isn't very open-minded, and she'd like to change. What kinds of actions can she take to help her see both sides of an issue?

3. Think of a time in your life when someone made you feel important. How did that person do it?

DISCUSSION STARTERS

1. Of the personal traits listed on page 134, which do you think are most important in a friendship? on the job? in school? Explain the reasons for your choices.

2. In this chapter you read about more than a dozen ways to influence, or persuade, people. Think about a situation in which someone used one or more of these methods (or a situation in which someone used just the opposite methods). Explain the behavior of those involved (omitting names, of course). Were the techniques employed effective? Why or why not?

BUILDING BASIC SKILLS

Math

1. You have taken a job at Liscinsky's Market. Mr. Liscinsky says he wants you to work 30 percent of your time stocking shelves, 25 percent cleaning the aisles, and 45 percent bagging. If you work 25 hours a week, how much time will you spend at each task?

2. Because you work at Scanlon's Department Store, you get a 20-percent discount on all merchandise you buy there. You plan to purchase a $35 sports shirt and some shoes priced at $46. What will you pay for them under the following circumstances?

   • You buy the items today, claiming the standard employee discount.

   • You wait one week so that you can take advantage of Scanlon's Scandal, an annual one-day sale during which all merchandise is one-third off.

Human Relations

3. Your friend Rosalie never seems to listen when you talk to her. She just waits for you to finish so that she can go on talking about herself. It's annoying, but you like Rosalie and don't want to give up her friendship. What improvements would you suggest in Rosalie's behavior, and how exactly would you suggest them?

Leadership

4. You are in charge of fund raising for the cyclists' club at school. The club is selling candy bars so it can send a team to the state competition, but you seem to be the only one doing any selling. How can you motivate the others to work harder?

SUGGESTED ACTIVITIES

1. Choose a group of people and a time to observe them—for example, students in your school during class, teachers in the corridors between classes, patrons shopping at a local supermarket. Analyze the body language of at least six subjects (identify them by number and gender only). Consider such things as posture, gestures, and facial expressions. Write a short paragraph for each subject, summarizing your observations and conclusions.

2. Think of something reasonable that you would like a friend or family member to do. Then try to influence that person to do as you wish. Use as many of the techniques for influencing others as seem appropriate. Don't rush the person. After a while, consider whether these approaches work better than your usual way of trying to influence others. Compare your experiences with those of your classmates.

Your Personal Health and Safety

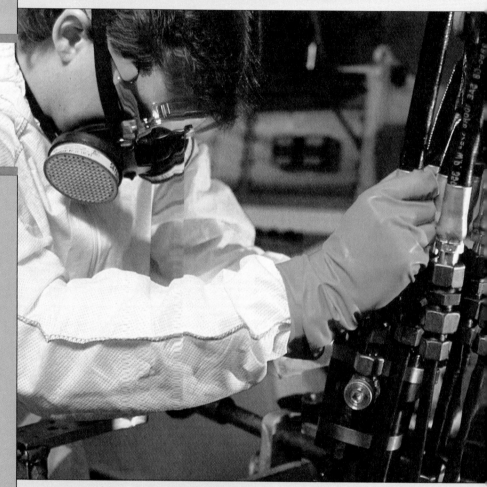

*I*n the last few chapters, we've considered how to be successful on the job. We've talked about what you'll have to do to get along with your co-workers, meet your employer's expectations, and get a raise or a promotion. What we've assumed, however, is that you will have the physical and mental energy to do these things. We've assumed that you'll have good health.

Good health is a result of a combination of factors—heredity, environment, and personal choice. In this chapter we'll concentrate on the last two. We'll provide some personal health guidelines. We'll also explore the costs, causes, and prevention of one of the most serious health risks in our society—the risk of accidents, both on and off the job.

1 What It Takes to Be Healthy

Being healthy means more than not being sick. It means having energy and a sense of well-being. It means feeling good about yourself and taking pleasure in the company of others. Truly good health, in other words, involves both mind and body.

Without good health, life is much less pleasant—and work may be impossible. Therefore, if you care about your future, you will do all you can to maintain and improve your health. In this lesson you'll be given some guidelines that will help.

A Balanced Diet

You are what you eat—it's a cliché, but it's true. A good diet, one containing a balance of foods and the nutrients in them, is necessary for good health. You can achieve this "balance" by including foods from the four basic food groups (Figure 9-1) in each of your meals. For teens it is recommended

A Balanced Diet

Basic Food Groups	Recommended Daily Servings	Serving Size
Fruits and Vegetables	4 or more	1 small whole fruit 1/2 grapefruit/banana 1/2 cup sliced fruit 3/4 cup fruit juice 1/2 cup cooked vegetable 3/4 cup vegetable juice
Breads and Cereals	4 or more	1 slice bread 1 small roll 1/2 cup cooked cereal/rice/pasta 1 cup ready-to-eat cereal
Milk and Dairy Products	4 (teens) 3 (children) 2 (adults)	1 cup milk 1 cup plain low-fat yogurt 1 ounce hard cheese
Meat, Fish, and Poultry (Group also includes meat substitutes like dried beans or peas, eggs, and peanut butter.)	2	3 ounces cooked meat/poultry/fish 2 medium eggs 3/4 cup cooked dried beans/peas

Figure 9-1 Meals containing items from each of the four basic food groups are the basis of a healthy diet. Suggest a breakfast that meets this standard.

that a day's meals contain two servings from the meat, fish, and poultry group and four servings from each of the remaining groups.

How much food you need will depend on your age, sex, height, weight, and activity level. The last factor is particularly important. If you are very active—for example, if you walk a great deal on your job or do heavy, physical work—you will need to eat more. If you sit most of the day, you will need to eat less.

Why is this true? Almost any food contains calories. A **calorie** is a measure of the energy that food supplies. As the fat, starch, and sugar content of food rises, so does its calorie count. For example, a cup of green beans will contribute 30 calories to your diet; but three ounces of lean ground beef will add more than six times that amount (185 calories)—and a half cup of whipping cream will pile on 420 calories more! It should be obvious that a fat-laden meal like a hamburger, french fries, regular soda, and ice cream sundae could add more than 1,000 calories to your daily total.

What happens if you consume more food than your body needs to maintain itself and provide for your daily activities? You gain weight. The excess food energy is stored as fat. You can avoid this state of affairs by observing these guidelines:

- Eat a variety of foods to get the nutrients you need.
- Control the quantity of food you eat according to how active you are.
- Reduce the amount of fat (especially animal fat), salt, and sugar in your diet.
- Increase the amount of fruits and vegetables (and hence fiber) in your diet.
- Schedule meals at regular times, if possible.
- Eat at a leisurely pace.

If you do find yourself in the position of being overweight, avoid the temptation to go on a crash diet. Doctors and nutritionists warn that it is unsafe to consume fewer than 1,200 calories per day. To do so is to risk damage to vital organs like the heart. Rather, concentrate on reducing portions of the foods you do eat and increasing your level of physical activity.

Exercise

Becoming more physically active is not easy in today's world. Jobs are more **sedentary** (that is, they require a great deal of sitting). People rely on cars and public transportation (also sedentary) to make long, time-consuming, daily commutes. Once people are home, they find that the accumulated demands of family life leave little time for exercise.

Today, however, people are more aware than ever of the importance of physical fitness to their long-term health. They know that a good physical fitness program will help them to

- maintain weight by burning off excess calories,
- develop muscle tone and definition,
- increase strength and endurance,
- lower the risk of heart disease,
- improve body coordination,
- stimulate mental alertness, and
- reduce stress.

You can start an appropriate physical fitness program at any age. It's best, however, to start such a program when you're young and continue it throughout your life.

If you have any health problems, you might want to check with a doctor first to be sure the type and amount of exercise you want to do will not aggravate them. There are other considerations as well. The activity you choose should be one you will enjoy. If you like what you're doing, you'll be less tempted to slack off or abandon your program entirely. It should also be an activity that is suitable for the location in which you live. If you live in an area where it is extremely hot in the summer and/or extremely cold in the winter, you may want to consider only those activities that can be done indoors.

When it comes time to begin your exercise program, these guidelines will help:

- *Set goals for yourself, and draw up a plan to achieve them.* You can use many of the same techniques here that you used in drawing up a plan of action for achieving your career goal. Structure your plan around short-, medium-, and long-range goals that are specific and realistic.
- *Schedule your exercise.* Find a time for exercising, and make it part of your routine.
- *Begin slowly.* This applies to your overall program and to individual exercise sessions as well. If, for example, you want to run five miles three times a week, start with shorter distances. Before doing any strenuous physical activity, warm up by doing exercises to

Many people today, despite the sedentary nature of their jobs, are committed enough to physical fitness that they find time for it. What solution has one of the office workers shown here found? Can you name some others?

stretch the muscles you will be using. (*Note:* You should finish an exercise session exactly the same way you began it—slowly. You should cool down by gradually decreasing your level of activity rather than simply stopping all at once.)

• *Reward yourself for progress made.* This is part of the enjoyment that will keep you going and committed to your program.

Disease Awareness and Prevention

Not all the things you must do to maintain your health require as much effort as committing yourself to a physical fitness program. Sometimes simply being aware of the potential for a problem is

enough to avoid it. This is true of any number of conditions that pose serious health threats to people.

Physical Illness　In the United States, more people die from heart disease than any other ailment—976,000 in 1988 alone. Nearly 67 million Americans are considered potential victims of heart attack. Of them, one-fifth will be stricken before the age of 65.

If you have a family history of heart disease, you should practice prevention. Fortunately, the guidelines for avoiding heart disease are similar to those for maintaining general good health—eat a balanced diet (low in fat, salt, and sugar and high in fiber) and exercise regularly (three times a week for at least 20 minutes). These precautions will control your weight, keep your heart strong, and reduce the possibility that blockages will develop in your blood vessels. You should also avoid smoking, try to reduce stress in your life, and have your blood pressure checked regularly by a physician.

Cancer ranks second after heart disease as a cause of death in the United States. In 1989 a half million Americans died of cancer.

Most cancers develop over a long period of time. The exact causes of the disease are not known, but it is believed that diet, personal habits (smoking and drinking), heredity, and environmental factors (exposure to cancer-causing agents) play a role.

Clearly, some of these factors—like heredity—cannot be controlled; others can be. Even if you do not have a family history of cancer, you should avoid smoking—including the breathing in of secondhand smoke. You should limit the fat content of your diet. Finally, you should keep yourself informed about the potential for exposure to cancer-causing agents in your environment. These might include pesticides, building materials, food addi-

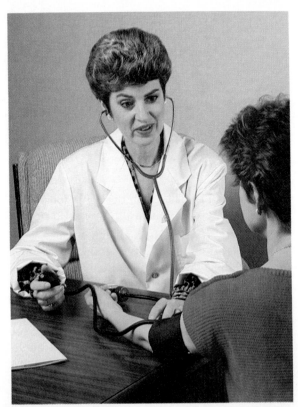

Even without a history of heart disease in your family, you should have your blood pressure checked regularly. Why?

tives, and water or air pollutants. If you feel that the threat from such exposure is substantial, you should try to remove the cancer-causing agent from your environment. This might mean tearing out insulation material, discarding an appliance, using fewer (or no) chemicals for gardening, or installing a water filtration system. If actions like these are not possible, then you might want to consider moving yourself away from the exposure.

Despite their status as the leading causes of death among adults in the United States, heart disease and cancer do not get the most attention in the media today. The headlines are reserved for two other problems—drug addiction and AIDS.

Abuse of drugs is not limited to illegal substances like cocaine and heroin. People can become addicted to certain prescription drugs, alcohol, and tobacco. This means that they crave the substance, that their bodies cannot do without it. When the substance is withheld, the victim of addiction suffers symptoms that can be as mild as nervousness or sleep loss or as severe as nausea, vomiting, trembling, and cramps.

People often get involved with addictive substances out of curiosity or out of a desire to be like their peers. Then, once they start, they can't stop. Their addiction often costs them more than money. It costs them their jobs, their families, their health, and sometimes even their lives. Recent research indicates that some people may be predisposed to addiction by heredity. Perhaps you're not among them, but it may be best not to take the chance. Avoid experimenting with addictive substances. Use prescription drugs only as directed and only for the condition and length of time specified.

Acquired immunodeficiency syndrome (AIDS) is a problem often discussed in the same breath with drug use and addiction. AIDS is principally a sexually transmitted disease, but certain practices of drug users (mainly sharing needles) put them at high risk of infection. Nonaddicts leading healthy life-styles are not likely to contract the disease. Only blood transfusions from infected individuals pose a risk to such people, and today blood is carefully screened to prevent the spread of AIDS.

Ironically, though, blood donations are down because many people fear that *giving* blood will somehow expose them to the disease. This has prompted some doctors and hospitals to recommend that patients contemplating elective surgery donate blood for themselves in advance. A better

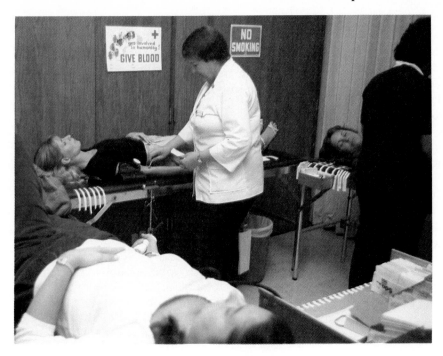

In the atmosphere of fear generated by the AIDS epidemic, blood donations in many communities have suffered. Why is this fear irrational?

idea might be for all people determined to maintain and improve their health to donate blood regularly as part of their life-style. The idea behind blood banks is that donors give when they can against the time when they themselves may be in need. In this sense, blood donation can be considered a form of planning for one's future health.

Mental Illness Mental ailments are often more difficult to identify and treat than physical ailments. This does not mean that they have less impact on health or that they should be ignored. Left untreated, severe forms of mental illness can not only disrupt lives but also take a toll on physical well-being.

Depression is one of the most common forms of mental illness. Its symptoms can range from mild and persistent feelings of sadness to intense, suicidal despair. It is estimated that 20 million Americans will be affected by depression at some time in their lives.

You should be able to recognize the warning signs of depression. They include the following:

- Persistent sadness, anxiety, or moodiness
- Feelings of hopelessness or lack of worth
- Sleep disturbances (oversleeping or lack of sleep)
- Loss of interest in friends or pleasures
- Unusual increase or decrease in appetite
- Difficulty in concentrating, remembering, or making decisions
- Neglect of appearance or routine responsibilities
- Physical symptoms, such as headache or pain
- Tiredness or lack of energy

Granted, many of these symptoms could have other causes. Should they occur together and persist over a long period of time for no obvious physical reason, however, you should consult a mental health professional.

✔ CHECKING UP

1. List three areas around which you could build a plan for maintaining good health, and briefly explain what you would do in each area.
2. What is the easiest way to ensure that your diet is balanced?
3. The use of illegal substances is called drug abuse—true or false? Explain.

2 *Accidents*

In 1988 an average of 11 accidental deaths occurred each hour in the United States. The total for the year was 97,500 fatalities. This number may appear small when compared with the 2,171,000 deaths reported for the year from all causes. However, accidental deaths were disproportionately concentrated in one age group—they were the leading cause of death among people under the age of 24.

It is estimated that in 1989 the financial cost of accidents was $148.5 billion. This figure includes lost wages, medical expenses, and insurance administration costs. It is a huge sum, but it represents only one part of the cost of accidents. The other part is the human cost.

An accident that results in long-term disability can cost you your job. This can take a heavy toll on other family members in terms of additional responsibility and stress. A permanently disabling accident can cost you even more. It can cost you the career for which you've planned for years. It can cost you your dreams and even some of the most basic pleasures of life. Consider these examples:

- The teenaged athlete who dived into a pool and hit bottom, fracturing his neck and paralyzing him for life
- The young mother blinded by an explosion in her gas oven, who will never see her husband or baby again
- The ten-year-old who lost all of his fingers when the firecracker he had lit went off in his hands

When human suffering is considered, the cost of accidents truly becomes impossible to calculate.

Case Study 1

Sam thought he was very lucky when he signed a six-month contract to sing at the Valley Theater. He was even happier when the audience liked his act. Many people said Sam was good enough to be a star.

Next to singing, Sam's favorite activity was motorcycle riding. The speed thrilled him. On one of his days off, Sam decided to ride to a city 60 miles away (he was a good rider and had no fear of traffic).

On the way home, it began to rain. Four blocks from his apartment, a car turned in front of Sam, and his bike skidded on the wet pavement. As a result of the accident, Sam was hospitalized for four weeks.

Sam's employer needed a singer, and the job couldn't wait for Sam to get better. Sam probably hasn't lost his singing voice, but it may be hard for him to get another steady singing job.

The cost of an on-the-job accident may only start with medical expenses and lost wages. What are some other possible costs?

Where Accidents Occur

You are never totally free from the possibility of being involved in an accident. An accident can happen anyplace and anytime.

At Home Accidents in the home result in more injuries than accidents that occur anywhere else. According to the National Safety Council, 22,500 deaths and 3.4 million disabling injuries occurred at home in 1989. Falls (on stairs, ladders, and roofs) accounted for the greatest number of deaths, followed by fires and accidental poisonings. The largest number of fatalities occurred in two groups—people 25 to 44 years old and those over 75.

In Motor Vehicles Can you imagine a city of nearly 47,000 people simply disappearing? In a sense that's what happens every year as a result of automobile accidents. Motor vehicles cause that many deaths.

Figure 9-2 shows that motor vehicles are the leading cause of accidental deaths in the United States. In 1989, automobiles were involved in almost half of accident fatalities. It is estimated that these accidents cost $72.2 billion.

Here are some additional facts about automobile accidents that may surprise you.

- Drivers between the ages of 15 and 24 have the highest accident rate of any age group.
- The accident rate for male drivers is twice that of female drivers.
- Improper driving is responsible for 64 percent of all accidents.
- The use of alcohol is a factor in at least half of all motor vehicle deaths.
- The most dangerous time to drive is between 12 midnight and 2 a.m. on Sunday morning.
- More motor vehicle deaths are reported in July and August than in any other months.
- Labor Day is one of the most dangerous days to be on the road.

On the Job Jobs in some industries are more dangerous than jobs in others. To protect your health and safety, you must know how dangerous your work really is.

On-the-job fatalities occur most often in mining and agriculture. The aircraft and communications industries have the lowest fatality rates. In recent years, the construction and transportation industries have had lower rates, but their figures are still high.

Accidental Deaths and Injuries (1989)				
Class of Accident	Deaths	Change from 1988	Deaths per 100,000 Persons	Disabling Injuries
All classes	94,500	–2%	38.1	9,000,000
Motor vehicle	46,900	–4%	18.9	1,700,000
Public nonwork	42,800			1,500,000
Work	3,900			200,000
Home	200			*
Work	10,400	–4%	4.2	1,700,000
Nonmotor vehicle	6,500			1,500,000
Motor vehicle	3,900			200,000
Home	22,500	0%	9.1	3,400,000
Nonmotor vehicle	22,300			3,400,000
Motor vehicle	200			*
Public	19,000	+3%	7.7	2,400,000

*Less than 10,000.
Source: National Safety Council

Figure 9-2 While auto accident deaths have declined over the last few years, they still account for the largest portion of accident fatalities. What is the exact percentage of total deaths that motor vehicles are responsible for? In what other areas have the number of accidental deaths declined?

Strive for Success

She's MADD at Drunk Drivers

The killer was everywhere, in every community in America, and the killer was very efficient. During the decade of the 1980s alone, the killer took an estimated 240,000 lives. Police seemed powerless even to slow the killer down. Then one woman in her grief decided to make a stand against the killer. Her efforts made a difference. The killer was drunk driving, and the woman who took on the challenge of doing something about it was Candy Lightner.

Lightner's fight against drunk driving began in 1980. She was spurred into action after a drunk driver struck and killed her 13-year-old daughter, Cari. The man who sped away from the scene of the accident had four prior arrests for driving while intoxicated but was still on the road.

This crisis might have crushed Lightner, a California real estate agent, but instead it led her to fight back. She didn't get even; she got MADD. Lightner founded Mothers Against Drunk Driving (MADD), an organization devoted to doing something about the fact that, as Lightner puts it, "death caused by drunk drivers is the only socially acceptable form of homicide."

MADD set out to lobby legislators to pass stricter laws and tougher penalties for dealing with the problem of drivers who drink. To achieve these goals, MADD would have to grow, and grow it did. Within just a few years, thousands of others who, like Lightner, had lost a family member or loved one to a drunk driver joined MADD. Soon there were chapters of the organization in almost every state in the union.

The organization has had many successes. It has helped raise the minimum drinking age to 21 in all states. In 15 states it has gotten required jail time for anyone proved guilty of a first drunk driving offense.

Although no longer a member of MADD, Lightner continues the fight through public speaking engagements and other efforts. She admits that, in a country where someone dies every 27 minutes in a car accident involving alcohol, there's still much to be done. However, she points out, "If not for MADD, there would be a lot more tombstones today."

Why do some companies have more accidents than others? Obviously, some are involved in more dangerous work than others. Some use less safe equipment. Others provide little or no training, including safety education.

We don't always realize the importance of health and safety in our lives. We usually feel that nothing will ever happen to us, that it will happen to someone else. However, accidents can and do happen to everyone. We must all think of the value of our health and safety. We must try our best to protect ourselves and others at all times.

Causes of Accidents

Those who study safety say that there are two main causes of accidents. The first is human error —everyone makes mistakes. The second is unsafe environment. Whether you are at home, work, or play, your environment may be unsafe.

Human Error Most accidents, both on and off the job, are caused by human error. There are several types of human error, any one of which could result in unsafe behavior.

Think about an accident you or someone you know has had. Chances are it happened for one of the following reasons:

- *Poor safety attitude.* Someone who does not care about safety has a poor safety attitude. Because such people are far more likely to be involved in accidents, much research has been done to identify them. Researchers have found that people who are excited, angry, depressed, or tired are less likely to be concerned with safety. The use of drugs or alcohol has also been linked to poor safety attitudes.
- *Lack of knowledge.* Many workers are not aware of the potential for injury that exists

Some industries are more dangerous to work in than others. What might make jobs in the areas shown here particularly hazardous?

from the machines or materials they use on the job. New workers are especially at risk. Even if trained, they are seldom aware of everything they need to know to be safe. This is because a certain amount of learning must take place on the job.

- *Lack of skill.* This is the most common cause of accidents. Usually an emergency creates a situation that requires a skilled response, which the accident victim can't provide. A driver brakes to avoid an obstacle and skids out of control. A new skier can't change direction well enough to avoid someone in his or her path.
- *Physical limitations.* A **physical limitation** is the inability to do certain physical tasks. Many accidents occur because people are not strong enough or quick enough to prevent them. A swimmer lacks the strength to swim to safety. Alcohol slows a driver's response, making it impossible for him to avoid a collision.

Unsafe Environment   Not all accidents are the fault of the victim. Some are caused by the victim's environment.

For example, it was noted earlier that some industries are by their very nature less safe to work in than others. Consider meat packing. The employees in packing plants work with knives, cleavers, saws, and meat hooks. They must work fast, paced as they are by a number of conveyer systems. Temperatures (of both the meat and the rooms in which it is handled) are often below the comfort zone. The noise level (from the conveyers and saws) is fairly high. By almost anyone's standards, this would be considered a hazardous work environment. Any kind of mishap that occurred here would be potentially very serious.

Sometimes it is the materials or products that people work with that present the greatest hazard in the job environment. For example, service people who work with electricity, gas, oil, and certain kinds of chemicals face risks that office workers and store clerks do not.

Weather is a final factor that could make for an unsafe environment, both on and off the job. Snowy or icy conditions, for example, would make it difficult for all but the most experienced and skilled drivers to commute safely. It is not unusual for accident rates to soar when such conditions prevail.

Case Study 2

Bill finished truck-driving school a month ago and began driving an 18-wheeler almost immediately. In two weeks he had made a few panic stops, but he had had no serious emergencies.

Then it happened. The left front tire blew out. Bill could not control the truck, and it ran into the median strip of the highway.

Bill was lucky—there was little damage to the truck, and no one was hurt. However, Bill's lack of driving skill could have caused a tragedy. The blowout could have happened in heavy traffic or on a bridge. Bill felt he had learned from this experience. He knew he had to improve his skill so that he could handle future emergencies better.

Accident Prevention

Preventing accidents on the job is not something that individuals can do alone. It is and must be a cooperative effort among employers, employees, and government.

What Employers Can Do   Employers have a number of tools that they can use to ensure workplace safety. Principally, they can provide their employees with safety equipment and training and then back these efforts up with an enforcement program.

Employers should do more than teach employees the right way to do things. They should make employees aware of the consequences of doing things the wrong way—especially if those consequences include physical harm. Employees should also be provided with safety equipment—hard hats for work areas where falling objects might be a hazard, goggles or safety glasses for those working with cutting tools, and seat belts in any vehicles that must be driven on the job. Finally, use of both the procedures and the equipment should be enforced by supervisory personnel.

Employers can also take advantage of the services offered by safety specialists. They can consult with engineers to remedy safety problems with equipment. They can implement the recommendations of government inspectors who visit their facilities. They can employ their own safety inspectors or participate in voluntary inspection programs sponsored by their industry.

What You Can Do   An employer can do only so much to protect his or her workers. After that, the workers must protect themselves. They must accept responsibility for their own safety.

Here are some minimal safety guidelines that you should observe on any job:

- *Use all safety equipment provided.* This should be of more interest to you than it is to your employer. After all, if you are injured on the job, your employer can only lose money (to pay for your medical expenses or disability coverage). You, however, could lose your health—perhaps for a lifetime.

- *Know your equipment.* This means more than knowing how to use a particular machine or tool properly. It means understanding its potential for harm and knowing what to do if anything does in fact go wrong.

- *Know the materials you must use.* Be especially careful with chemicals. Read the instructions on the container or package, paying

particular attention to any precautions for use. Note whether the material is flammable or corrosive, whether it must be used in a well-ventilated area, what it can be used on, and what it can or can't be mixed with.

- *Know your limitations.* Overcome them if you can. If not, accept them. By pushing yourself beyond your limits, you risk injuring yourself and possibly even others.

MAKE A DECISION

You have a summer job working on a factory assembly line. You were told to wear safety goggles because of some grinding and drilling that is done at various places along the line. Many of the workers don't wear the goggles because they're hot and uncomfortable. You don't want to take a chance on seriously hurting your eyes, but you hate wearing the goggles. What's your decision—to wear them all the time or to take them off when the supervisor isn't around? Give the reasons for your decision.

Safety is as much an employee's responsibility as an employer's. In what ways are these workers showing that they accept this responsibility?

- *Look out for your co-workers.* You should try to be as skilled and knowledgeable about your work as possible. You should also try to notice when others lack skill and knowledge and try to help them. This could avoid an accident and thus ensure everyone's safety.
- *Come to work physically and mentally fit.* This means refraining from the use of alcohol or similar substances during work and possibly during the entire work week. Such substances can affect your alertness, reaction time, and judgment. For these reasons, they could pose a severe threat to you and to everyone who works with you.

SITUATION
SOLUTION

Confronting Drug Use on the Job

You work on an auto assembly line installing transmissions. You've become aware that several people on the team just up the line from you are doing drugs during working hours. You're not sure whether management is aware of the situation. You've noticed some sloppy work, but nothing's fallen off a car body coming from the team's station, and nothing's happened that's endangered you or anyone else on another team.

You are beginning to wonder, though, if it just isn't a matter of time. Last week one of the welders on the team dropped his torch (fortunately it's suspended from the ceiling, so it didn't go far). Also, a few times team members have drifted over into your station because they couldn't keep up with the line. Everyone treated it as a joke.

That's the problem, though. No one seems ready to take the situation seriously or really do anything about it.

1. Would you say anything to your supervisor or union representative at this point? Why or why not?
2. Would you say anything to the employees who are involved or their team members? Why or why not?
3. What precautions would (or could) you take to protect yourself and your team members from safety problems growing out of the other team's conduct?

Many of these guidelines can carry over into your personal life. Just consider a few variations: Use safety equipment in your car—buckle your safety belt. Don't drink and drive. Read the labels carefully on household products and over-the-counter drugs; store both in safe places, well out of the reach of young children. Read the owner's manual before you operate any new appliance. Don't try to lift more than you can carry without difficulty.

You can't eliminate every potentially unsafe condition from your environment. That's not practical, even if it were possible. You should, however, do what you can to make your environment safer and prevent accidents. Safety is everyone's job. It's also a job that lasts 24 hours a day—not just from nine to five.

Government's Role   Work in the nineteenth century was often very hazardous. Early railroads and industrial plants were especially dangerous, and there was very little safety engineering. There were few safety laws regulating dangerous occupations, such as mining. Miners had to deal with cave-ins, explosions, and a debilitating disease called black lung.

Over time companies were pressured to prevent accidents and eliminate health hazards. Accidents were studied. Many new practices were put into effect to reduce on-the-job dangers. Safety education programs were started by labor unions and management, especially in the larger industries.

Much of the impetus for these measures came from government. It's part of government's role to make and enforce laws that promote health and safety. Two federal agencies have special responsibilities in this area.

The **Occupational Safety and Health Administration (OSHA)** was created by Congress in 1970 to determine safety and health standards for the world of work. OSHA decides what the lowest acceptable levels of safety will be. The agency's inspectors can force company officials to appear in court when they find workplaces that do not meet the minimum standards.

The legislation that created OSHA states that both employers and employees have responsibilities as well as rights. It says that each employer must provide a job site free from safety and health hazards. It also says that employees must obey the rules listed in the Occupational Safety and Health Act. For example, where required, workers must use protective equipment. For OSHA rules applicable to your job, see the OSHA poster at your job site.

The **Environmental Protection Agency (EPA)** is another government agency that makes our country safer for everyone. The EPA tries to protect the environment. By doing this, it protects our health. Reducing air and water pollution is one of the main goals of the EPA.

Many scientific groups wrote reports that showed the need to protect the environment. These scientists studied air pollution in large cities. They analyzed water pollution in rivers and lakes and found that pollution, which can cause serious diseases, had reached dangerous levels in some areas.

As a result of these studies, the EPA was given certain powers. Among them was the power to limit the amount of smoke and fumes released into the environment by automobiles and factories.

When an Accident Occurs

Despite all the safety precautions you take, accidents will still happen. When they do, you should know how to help the victim until a medical professional can arrive on the scene. What

you do in the first five minutes of an emergency can mean the difference between life and death for an accident victim.

First Aid Should an injury accident occur either at home or on the job, you must remain calm and act quickly. The guidelines below can help. They reflect standard first aid practices and priorities.

- *Rescue promptly.* Should you move someone who is injured? The answer is yes—but only to save the person's life. You would remove an auto accident victim from a burning vehicle or a drowning victim from the water. However, you would treat someone who fell from a ladder where he or she lay, provided there was no danger from falling debris.

- *Check breathing.* A person can live for only four or five minutes without oxygen. You should therefore check first to see if an accident victim is breathing. Look for the rise and fall of the chest, listen for the sound of inhaling or exhaling, and feel for exhaled air on your cheek. If none of these indications is present, verify that the victim's airway is open. Clear it if it isn't. Then provide artificial respiration, or breathing (Figure 9-3).

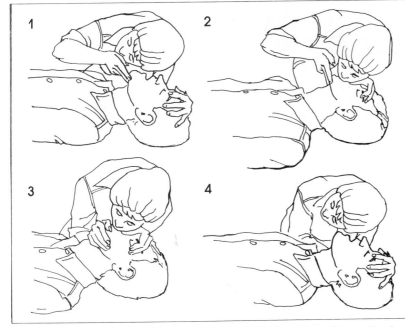

Artificial Respiration for Adults

1. Position head to clear airway. Then pinch nostrils shut with index finger and thumb.
2. Keeping nostrils pinched shut, place your mouth over the person's mouth, forming a seal.
3. Give the person two breaths (1-1.5 seconds each). Allow deflation between breaths.
4. Keep head tilted. Look, listen, and feel again for signs of breathing.
5. Continue at the rate of 1 breath every 5 seconds.

Figure 9-3 Breathing for an accident victim who cannot breathe for him- or herself is one of the top priorities in first aid. Judging from the illustrations, what does it mean to "position the head to clear the airway"?

- *Control bleeding.* If bleeding is bright red and spurting, it is severe and should be controlled quickly. This is done by applying direct pressure. Place a thick, clean cloth over the wound, and press firmly with the palm of your hand. (*Note:* If possible, you should raise the injury site above the level of the victim's heart—unless the bleeding involves a broken bone.)

- *Treat poisoning.* If the victim has come into contact with a poisonous substance, call the local poison-control center. Provide as much information about the accident and the victim as you can, and follow the instructions you are given.

These procedures are your first priorities in giving aid because they ensure the victim's safety and life-support systems. Once these procedures have been carried out, you should summon medical help and keep the victim still and warm.

Artificial respiration, described briefly earlier, is not the only procedure that can be used to help an accident victim who is not breathing. Victims of heart attack, electrical shock, drug overdose, smoke inhalation, and drowning—people whose hearts have stopped beating—are today often helped by a technique called **cardiopulmonary resuscitation (CPR).** CPR does more than help a victim breathe. By applying pressure to the chest (see Figure 9-4), it forces the heart to pump blood as well. In other words, it provides artificial *circulation.*

Only someone who has successfully completed a CPR course can perform the procedure. Such courses are offered throughout the country by the American Red Cross and the American Heart Association. To be certified to perform CPR, you must pass both a written and a performance test.

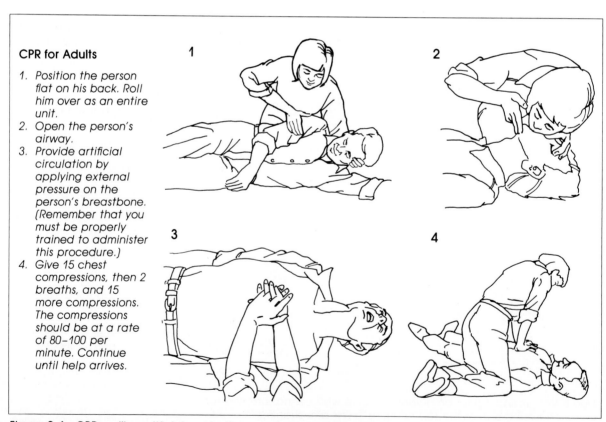

CPR for Adults

1. *Position the person flat on his back. Roll him over as an entire unit.*
2. *Open the person's airway.*
3. *Provide artificial circulation by applying external pressure on the person's breastbone. (Remember that you must be properly trained to administer this procedure.)*
4. *Give 15 chest compressions, then 2 breaths, and 15 more compressions. The compressions should be at a rate of 80–100 per minute. Continue until help arrives.*

Figure 9-4 CPR, unlike artificial respiration, requires special training. Judging from the illustrations shown here, why do you think this is so?

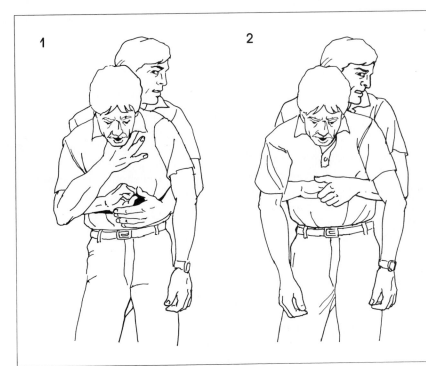

First Aid for Choking in Older Children and Adults (Conscious Victims Only)

1. *Wrap arms around the victim's chest with the thumb side of your wrist against the person's abdomen. Place your hand just above the navel.*
2. *Grasp your fist with your other hand and press into the abdomen with quick, upward thrusts until successful.*

Figure 9-5 The Heimlich maneuver, shown here, is intended as immediate first aid for a choking victim. The procedure can also be self-administered if no one is around to help. Judging from these illustrations, how?

A final procedure commonly used in first aid is called the **Heimlich maneuver** (Figure 9-5). This technique employs abdominal thrusts to help victims of choking. Choking is the sixth leading cause of accidental death in the United States. More than 3,000 Americans die each year as a result of choking.

Choking occurs when an object (usually a piece of food) becomes lodged in a person's windpipe, cutting off the flow of air. The Heimlich maneuver works by abruptly forcing air out of the lungs to clear the windpipe. A person using the technique may have to repeat it ten or more times before he or she is successful.

Emergency Facilities Accident victims who can walk or have someone to transport them can seek first aid and/or treatment at the emergency room of the nearest hospital. Such facilities, however, may be overcrowded—especially if you live in a large urban area. Their services may also be extremely expensive.

One alternative for care that has emerged in recent years is the walk-in clinic. Usually this is a freestanding medical facility—that is, it is not associated with a hospital as most other kinds of clinics are. Walk-in clinics primarily serve people who have minor medical emergencies. Their principal advantages are convenience and low cost. Clinics are open 365 days a year, usually from early in the morning until late at night. Charges are often less than half of what they would be at the local hospital emergency room.

✓ CHECKING UP

1. People who have a poor safety attitude are just selfish; they'd rather let the other guy do it—true or false? Explain.
2. List three things you can do on the job to ensure your safety. Then describe what would be equivalent behavior at home.
3. You find someone lying unconscious and bleeding in the middle of your front lawn. What would you do first and why?

Review Your Learning

CHAPTER SUMMARY

In order to pursue your career goal, you'll need good health. This means that throughout your life you'll need to monitor yourself in three areas—diet, exercise, and disease awareness and prevention.

In the area of diet, you should eat a variety of foods (some from each of the four basic food groups at each meal). You should also limit the amount you eat according to how active you are; reduce the amount of salt, sugar, and animal fat in your diet; and increase the amount of fiber. You should exercise regularly (at least three times a week for 20 minutes). Finally, you should be aware of the causes of major ailments like heart disease and cancer. You should try to eliminate those causes from your life-style.

Accidents—at home, at work, and on the road—are another serious health risk that you can take steps to reduce. This is because most accidents are caused by human error. People are hurt because they are careless (have a poor safety attitude), lack necessary knowledge or skills, or fail to recognize their own limitations. Fewer accidents are caused by unsafe conditions in the environment.

Preventing accidents on the job must be a cooperative effort among employers, employees, and government. Employers can provide safety equipment and training. Employees can come to work physically and mentally fit, use the equipment and training provided, and look out for each other. Government, through OSHA and the EPA, can ensure that specific workplaces and the environment in general are not hazardous to people carrying out their daily activities.

Finally, you should know the basics of first aid so that if an accident does occur you will be able to act quickly and calmly to help the victim(s). You should proceed in the following order: (1) rescue promptly, (2) check breathing, (3) control bleeding,

and (4) treat poisoning. You should then summon professional medical help or seek it at the nearest emergency room or walk-in clinic.

TERMS TO KNOW

On a separate sheet of paper, write definitions for each of the following terms:

calorie
sedentary
depression
physical limitation
Occupational Safety and Health Administration (OSHA)
Environmental Protection Agency (EPA)
cardiopulmonary resuscitation (CPR)
Heimlich maneuver

STUDY QUESTIONS

1. What is a balanced diet?
2. Why do people gain weight?
3. What are the benefits of a physical fitness program?
4. Which diseases are the two leading causes of death in the United States?
5. What are the warning signs of depression?
6. Where do the greatest number of accident injuries occur?
7. Name the two major causes of accidents.
8. List three things employers can do to ensure a safe workplace for their employees.
9. What is the main purpose of OSHA? of the EPA?
10. Why is it so important to verify that an accident victim is breathing before giving any other kind of first aid?
11. When do you use the Heimlich maneuver?
12. What are the two principal advantages that walk-in clinics have for patients over hospital emergency rooms?

CRITICAL THINKING

1. Is it possible for someone to eat more yet still lose weight? How?
2. What is the cartoon below saying about individual responsibility and accidents?

3. What is the main difference between CPR and artificial respiration?

DISCUSSION STARTERS

1. Many people are far more reluctant to seek treatment for mental problems than physical ailments. Why do you think this is so? What evidence do you see that such attitudes are (or are not) changing?
2. How should society treat those people who are found to be driving under the influence of alcohol or drugs?
3. Businesses usually pass the cost of meeting OSHA standards on to consumers in the form of higher prices. Is the extra cost worth it? Explain your reasoning.

BUILDING BASIC SKILLS

Math

1. Medical authorities recommend that Americans modify their diets so they get no more than 30 percent of their calories from fat. In fact, average Americans get more than 40 per-cent of their calories from that source, while average Japanese get only 20 percent. If your total calorie intake for a day is 1,960 calories (of which 730 come from fat), which dietary pattern do you fit—American or modified American? By how many calories would you have to reduce your fat intake to meet the Japanese norm?

Computer Literacy

2. Keep track of all the food you eat for one day. Then use a computer program like Pillsbury's "Eat Smart" to analyze your food choices. In what areas, if any, did the program recommend reductions or additions? (*Note:* If you are using a home computer or if computer time is available in your school's computer lab, experiment with modifying your diet. Try adding or subtracting snacks, and note the effect on the program's recommendations. Try a diet based entirely on "grazing" [eating several small meals each day rather than three large ones]. Which dietary patterns yielded the most favorable results?)

Human Relations

3. Your grandfather is exhibiting many of the warning signs of depression, and you are concerned that he is going untreated. How can you convince him that he should get medical help? Who else might you enlist in your efforts?

SUGGESTED ACTIVITY

Investigate at least three physical fitness programs available in your community. Compare the programs in terms of facilities, quality of instruction, atmosphere, and cost to determine which would be the best for you. Describe your decision-making process to the class in a brief oral report.

UNIT
Three

Developing Your Skills and Understanding

Communication Skills

Communication is the process of exchanging information. It is how we transmit thoughts and ideas from one person to another.

There are four primary communication skills: speaking, listening, writing, and reading. These skills are necessary in almost every work situation. Almost without exception, those who rise to the top of any career are those who communicate well.

There are two parts to communicating a message. Every message must be sent, and it must be received. Some people think that just because they say something, they are communicating. They forget that unless someone understands what they are listening to or reading, no communication has taken place. It takes at least two people to communicate a message.

In this chapter you will learn how to improve your communication skills. You can then begin working and practicing to become a better communicator. The work you do to improve these skills may be just as important as the work you do on the job.

1 Speaking

Your ability to communicate orally, or to speak, will have considerable influence on your success in the world of work. Some careers require more speaking skills than others. Whatever your career, though, you will need to express yourself clearly so that your supervisor and co-workers understand the message you are sending.

In this lesson, you will learn how to speak, and therefore communicate, more effectively. You will learn how to establish a purpose in speaking, plan what you say when speaking formally, and use good speaking habits.

Establishing Your Purpose

Always keep in mind why you are speaking. In most cases we speak to inform, to persuade, or to entertain.

Speaking to Inform The main purpose of most conversations is to inform one or more of the people involved in the conversation. The participants exchange information, frequently changing roles from receiver to sender and back again.

When your purpose in speaking is to inform, get right to the point. Try not to give others unnecessary information which may waste their time. Be direct—say what you want to say clearly and quickly.

Speaking to Persuade In many careers it is necessary to persuade others to see or do things your way. In Chapter 8, you learned some methods for understanding and influencing others. Several of the hints in that chapter provide a good background for persuading others through spoken communication.

Use as many of these strategies as you can. Some, like smiling, are easy. Perhaps the most important is learning the needs of the listener, then showing how you can satisfy at least one of those needs.

Speaking to Entertain Sometimes the purpose of a conversation is to entertain. Sometimes speaking to entertain can also help inform or persuade. In many careers, such as sales, it is necessary to entertain clients. Meeting with business associates, including your boss and those you supervise, provides other situations in which you will need to talk to and entertain others.

Few of us are really comedians, but it is fun to talk, tell stories, and joke with friends. You may use slang expressions or even special words that only you and your friends know. This kind of speaking is usually quite informal.

Using a Plan

You may not give many formal speeches, but in the world of work many spoken messages are at

Good speaking skills are essential in many jobs. How is this police officer affected by how well he speaks to others?

Strive for Success

The Remarkable Communicator

One of the most remarkable women in history, she was once legally classified as an idiot. For a period of approximately five years, she grew up as she later described herself "wild and unruly, giggling and chuckling to express pleasure; kicking, scratching, uttering the choked screams of the deaf-mute to indicate the opposite."

Helen Keller was born in 1880. Blind, deaf, and unable to speak, she was virtually cut off from the world. However, with the love and assistance of a remarkable teacher named Anne Sullivan, she accomplished what many at the time considered impossible. She not only learned to read (using the braille system) but also to write and to speak.

When Sullivan first came to teach Keller, she was the wild child of her own description, living in a world of darkness and silence she could not understand. Sullivan made contact with Keller by spelling words, such as *doll, puppy,* and *water,* into Keller's palm and then allowing Keller to touch that particular item. At first, this made no sense to Keller. Then one day she finally made the connection between the letters that were spelled in her palm and the water that Sullivan was pumping to her hand.

This event opened the door to a world of learning for Keller, and she was ready to take advantage of the chance. Within three years, she knew the alphabet and could read and write in braille. She could also speak, using sign language.

By the time she was ten years old, Keller had decided that she would also learn to speak aloud and began lessons with a teacher of the deaf. In 1900 she enrolled at Radcliffe College, where Sullivan helped her by spelling the lectures in her hand. She wrote her first book, *The Story of My Life,* in 1902 and graduated with honors from Radcliffe in 1904.

Already Keller's book and her accomplishments had brought her worldwide acclaim. She chose to make use of her fame by devoting her life to helping blind and deaf people. She took an

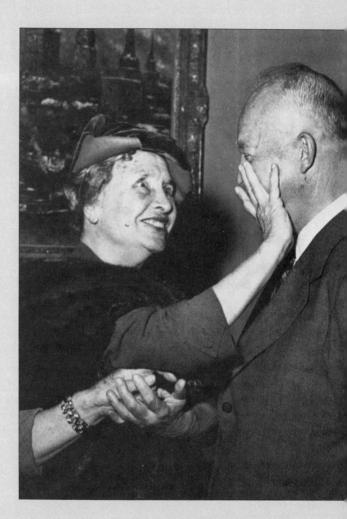

active role on the staffs of the American Foundation for the Blind and the American Foundation for the Overseas Blind. She became a prolific author, writing essays, articles, and books, as well as a well-traveled lecturer. With each stop or new publication, she furthered the cause of blind and deaf people not only in this country but also throughout the world.

least semiformal. Jobs in business, engineering, education, health, and many other careers require people to deliver messages in such a way that others will listen and understand them. When you speak to others on the job, you will want them to listen to what you are saying. A well-organized spoken message always receives more attention than one presented in a haphazard way. Some basic organizational patterns you can use are discussed below.

Enumeration   Enumeration is the process of listing several items in a particular order. When you become a supervisor, you may tell a new worker, "There are six steps in handling this task." Then the new worker will know to listen for six separate, but related, things to do. They will be easier to understand because the listener is expecting them. Using signal words such as *first, second, third,* and *next* will also help the listener.

Generalization with Example   Speakers often use generalizations to make a point. Good speakers support their generalizations with examples and evidence. If you work for an insurance company, you won't simply say, "Motor vehicles are the leading cause of accidental deaths in the United States." You will also present evidence: "Of all accidental deaths in the past year, almost half were the result of auto accidents." Evidence in

support of generalizations clarifies the message and helps the listener remember the main points. Use signal words such as *for example* and *for instance.*

Cause and Effect   An effective way of explaining a topic is to discuss it in terms of cause and effect. This pattern leads the listener from the cause of something to the result. This method can also be used in reverse by presenting an effect and then considering possible causes. Signal words are *as a result, therefore, accordingly,* and *consequently.*

Comparison and Contrast   Comparison and contrast is another technique for explaining something. An effective way of explaining new concepts is to show how they are similar to concepts already known to the listener. Use words like *however, nevertheless,* and *on the other hand.*

Using Good Speaking Habits

To speak as effectively as possible, you should use certain methods of oral, or spoken, communication. A few tips for proper speech are presented here. Try to develop these tips into personal habits that will make you a better communicator.

Standard English   When you talk with friends, you can use slang expressions to spice up the conversation. However, on the job in most

Even though the worker on the left is speaking informally, he has organized his presentation for his colleague. How do you know? How does this type of presentation benefit both the workers and the company that employs them?

companies, people are expected to use standard English. This will reduce the chances of your being misunderstood.

Voice Quality   A pleasant voice is not pitched too high or too low. Compared to music, the pitches of voices could range from a tenor flute to a bass drum. You may have heard someone whose voice was so highly pitched that you didn't really want to listen to what that person said. Think about the pitch of your voice. Would it be more pleasant if it were higher or lower?

A relaxed voice is more attractive than a tense one. A voice sounds relaxed when a medium tone is combined with smoothness. When you are tense, you usually speak in a higher voice and your voice may sound shaky.

As a speaker, you can use inflections to make your voice more interesting. **Inflection** is the use of the voice to alter the meaning of a spoken message. You can use inflections for emphasis and interest by placing stress on certain important words and syllables. This helps make your meaning clear.

The volume, or loudness, of your voice is also important. No one likes to strain to hear what is said or ask that the message be repeated. On the other hand, speaking in a very loud voice will cause people to avoid listening to you.

Pronunciation, Enunciation, and Speed
Good speaking habits also include using correct pronunciation and enunciation. **Pronunciation** refers to the way a word sounds. Always try to say the sounds of words correctly. Correct **enunciation** means speaking each syllable clearly and separately.

Speaking too fast or too slowly is a speaking habit that needs attention. Talking too fast can make you difficult to understand, and talking too slowly can make you boring to listen to. A moderate speed that is neither hurried nor drawn out is best. Remember, however, to vary the speed to keep your listener interested.

Telephone Technique   A great deal of work in the business world is done over the telephone. How effective you are in speaking on the phone can affect your success. This is especially true if you are an office worker.

When you speak on the telephone, your voice becomes even more important than in face-to-face conversations. In face-to-face conversations, facial expressions and body language help you get your message across. In phone conversations, the person with whom you are speaking can't see you. In these situations a pleasant voice can have the same effect as a smile or a friendly gesture.

When your phone rings, answer it right away. People who are kept waiting on the phone are frequently not as cooperative as they would be otherwise. When you answer, give the name of your company or department first. Then give your name: "Maddox Company, Ms. Jones speaking."

Ideas about proper phone etiquette do vary, however. It's a good idea to ask your employer how you should answer the phone.

When you speak on the phone, speak clearly and directly into the mouthpiece. Talk loudly enough so the other person doesn't have to strain to hear you, but don't yell. Develop the habit of being courteous, and never interrupt the other person.

Answering the phone in a professional manner is an important part of business communication. Do you think this worker is a good communicator? Why or why not?

✓ CHECKING UP

1. What are the three main purposes for speaking?
2. Describe the four basic organizational patterns used when speaking.
3. Why do speakers use inflections?

2 *Listening*

As stated earlier, there are two parts to communicating a message—sending and receiving. Receiving a message actually involves more than hearing or reading it. The receiver must be able to understand the sender's message. Communication means both the sender and the receiver understand the message in the same way.

Listening—like speaking, reading, and writing—is a skill. Skillful listeners receive messages and understand them. These people are usually very successful in the world of work, and they often appear more intelligent than the rest of us. Those who develop high-level listening skills become far more knowledgeable than those who don't. How would you rate your listening skills? Are you a good listener?

Many people have never learned to listen well. Do you know anyone so interested in speaking that he or she hardly listens at all? These people haven't learned the difference between hearing and listening. Hearing is simply the physical process. Only your ears are involved. Listening is a mental process, requiring the use of your brain.

It's so easy to misunderstand a message. You must work hard mentally to listen with understanding. There are some listening strategies, or skills, that can help you understand the messages sent to you. These strategies deal with what to listen for and what to do in your mind while listening.

Recognize the Purpose

Sometimes you will know the purpose of a message before the person begins to speak. If so, think about how a clear understanding of that message may help you. If you don't know the purpose, make a quick mental note of how understanding might help you as soon as you realize the purpose. When you know how a clear understanding of the message can help you, you can better concentrate all your mental energy on the message.

Look for the Plan

You may recall that in formal, structured speeches there is usually some kind of plan. For example, the speaker may use enumeration, generalization, cause and effect, or comparison and contrast. Informal talks may include a plan as well. Your boss may use enumeration in his or her explanation of how to carry out your work responsibilities.

Recognizing the signal words discussed earlier can help you identify the plan. Knowing the plan can greatly improve your understanding of the message being communicated. You will also remember the message longer.

Give Feedback

Feedback is the receiver's response to the sender's message. Feedback makes it possible for the sender to determine whether or not a receiver understands a message. As a listener, you can speed things up and improve understanding by sending signals back to the speaker. Nod your head to show that you are getting the message. A raised eyebrow or quizzical look will tell the speaker to slow down or repeat a complicated part of the message. With these small gestures and a quick summary of your understanding at the end, you can make sure that you and the speaker understand the message in the same way.

This speaker is trying very hard to communicate with her listeners. Do you think she is succeeding? Why or why not?

Make Distinctions

As a skilled listener, you should distinguish between fact and opinion. Usually facts are more important than opinions. Listen to some radio and television commercials. How much is fact and how much is opinion? Can you always tell the difference? Facts are truths. Opinions differ from one person to the next.

Of course, "expert" opinion is often considered the next best thing to facts. When your boss gives you his or her opinions about how you should do your job, you will probably consider those opinions just as important as facts.

You should also distinguish between what is important and unimportant. You can't remember every word a person says. Try to sort out what is important and what is unimportant. Then discard what's unimportant.

Listen for More than Verbal Content

There is much more to a speaker's message than the meanings of the words used. The way in which someone speaks and his or her body language are major parts of the message.

You may recall that speakers use inflection for emphasis and to make meaning clearer. By using inflection people can create several different meanings for the same sentence. They can say it loudly or softly. They can pick out one or two words and say them much louder than the others.

As a listener, you must pay attention to inflection. The speaker's inflection will give you valuable clues to the real meaning of the message. Anger, fear, and other emotions that are important to your understanding will come through inflection.

Observing the speaker's body language will also help you understand the message. You read about the importance of body language in Chapter 8. Even though you don't hear gestures and body movements, taking them into account makes you a better listener.

Additional Skills

There are additional skills that will help you remember what you listen to. If you use them consistently, you will become a more skilled listener and a better communicator. These skills include asking questions, taking notes, listening for a conclusion, and using the dictionary.

Ask Questions   If you can, ask questions whenever you don't understand something. Some people are afraid they will embarrass themselves if they ask questions. Don't worry about that. On the job, especially, it's far better to ask questions and make sure you know what you are supposed to do than to risk doing your job wrong because of a misunderstanding.

Take Notes   If you have a chance, make written notes on the speaker's main points. Then you can review them one at a time later. If you can't write down the main points, make mental notes. Say the main points in your own words, in your mind. Try to relate the speaker's message to your own experiences. This rewording and repetition will help make certain things clearer and will also help you remember important items.

Listen for a Conclusion   If no conclusion is given, mentally summarize the speaker's main points and draw your own conclusion. You may need or want to take some kind of action based on this conclusion.

Use the Dictionary   We all hear words that are new to us. Often we need to know these words to understand the meaning of the message. Don't let yourself be confused twice by the same word. If someone uses a word you don't know, look up the meaning in a dictionary the first chance you get. If you make this a habit, you will improve your vocabulary. This will go a long way toward making you a better listener.

Overcoming Blocks to Listening

Some things commonly prevent people from being good listeners. We call them blocks to listening with understanding. If you can avoid these blocks, you can concentrate your attention on listening and understanding.

Distractions   Distractions are noises, thoughts, or anything that prevents you from concentrating on what the speaker is saying. Some people are bothered more by distractions than others.

Being able to block out distractions is mostly a matter of concentrated effort. You can do it if you focus all your mental energy on what the speaker is saying.

Both the sender and the receiver of a message have a responsibility to see that communication takes place. If this worker doesn't understand her supervisor's explanation, how can she communicate this fact?

Emotional Blocks   If you don't like the speaker or strongly disagree with his or her ideas, you may find it difficult to listen. In the world of work, though, if you don't understand the message, you may not be able to do your job correctly. If you disagree with the speaker's ideas, it is especially important to listen and to understand. Otherwise you will be unable to respond in a meaningful way. When you know the value of listening in these situations, you can usually prevent emotional blocks.

Many people block out emotionally painful messages by hearing what they want to hear. The speaker says one thing, but the listener hears another. This may avoid the problem for a while, but it won't make it go away. It's better to listen and deal with the situation right away than to deal with a bigger problem later.

Planning a Response   One of the most frequent blocks to listening is planning what you will say next. The mind works much faster than the mouth, and you can easily jump ahead of the speaker in many situations. When the speaker says something you want to respond to, it's tempting to think about your response and tune out the speaker. By doing this, however, you may miss out on a key piece of information. Then your reply will not be appropriate. Only by listening to and understand-

ing the entire message can you make a good response.

MAKE A DECISION

Your boss is the slowest talker you have ever encountered, and he repeats every instruction over and over. You almost always know what he wants you to do after listening to his first few words, but he talks on and on. You find yourself thinking of other things, though you know you should pay attention. What's your decision—will you listen carefully to every word, or will you block out the boss and think of other things? Give the reasons for your decision.

✓ CHECKING UP

1. What are some of the strategies that listeners can use to understand spoken messages better?
2. What is feedback?
3. Describe the blocks that prevent people from being good listeners.

3 *Writing*

The simplest and fastest way to communicate with someone is to have a conversation. With a telephone we can send or receive messages instantly, even if the other person is thousands of miles away. There are times, though, when writing is a better way to communicate than speaking.

Writing out your message is the best way to organize your thoughts. It gives you a chance to revise your message before sending it. Often, when you see your thoughts in writing, you will think of ways to improve your message. Maybe you can say it in a clearer way or give it more impact.

A written message is an exact record of your message. It's easy to make copies for whoever needs to read it. By filing a copy you have a dated record of when it was written.

In conversations, we tend to hear what we want to hear and forget the rest. When you write a message down in black and white, however, it's all there. It can't be easily ignored. The receiver is more likely to take appropriate action than if he or she had received the same message in a conversa-tion. The impact of a written message also lasts longer since the message can be kept permanently.

There will be many occasions for writing in your personal life. Writing is also an important function on most jobs. Therefore, good writing skills will be very useful. In this lesson you will learn writing skills that will help you become a better communicator.

Basic Considerations in Writing

Before you can begin writing, you must consider three basic things. These are the reader, your purpose in writing, and the subject. This section tells you how to consider each to write most effectively.

Know Your Reader   Before you write anything, give some thought to those who will be reading your message. Who are they? Why will they be reading your message? What do they already know about the subject? The answers to these questions, and any others you can think of in each situation, will help you to know the reader better. When you understand the needs of the reader, you can write a more meaningful message.

Written messages have several benefits over spoken messages. What benefits are suggested by the situation shown here? What other benefits might there be?

Case Study *1*

Jill Byers never cared much for writing. When writing assignments were given in her English classes, Jill did the very minimum to get a passing grade. "Besides," she thought, "I'm going to be a horse trainer, and I won't have to do any writing."

Jill did become a horse trainer. Only then did she learn the importance of writing. When she entered her horses in races, she had to write out the information for the racing secretary at Hollywood Park. Every month she wrote statements showing what each horse owner owed for training, horseshoeing, and veterinary charges. On one occasion she had to send a letter to a mail order house in the Midwest to complain about some defective stable supplies and to request replacements. Her activities at horse sales also required a great deal of writing.

Jill was quite surprised by the amount of writing she was doing. She wished she had given it more attention in high school. When Jill was back home for a week, she stopped by to see her former English teacher. Jill offered to come and talk with students about the importance of improving their writing skills.

Know Your Purpose   The second thing you will consider as you begin your writing is the purpose of your message. Most writing is done in order to

- inform,
- request,
- confirm,
- persuade,
- inquire, or
- complain.

Stop and think about your purpose before you start. This will probably affect the tone of your writing. For example, if you're writing to persuade, your message would sound friendlier than if you were writing to complain. Make sure you know why you are writing your message.

Know Your Subject   You will need to know your subject well in order to write about it. On the job you may learn enough about the subject that no further research is necessary. If you are still new on the job, though, you may want to do some reading before you write certain messages. When you know your subject well, you will feel more confident as you write.

Writing Style

Some years ago, much of the writing in the business world was formal and stiff. The trend in recent years has been toward more informal business writing. Of course, company executives usually set the tone and style of writing for their companies, which means the style will vary from one office to the next. You will probably have an opportunity to read company letters, memos, and reports before writing any. This will give you a chance to see how formal the writing style is where you work.

Most companies today emphasize simple, direct, clear writing. This means writing in a conversational style, using words you would use if you were speaking. For example, you would write, "I believe" rather than "It is believed."

Any written message is a reflection of the writer. When your writing is a neat, well-organized message, others see you as a neat, well-organized person.

As you write, keep in mind your main purpose in writing—to communicate something to another person. Select individual words that will make the message clear to the reader. Don't try to impress the reader with your vocabulary.

In some cases it is necessary to use jargon when writing. **Jargon** consists of words or phrases that have meaning only within a particular career field. Think of it as a kind of verbal shorthand used to speed communication between people who work in the same field. For people outside the field, however, jargon is a stumbling block to communication. You should therefore avoid jargon when writing to people not involved in your area of work.

The one word you can use in a written message that best aids communication is the name of the person who will read it. You know the importance of saying others' names in spoken conversations. Writing the name of the person who will receive your written message helps personalize it. The person reading the message will have a warmer feeling toward you.

Good Writing Skills

Good writing rarely comes easily. Because it is so difficult to achieve for so many people, those who can write well are usually very successful in the world of work.

In many cases the most difficult part of writing is getting started. If you are having trouble, make yourself write your ideas down on paper, even if they are rough. Walk away from what you've written for a short time. Then come back and try to improve part of your message. Repeat this process until you build up some momentum.

If you are not satisfied with your writing ability, you can improve. Follow the rules below—and practice.

Spell All Words Correctly   The most obvious errors in any written message are the spelling errors. When these errors appear, those reading the message usually form a negative opinion of the writer and the writer's message. Look up all the words you are not sure of in the dictionary.

Use Correct Grammar   This rule refers to all the composition rules you've been learning in school. Messages with poor grammar, like messages with misspellings, are often received negatively. (Consider Figure 10-1.) If you have questions about grammar rules, talk to your teacher or librarian about reference books they would recommend.

Get to the Point   In writing, as in speaking to inform, it is important to say what you want to say as directly and concisely as possible. Do not give the reader any unnecessary information. Keep it short and simple (see Figure 10-2). This is

Figure 10-1 Good writing skills include spelling correctly and using correct grammar. The person receiving this sample letter might make a donation. What, however, do you think will be his reaction to the writer and the organization she represents? If you were to rewrite the letter, what would you change?

```
                                    1408 Buncombe Drive
                                    Atlanta, GA  30360
                                    September 8, 1991


Mr. Joseph McGill
11377 Peachtree Avenue
Atlanta, GA  80369

Dear Mr. McGill:

    I was given your name by Coach Smith as a person to contact
about donations of softball equimpment for a new community center
softball teem this is for the Peachtree Community Center.  Coach
Smith thought that because you have donated generosely in the past
you might be willing to help some more.

    We specially need gloves bats and batting helmuts.  If you
could help.  Please let me know.

                                Sincerely,

                                Janice Mitchum

                                Janice Mitchum
```

DuPres
Associates

299 Alexander Street • Suite 1246 • Circleville, Ohio 43113 • (614) 838-3666

March 12, 1991

Megabyte Computers, Inc.
1700 Kellogg Boulevard
Wichita, KS 67213

Dear Sir:

    After reading about the new Dream Machine computer
that you advertised in the March issue of Business World
Computing, I would like a price list and specifications
on each model. We plan to replace several of our microcomputers, and I would like our Board of Directors to
consider the Dream Machine.

    Do you have a sales representative on the West Coast?
If so, I would appreciate receiving a call from him or her.

                              Yours truly,

                              Grant Kinsey

                              Grant Kinsey
                              President

GK:sm

Figure 10-2   This is a well-written business letter because it is brief and
to the point. What is the purpose of this letter? Which sentence or
sentences describe its purpose?

especially important in the world of work, where people are busy and often labor under deadline pressure.

Organize Your Ideas Logically If you were saying the numbers from one to ten, you wouldn't say six and then three. When you write a message, present your ideas in the order in which they will make sense to the reader. Sometimes you won't know the most logical order until you write your entire message and reread it. The paragraphs of your message should progress logically from one to the next.

Reread and Rewrite Very few people get it right the first time. Almost all good writers rewrite their letters, memos, and reports. They read their first attempt as though they were the people who will receive the message. As they read, they ask themselves, "Will the reader understand that? Does it make sense? Will he or she know exactly what I mean?" Not until all the answers are yes is the written message finished.

Forms of Written Communication

There are many forms of written communication. Which form you use in a particular situation usually depends on the kind of information you are communicating. Sometimes a simple handwritten note is all that's required. In business, most written messages are in the form of letters, memos, or reports.

Business Letters Business letters will be your main form of written communication with people outside your own company. You can use letters to inform, request, confirm, persuade, inquire, or complain. The main parts of a business letter were described in Chapter 5. Business letters are always typed.

Memos A memo is a written message to someone in your own company. Memos are usually brief and often cover only one topic. Much of the important communication that takes place within companies is done in memo form.

Like business letters, most memos are typed. What makes memos so much simpler to prepare is their format. Memos begin with a standard set of headings which the user simply fills in (see Figure 10-3). The memo's message follows in paragraph form.

Reports A business report is often written to explain certain things. Usual topics for reports include yearly sales, problems that need attention, results of studies or surveys, and results of special projects. Some reports are in-house reports, to be read only by company employees. Others are written for a wider audience, such as stockholders, investors, or government agencies.

Some long, complex reports are organized formally with a table of contents, introduction, body, and summary. Others are short, informal reports consisting only of the body, similar to the body of a letter. Before you begin preparing a report, learn whether your company has a preferred way of organizing such a document.

SITUATION
SOLUTION

In Over Your Head?

You have really enjoyed working in sales for O'Connor Computers, and the company is impressed with your performance. Mr. O'Connor wants to promote you to district sales manager, which will mean responsibility for writing monthly sales reports as well as evaluations of over 20 salespeople. You barely made passing grades in English and are frightened at the prospect of all this writing.

1. Should you decline the promotion and try to sell more computers so that you make as much money as you would have in the new job? Explain why or why not.

2. What could you do to accept the promotion and at the same time feel comfortable with your additional writing responsibilities?

3. Mr. O'Connor has learned that you are nervous about taking the new position and is considering offering the promotion to someone else. What can you say to reassure him you can do this new job well?

M E M O R A N D U M

Date: January 6, 1991

To: George Byerson

From: Cindy Marshall   *CM*

Subject: Reserving parking spaces for staff

As you know, we have 14 employees, and the company parking lot
will accommodate 16 cars. Several of us must make calls during
the day, and when we return to the office, the lot is often full.
It appears that shoppers in the area are parking in our company
lot while they are at the mall.

I suggest that we have each employee's name painted on a small
sign and placed in front of his or her space. In addition, we
could place a larger sign at the entrance of the parking lot that
says something like "Byerson and Marshall, Inc., Parking for
Employees Only." Maybe we should add, "All other cars will be
TOWED AWAY!"

Figure 10-3   Memos are written messages to a
person or people in your own company. This
memo addresses a parking situation that affects
just company employees. How would you rewrite
this message if you were sending it to the local
police department so that they might take
action?

✓ **CHECKING UP**

1. Why are the three basic considerations
    in writing important?
2. Why is it important to spell all words
    correctly in a business letter?
3. What is the difference between a letter
    and a memo?

4 *Reading*

Reading, like listening, is a mental process of trying to understand a message. Reading with understanding is important in all phases of life. It's a necessity in most careers. In fact, it's rare for anyone to get a job without being able to read. An efficient plan for finding and applying for a job requires reading. You begin by reading the help-wanted ads. Then you read the job application forms.

The importance of good reading skills cannot be stressed too much. There are reading skills that can make understanding what you are reading easier and more meaningful. Some of these are presented here.

Previewing

You can improve your understanding by always being aware of why you are reading. Asking yourself this question will help you decide how you will read something. For example, if you're reading a job application form or a warranty on something you may buy, you read every word. You will probably even reread several sentences to be sure of their meaning.

When you know why you are reading something, you can often save time by previewing. **Previewing** means reading only those parts of a document that outline or summarize its contents.

Suppose that you work for an advertising agency. Your boss, Ms. Gordon, is planning a series of magazine ads for a company that manufactures recreational equipment. She has learned that, as we near the turn of the century, many groups are planning national campaigns with a colonial American theme.

Ms. Gordon asks you to look for information on forms of recreation in colonial America. You probably won't find any entire books on this topic, but you will find many books on recreation and other books on colonial America.

In this situation you can save yourself quite a bit of time by previewing. First, check the book title. Does it sound like it might have information on recreation in colonial America? If not, you may not even want to open the book. If it does, look at the table of contents. Most books list chapter titles, or at least the major topics covered in the book, in the

People read many different things for many different reasons. How does what a person is reading affect the way he or she reads?

table of contents. Many books have an index in the back of the book that lists most topics covered, even if they are mentioned only briefly. If what you're looking for isn't listed, then go on to another book. This is previewing.

You may find several books with chapters devoted to your subject. Some may only have part of a chapter on your topic. Other books may show one or two references to your subject in the index. By previewing the table of contents and index in this way, you can find the information you want without reading the whole book.

Skimming

Another reading skill that can save you time is skimming. **Skimming** means reading through something very quickly, picking out the key points. You are skimming when you look up words in the dictionary or read headlines in the newspaper to find articles you want to read. When your time is limited, you may also skim newspaper articles. You may skim a chapter of a book now and then.

When skimming, you will usually be looking for the topic sentence in each paragraph. The topic sentence, usually the first sentence, is the sentence that states the main idea of that paragraph. If the topic sentence is about something you already know, or if it isn't interesting, skip on to the next one. If the topic is interesting, read the whole paragraph. In this way you can read a great deal more of what you want and need to read.

Reading for Meaning

Good readers understand the message sent by the writer. Four activities that will help you better understand the writer's message are listed below.

- Focusing your mind
- Forming pictures
- Forming patterns
- Improving your vocabulary

Focusing Your Mind   Do you use a camera? You probably know that cameras must be focused in order to get a clear picture.

When we read, our minds are like cameras. They must be focused, or we will not clearly see and understand what we are reading. Focusing your mind requires constant concentration. This is why you should be constantly aware of what's on your mind. If your mind wanders from the subject you are reading, you need to refocus.

Forming Pictures   Do you imagine what you're reading? If not, try to form pictures in your mind as you read. The message may describe things, places, situations, people, or actions by certain people. When you picture the message in your mind, it becomes clearer.

Forming Patterns   Try to separate the main ideas from the details. Then, in your mind, outline the writer's organization of ideas. When you can see the relationship of ideas and details, you will have a more complete understanding of the message. The message becomes even more meaningful if you can relate the ideas, or even some details, to your own life. This will also help you remember the message longer.

Improving Your Vocabulary   As we read, we all come across words we don't know. Many times we can determine the meaning of a new word from the way it's used in a sentence or paragraph. If this doesn't work, it's important to find out what the word means. The best way to check on the meanings of words is to consult a good dictionary.

As you take your place in the world of work, you will encounter words that relate especially to the type of work you do. As you know, these words are called jargon. Whatever career field you enter, you will probably have to learn some jargon to read and understand job-related materials.

When you first begin working, you may feel a little embarrassed to ask the meaning of words. However, it is better to ask what a word means than to make a serious error in carrying out your work responsibilities.

✓ CHECKING UP

1. How can being aware of why you are reading help you improve your understanding of what you are reading?
2. How is previewing different from skimming?
3. Name the four activities that will help you understand the writer's message.

CHAPTER SUMMARY

Communication—the process of exchanging information by sending and receiving messages—is an important part of the world of work. You can improve your chances for success by developing your speaking, listening, writing, and reading skills.

People speak for three reasons—to inform, to persuade, and to entertain. You can use the techniques of enumeration, generalization followed by example, cause and effect, and comparison and contrast to organize your formal speeches. Good speaking habits include using standard English, developing and using an attractive voice, using correct enunciation and pronunciation, and not speaking either too fast or too slowly.

There are several strategies for improving your listening skills. They include recognizing the purpose of the speaker, looking for a plan, giving feedback, making distinctions, and listening for more than verbal content. Additional skills include asking questions, taking notes, listening for a conclusion, and using the dictionary. By using these strategies and avoiding the blocks to listening—distractions, emotional blocks, and planning a response—you can become a better listener.

There are several advantages to writing messages rather than speaking them. Writing helps you organize your thoughts, it provides a lasting record of your message, and it helps initiate action. Good writing skills include spelling correctly, using correct grammar, getting to the point, organizing ideas logically, and rereading and rewriting what you've written. Three things to consider before you write anything are your reader, your purpose, and your subject. It's best to write in a friendly, conversational style unless your company executives prefer a more formal style. Your writing will primarily be in the form of letters, memos, and reports.

You can improve your reading skills by making sure you know why you are reading. Then you can use such techniques as previewing and skimming to save time and find the information you need. Focusing your mind, forming pictures, forming patterns, and improving your vocabulary are four techniques that will help you read for meaning.

TERMS TO KNOW

On a separate sheet of paper, write sentences for each of the following terms:

communication
inflection
pronunciation
enunciation
feedback
jargon
previewing
skimming

STUDY QUESTIONS

1. What is the main purpose of most conversations?
2. Why should you use standard English on the job?
3. What are four techniques that make a speaking voice attractive?
4. Name three good speaking habits.
5. What is the difference between hearing and listening?
6. List nine strategies that will help you improve your listening.
7. What are two things that can cause emotional blocks to listening?
8. Describe five good writing skills.
9. Name at least three advantages of a written message over a spoken message.
10. Name the three common considerations in every kind of writing.

11. What are the three most common forms of writing in business?
12. What question can you ask yourself that will help you improve your understanding when reading?

CRITICAL THINKING

1. You have been asked to speak to some of the older adults in your community about sponsoring a new recreation center. What might you say to them? What plan would you use?
2. A fairly well-known jazz guitar player is speaking at a local college about jazz guitar techniques. He has recently released a new CD, and you suspect he will just be trying to promote it. If you are very interested in learning more about guitar techniques, which listening skills can you use to get the most from his talk?
3. Your sister has been asked to write a report on a new procedure she has developed at work. When she has finished, she asks you to critique the report. What will you look for?
4. Your civics teacher has asked you to compare and contrast two candidates running for governor. While researching this report, how would you use previewing and skimming?

DISCUSSION STARTERS

1. How do you rate yourself as a listener? What makes listening difficult for you? How could you improve?
2. How do you rate yourself as a reader? What makes reading for meaning difficult for you? How could you improve?
3. How do the qualities of a good listener compare with the qualities of a good friend?
4. You've been invited to study at a friend's house, but you know she studies and watches television at the same time. Do you think this practice might affect your work? Why or why not?
5. Which of the four primary communication skills do you think is most important in the world of work? Explain.

BUILDING BASIC SKILLS

Math
1. Suzy is very excited about her new job as an assistant clerk for a public relations firm. She must send out 75 letters every day for the next three weeks. If she works five days a week, how many letters will she have sent out at the end of three weeks?

Communication
2. As correspondence secretary for your school's FHA chapter, you have been asked to write letters of invitation to the club's annual spring picnic. The list of people to invite includes teachers, alumni, and local business people. Write a short letter including all the necessary information.

Human Relations
3. In your job you supervise five employees. Two of them, Lucy and Michael, are good friends and seem to talk to each other in a language all their own. Other employees have become confused about their responsibilities after talking to Lucy or Michael. Your entire group works well together, and you don't want to embarrass anyone. What would you say and to whom in order to encourage better communication among your employees?

SUGGESTED ACTIVITIES

1. Select a product you would like to know more about. Then write a letter requesting information about the product.
2. Listen to ten or more TV commercials. Then write down everything you can remember about the products advertised in four of them.
3. Ask a worker how communication skills are important on his or her job. Note some specific examples of how this worker uses these skills, and prepare a short oral report.
4. There are hundreds of books written about different aspects of the world of work. Ask your teacher or librarian for suggestions and pick a book to read. Write a short report on what you learned.

Math Skills

*I*n the first ten chapters, we've discussed many kinds of skills needed to choose a career, find and apply for a job, and be successful on the job. You may feel that employers expect a great deal from their workers, and they do.

In a recent survey employers said that more than anything else new workers needed better math skills. Almost all careers require a good understanding of basic math. Almost all workers must have the ability to calculate simple problems quickly and accurately.

In this chapter, we will review the basic arithmetic skills you need to be successful on the job. We will also look at a few ways in which you will use these skills in the world of work.

1 *Reviewing Basic Skills*

Most of what you are about to read, you have already learned. Use this section as a review of your basic skills and a self-check for weaknesses. If some part of the review gives you trouble, you probably need to get help from a teacher or other qualified person. These basic math skills must be automatic in the world of work.

Case Study 1

DeEtta and Jean were friends all through high school. They often studied math together, especially when a test was coming up. At home around the dining room table, both girls were able to do the problems they thought might be on the next test. When test day came, though, DeEtta always scored higher than Jean.

During their senior year, DeEtta and Jean were both hired for part-time jobs in a fabric store. It was a busy store, and often there were lines of people with yard goods waiting to make their purchases. DeEtta was very quick with her work. Jean, though, seemed unsure of herself and made numerous errors. Afraid she might be fired, Jean asked DeEtta, "You've always been so good in math. How do you do it? How can you do all that figuring when there are a dozen people watching and waiting?"

After a moment's thought, DeEtta answered. "I never talked about it much, but I've always been afraid the stress of taking a test would make me do badly. That's why every night for four or five days before a test, I study over and over the things I've already learned. I call it 'over learning,' and it's helped me understand math so well that nothing interferes with my working out the problems. I think that's why all those customers waiting in line—here on the job—don't bother me either."

Our system of numbering is made up of ten basic symbols: 0, 1, 2, 3, 4, 5, 6, 7, 8, and 9. These numbers are called digits, and they can be com-

bined to make larger numbers, such as 36, 456, 3,914, and 14,672.

All the numbers above are called whole numbers—they are numbers that contain no fractions or decimals. Each digit in each whole number tells how many of something. Look at the number 36, for example. It's the same as 30 + 6. It's not the same as 63. The placement of each digit makes a difference.

The digit on the far right tells us the number of ones. The next digit left tells us the number of tens. Thus, in the number 36 we know there are 6 ones and 3 tens.

You sometimes need to know the names of each placement spot for digits. When writing checks for example, you must write numbers in words. To do this, you must know the placement names.

Here are some rules that will help you write whole numbers in words.

- Translate the number in groups of three digits: millions, thousands, units, and so on.

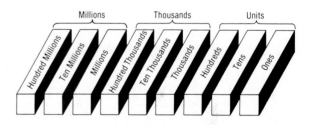

- Separate the groups with commas.

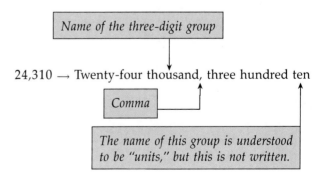

- The word *and* is never used when writing whole numbers.

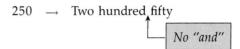

- Use hyphens in numbers less than 100 when two words are involved.

36   →   Thirty-six

> Use a hyphen.

- When a three-digit group consists of all zeros, the name of the group is not written.

2,000,115   →   Two million, one hundred fifteen

> No words appear for the thousands group.

Examples:

67   →   Sixty-seven

> Don't forget the hyphen.

346   →   Three hundred forty-six

> No "and" appears.

4,211   →   Four thousand, two hundred eleven

> A comma after "thousand"

24,006   →   Twenty-four thousand, six

> No word appears for hundreds.

Practice Set 1

Write the following whole numbers in words. DO NOT WRITE IN THIS BOOK. For all practice problems in this book, use a separate sheet of paper. Check your answers on page 206.

a. 5,010	d. 44,902	g. 7,000,015
b. 638	e. 308,012	h. 23,624,983
c. 2,007	f. 500,264	

Addition

Addition is the process of combining numbers to get a total. The total is called the **sum**. Addition is the most basic and frequently used arithmetic operation. A small symbol called a plus sign (+) indicates addition.

When adding without a calculator, arrange the numbers vertically in columns. Then use the following procedure:

- Count the number of ones in the column to the far right.
- If the column total is one digit, write it down, and go on to the next column to the left.
- If the column total is more than one digit, write down only the ones digit, and carry the number of tens or hundreds over to the next column on the left.
- Continue in this manner until all columns have been added.

Examples:

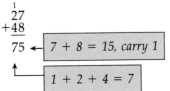

$$\begin{array}{r} 4\ 7 \\ +2\ 1 \\ \hline 6\ 8 \end{array}$$

Tens column — 4 + 2 = 6   Ones column — 7 + 1 = 8   The sum is 68.

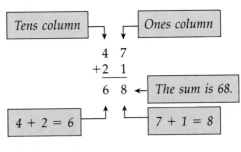

$$\begin{array}{r} \overset{1}{} \\ 27 \\ +48 \\ \hline 75 \end{array}$$

75 ← 7 + 8 = 15, carry 1

1 + 2 + 4 = 7

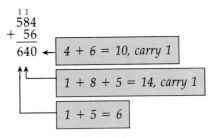

$$\begin{array}{r} \overset{1\ 1}{} \\ 584 \\ +\ 56 \\ \hline 640 \end{array}$$

640 ← 4 + 6 = 10, carry 1

1 + 8 + 5 = 14, carry 1

1 + 5 = 6

Practice Set 2

Add these numbers. Remember—DO NOT WRITE IN YOUR BOOK.

36	16	46	58	75
+45	+38	+29	+69	+49
417	864	219	765	436
+266	+916	+784	+544	+988

Check your answers on page 206. If you missed more than two, ask your teacher to watch you add a few numbers to determine where you are having difficulty. The most common problems are not carrying over correctly to the next column or not knowing the combinations of basic numbers.

Practice Set 3

Check yourself by working these problems as fast as you can. How long does it take you?

2	4	4	5	6	8	7
+3	+3	+5	+3	+4	+6	+5

9	3	5	9	7	9	8
+7	+6	+7	+6	+6	+9	+4

If you really know these combinations, you should be able to answer all of them in 15 seconds. Check your answers on page 206. If you missed more than one or took more than 25 seconds, you need to practice.

Practice Set 4

If the combinations above were easy for you, do the following problems as fast as you can. Check your time.

41	16	71	67	34	19
26	29	62	91	17	82
39	71	38	43	28	76
+62	+46	+14	+22	+63	+48

87	79	58	89	78	85
66	68	95	74	99	97
47	84	89	98	87	73
+91	+76	+63	+85	+92	+98

Check your answers on page 206. If they are all correct and you finished in less than two minutes, you probably have little or no difficulty with addition. If you missed more than one answer or required more than two minutes to finish, you need practice.

Subtraction

Subtraction is the process of deducting one number from another. The result of subtracting is called the **difference.** A symbol called a minus sign

(−) located to the left of a problem indicates subtraction.

When subtracting without a calculator, arrange the numbers vertically in columns with the larger number on top. Then use the following procedure.

- Begin with the ones. If the bottom number is less than the top number, subtract and go to the next column to the left.
- If the bottom number is larger than the top number, borrow 10 from the next column to the left. To borrow, make the top number of the next column one less and add 10 to the number from which you are subtracting.
- Continue this procedure until all columns have been subtracted.

Examples:

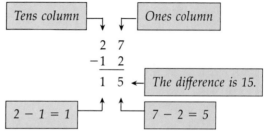

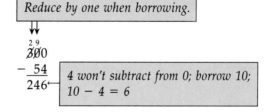

Practice Set 5

Subtract these numbers.

29	38	46	52	47
−15	−21	−36	−23	−29

114	165	258	753	641
− 90	−146	−199	−545	−155

Check your answers on page 206. If you missed more than two, ask your teacher to watch you subtract to determine where you are having difficulty. The most common problems are not borrowing correctly or not knowing the differences of basic numbers.

Practice Set 6

   Check yourself by working these problems as fast as you can. How long does it take you?

8	7	9	16	13	18	14
−2	−5	−5	−7	−9	−9	−8

12	15	17	13	11	16	17
−8	−9	−8	−6	−4	−8	−9

If you really know these basic differences, you should be able to answer all of them in 20 seconds. Check your answers on page 206. If you missed more than one or took more than 30 seconds, you need to practice.

Practice Set 7

   If the subtraction of the basic numbers above was easy for you, subtract these numbers as fast as you can. Check your time.

86	75	95	115	250	160	500	75
−50	−66	−54	− 85	−165	−145	−155	−48

47	85	66	758	315	130	404	80
−39	−36	−27	−169	−255	− 95	−135	−18

Check your answers on page 206. If they are all correct and you finished in less than one minute, you will have no difficulty with subtraction. If you missed more than one answer or required more than one minute to finish, you need to practice subtraction.

Multiplication

   Multiplication is actually a shorthand way of adding. For example, you could add 361 + 361 + 361 + 361 + 361 + 361 + 361 and get 2,527. You could also multiply 361 by 7 and get the same answer. In multiplication the answer is called the **product.**

When multiplying without a calculator, arrange the numbers vertically. Then use the following procedure:

- Begin by multiplying the ones digit of the top number by the ones digit of the bottom number.
- If the product is a one-digit number, write it down. If the product is a two-digit number, write down only the ones digit. Then, after the next multiplication, add the tens digit of this number to the new product.
- Multiply the tens digit of the top number by the ones digit of the bottom number.
- Continue this procedure until each digit of the top number has been multiplied by the ones digit of the bottom number.
- If multiplying by a two-digit or larger number, multiply each digit of the top number by the tens digit of the bottom number using the same procedure you used before. The only difference is that in writing down the product you must indent your answer one digit to the left. In other words, the ones digit of this product is placed under the tens digit of the first product.
- Continue multiplying until all top digits have been multiplied by each digit of the bottom number. Continue indenting each new product one place to the left.
- Add all products together to get the final answer.

Examples:

```
   4              1 4
 361            526
× 7           × 71
2,527           526
               3682
              37,346
```

Practice Set 8

   Multiply the numbers below.

35	41	55	73	96	68	125
× 8	× 6	× 7	× 5	× 4	× 9	× 3

85	37	75	174	213	389	768
×12	×16	×25	× 38	× 47	× 96	× 35

Check your answers on page 206. If you missed more than three, ask your teacher to watch you multiply some numbers to determine where you are having difficulty. Multiplication is harder than either addition or subtraction. The most common problem is not knowing the multiplication tables.

Practice Set 9

Check yourself on the multiplication tables by multiplying the numbers below as fast as you can. How long does it take you?

5	7	6	4	9	8	3	9	7
×4	×3	×8	×7	×5	×7	×5	×4	×5

6	7	4	9	6	9	3	9	8
×7	×7	×6	×7	×9	×8	×9	×9	×8

If you really know these combinations, you should be able to answer all of them in 20 seconds. Check your answers on page 206. If you missed more than two or took more than 30 seconds, you need to work on the multiplication tables.

Practice Set 10

If the combinations above were easy for you, multiply these numbers as fast as you can. Check your time.

654	395	506	419	725	386	853
× 37	× 24	× 34	× 25	× 36	× 21	× 74

742	905	186	614	372	125	498
× 16	× 37	× 79	× 83	×145	×346	×125

Check your answers on page 206. If they are all correct and you finished in less than six minutes, you will have no difficulty with multiplication. If you missed more than two or took more than ten minutes, you need to practice multiplying.

Division

Division is the reverse of multiplication. By dividing a number, you can separate it into equal parts. The answer to a division problem is called the **quotient.**

Suppose you wish to divide 273 into 21 equal parts. You would use the following procedure:

- Place the number to be divided (273, called the dividend) inside the division sign and the number by which you will be dividing (21, called the divisor) outside the division sign. (See below.)
- Try to find a number you can multiply by the divisor to get a number that is equal to or slightly less than the dividend. Begin by finding digits on the *left* side of the dividend that form a number equal to or slightly larger than the divisor. For example, 21 goes into 27 one time, so 1 is placed at the top of the division sign over 27. You would then multiply 1×21, place this product, 21, under 27 and subtract. Bring down the next number to the right, which is 3, and start the process again.
- If the product is equal to the dividend, you have completed the division problem. If the product is less than the dividend, subtract, and place the difference over the divisor to make a fraction. This fraction then becomes part of the quotient.

Examples:

$$
\begin{array}{r}
13 \\
21\overline{)273} \\
21 \quad \leftarrow 21 \times 1 \\
\hline
63 \\
63 \quad \leftarrow 21 \times 3 \\
\hline
0
\end{array}
$$

$$
\begin{array}{r}
307 \\
15\overline{)4605} \\
45 \quad \leftarrow 15 \times 3 \\
\hline
10 \\
0 \quad \leftarrow 15 \times 0 \\
\hline
105 \\
105 \quad \leftarrow 15 \times 7 \\
\hline
0
\end{array}
$$

$$
\begin{array}{r}
2014\frac{9}{36} = 2{,}014\frac{1}{4} \\
36\overline{)72513} \\
72 \quad \leftarrow 36 \times 2 \\
\hline
5 \\
0 \quad \leftarrow 36 \times 0 \\
\hline
51 \\
36 \quad \leftarrow 36 \times 1 \\
\hline
153 \\
144 \quad \leftarrow 36 \times 4 \\
\hline
9
\end{array}
$$

Practice Set 11
  Divide these numbers.

  $6\overline{)54}$ $7\overline{)42}$ $9\overline{)108}$ $8\overline{)56}$ $12\overline{)96}$ $13\overline{)273}$

  $16\overline{)128}$ $19\overline{)475}$ $24\overline{)264}$ $35\overline{)630}$ $46\overline{)1,430}$ $18\overline{)220}$

Check your answers on page 206. If you missed more than two, ask your teacher to watch you divide some numbers to determine where you are having difficulty.

MAKE A DECISION

You like your job as a salesclerk in a clothing store because you enjoy talking to all the people and you like clothes. You were never very good at math, though, and you seem to be constantly embarrassing yourself by making mistakes in figuring sales totals. You don't want to take a basic math course or ask someone to tutor you, but you'll quit your job rather than continue to make so many simple mistakes. What's your choice—a new job without so much math or relearning some basic arithmetic? Give the reasons for your decision.

Fractions

Fractions are numbers used to describe a part of some standard amount. For example, the shaded area in this rectangle is 3/5 (three-fifths) of the total rectangle.

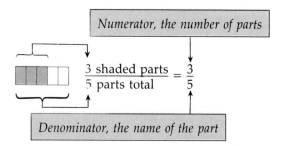

Numerator, the number of parts

$$\frac{3 \text{ shaded parts}}{5 \text{ parts total}} = \frac{3}{5}$$

Denominator, the name of the part

It is especially important that you understand fractions since most calculators cannot work with them. This means you will have to do all computations involving fractions on your own or convert them to a form calculators can use.

Examples:

Write a fraction to describe the shaded part of each of the following.

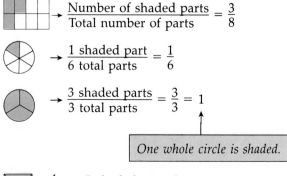

$$\rightarrow \frac{\text{Number of shaded parts}}{\text{Total number of parts}} = \frac{3}{8}$$

$$\rightarrow \frac{1 \text{ shaded part}}{6 \text{ total parts}} = \frac{1}{6}$$

$$\rightarrow \frac{3 \text{ shaded parts}}{3 \text{ total parts}} = \frac{3}{3} = 1$$

One whole circle is shaded.

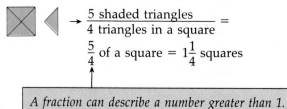

$$\rightarrow \frac{5 \text{ shaded triangles}}{4 \text{ triangles in a square}} =$$

$$\frac{5}{4} \text{ of a square} = 1\frac{1}{4} \text{ squares}$$

A fraction can describe a number greater than 1.

Practice Set 12
  For each group below, what fraction of the total number of shapes are triangles?

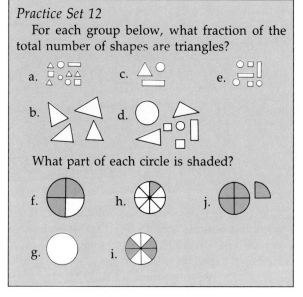

What part of each circle is shaded?

Check your answers on page 206.

Decimal Numbers

On some jobs it is necessary to add, subtract, or multiply fractions. In some cases it may even be necessary to divide fractions. It is much easier, however, to perform these operations if the fraction is first converted to a decimal number. A

decimal number is a fraction or mixed number (whole number and fraction together) whose denominator is a multiple of ten. If you are using a calculator, converting to decimals is probably the only way you can do the problem.

To convert a fraction to a decimal number, divide the numerator (top number) by the denominator (bottom number). For example, to convert 1/4 to its decimal equivalent, divide the 1 by 4.

$$
\begin{array}{r}
.25 \\
4\overline{)1.00} \\
\underline{8} \\
20 \\
\underline{20}
\end{array}
$$

Decimal numbers are very important in the world of work. On many jobs you might use a conversion table to look up the decimal equivalents of common fractions. If you know how to convert fractions to decimals, however, you will not need to depend on a table.

Reading and Writing Decimal Numbers

A decimal number is sometimes called a decimal fraction. The decimal number 3.7 is

$$3 + .7 \text{ or } 3 + \frac{7}{10} \text{ or } 3\frac{7}{10}.$$

You say and write decimal numbers in much the same way you would whole numbers. The decimal number 935.47 can be broken down as follows:

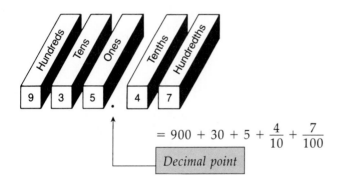

$$= 900 + 30 + 5 + \frac{4}{10} + \frac{7}{100}$$

Decimal point

To find the name in words of any given decimal place, follow this procedure:

- Write zeros under each digit to the right of the decimal point.
- Write a 1 directly under the decimal point.

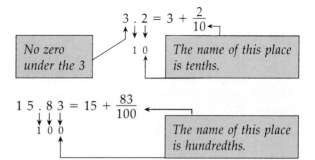

To read or write a decimal number in words, follow the procedure below. Use 15.83 as an example.

- Write the number to the left of the decimal point as whole number (fifteen).
- Write *and* for the decimal point.
- Write the number to the right of the decimal point as a whole number (eighty-three).
- Write the name of the decimal place of the right end digit (hundredths).

The result is fifteen and eighty-three hundredths.

Examples:

3.6 → | *Three and six-tenths* |

324.57 → | *Three hundred twenty-four and fifty-seven hundredths* |

The sum of money $324.57 would be written on a check as follows:

Three hundred twenty-four and 57/100

> **Practice Set 13**
> Write these decimal numbers in words. Check your answers on page 207.
>
> | | | |
> |---|---|---|
> | a. 6.7 | e. 2.13 | h. 38.59 |
> | b. 0.9 | f. 8.09 | i. $201.38 |
> | c. 15.3 | g. 12.44 | j. $338.97 |
> | d. 0.05 | | |

Adding or Subtracting Decimal Numbers

To add or subtract decimal numbers, first line up the numbers vertically. Make sure you keep the decimal points in the same vertical column. Then add or subtract, the same as you would with whole numbers.

Examples:

1.45 + 3.4 = ?

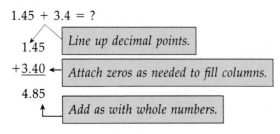

13.4 − 7.56 = ?

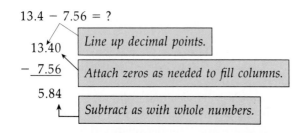

Practice Set 14
Do the following addition and subtraction problems with decimal numbers. Check your answers on page 207.

a. 4.2 + 7.3 =
b. 5.6 + 9.1 =
c. 8.8 + 6.7 =
d. 23 + 5.8 =
e. 15.6 + 3.67 =
f. 5.08 + 67.2 =
g. 0.6 + 1.44 + 3 =
h. 3.8 − 2.6 =
i. $4 − $3.68 =
j. 32.7 − 6.45 =
k. 19.4 − 7.361 =
l. 12.37 − .055 =

m. In August, Yolanda's Ice Cream Shop paid $44.38 for electricity, $32.79 for telephone service, $38.16 for insurance, and $450 for rent. What was her total for these expenses?
n. From a 16-meter length of wire, an electrician cut two pieces 3.86 meters and 8.27 meters long. How much wire was left?

Multiplying Decimal Numbers To multiply decimal numbers, use the following two-step procedure.

- Multiply the two numbers as if they were whole numbers. Pay no attention to the decimal points yet.
- Add the number of decimal places in the two numbers being multiplied. Then, starting from the right, count off this number of decimal places in the product. Insert the decimal point.

Examples:

3.2 × 0.41 = ?

$$\begin{array}{r} 3.2 \\ \times .41 \\ \hline 32 \\ 128 \\ \hline 1312 \rightarrow 1.312 \end{array}$$

3.2 ← 3.2 has one decimal place.
.41 ← .41 has two decimal places.

Answer must have three decimal places.

9.05 ×. 4.31 = ?

$$\begin{array}{r} 9.05 \\ \times 4.31 \\ \hline 905 \\ 2715 \\ 3620 \\ \hline 390055 \rightarrow 39.0055 \end{array}$$

9.05 ← 9.05 has two decimal places.
4.31 ← 4.31 has two decimal places.

Answer must have four decimal places.

Practice Set 15
Do the following multiplication problems with decimal numbers. Check your answers on page 207.

$$\begin{array}{r} 4.1 \\ \times\ 8 \end{array} \qquad \begin{array}{r} 7.4 \\ \times 5.1 \end{array} \qquad \begin{array}{r} 23.4 \\ \times\ 9.8 \end{array}$$

$$\begin{array}{r} 4.05 \\ \times 0.86 \end{array} \qquad \begin{array}{r} 3.96 \\ \times\ 2.3 \end{array} \qquad \begin{array}{r} 0.723 \\ \times\ 6.01 \end{array}$$

3.5 × 8.7 =   0.63 × 0.02 =

a. If you earn $6.27 per hour, how much pay should you receive for 38 hours of work?
b. At Dante's Pizza Place, the estimated cost of delivering orders is $.42 per mile. If the delivery van averaged 329.8 miles per day last week, what is the average daily cost of making deliveries?

Dividing Decimal Numbers Division of decimal numbers is similar to the division of whole numbers. Follow the steps below to divide decimal numbers.

- Set up the division problem as you would with whole numbers.

69.7 divided by 1.7 $= 1.7\overline{)69.7}$

- Shift the decimal point in the divisor so that it becomes a whole number. Then shift the decimal point in the dividend the same number of decimal places.

$1.7\overline{)69.7} \rightarrow 17.\overline{)697.}$

Shift the decimal point one place to the right.

- Place a decimal point in the answer space directly above its new position in the dividend. Then divide as with whole numbers.

$17\overline{)697.}$

$$\begin{array}{r} 41. \\ 17\overline{)697.} \\ \underline{68} \\ 17 \\ \underline{17} \\ 0 \end{array}$$

Examples:

$16.38 \div 6.5$

$$\begin{array}{r} 2.52 \\ 6.5\overline{)16.380} \\ \underline{130} \\ 338 \\ \underline{325} \\ 130 \\ \underline{130} \\ 0 \end{array}$$

Attach an extra zero if necessary.

$65 \times 2 = 130$

$65 \times 5 = 325$

$65 \times 2 = 130$

$8.91 \div 0.054$

$$\begin{array}{r} 165. \\ 0.054\overline{)8.910} \\ \underline{54} \\ 351 \\ \underline{324} \\ 270 \\ \underline{270} \\ 0 \end{array}$$

Attach an extra zero.

$54 \times 1 = 54$

$54 \times 6 = 324$

$54 \times 5 = 270$

SITUATION
SOLUTION

Underpaid!

You open your pay envelope one week to find you have been paid for only 17 hours, although you worked 21. When you ask your supervisor about it, he shows you your time card. Apparently you forgot to clock in and out one day. The supervisor, who has never been friendly to you, remembers your being at work that day, but he says if you don't clock in you don't get paid.

1. There is a grievance committee at the store that you could appeal to, but you are sure your supervisor would be really hard on you if you did. Will you appeal? Why or why not?
2. You have the opportunity to speak to the district manager about your paycheck without your supervisor's knowledge. What do you say to her?
3. Others at work say they will punch in for you an hour early all next week to make up the difference. You think you could get away with it. Will you let them do it? Explain your answer.

Practice Set 16

Do the following division problems with decimal numbers. Check your answers on page 207.

$0.57 \div 1.9 =$ $3.78 \div 2.8 =$

$1.573 \div 4.84 =$ $9.6 \div 0.016 =$

$0.036 \div 1.2 =$ $6.004 \div 0.2 =$

a. The HMS Corp. paid $253.64 for printer paper. If the paper costs $7.46 per box, how many boxes did they buy?
b. Pat averages 4.7 pages per hour when typing budget tables on a word processor. How long will it take her to type 200 pages?

✓ CHECKING UP

1. If you were to make out a check for $431.26, what words would you write on the check to describe the amount?
2. What is the first step you would take if you wanted to multiply two fractions and you were using a calculator?
3. Describe the steps you would take to subtract decimal numbers.

2 *Surface and Volume Measurement*

In many jobs, you have to be able to measure surfaces and volumes. People in the carpet business, for instance, need to be able to calculate the total area of a floor surface. Builders need to know the size of the area where they will be building and the volume of concrete they must order for a foundation. The following formulas and examples will help you compute surface and volume measurements for the most common shapes.

Surface Measurements

Surface measurements measure either the distance around a shape or the area the shape covers. They are computed differently for different kinds of shapes.

Rectangles and Squares   To measure the **perimeter,** or distance around, a rectangle or square, simply add together the lengths of all four sides. The formula for this procedure is

$$P = l + l + w + w$$
or
$$P = 2 \times (l + w)$$

where P stands for perimeter, l for length, and w for width.

Example:

Find the perimeter of the rectangle below.

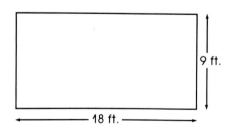

$$P = 18 + 18 + 9 + 9$$
$$P = 54 \text{ feet}$$

or

$$P = 2 \times (18 + 9)$$
$$P = 2 \times 27$$
$$P = 54 \text{ feet}$$

Because all the sides of a square are the same length, it is easy to calculate a square's perimeter. The formula you use is

$$P = 4 \times l$$

where l represents the length of one side.

Example:

Find the perimeter of the square below.

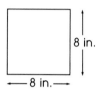

$$P = 4 \times 8$$
$$P = 32 \text{ inches}$$

Practice Set 17

Determine the perimeter of each rectangle if its dimensions are as given below. Check your answers on page 207.

a. 27 ft. long and 16 ft. wide
b. 97 in. long and 53 in. wide
c. 62 in. long and 17 in. wide
d. 7 ft. long and 4 ft. wide

Determine the perimeter of each square if the length of a side is as given below. Check your answers on page 207.

e. 4 inches   h. 76 inches
f. 10 feet   i. 33 feet
g. 14 feet   j. 104 feet

The **area** of a surface is the number of squares of a certain measure that the surface covers. If you have been measuring the length and width in feet, your area will be expressed in square feet. If you have been using inches, it will be expressed in square inches.

To compute the area of a rectangle or square, you multiply the length of one side by the length of the side next to it. The formula for the area of a rectangle is

$$A = l \times w$$

where A stands for area, l for length, and w for width.

Examples:

Find the area of the rectangle in the previous set of examples.

A = 18 × 9
A = 162 square feet

Find the area of the square in the same set of examples.

A = 8 × 8
A = 64 square inches

Practice Set 18

Using the following dimensions, determine the area of each rectangle. Check your answers on page 207.

a. 27 ft. long and 16 ft. wide
b. 97 in. long and 53 in. wide
c. 62 in. long and 17 in. wide
d. 7 ft. long and 4 ft. wide

Determine the area of each square, if the length of a side is as given below. Check your answers on page 207.

e. 4 inches   h. 76 inches
f. 10 feet   i. 33 feet
g. 14 feet   j. 104 feet

Circles Circles are slightly trickier than squares or rectangles because they are composed of a single line. This is called the **circumference** (the word we use for the perimeter of a circle). In order to compute the circumference and area of a circle, you will need to use a number called pi, which is written as π. The value of pi (π) is approximately 3.14, which represents the relationship that always exists between the circumference of a circle and its diameter. The diameter is an imaginary line that passes through both edges and the center of any circle.

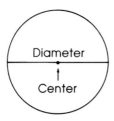

To find the circumference of a circle, multiply π by the circle's diameter. The formula is

$$C = \pi \times d$$

where C represents the circumference and d represents the diameter.

Example:

Find the circumference of a circle whose diameter is 12 inches.

C = 3.14 × 12
C = 37.68 inches

To compute the area of a circle, it is necessary to know its radius. The radius of a circle is half its diameter, or the length of a line from a point on the edge of the circle to its center.

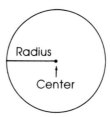

To find the area of a circle, use the following procedure:

• Multiply the length of the radius by itself. This is an operation known as squaring the number.
• Then multiply the product of that operation by pi, 3.14, to get the area.

The formula for the area of a circle is

$$A = \pi \times r^2$$

where A stands for area and r stands for radius. The superscript (the little two written above and to the right of the r) is a symbol meaning squared, or multiplied by itself.

Example:

Compute the area of a circle whose diameter is 12 inches. The radius of such a circle would be 6 inches (half of 12).

A = 3.14 × 6²
A = 3.14 × (6 × 6)
A = 3.14 × 36
A = 113.04 square inches

Strive for Success

A Mind for All Time

Though his legs are paralyzed, his mind has traveled the cosmos. Though he is unable to speak, he has communicated to us the answers to the mysteries of time. Though he cannot stand, his accomplishments rise up as testimony to his courage, his determination, and his genius.

He is Stephen Hawking, the best-selling author of *A Brief History of Time,* which was published in 1988. A victim of amyotrophic lateral sclerosis (often called Lou Gehrig's disease), Hawking is unable to move anything except his eyes and three fingers of his right hand.

His physical limitations, however, have in no way slowed down his incredible mind. His achievements have helped both scientists and laymen better understand the physical nature of our world, our universe, and even time itself.

Hawking gets around with the use of a motorized wheelchair that he steers using a joystick. This is relatively easy compared to the pains he must take to communicate. His communication is made possible through the use of a specially built word processor. This computer allows him to scan 2,600 preprogrammed words. By squeezing a switch held in his lap, he is able to choose the words he uses to construct sentences. He can operate this device at a speed of approximately ten words a minute. Once he has constructed a sentence, a built-in speaker broadcasts his words to whomever Hawking is "talking" to.

Hawking's most famous work has been on the nature of black holes. Black holes are regions in space of extremely dense matter in which gravity is so strong that nothing—not even light—can escape.

Almost as amazing as Hawking's complex work is his ability to explain it to nonscientists. "My goal," Hawking has said, "is a complete understanding of the universe, why it is as it is and why it exists at all." Despite his physical condition, Hawking has moved us all a little closer toward his goal.

Check your answers on page 207.

Volume Measurements

Surface measurements, as their name implies, measure flat surfaces. **Volume** measurements, on the other hand, measure the space inside various shapes—like shoe boxes, soft drink cans, basketballs, and even whole rooms. While a surface has two dimensions, length and width, it has no depth. A shape that has volume will always have depth. It has three dimensions, not two.

The most common shapes for which we measure volume are cubes and other rectangular boxes. A cube is a box whose length, width, and depth are all the same—each of its sides is a square. To find the volume of a cube or other rectangular box (how much it will hold), we multiply the length by the width to find the area of one side. Then we multiply that number by the height. The answer is expressed in cubic units, such as cubic inches, cubic feet, or cubic yards. The formula for computing the volume of a rectangular box is

$$V = l \times w \times h$$

where V stands for volume, l for length, w for width, and h for height.

Examples:

Compute the volume of the box below.

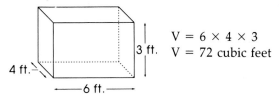

$V = 6 \times 4 \times 3$
$V = 72$ cubic feet

Compute the volume of the cube below.

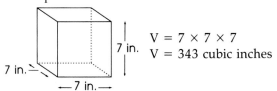

$V = 7 \times 7 \times 7$
$V = 343$ cubic inches

Another formula used only for cubes is

$$V = l^3$$

where V stands for volume, l for the length of each side, and the superscript (3) for cubed (or multiplied by itself twice).

To find the volume of a cylinder, such as a soft drink can or an oil drum, you must first find the area of the circle that is one end of the cylinder. Then you multiply that number by the height of the cylinder. The formula for this is

$$V = \pi \times r^2 \times h$$

where V represents the volume, r the radius, and h the height.

Example:

Compute the volume of the tank below. Since the tank has a diameter of 12 feet, its radius is 6 feet.

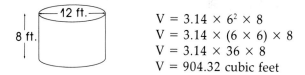

$V = 3.14 \times 6^2 \times 8$
$V = 3.14 \times (6 \times 6) \times 8$
$V = 3.14 \times 36 \times 8$
$V = 904.32$ cubic feet

There are formulas for finding the volumes of many other shapes, but these are the ones you are most likely to need in the working world.

✓ CHECKING UP

1. How is the perimeter of a square or rectangle determined?
2. How is the circumference of a circle computed?
3. What is the difference between surface and volume measurements?

3 *Using a Calculator*

Calculators have become essential tools for workers in almost every occupation—from order clerks to engineers, from tellers to bank presidents. If you are to use a calculator correctly in your work, you must be able to do the following:

- Multiply and add one-digit numbers quickly and correctly
- Read and write any whole number, decimal number, or fraction
- Convert fractions to decimal numbers
- Estimate answers and check your work

You may wonder about the importance of estimating an answer before doing a problem. The value of an estimate is in knowing whether an answer is reasonable. If you were multiplying 3 × 4, you would know that 120 was not a reasonable answer. If you were multiplying much larger numbers, however, you might not notice an unreasonable answer. A very good rule—especially when using a calculator—is never to work an arithmetic problem until you know roughly what the answer will be. Use the following "Guess 'n Check" method:

- Estimate the answer.
- Work the problem.
- Check your answer by comparing it with the estimate. If the answer and estimate are far apart, repeat all three steps.

Examples:

387
+998
1,385 ← | Estimate: 400 + 1,000 = 1,400

Check: 1,385 is roughly equal to 1,400. The answer is reasonable.

87
+244
331 ← | Estimate: 100 + 200 = 300

Check: 331 is roughly equal to 300.

Here are a few hints to help you use your calculator effectively.

- Always check the display after you have entered a number and before you have entered the operation to be certain you are using the correct number. If you have made a key-press error, use the "clear entry" key ([CE] or [C])

to remove this last entry. For example, if you wanted to enter 3.8 × 1.2 but you mistakenly entered ③ [.] ⑧ [×] [.] ① ②, pressing [CE] will delete the last three key strokes. You can reenter the second number. The first number will remain in the calculator work area. Press the [=] key and the answer will be displayed [**4.56**].

- Always estimate your answer before you do the calculation. In the problem given above you would estimate that the correct answer is about 4 × 1, or 4. If you had not noticed the key-press error, the calculator would display [**0.456**]. Your estimate would be an immediate warning that something was wrong.

- Don't worry about leading zeros (those to the left of the decimal point, as in 0.5 or 0.664) or final zeros after the decimal point, (those as in 4.70 or 32.500). You need not enter these. The calculator will display all the digits needed.

Number	Enter	Display
0.5	[.] ⑤	0.5
0.664	[.] ⑥ ⑥ ④	0.664
4.70	④ [.] ⑦	4.7
32.500	③ ② [.] ⑤	32.5

- Express fractions in decimal form. Divide the numerator by the denominator before entering. For example, 4 1/4 is entered as [**4.25**], and 5 2/3 is entered as [**5.6666667**].

- When you solve a problem using a calculator, the display will usually *not* give the answer in a finished form. You must often interpret the answer. For example, if you solve a business problem that requires an answer in dollars, you would have to interpret the display as indicated below.

Display	Answer
3.2	$3.20
23.462012	$23.46 *(rounded to the nearest cent)*
35.027	$35.03 *(rounded to the nearest cent)*
14250.2	$14,250.20

- A calculator can operate on only two numbers at a time. You can, however, perform a long and involved string of calculations on more than two numbers without pausing, if you are careful. The calculator will do them in order as the numbers are entered.

Example:

4.1 $\boxed{+}$ .72 $\boxed{+}$ 12.68 $\boxed{-}$ 5.032 $\boxed{=}$ → $\boxed{\textbf{12.468}}$

450 $\boxed{\times}$ .81 $\boxed{\div}$ 4 $\boxed{\times}$ 1.2 $\boxed{=}$ → $\boxed{\textbf{109.35}}$

21 $\boxed{\div}$ 3 $\boxed{\times}$ 13 $\boxed{-}$ 38 $\boxed{=}$ → $\boxed{\textbf{53.}}$

Practice Set 21

Work these problems using a calculator. Check your answers on page 207.

a. The Candy Shop paid $8,813 for a shipment of 27 storage cases, each one the same model. Find the cost of each case.

b. If weekly sales receipts for the Turner Gas Station are $1,875.37, $3,168.19, and $2,046.82, what income is needed in the fourth week to meet a four-week goal of $10,000?

c. Find the cost of 435.8 gallons of truck fuel at $1.13 per gallon, rounded to the nearest cent.

d. What is Rueben's pay on a construction job if he works 28 3/4 hours per week for six weeks at an hourly rate of $7.46 per hour?

Working with Percentages

The word **percent** comes from a Latin word meaning "by the hundred" or "for every hundred." A number expressed as a percent is being compared to some standard divided into 100 parts.

For example, suppose you wanted to give 25 percent of your birthday cake to your best friend. This would mean that if the cake were divided into 100 parts, you would give your friend 25 of the parts. A certain percent is a certain part of a whole, using 100 total parts as a basis for comparison.

To write a decimal number or whole number as a percent, multiply it by 100 and add a percent sign. This is equivalent to moving the decimal point two places to the *right*.

Examples:

0.60 = 0.60 × 100 = 60%   or   0.60 = 60.%
0.02 = 0.02 × 100 = 2%   or   0.02 = 2.%
3.4 = 3.4 × 100 = 340%   or   3.40 = 340.%

To write a fraction as a percent, first write it in decimal form (using your calculator if necessary). Then multiply by 100 and add a percent sign.

Examples:

$\dfrac{1}{2}$ = 0.5 → 0.5 × 100 = 50%

$\dfrac{3}{20}$ → 3 $\boxed{\div}$ 20 $\boxed{=}$ → $\boxed{\textbf{0.15}}$
→ 0.15 × 100 = 15%

$2\dfrac{3}{8}$ → 3 $\boxed{\div}$ 8 $\boxed{+}$ 2 $\boxed{=}$ → $\boxed{\textbf{2.375}}$
→ 2.375 × 100 = 237.5%

$\dfrac{2}{3}$ → 2 $\boxed{\div}$ 3 $\boxed{=}$ → $\boxed{\textbf{0.6666667}}$
→ 0.6666667 × 100 = 66.66667% or 66.7%

To change percentages to decimal numbers, divide the percentage by 100. This is equivalent to moving the decimal point two places to the *left*.

Examples:

14.8%   14.8 $\boxed{\div}$ 100 $\boxed{=}$ → $\boxed{\textbf{0.148}}$
or 14.8% = .148

1.5%   1.5 $\boxed{\div}$ 100 $\boxed{=}$ → $\boxed{\textbf{0.015}}$
or 01.5% = .015

$9\dfrac{3}{4}$%   3 $\boxed{\div}$ 4 $\boxed{+}$ 9 $\boxed{\div}$ 100 $\boxed{=}$ → $\boxed{\textbf{0.0975}}$
or 09.75 = .0975

$\boxed{\textit{Write the fraction as a decimal.}}$

Practice Set 22

Write each of these numbers as a percent.

0.25	0.06	0.7	2.7
0.98	2.16	0.01	4.75

Write each of these fractions as a percent.

$\dfrac{3}{4}$	$\dfrac{9}{10}$	$2\dfrac{3}{25}$	$\dfrac{7}{8}$	$\dfrac{5}{6}$

Write these percents as decimal numbers.

10%	6%	2.5%	$6\dfrac{1}{2}$%
$12\dfrac{3}{4}$%	120%	200%	0.5%

Check your answers on page 207.

Percent Problems

When percent problems appear in on-the-job situations, they do not come neatly packaged with careful instructions, as they do in textbooks. This means that you must first be able to understand the problem. You must then set it up in a mathematical form and solve it. In this section we will review a few of the basic concepts and typical uses of percent in business.

For example, if you earn $8.74 per hour and receive a 4 percent raise, by how much will your pay be increased? To solve the problem, follow this procedure:

- *Estimate the answer.* Ten percent of $8 is 80 cents. Since 4 percent is less than half of 10 percent, the answer will be about half of that, or 40 cents.
- *Translate the problem into a math statement.*

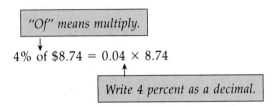

"Of" means multiply.

4% of $8.74 = 0.04 × 8.74

Write 4 percent as a decimal.

- *Do the arithmetic with a calculator.*

0.04 ⊗ 8.74 ⊜ → **0.3496**

- *Round the answer to the nearest cent, and check it against your estimate.* The pay raise is 35 cents per hour.

Examples:

Find 73 percent of 285.

Estimate: 70 percent of 300 is 210.

0.73 ⊗ 285 ⊜ → **208.05**

If the sales tax on a purchase is 6 1/2 percent, what tax would you pay on a camera costing $129.95?

Estimate: This is a tax of about 6¢ on each dollar, or $6 on $100. The tax will be a bit over $6.

$6\frac{1}{2}$% of 129.95 = 0.065 ⊗ 129.95 ⊜
→ **8.44675**

The tax would be $8.45.

To improve sales, merchants often sell items at less than their regular, or list, price. The amount of money subtracted from the list price is called a discount. The discount is usually given as a percentage of the list price. By subtracting this percent from the list price you arrive at the sale price.

Example:

A bicycle regularly priced at $159.75 is advertised for sale at 35 percent off. What is its sale price?

- *Estimate the answer.* Thirty-five percent is about one-third, and one-third of $150 is $50. Subtracting $50 from $150 leaves about $100.
- *Write 35 percent as a decimal.*

35 ÷ 100 ⊜ → **0.35**

- *Figure the discount.*

0.35 ⊗ 159.75 ⊜ → **55.9125**

The discount would be $55.91.

- *Figure the sale price.*

159.75 ⊖ 55.91 ⊜ → **103.84**

The sale price would be $103.84.

Salespeople are often paid on the basis of their success at selling. They receive a commission, which is a fee they are paid for their work. Commissions are usually figured as a percentage of the salesperson's total sales.

Example:

The Happy John Used Car Company pays each salesperson a 4.5 percent commission on his or her sales. If you were a salesperson for Happy John, what commission would you expect to receive on weekly sales of $7,240.63?

- *Estimate the answer.* Ten percent, or one-tenth, of $7,000 is $700. Since 4.5 percent is about half of 10 percent, you should get about half of $700, or $350.

MAKE A DECISION

Suppose you are offered a choice between two sales jobs. Both jobs involve about the same kind of work. One pays a salary of $1,500 a month. The other pays a salary of $800 a month plus a commission of 5 percent of sales. Other salespeople average between $7,500 and $15,000 in sales per month. What's your decision—the straight salary or the salary and commission? Give the reasons for your decision.

Percentages are a part of many jobs in the service sector. What role do they play in this job? How would they most likely be figured?

• *Calculate the commission.*

0.045 ⊗ 7240.63 ⊜ → 325.82835

The commission would be $325.83.

In Chapter 18, you will read about the money banks pay on savings accounts and collect on loans. These payments are called interest. Interest is usually expressed as a percentage. A bank loan might involve a 15 percent per year interest payment, while a credit card loan might require 1.75 percent interest per month.

You will learn more about how interest works in Chapter 18. Here you will do a few practice problems. The formula for figuring interest is

$$I = p \times r \times t$$

where I stands for interest, p for principal, r for rate, and t for time.

Example:

Calculate the interest on a loan of $725 at 14.6 percent interest repaid over two years.

• *Estimate the answer.* The rate, 14.6 percent, is about one-seventh. Therefore, the interest will

be about one-seventh of $700, or $100, per year, or a total of $200.

• *Write 14.6 percent as a decimal.*

14.6 ⊘ 100 ⊜ → .146

• *Calculate the interest.*

725 ⊗ 0.146 ⊗ 2 ⊜ → 211.7

⬑ *Time in years*

The interest is $211.70.

Practice Set 23

Do the following problems involving interest. Check your answers on page 207.

a. A VCR that sells for $565 is reduced in cost by 20 percent. What is the new selling price?
b. If Murphy's Ice Cream Store borrows $4,580 at 16 1/2 percent interest for one year, how much interest must they pay?
c. Calculate the commission that a salesperson will receive for selling ten rowing machines at $286.90 each if the company pays a 40 percent commission.
d. How much will be discounted off a car that has a list price of $8,695 and a discount rate of 18 1/4 percent?
e. Roberto earns a 9 percent commission on his weekly sales. What was his commission for a week in which he sold $2,847.65 of merchandise?
f. What is the interest on a loan of $750 at 14 1/2 percent to be repaid in one year?
g. Figure the interest on a car loan of $5,900 at 16 3/4 percent to be repaid in three years.

✓ **CHECKING UP**

1. Describe four things that will help you use your calculator more effectively.
2. How would you estimate a 45 percent increase in bus fares that have been $.80?
3. Describe the steps to calculate the price of a pair of $55 jeans now discounted 30 percent.

4 *English and Metric Measurements*

The system of measurement that we use most often in the United States is called the English system. It includes the common measures we all had to memorize in elementary school—pints, quarts, inches, feet, miles, and so forth. In the rest of the world, however, the most common system of measurement is the metric system.

Metric measurement is based on the decimal system and is therefore much simpler to learn than the English system. The U.S. government has made a commitment to change to the metric system eventually. You may already have seen road signs showing distances in both miles and kilometers. The latter is a metric measurement. Also, look at the volume measurement the next time you buy a soft drink in a can or bottle. Chances are it will be in milliliters, another metric amount. Scientists and auto mechanics working on foreign cars have been using the metric system for a long time.

A conversion table is a useful tool for estimating metric amounts from their English equivalents or vice versa. Such a table is shown in Figure 11-1. These equivalents are not exact, however. For exact conversions, you would need to have the conversion factor extended three or four places to the right of the decimal point.

One measure of the U.S. commitment to switch to the metric system is the inclusion of metric equivalents on many grocery items. Which two measurements are used here? Verify the equivalence using information from Figure 11-1.

✓ CHECKING UP

1. What are some of the measures used in the English system of measurement?
2. What are some of the measures used in the metric system of measurement?
3. Why is the metric system considered easier to learn than the English system?

From Metric to English

	When You Know	Multiply by	To Find
Length	millimeters	0.04	inches
	centimeters	0.4	inches
	meters	3.3	feet
	meters	1.1	yards
	kilometers	0.6	miles
Area	square centimeters	0.16	square inches
	square meters	1.2	square yards
	square kilometers	0.4	square miles
	hectares (10,000 m²)	2.5	acres
Mass (weight)	grams	0.035	ounces
	kilograms	2.2	pounds
	tonnes (1,000 kg)	1.1	short tons
Volume	milliliters	0.03	fluid ounces
	liters	2.1	pints
	liters	1.06	quarts
	liters	0.26	gallons
	cubic meters	35	cubic feet
	cubic meters	1.3	cubic yards
Temperature (exact)	Celsius temperature	9/5 (then add 32)	Fahrenheit temperature

From English to Metric

	When You Know	Multiply by	To Find
Length	inches	2.5	centimeters
	feet	30	centimeters
	yards	0.9	meters
	miles	1.6	kilometer
Area	square inches	6.5	square centimeters
	square feet	0.09	square meters
	square yards	0.8	square meters
	square miles	2.6	square kilometers
	acres	0.4	hectares
Mass (weight)	ounces	28	grams
	pounds	0.45	kilograms
	short tons (2,000 lb)	0.9	tonnes
Volume	teaspoons	5	milliliters
	tablespoons	15	milliliters
	fluid ounces	30	milliliters
	cups	0.24	liters
	pints	0.47	liters
	quarts	0.95	liters
	gallons	3.8	liters
	cubic feet	0.03	cubic meters
	cubic yards	0.76	cubic meters
Temperature (exact)	Fahrenheit temperature	5/9 (after subtracting 32)	Celsius temperature

Figure 11-1   A conversion table can take the pain out of moving back and forth between English and metric measurement. Prove it to yourself. Try these problems: (1)The temperature on the thermometer says 37° C. Do you have a fever? (2) The road sign says 40 miles to Vancouver. What would it say in metric measurement?

CHAPTER SUMMARY

Almost all workers must be able to solve basic math problems. Employers say that the ability to use math on the job is an important skill that many employees lack. If you cannot use basic math, you need to learn and practice your skills now.

Addition, subtraction, multiplication, and division are the basic math operations you need to know. You should understand fractions and decimals and be able to convert a fraction to a decimal number. You should also be able to calculate surface and volume measurements for various shapes. These are skills necessary in many occupations.

Much of the drudgery of math has been eliminated by the calculator. Still, you must understand basic math to use the calculator correctly. A good habit to develop when using a calculator is estimating your answer before you begin. Estimating will help you eliminate obvious errors. Among the types of problems you should be able to do on the calculator are percent problems, such as figuring discounts and commissions.

The English system of measurement is the most common system used in the United States, but the rest of the world uses the metric system. It is based on the decimal system and is therefore easier to use. A conversion chart is a useful tool for comparing amounts from the two systems.

TERMS TO KNOW

On a separate sheet of paper, write two paragraphs—the first a math problem, the second a description of its solution. Use all of the following terms:

sum
difference
product
quotient
decimal number
perimeter
area
circumference
volume
percent

STUDY QUESTIONS

1. Write the following numbers in words.

   76   436   3,511   34,005   999

2. Solve the addition problems below.

27	29	15	28	30
19	31	40	16	41
32	41	19	64	35
+31	+48	+52	+39	+62

3. Solve the subtraction problems below.

887	795	658	418	666
−188	−713	−511	−365	−319

4. Solve the multiplication problems below.

753	518	628	555	425
×354	×687	×674	×789	×698

5. Solve the division problems below.

   $68\overline{)3,536}$ $17\overline{)765}$ $58\overline{)2,494}$ $25\overline{)705}$ $85\overline{)1,275}$

6. Write the following decimal numbers in words.

   29.6   14.25   8.07   12.10   139.99

7. Solve the following problems with decimal numbers.

15.32	13.05	28.6	14.9	$4.32\overline{)1.9872}$
+49.07	− 7.29	× 7.8	×7.01	

8. Write the following numbers and fractions as percents.

   0.08 $\dfrac{7}{10}$ 2.0 $\dfrac{1}{4}$ $\dfrac{15}{16}$

9. If the interior of your refrigerator measures 24 inches wide, 48 inches high, and 18 inches deep, what is the volume of your refrigerator in cubic feet?

10. A sign on a dress rack says "30 percent off all dresses!" The price tag on the dress you like is $49.99. How much will this dress cost you? Don't forget the sales tax (4 percent).

CRITICAL THINKING

1. How are fractions and decimal numbers alike? How are they different?

2. For your father's birthday, you would like to build a bookcase in his study. This bookcase will be built onto the wall between the door and the window, and it will reach from floor to ceiling. Which measurements and formulas will be of most use to you as you draw your plans?

DISCUSSION STARTERS

1. Your friend Mason won't study for his math class and is convinced that he can find a job that requires no math skills. What examples can you give him to show that math is part of his everyday life, even if he doesn't have to use it very much at his job?

2. American high school students score much lower on math tests than students in Europe and Asia do. How do you think this will affect the future of American business?

BUILDING BASIC SKILLS

Math

1. You have started working as a carpenter for your parents' contracting business, and you will be buying some of the materials. You need plywood roofing for a room addition, and the roof to be built is 27 feet by 33 feet.

   • What is the area of the roof?
   • If each sheet of plywood is 4 feet by 8 feet, how many sheets must you buy to cover the area of the roof?

Communication

2. Every time Marilu takes a break at the Ice Cream Palace, she takes a dip of ice cream without paying for it. Three or four of the other employees have started doing the same thing, and Marilu asks you why you never have one. "It's no big deal," she says. "No one's going to care about one scoop of ice cream." What would you say to her?

Decision Making

3. Your neighborhood has decided to organize a recycling program for everyone in the area to use voluntarily. Several barrels will be set up behind a neighbor's garage as a drop-off point. You are in charge of getting and setting up the barrels. The following are available:

   • Six barrels that are 54 inches high and 30 inches in diameter
   • Eight barrels that are 48 inches high and 56 inches in diameter

   Which would you choose? Why?

SUGGESTED ACTIVITIES

1. Do a research project to find out how math skills are used in a wide range of occupations. Make a list of 25 occupations. Try to include as many different kinds of work as possible. Then gather information through interviews and reading to determine the different ways math is used in each occupation. Are there any occupations in which no math is needed?

2. As you may know from a job experience, the real math challenge in the world of work is being able to solve problems quickly while people are waiting for you to finish. Divide into groups of four or five, and act out some work situations in which you must use math. Each person should take a turn at being the worker who must solve the problems. After each person has taken a turn, discuss with the entire class the various reactions to such pressure.

Answers to Practice Set Problems

Practice Set 1 (page 186)
a. Five thousand, ten
b. Six hundred thirty-eight
c. Two thousand, seven
d. Forty-four thousand, nine hundred two
e. Three hundred eight thousand, twelve
f. Five hundred thousand, two hundred sixty-four
g. Seven million, fifteen
h. Twenty-three million, six hundred twenty-four thousand, nine hundred eighty-three

Practice Set 2 (page 186)

81	54	75	127	124
683	1,780	1,003	1,309	1,424

Practice Set 3 (page 187)

5	7	9	8	10	14	12
16	9	12	15	13	18	12

Practice Set 4 (page 187)

168	162	185	223	142	225
291	307	305	346	356	353

Practice Set 5 (page 187)

14	17	10	29	18
24	19	59	208	486

Practice Set 6 (page 188)

6	2	4	9	4	9	6
4	6	9	7	7	8	8

Practice Set 7 (page 188)

36	9	41	30	85	15	345	27
8	49	39	589	60	35	269	62

Practice Set 8 (page 188)

280	246	385	365	384	612	375
1,020	592	1,875	6,612	10,011	37,344	26,880

Practice Set 9 (page 189)

20	21	48	28	45	56	15	36	35
42	49	24	63	54	72	27	81	64

Practice Set 10 (page 189)

24,198	9,480	17,204	10,475	26,100	8,106	63,122
11,872	33,485	14,694	50,962	53,940	43,250	62,250

Practice Set 11 (page 190)

9	6	12	7	8	21
8	25	11	18	$31\frac{2}{23}$	$12\frac{2}{9}$

Practice Set 12 (page 190)
a. $\frac{4}{10}$ (or $\frac{2}{5}$) b. $\frac{4}{4}$ (or 1) c. $\frac{1}{3}$ d. $\frac{2}{7}$ e. 0

f. $\frac{3}{4}$ g. No parts shaded h. $\frac{1}{8}$ i. $\frac{4}{8}$ (or $\frac{1}{2}$) j. $\frac{5}{4}$ (or $1\frac{1}{4}$)

Practice Set 13 (page 191)

a. Six and seven tenths
b. Nine tenths
c. Fifteen and three tenths
d. Five hundredths
e. Two and thirteen hundredths
f. Eight and nine hundredths

g. Twelve and forty-four hundredths
h. Thirty-eight and fifty-nine hundredths
i. Two hundred one dollars and thirty-eight cents
j. Three hundred thirty-eight dollars and ninety-seven cents

Practice Set 14 (page 192)

a. 11.5   b. 14.7   c. 15.5   d. 28.8   e. 19.27   f. 72.28   g. 5.04
h. 1.2   i. $0.32   j. 26.25   k. 12.039   l. 12.315   m. $565.33   n. 3.87m

Practice Set 15 (page 192)

32.8	37.74	229.32	a. $238.26
3.483	9.108	4.34523	b. $138.52
30.45	0.0126		

Practice Set 16 (page 193)

0.3	1.35	a. 34
0.325	600	b. 42.553 (or 43) hrs.
0.03	30.02	

Practice Set 17 (page 194)

a. 86 ft.   c. 158 in.   e. 16 in.   g. 56 ft.   i. 132 ft.
b. 300 in.   d. 22 ft.   f. 40 ft.   h. 304 in.   j. 416 ft.

Practice Set 18 (page 195)

a. 432 sq. ft.   e. 16 sq. in.   h. 5,776 sq. in.
b. 5,141 sq. in.   f. 100 sq. ft.   i. 1,089 sq. ft.
c. 1,054 sq. in.   g. 196 sq. ft.   j. 10,816 sq. ft.
d. 28 sq. ft.

Practice Set 19 (page 197)

a. area—1,133.54 sq. in., cir.—119.32 in.
b. area—1,519.76 sq. ft., cir.—138.16 ft.
c. area—3,419.46 sq. ft., cir.—207.24 ft.
d. area—63.585 sq. in., cir.—28.26 in.
e. area—1,962.5 sq. miles, cir.—157 miles
f. area—10,930.34 sq. ft., cir.—370.52 ft.

Practice Set 20 (page 197)

a. 432 cubic in.   b. 2,197 cubic ft.   c. 87.92 cubic in.

Practice Set 21 (page 199)

a. $326.41   b. $2,909.62   c. $492.45   d. $1,286.85

Practice Set 22 (page 199)

25%	6%	70%	270%	
98%	216%	1%	475%	
75%	90%	212%	87.5%	$83\frac{1}{3}$%
0.1	0.06	0.025	0.065	
0.1275	1.2	2	0.005	

Practice Set 23 (page 201)

a. $452   c. $1,147.60   e. $256.29   g. $2,964.75
b. $755.70   d. $1,586.84   f. $108.75

Computer Literacy

OBJECTIVES

After studying this chapter and doing the activities, you will be able to:

- describe how computers are changing our lives;
- outline the history of computer technology;
- explain how a computer works;
- discuss the various types of application software and their uses; and
- tell which computer languages are best for certain applications.

TERMS TO KNOW

modem
database
micros
hardware
disk drive
floppy disks
software
boot
CAD and CAM

*I*mportant inventions often dramatically change the way we live and work. The electric light bulb changed night into day. The internal combustion engine, the airplane, and the telephone brought us all closer together and made things happen much faster.

Today another invention, the computer, is changing the way we live and work. Computers are eliminating old jobs and creating new ones. Almost everyone now needs to have some level of computer knowledge and skill. Certainly everyone needs to understand what computers can do, how they are used, and how they will continue to change our lives. This understanding is called computer literacy.

In this chapter, you will learn about the development of computers and how they've changed our lives. You will also learn about the basic components and operation of computer systems. After reading this chapter, you will have a general understanding of computers to take with you into the world of work.

1 Computers in Everyday Living

Computers have been influencing our lives for years. At school, in the supermarket, on the telephone, at the bank, and in many other places, computers are making an impact on our society.

Computers are powerful tools. They improve the quality of our life, but they also have the potential to control our lives in many ways. This is one reason why it's important for all of us to understand how computers work and how they are being used. A second reason can be found in the changes that are taking place in the world of work. Today more and more jobs require computer knowledge and some level of computer skill.

In this lesson, you will read about the many ways computers have become part of our everyday lives. As you read, think about your career interest areas—how computers are influencing those areas and how learning about computers will help you in your career choices.

Education

Today students come into contact with computers very early in their school careers. Often students' enrollment in school is projected by computer even before they ever set foot in a school building. Once enrolled, students are tested and their scores tallied, recorded, and even analyzed by computer. As early as the elementary grades, students are taught how to use computers. They may even be taught *by* computers.

Computer-assisted learning can take a number of different forms. Most commonly a student is guided through a learning process by a computer program. The program's questions get easier or harder, depending on the student's responses. This allows the student to progress at his or her own pace.

Students may even have their attendance monitored by computer. Some school systems use computers to verify absences. Every evening a computer calls the parents of students who have missed classes. It dials the number and provides a taped message when someone answers the phone. If the line is busy, the computer dials again and keeps dialing until it gets an answer. In schools where this system has been used, absences have dropped sharply.

Business

Every time you go into a store to buy something, you are affected by the computer. For example, think about the supermarket where you buy groceries. The lines move faster now because scanners connected to a computer read the prices. Most products are imprinted with a universal product code (UPC). The checker passes the item across the scanner, and a computer records your purchase. (We will discuss scanners in greater detail later.)

The data read by the scanner is stored in the computer and used for several purposes. First, you will receive a printed record of what you bought. You will see not only the prices and the total but also a description of each item. Next, the computer will list the items you bought and file this list for later use. Finally, the computer will dial the warehouse and order replacement goods for all the items in short supply.

Another example of how the computer affects retail sales is the computer's role in credit card purchases and check cashing. The store clerk will enter the numeric data on the credit card or check into a computer. The computer will dial another computer to be sure that the credit card is valid for the purchase or that the checking account has the money to honor the check. In just a few seconds, the computer will tell the store clerk that the purchase can be completed.

Banks use the computer to process checks. A scanner reads special numbers along the bottom edge of a check and deducts the amount from the appropriate account. Automatic teller machines (ATMs) are special-purpose computers that allow you to withdraw cash from your account or make deposits at any time of the day, even when the bank is closed. Many people have their paychecks deposited directly to their bank accounts with electronic fund transfer (EFT) entries made between different computers over telephone lines.

The computer has changed almost every type of business. On some dairy farms, an electronic collar is placed around each cow's neck. When the cow comes to the stall for food, she is given a specially prepared ration custom-blended for her own needs and different from that provided for any other cow. At the same time, the milking machine is custom-configured and attached. This individual treatment would be impossible without the computer's keeping track of the various factors of milk production.

Computers offer us more conveniences than ever before. How is a computer providing a service in this picture? How is this person benefitting from a computer?

Even the basic structure of business is being changed by the computer. A new type of organization is emerging that has fewer levels of management. Using computers for written and video communication, company presidents now communicate more directly with their employees.

Many manufacturing companies now have less money tied up in inventory thanks to computers. Computerization allows them to use an inventory system called the just-in-time (JIT) method. By closely monitoring inventory levels, computers allow manufacturers to keep less inventory on hand. They simply order smaller amounts more frequently. If their suppliers are dependable, the production lines never run out of parts.

Health Care

Computers are used to study the causes of diseases and the effectiveness of treatments. Case histories of millions of people have been entered in computer files. Scientists study this information to find relationships between possible causes and certain diseases. Computers make this possible because they can sort through huge amounts of information much faster than people can.

Computerized axial tomography (CAT) uses a scanner to x-ray thin sections of the body. Another procedure, magnetic resonance imaging (MRI), does the same sort of thing but avoids some of the problems associated with using X rays. In both processes, a computer assembles multiple images into three-dimensional pictures. Thus, the whole interior of the patient's body can be seen, something that would not have been possible before without exploratory surgery. The information CAT and MRI scanners provide helps in the diagnosis of many kinds of diseases.

Doctors sometimes fasten a recording device to the body of a recovering heart patient. The device is then connected to a telephone so that it can transmit heart activity over the phone to the doctor's office. There a computer analyzes the information to see if there is a problem. If there is, the doctor is summoned at once by the computer.

The vital signs of patients in intensive care are often monitored by computer. If a problem arises, the nearest nurse's station is notified by the same computer.

Law Enforcement and Government

A police officer in a patrol car is now the first link in a chain of computer-assisted law enforcement activities. Officers needing information enter their request on a computer console in their patrol car. The computer radios the request to a computerized data bank which sends the requested information back to the officer's car almost immediately.

Judges use computers to issue arrest warrants. Time is critical since the suspect may be fleeing at the moment the warrant is issued. In the old (paper) warrant system, it could take a week for a warrant to be issued and the information given to law enforcement agencies. Modern warrant systems do this in a matter of seconds.

Crime labs use computers for many things. For example, fibers are analyzed and compared with known samples. Often the lab can tell if a suspect was at the crime scene. Analysis of compounds called DNA allow hair and tissue samples to be positively identified and linked to a particular person, establishing the identity of a victim or a suspect.

Governments at all levels could not function in today's society without computers. Computer storage of vast amounts of information has made it possible for governments to keep track of the growing population. For example, income tax and social security records for every worker in the country are stored in government computers.

Legislatures are drafting laws that protect access to information stored in computers. In many states it is a serious crime to gain unauthorized access to a computer. In the 1980s, some people thought it a challenge to break into someone else's computer bank, so they did it just for fun. Now when this happens, the guilty party usually loses his or her computer equipment and is fined. Some individuals have even gone to jail.

Computers have also been essential to our efforts in space. Computers chart the movement of space vehicles using numbers and formulas that would take months to compute by hand. Returning to earth would be impossible without computers to plot the angle of reentry.

Closer to earth, navigational computers can guide aircraft from one point to another with little or no help from people. New military aircraft are so fast and agile that the flight controls must be corrected more than 50 times each second. These corrections are made by a computer. If left to the human pilot alone, the plane would literally disintegrate.

Communication

A society's progress is often measured by its ability to communicate, both internally (among its own members) and externally (with other societies). Computers affect everyone in this process. In the United States, for example, most of the switching of telephone calls and the routing of mail depends on computers.

Computers can assist police officers in investigating crime. How would having a computer in a patrol car assist this officer?

Computers also communicate with one another. This saves a great deal of time and reduces errors. For example, branch offices of businesses once had to prepare long reports and mail them to main offices. These reports were then typed into a computer for analysis. Today, a branch office computer can provide all the needed data directly to a main office computer.

In most cases, computers communicate over telephone lines. Some lines require that computers use a modem, which is short for MOdulator-DEModulator. A **modem** is a special piece of computer equipment that connects a computer to a telephone line. More modern telephone lines, however, can accept transmissions directly from a computer. To establish contact at the other end, the computer dials a telephone number, just as you would for a regular phone call. Once the connection is made, you can send information from your computer to the receiving computer and wait for an answer.

An example of this technology is a facsimile, or FAX, machine. This machine looks like a small copier. Instead of copying the page to a sheet of paper, however, the information is sent over a telephone line and printed on a sheet of paper at its destination. Many businesses are now dependent on this ability to transmit documents over long distances in a matter of minutes.

Cellular telephones allow communication to be established from personal automobiles. The call is made much the same as with a regular telephone, but the voices are transmitted by radio to a receiver. This receiver hooks the caller into the regular telephone lines so that any telephone number may be called. If the caller gets too far from a receiving tower, he or she is automatically handed off to the next receiving tower. All this activity must be processed by special-purpose computers.

This explosion of communication capabilities has added to the load telephone lines must carry. The old metallic lines no longer have the capacity to handle all the traffic. Modern telephone lines are therefore often made up of glass fibers that carry voice and data in the form of waves of light. A computer must convert voice and data to this light wave and then convert it back to voice and data at the other end.

The process of using telephone lines to link computers provides access to massive amounts of information. A collection of stored, computerized information is called a **database.** There are a number of very large databases available over phone lines to anyone with a computer. For example, some databases keep copies of articles from thousands of magazines. It's possible to obtain a copy of an article on any subject you can think of from such sources, and it's available in minutes.

MAKE A DECISION

You are planning your schedule for the second semester at the local junior college. You have room left for one three-hour elective, and you are considering either an introductory computer programming course or a speech course. Both would be challenging courses, and both would help you when it came time to look for a job. What's your decision—the computer course or the speech course? Give the reasons for your decision.

In the Home

Computers have changed the way people live and work. For example, some people have used computers to eliminate commuting. These people have computer terminals at home that they use to communicate with their workplace computer and co-workers. This helps relieve such urban problems as traffic jams, smog, and crowded parking lots.

Computers also help prevent fires and burglaries. In some newer, planned communities, for example, video cameras watch homes while owners are away. People who are in poor health can benefit from similar monitoring. By simply pushing a button on a device worn around their necks, they can summon police, medical, or other emergency services. All of these devices depend on small computers to transmit, receive, and process information.

✓ CHECKING UP

1. Give four examples that show how businesses use computers.
2. How are doctors benefitting from computers?
3. How have computers changed the way some people work?

2 *The Development of Computer Technology*

The development of calculators took thousands of years. The computer, though, is a product of this century.

The military needs in World War II brought about the development of the first computers. The speed of battle, particularly in the air, surpassed the ability of the mind to calculate the proper position of guns. Single-purpose computers, operating much faster than the human mind, were developed as a defensive aid.

After the war, engineers began using computers to design new products. Computers became the brains for engineers, but they were still too expensive for other business uses.

Since then the computer has seen four generations of development. With each generation, the physical size of the computer has decreased, while the computer's capacity has at least stayed the same or even increased. Technological ad-

vancements have also made the computer more affordable for more people. Both businesses and individuals have benefitted from computer development.

The First Three Generations

Most people consider ENIAC (Electronic Numerical Integrator and Computer) to be the first modern, multipurpose computer. ENIAC was designed and built at the University of Pennsylvania in the mid-1940s. ENIAC worked about a thousand times as fast as the most advanced computers at that time.

Computers such as ENIAC were huge—some as big as a house! The largest, weighing 175 tons, is now on display in the Computer Museum in Boston. Only a few large businesses—those with a pioneering spirit—used these computers, which are referred to as Generation I computers.

In the 1960s a new type of computer was ready. The Generation II computer used transistors instead of vacuum tubes. The new machines were

The first modern computers, such as ENIAC shown here, were enormous. Although they could do calculations much faster than people, they broke down frequently and required constant maintenance. Based on what you've read so far and your own experiences with computers, how would you say computers have changed?

Strive for Success

Rocky Raccoon, Computer Whiz

He has been described as everything from a high-tech hero to an entrepreneurial wonder. To those in the computer business he is simply known as the Woz. To the faculty at the University of California at Berkeley, he was known as Rocky Raccoon Clark. His real name is Steve Wozniak, and he may just be the richest elementary school teacher in America.

In 1976 Wozniak and friend Steve Jobs co-founded Apple Computer in a California garage. The company's first major product was the Apple II personal computer. The Apple II was small, relatively inexpensive, easy to use—and an incredible success. The Apple II soon became *the* personal computer for home or educational use. Its success started a boom in personal computers and created major tremors at the offices of IBM, the industry giant.

In 1979 Wozniak and Jobs decided to take the company public. They listed it on a stock exchange and allowed outsiders to invest in it by buying stock, Wozniak instantly pocketed $150 million—not bad for a person only 29 years old!

Before leaving Apple in 1985, Wozniak was also instrumental in the development of the company's next successful product—the Macintosh personal computer. Although sales got off to a slow start, the Macintosh too has proved to be an immensely successful product.

Wozniak left Apple in 1985, looking for new worlds to conquer. That same year, he was awarded the National Medal of Technology by then president Ronald Reagan. Young, rich, and decorated, Wozniak immediately set out to achieve the one goal that had thus far eluded him—to graduate from college.

Wozniak enrolled at the University of California at Berkeley to seek a degree in computer science and electrical engineering. He worried, however, that his famous name and success might lead to unintentional favoritism from the professors. In order to avoid this, he decided to enroll under a false name. The name he chose was Rocky Raccoon Clark.

Wozniak described his graduation as his crowning achievement. Since then he has been involved in everything from advanced television remotes to rock concerts to U.S.-Soviet relations. Currently, however, he spends a great deal of his time as a volunteer teacher at kindergartens in the Silicon Valley area of California. Instead of Rocky Raccoon, computer whiz, his students just call him Mr. Wozniak.

hundreds of times smaller, used much less energy, and were reliable for thousands of hours of operation.

The 1970s saw the development of improved computers with smaller devices that could sit on a desktop. These Generation III computers used a revolutionary part called an integrated circuit (IC). The first ICs contained only a few transistors in a small case. Soon, however, large-scale integrated circuits were developed on thin slices of silicon. These were commonly called chips. The chips had several different layers of other materials deposited on them. The pattern of these materials caused them to act like thousands of electronic components.

The Fourth Generation

In the 1980s the small desktop units developed into fully capable Generation IV computers. Generation IV computers use very large-scale integrated circuits containing thousands of electronic circuits. Each circuit is as complex as a complete computer once was. These computers have now become so inexpensive that many people own them for personal use in their homes.

Mainframes As the technology improved and small computers were developed, the very large computers came to be called mainframes. These are the large computers that are placed in special rooms where special conditions can be maintained. Mainframe computers can do a great deal more work than smaller computers. They are usually operated only by highly trained professionals.

Micros The terms *desktop computer, personal computer,* and *microcomputer* may have different meanings to some people, but basically they all refer to the same type of machine—a small computer that can be easily carried in the trunk of a car or placed on a desk. For simplicity, we will call such machines microcomputers, or **micros.**

A process called distributive processing can link a micro with a mainframe computer. This can be done either with a direct cable or over phone lines. The micro can be a stand-alone computer one minute and an intelligent terminal talking with the mainframe the next minute. Small jobs can be done on the micro under local control. Larger jobs, requiring the sharing of common data, can be transmitted to the mainframe.

Advances in technology have quite literally dropped amazing computer capabilities into our laps. Suggest some workers who might benefit from having a computer like this one.

The laptop computer is considered to be a microcomputer. These micros are so small, they can be used while they are resting on your lap. Weighing less than ten pounds, laptops operate on batteries and can fit inside a briefcase.

While you can choose from hundreds of brands of micros, most follow one of two standard designs. They are compatible with either the IBM-PC or the Apple computer. The most popular standard design used in business is the IBM, although many businesses use the Macintosh by Apple, particularly for publishing and design functions. In education, smaller Apple computers were by far the most popular throughout the 1980s. However, many schools have more recently purchased computers that are IBM compatible.

✓ CHECKING UP

1. Describe the development of the computer since the 1940s in terms of size and capacity.
2. Describe the characteristics of a Generation IV computer.
3. What is a laptop computer?

3 *Data Processing*

We've discussed how computers have changed our lives and how they were developed. Now it's time to learn what a computer is, how it works, and what it can do.

You've probably had at least one or two opportunities to work with a computer. If someone were to ask you what a computer is, what would you say? How would you describe what one does?

A computer is an electronic device that stores and processes data. Data are facts, small pieces of information such as dates, numbers, and names. Computers take pieces of data and manipulate and change that data into usable information. This process of changing data into information that people can use is called data processing.

How do computers do this? To answer this question you need to know about information systems and how they work.

Information Systems

A complete data processing system can be separated into four functions: input, processing, output, and storage. These four functions were used to process data long before there were computers. In fact, we all use these functions in processing data every day. The brain serves as the processor. Whether we use a computer, a pencil and paper, or simply "do it in our head," the basic functions are the same.

Input   The first step in processing data is to input it (to put it into the system). Input is a recording function. This means that we must record the data in usable form. If we are using a computer, we must record the data in a form that the computer can understand.

Processing   In the second step, processing, the data is changed to a more useful form. This function is the real heart of the information system. It can be broken down into five functions:

- Classifying
- Sorting
- Calculating
- Comparing
- Summarizing

The classifying function identifies the data. You are already familiar with this function. You classify people every day as men, women, children, family members, friends, and teachers.

People, as well as computers, can process data into usable information. How has this student operated as an information system?

The sort function arranges data by classification. Telephone directories sort names alphabetically. Can you imagine finding someone's number if all the numbers were listed randomly?

The calculate function involves adding, subtracting, multiplying, and dividing. The computer calculates with incredible speed and accuracy. It can use math formulas to solve complicated problems because the formulas are simply combinations of the four basic math functions.

The compare function means checking one piece of data against another. Suppose you want to pay your workers $10 an hour for all hours worked up to 40 hours. You want to pay $15 an hour for each hour above 40 hours. Before you could calculate the worker's pay, you would need to compare the hours worked by each employee with the number 40.

The summarizing function often provides information for decision making. Suppose the president of Lectrik Shavers is concerned about cutting production costs. It would be impossible to determine where costs should be controlled simply by looking at individual checks. The totals, or summaries, however, would show how much is spent in each area of company expense. This information might be the basis for a decision to buy materials from a different supplier or to lay off some workers.

Output The output function delivers information to users who need it. People output messages in different ways. We speak or point or write a letter so that other people know how we have processed the input that has come to us.

Computer output is usually communicated to users in the form of documents or displays. Documents are permanent records printed on paper. Displays are temporary visualizations, such as those on computer monitors or video screens.

When one computer communicates with another computer, the output is in the form of machine-readable electronic signals that the computer can process. Output can be in any form that delivers information where it is needed in a way that it can be understood.

Storage The storage function really involves both storing and retrieving information. Storing, of course, means placing the information where it can be found later. Retrieving means finding the information and outputting or processing it as needed.

Records stored in information systems provide the basis for doing business in the United States and around the world. Major businesses would collapse if their records were destroyed. Records stored in computer files must be protected from fire and other hazards and from those who might profit from stealing the information in them. Copies of records are often kept in another place. The data is protected by allowing access only to those who need to retrieve it.

Computer Systems

A computer system is one kind of information system. A computer system consists of separate, yet carefully-linked components, or pieces. There are four kinds of components:

- Input devices
- Processors
- Output devices
- Secondary storage devices

A computer system is similar to a system of stereo components. Each component has a job to do to make the whole system work. The components making up a computer system are often called **hardware.**

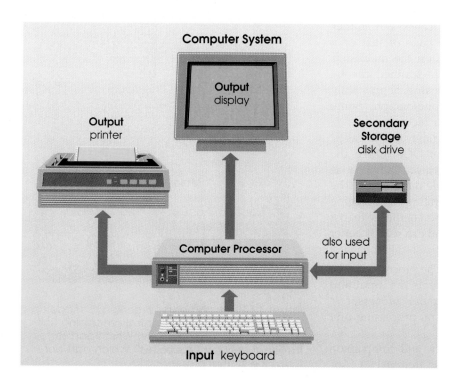

Computer System

Output display

Output printer

Secondary Storage disk drive

Computer Processor

also used for input

Input keyboard

Figure 12-1 This computer system consists of five components: keyboard, processor, printer, display screen, and disk drive. Each component performs a function. How might a CD player function like a computer system? Which components of a CD player perform which functions?

Input Equipment   Once data is in a computer, it can be used with little effort. Getting the data into a computer without errors is often the most expensive and time-consuming part of operating a computer.

The two most frequently used methods of inputting data are keying and reading. Keying inputs data one character at a time, through a typewriter-like keyboard. This process can produce machine-readable media, such as magnetic tape.

Key-disk or disk drive machines place tiny magnetic signals in specific spots on computer disks. The **disk drive** is the device that receives and operates the disk. You can think of the disk drive as being similar to a CD player.

Key-tape machines place the same kind of signals on tape. Much of this computer tape is just like the cassette tapes you buy at the music store. Sometimes it comes in giant 2,400-foot reels.

Another keyboard device, the computer terminal, can be used to input data directly into the computer. This eliminates the need to record on paper or magnetic media. The terminal is replacing other forms of inputting data for many applications.

Another piece of input equipment is a scanner. It uses the method of reading rather than keying to convert pages of text or graphics into computer data.

One example is the scanner at the grocery store that reads the UPCs as you check out. Other similar devices scan an entire page of text or a graphic as it is laid face down on the machine's glass top. The graphics that are scanned can be either line, such as a cartoon drawing, or gray scale with subtle shadings, like a photograph. Some scanners can even capture color pictures.

The reading technique a scanner uses is called optical character recognition, or OCR. Often the machine must be assisted in this task. A smudge on the page or an unusual type style may confuse the machine. After the person operating the machine corrects the scanned image, the computer learns about any unusual type style and can read it better the next time.

Processing Equipment   The processor is the heart of every computer. It accepts the input and processes the data. The computer processor is made up of two parts: the central processing unit (CPU) and the main memory.

The CPU performs arithmetic and comparison functions in its arithmetic-logic unit (ALU). An-

other part of the CPU, the control unit, accepts the input and places it in main memory to await actual processing. The control unit also controls the communication between the processor and the other devices in a computer system.

The devices connected to the computer processor are called peripherals. (Peripheral means around and close to a central object.) Peripheral devices are connected to a processor that is the center of the computer system.

Main memory, or primary memory, consists of Read Only Memory (ROM) and Random Access Memory (RAM). ROM is usually programmed into the machine at the factory. It contains a limited amount of instruction to the computer. You cannot change the content of ROM; it remains there forever.

The greater portion of main memory is RAM. You can store instructions and data in RAM and then tell the computer to process what is in RAM. When you have finished, you can replace the contents of RAM with something new. Whatever is stored in RAM is lost when the machine is turned off.

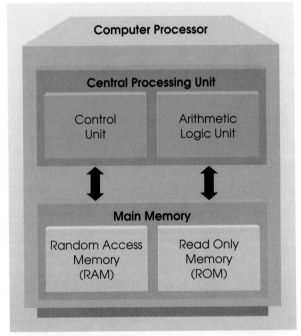

Computer Processor

Central Processing Unit

Control Unit   Arithmetic Logic Unit

Main Memory

Random Access Memory (RAM)   Read Only Memory (ROM)

Figure 12-2   A computer processor is made up of two main parts—the central processing unit (CPU) and the main memory. Which part stores the input until it is processed? Which part performs the actual processing?

Case Study 1

Derrick began playing games on his father's home computer when he was only six years old. By the time he reached junior high school, he was using a word processing program to write his class papers.

In high school Derrick began looking for a part-time job. He gave little thought to his computer skills. However, during an interview he happened to mention his use of computers. The interviewer began to question him about this and 20 minutes later offered him a better-paying job than the one he had applied for. The job would make use of the computer skills he had already learned. Some additional skills would be needed, but the interviewer was sure that Derrick, with his basic knowledge of computers, could easily pick them up.

Computers have different memory capabilities. Mainframes have much more storage capacity than micros. Some micros have more memory than others. The memory capability for micros is usually measured in kilobytes, commonly called K, which represents 1,024 characters.

Output Equipment   Several types of output devices are used to transfer information from the computer processor to the computer user. As described earlier, the two types of output most often used are displays and documents.

A display provides output in the form of words, numbers, or graphics on some kind of electronic screen. A display is not a permanent record. Most screen displays are on a cathode ray tube (CRT), which is exactly like a television picture tube.

Documents are words, numbers, or graphics printed on paper. Unlike displays, they are permanent records. Documents can be produced by various types of printers.

Documents are also called hard copy. When you hear people talk about hard copy, they are usually talking about a printed version of information also stored on a computer disk.

Storage Equipment   We can store data offline (anyplace not connected to the computer itself) in secondary storage as well as in the computer's main memory. The disadvantage to using secondary storage is that it's much slower to access.

The most common secondary storage media is the magnetic disk. Data can be stored on the disk, which can then be used later for input by reading the data into the computer's main memory. In other words, the disk can be used for both storage and input.

Mainframe computers use hard disks. These disks are built into the disk drive and may or may not be replaceable.

Floppy disks, also called diskettes, are used on smaller systems. Floppy disks are not really floppy. They are magnetic media in the form of a flat disk encased in paper or plastic. They are called floppy in comparison to hard disks, which are not flexible.

Floppy disks cannot store as much data as hard disks. They are designed to be loaded and unloaded into a disk drive. Most floppy disks are currently made in 3½- and 5¼-inch formats.

The new technology in data storage for the 1990s is compact optical disks. This technology uses a disk similar to musical compact disks and can store vast amounts of data (often more than a billion characters) on a removable disk. Some newer computers will surely use optical disks instead of magnetic hard and floppy disks.

MAKE A DECISION

You've saved about $1,000. You were going to use it as a down payment on a new car, which you need badly, but you've noticed how important computers have become at work. You were thinking about using the money to buy your own personal computer so you can learn about computers at home on your own. What's your decision—a car or a computer? Give the reasons for your decision.

✓ CHECKING UP

1. What are the four components of a computer system?
2. How do these components relate to an information system?
3. What does the term *peripheral* mean, and what are peripheral devices?

4 Computer Software and Its Applications

Fancy machinery won't do anything for anyone without instructions on how it should function. This is why computers need programs. Programs are instructions that tell a computer how to do a certain task or group of related tasks. A program is often called **software.** Software is soft in comparison to the equipment, which is hard.

This lesson introduces you to the two basic kinds of software—operating system software and application software. We will also look at some specific application software, the linking of computers (called networking), and some of the things you need to know to write your own computer software.

Operating System Software

Operating system software consists of a set of instructions that causes a computer's components to behave as a system. The operating system software is usually provided by the manufacturer of the machine. The software manages the movement of data to and from peripherals through the computer's main memory.

Operating systems that include instructions for disk drive operations are called disk operating systems (DOS). The disk drive loads the DOS into the computer's RAM portion of main memory.

Most computers have an initial set of instructions built into the computer's circuitry. These built-in instructions cause the computer to locate and begin performing the rest of the operating system. The first sequence of instructions the computer reads is called a boot procedure. **Boot** simply means to load an operating system into the computer. This is usually done by placing the disk in the disk drive. It tells the computer what it must do to read the rest of the disk.

When a computer is turned off, the RAM portion of main memory is wiped clean. The system software must be saved, however, even when the power is turned off. It's kept in secondary storage that does not depend on continuous power.

Mainframe computers usually store software on hard disks sealed in plastic. Micros may use hard disk storage, but they usually use the less expensive floppy disks.

Many computer users store their work on floppy disks, regardless of whether or not their computers have hard disks. What do you think is the reason for this?

Once a computer is "up," or operating, it can perform a variety of tasks. Each kind of task, or application, requires its own application software.

Application Software

Mainframe computers use many kinds of application software in business, engineering, education, and other fields. Many of these programs are highly complex, and many are customized to the needs of specific users. Our concern here is to understand how application software is used. We will focus on typical software used in micros.

Application programs, too, are usually stored on disks. Application software may be purchased from the company that made the computer or from other sources. Hundreds of companies and individuals sell programs for micros. You may also write your own programs for your own applications if you have learned how to program computers.

Word Processing   There are many types of software on the market. Among the most popular types for micros are word processing programs. These programs tell the micro how to act like a very efficient typewriter. To print out what you type, you will need to hook up a printer to the micro.

Different word processing programs have different features, but they all let you type your document on the screen. You can then move sentences around until they say exactly what you want. Some of these programs will also check your spelling. When your document is exactly right, you print it out on your printer. You can also store your document so that you can work with it or print another copy at a later time. Writing letters and other documents is two or three times faster on a computer than on an electric typewriter.

Video Games   The micro that becomes a super typewriter with one piece of application software becomes an entertainment center with another piece of software. You can now play at home many of the games previously found only in video arcades. By inserting different disks, you can fly to Mars or explore caves inhabited by dragons. You can solve crimes or be eaten by a little screen image, all without leaving the safety of your home.

It all depends on the application software you insert.

Desktop Publishing   One of the fastest-growing applications is desktop publishing (DTP) software. Using DTP, you can produce documents with text that flows around graphics, such as pictures, charts, and photos. If you have a color printer, you can produce these documents in full color.

This software is called desktop publishing because many organizations that previously sent publications, such as sales brochures and financial reports, to outside printers to be produced are now producing them in-house, on a desktop. DTP is becoming so popular because it offers businesses and other organizations more control over the appearance of their publications. It can also save a business money because it can produce publications more quickly and economically using the business's own equipment.

CAD and CAM   Two exciting newer types of application software are called CAD and CAM. **CAD** stands for computer assisted design. CAD programs make work much faster for drafters, engineers, and designers of buildings, bridges, automobiles, and even airplanes. CAD programs make it possible to design in three dimensions

Desktop publishing software is becoming very popular, especially among businesses that frequently produce small publications, such as newsletters, financial reports, or sales brochures. Why would some companies choose to use DTP software? Why would some companies choose not to?

right at a computer terminal. Changes that used to require drawing whole new sets of blueprints are made just by entering a different measurement. There are special printers available that will print the designs in blueprint form, ready for use on a job site or in a factory.

CAM, which means computer assisted manufacturing, takes CAD one step further. These programs allow the designs produced using CAD programs to be output directly to electronic robots that carry out the actual manufacture of the items. CAM software is widely used in the automobile industry, where CAM-driven robots have replaced workers on many assembly lines.

Other Kinds of Software   Although word processing and game playing are the most popular kinds of application software for micros, there are dozens of others. Database management programs allow those without much knowledge of computers to do sophisticated file and data manipulation. Graphics software can make you an artist with the screen as the canvas. Spreadsheet software allows manipulation of vast amounts of data for budgeting and money management. With calendar software, you can budget your time in the same way that you budget your money. Electronic mail software lets people write to one another without putting a word on paper.

Networking

Another application of computer software is to link computers through a system called networking. Computers are very useful by themselves, but they can be even more useful linked together.

Networking computers can share data, software programs, and peripheral equipment, such as printers. If a computer operator in one office of a company wishes to send letters to a list of customers stored in a computer in another office, networking makes this possible. The customer information does not have to be entered into the second computer.

Networking computers can save a business money. Some computer software programs are very expensive. When computers are linked through networks, several computers can share software programs. Some printers are also very expensive. A laser printer may cost thousands of dollars. If computers are networked, many can share the same laser printer.

SITUATION
SOLUTION

Introducing New Technology

You have recently been hired at Abbeville Books as a part-time bookkeeper. The store is prosperous, and the owner, Mrs. Ingram, has until now done her own bookkeeping. She prefers the records be kept manually on file cards. You feel that keeping records in this fashion is very time-consuming and can easily lead to errors. However, Mrs. Ingram does not want to spend the money for a computer and the necessary software. She also can show that her records have always been very accurate.

1. You have a personal computer at home and the appropriate software. Should you take her records home and put them on your computer, even though it would take several hours without pay? Explain why or why not.
2. You have a personal computer at home that you would be willing to use, but you do not have the software. What might you say to convince Mrs. Ingram to buy the software and pay for your time spent at home?
3. In what other ways could Abbeville Books benefit from having a computer? What other uses might Mrs. Ingram find for it?

In addition to the special software required to control the movement of the information between computers, networking computers requires a wire to connect the computers and special hardware components. The process of setting up a computer network is complicated, but once it is done the system is easy for computer operators to use.

Computer Programming

Suppose you want to use a computer for a certain application, but there is no software program available that will direct a computer to perform the task. What do you do?

You could hire a programmer. A programmer is a person who prepares a sequence of instructions that enables a computer to perform some special task. These instructions may be written in an electronic code or in a computer language that the computer itself must translate.

If you know how to program computers, you can write the program yourself. An advantage of this is that you will have greater control over how the program works. By writing rather than buying the program, you'll also save money.

In 1985 there were 443,000 computer programmers. This number is expected to increase by 77 percent by 1995. Programmers must be able to think logically and pay very close attention to detail. If you have these abilities, a career as a computer programmer could be very rewarding.

Machine Language   Computers process data electronically. That is, data is processed through controlling thousands, even millions, of circuits and memory locations. These circuits and memory locations have only two states. They are either on or off. The computer recognizes these two states as either a 1 or a 0.

The language of computers, then, is expressed in groups of 1s and 0s. This is called binary coding. Since all computer functions depend on this coding, it is also called machine language. This is the only language a computer's basic circuits can understand.

Programming Languages   People, however, prefer to write in human languages. The first uses of human language instructions, instead of binary coding, were assembly languages. The computer converted assembly instructions into machine language with a special program called an assembler.

This made programming somewhat easier, but assembly languages were not too different from binary coding. Each computer operation required a separate command. There was a need for programs requiring fewer source instructions.

Compiler languages use Englishlike words and abbreviations. They have been developed to meet special computing needs. The most frequently used compiler languages are FORTRAN, COBOL, and BASIC.

FORTRAN is an abbreviation of FORmula TRANslator. Introduced in 1957, it was the first important compiler language. It is an efficient way to enter scientific equations and math formulas for processing. FORTRAN is still widely used for math and scientific applications.

COBOL stands for COmmon Business Oriented Language. It was developed for business data

processing and was first used in 1960. COBOL uses many common English words and was designed for use on many kinds of computers used in business. It handles very large amounts of input and output.

BASIC is an abbreviation for Beginners All-purpose Symbolic Instruction Code. It was designed to be easy to learn for the nonprofessional programmer. Most BASIC commands are written in common English. It is the most commonly used language for programming micros.

A programming language called C is an attempt to provide a language that can be used on all sizes of computers from the smallest micro to the largest mainframe computer. Several computer manufacturers have pledged to create C compilers on their full line of equipment.

Special Programming Languages   The compiler languages we have discussed are all procedural languages. That is, you must write instructions out step by step. Other languages are nonprocedural. RPG, standing for Report Program Generator, is a fill-in-the-blanks language. Special forms are filled in that are translated into instructions to the computer. If, for example, you want output without dollar signs, commas, or leading zeros, all you have to do is fill in a certain code on a form.

Program Development   The actual writing, or coding, of instruction is called program development. This may be done directly on the monitor if you have a micro or a mainframe computer terminal. It can also be done off-line, if you have no computer handy. In this case the program will have to be entered into the computer system as another step.

Program development also includes testing and debugging, which is the process of removing errors from the program. Testing and debugging are necessary because programs don't always work the way we think they will. The longer the program, the more likely it is that some sort of error will occur.

✓ CHECKING UP

1. What does software do?
2. Describe desktop publishing software.
3. Describe the three most frequently used programming languages.

Review Your Learning

CHAPTER SUMMARY

Computers are changing the way we live and work. In schools, computers are used to process information about students, encourage attendance, and even instruct. Businesses use computers to speed up checkout lines and help control inventory. Computers are also used in medical research, law enforcement, space exploration, communication, and in the home. Almost all aspects of life have been affected by computers.

The development of computer technology has seen four generations of computers. ENIAC was the first modern, multipurpose computer. Generation II computers, developed in the 1960s, were smaller and more efficient. Generation III computers were brought about by the integrated circuit. In the 1980s, Generation IV computers were developed. They were as complex as large computers once were but small enough to fit on desktops. Today they are known as microcomputers, or micros.

Computers process data to generate information that people can use. Computers are information systems that input, process, output, and store data. They utilize several pieces of equipment (keyboard, printer, and central processing unit) to do these things.

The instructions the computer needs to do its work are called programs, or software. Two basic kinds of software are operating system software and application software. Word processing, desktop publishing, CAD, and CAM are some specific kinds of application software. Networking, which also uses special software, is one way that several computers can work together.

TERMS TO KNOW

On a separate sheet of paper, write a paragraph about computer literacy, using all of the following terms:

modem
database
micros
hardware
disk drive
floppy disks
software
boot
CAD and CAM

STUDY QUESTIONS

1. Name three ways in which computers are used in schools.
2. How have computers improved law enforcement?
3. What device connects a computer with a telephone line?
4. What is the major difference between Generation I and Generation II computers?
5. What revolutionary part made the computers of the 1970s superior to those of the 1960s?
6. What is the basic difference between a mainframe computer and a microcomputer?
7. Which is most helpful to people—data or information? Why?
8. What are the four steps in an information system?
9. What are the five functions of processing?
10. What are the two kinds of main memory?
11. What are the two kinds of output?
12. What are the two basic kinds of software?
13. Name at least three kinds of application software.
14. What is networking?
15. Which program language was designed for science and math applications?

CRITICAL THINKING

1. During the summer, you teach swimming to the nine- through twelve-year-old swimming class. If you had access to a micro and the software of your choice, which software would you choose and what teaching materials would you produce?

2. In your job at the orchard, you are responsible for inspecting the apples and deciding which are in the right condition for shipping and which are not. You also decide which apples should be marked small, medium, or large. What processing function or functions are you performing at your job?

3. Because you like to write and draw, you decide to start a business producing newsletters for other businesses in your community. How can a computer assist you in developing and engaging in this kind of a business?

DISCUSSION STARTERS

1. If you had the choice of taking a math course from a teacher or a computer, which would you choose? Give the reasons for your decision.

2. If there is a computer in your home, what is it used for? How can a home computer be used to increase your efficiency or organize your life better?

3. What are the advantages and disadvantages in CAM programs in which robots take the place of people in manufacturing jobs?

4. Many schools are requiring computer courses for graduation. Do you think this is a good idea? Why or why not?

BUILDING BASIC SKILLS

Math

1. You and Marilyn are both sending out resumes to employers. Both of you make small document changes in each to customize it for a particular job opening. Because Marilyn does this on her electric typewriter, she has to type the entire resume over each time, which takes her 20 minutes. You use a computer, and making the changes and printing out the new resume takes you 5 minutes. If each of you applies for eight jobs, how much less time will it take you than Marilyn?

Communication

2. For your computer class, you have been asked to explain a magazine as an information system. Write out what you would say.

Decision Making

3. Your friend Ned is trying to decide which software to use to prepare his history report. His report includes many time lines. He is very familiar with a word processing program and somewhat familiar with a graphics program. Ned also has access to a desktop publishing program. It can be complicated to use, but it will produce a spectacular report. Which of these options should Ned choose and why?

   - Use the graphics program in combination with the word processing software.
   - Take the additional time necessary to learn to use the desktop publishing program.

SUGGESTED ACTIVITIES

1. For five days, keep a record of your encounters with computers. Write down the location and the use of the computer with each occurrence. At the end of the week, compare your list with the lists made by your classmates.

2. Make a class montage of photos representing the historical development of calculating machines and computers. Find as many different photos and drawings as possible. Arrange them with dates to show how the technology has progressed.

Our Economic System

*W*ould you try to drive a car if you didn't know the difference between red and green at a stoplight? What if you knew nothing about our highway system, even that in this country everyone is supposed to drive on the right? Without knowing the rules of the road, you would probably have a difficult time getting to where you wanted to go. In fact, there's a good chance you would never get there.

The same is true of your career goals and the need to understand a few basic facts about economics. You will be working within our economic system. To be successful, you will need to know why certain things are happening, such as why prices go up and down and why new jobs are created and old ones disappear. You will have a much better chance of reaching your career destination if you know why these things happen—if you know the economic "rules of the road."

In this chapter you will learn how our economic system works. You will learn why conditions change so rapidly. With a basic understanding of the system, you will be able to prepare yourself for the challenges such a system presents.

1 *Understanding Free Enterprise*

Every country needs an **economic system.** What is an economic system? It's everything that goes on in the world of work. Specifically, it is the method by which a society produces and distributes goods and services to the people who need and want them.

In the United States our economic system is known as free enterprise. The name is one that practically defines itself. You already know what the word *free* means. The word *enterprise* refers to an activity, effort, or attempt to accomplish something. Thus, in general terms, free enterprise means that people are free to attempt whatever activity they choose.

Choice and Constant Change

In economic terms **free enterprise** refers to a system in which people have the right to make their own economic decisions. They can decide what kind of work they want to do and where they want to do it. They can choose to start their own businesses or work for someone else. They can hold more than one job if they wish. They can acquire and sell property.

All countries do not operate under a free enterprise system. Some governments choose to organize people and their economic activities differently. Countries with communist governments, for example, have systems in which the government controls almost all economic activity. Under these systems the government decides what will be produced. The government also tells people where they will work and which jobs they will do. It often owns all the property. In recent years, countries with such systems have faced increasingly severe economic problems.

Free enterprise has proved to be more successful. In the United States, for example, it has provided most people with jobs and enough money to buy food, clothing, and shelter. Most people even have enough money left over to buy some of the luxury items and services available in the economy. Few countries in the world offer such a high standard of living for so many.

Still, our economic system is far from perfect. Under free enterprise, the economy changes constantly. Prices rise and fall. Old jobs in factories disappear, while new jobs in the service sector are created. Many workers in their forties and fifties must start over in entirely new careers. Many others cannot find jobs at all. They find themselves, perhaps for the first time in their lives, without enough food to eat or a place to live.

Changes like these make free enterprise appear risky, confusing, and unpredictable—and in some measure it is. There are more than 250 million people in the United States. All of them have their own wants and needs, and all are free to make their own economic decisions. With so many differences and so much freedom, the economy is bound to change rapidly and often. This does make the system difficult to understand—difficult, but not impossible.

MAKE A DECISION

In our free enterprise system, you can decide not only what you want to do but also where you want to do it. Suppose you find that you can get the type of job you want anywhere in the country—and even in a few foreign countries. You know that where you live will be a big factor in determining whether or not you are happy. What's your decision—where will you live and work? Give the reasons for your decision.

Economists (people who study economic systems) have been able to spell out a number of principles basic to the operation of a free enterprise system. In the next few sections you will learn about some of them.

Participants in the System

The best place to begin an explanation of any economic system is with the main participants. In the case of a free enterprise system, there are primarily two—consumers and producers.

Consumers A **consumer** is someone who consumes, who buys and uses goods and services. We are all consumers. We all use up thousands, even millions, of dollars in products over the course of our lifetimes. Two-thirds of all the goods and services produced are sold to individual consumers.

Consider these two contrasting scenes—the meat counter in a Soviet state-run market (above) and the meat counter in a U.S. supermarket (below). How has the Soviet economic system served its citizens compared to the free enterprise system in the United States?

The needs and wants of consumers play a major role in determining what happens in our economy. If consumers are willing to pay for a certain product, someone will probably provide it. If consumers suddenly change their minds and no longer want that product, the people providing it will soon stop.

Regardless of what consumers want, though, they can't buy goods and services unless they have enough money. How much money consumers have determines what and how much they buy. The more money they have, the more they buy. The less money they have, the less they buy.

Few people have as much money as they would like to have. This means that most consumers must be selective in what they buy. They choose the best-made product over the poorly made product.

They choose the cheaper product over the more expensive product. They usually choose the things they need over the things they want. Most consumers try to get the most they can in terms of quality and quantity for each of their hard-earned dollars.

Producers   The people who supply consumers with the goods and services they want are called producers. Producers are free to decide which goods and services they will produce. They are also free to decide how much they will produce.

To help them make these decisions, producers look to consumers. Producers try to determine what consumers want and need. When they think they know, they produce it.

Producers organize themselves into separate businesses, or companies. Usually each business concentrates on providing a certain kind of service or producing a certain kind of good. The local barbershop is a business specializing in the service of cutting people's hair. General Motors is a business that concentrates on producing and selling automobiles and trucks.

Everyone who works is a producer in some way. The owner of a business, the store manager or plant supervisor, the employees—all are producers. If you have a part-time job as a waiter or waitress, you are a producer. You produce a service for the people who eat in the restaurant where you work.

Producers who start new businesses are called **entrepreneurs.** These are the people who have ideas about how they can produce a needed good or service for consumers. An entrepreneur can be someone who invents something. An entrepreneur can also be someone, like the owner of a new restaurant, who believes he or she can do a better job than others running similar businesses.

How the System Works

Entrepreneurs are very important in our free enterprise system. In discovering new ideas and responding to the needs of consumers, they help set the economy in motion. They lead the way in creating new products and new jobs.

In establishing new businesses, entrepreneurs take a great many risks. Usually they must spend a great deal of money to produce the goods or services they believe consumers want. They must hire workers and pay them wages. They must buy tools, equipment, and materials and pay rent and utility costs. Once they start their businesses, they must pay for these things whether they take in any money or not.

If for some reason consumers don't buy their goods and services, entrepreneurs may go out of business. Many do in a very short time—and owing thousands of dollars. You will learn more about how to become an entrepreneur in the next chapter.

Resources In creating their new businesses, entrepreneurs must bring together many different resources. Probably the most important resource for any business is labor. Businesses cannot survive without labor. They need the hard-working, highly skilled workers who make up our labor force.

Our country has been fortunate in that many people have come here from other lands. These people have brought skills and know-how with them. As a result, our country's labor force is one of the most productive in the world.

SITUATION
SOLUTION

Working Under Deadline Pressure

You are the head of a group writing a sales report to be presented at the quarterly management meeting. The deadline is a week away, and it's becoming clear that you aren't going to make it, no matter how many hours you work. Management will not be able to make decisions for the coming quarter without your information.

1. Two of your co-workers have not been pulling their share of the load, and you've been trying to do it all. How can you motivate them to work harder?
2. You told your supervisor last week that the work was on schedule, though you were already falling behind. What will you say now?
3. If you're certain that the work cannot be finished by the deadline, how will you decide which work does get done?

Natural resources (land and those things grown on or taken from it) are also needed to produce many goods and services. For example, our entire economy uses a tremendous amount of energy, most of which is produced by burning fossil fuels such as oil and coal. Although we must import oil and many other resources, our country has been blessed with a great supply of natural resources.

Another necessary resource for businesses of all kinds is capital. **Capital** is anything other than land that is used to produce more wealth. Machines and buildings that can be used for production are capital. So is money used to pay for machines and buildings. The importance of capital in free enterprise is obvious when you remember that our economic system is also called capitalism.

The Profit Motive Why do entrepreneurs start new businesses? Why do they risk losing their money? Do they want to produce goods and services just for the purpose of satisfying consumers?

Most entrepreneurs and business owners are in business to make a profit. **Profit** is the amount of

Every business uses a particular combination of resources to provide goods or services to the consuming public. What combination is illustrated here?

money taken in that is more than what was spent. If you pay $10,000 for a car and sell it immediately for $15,000, you have made a profit of $5,000. This is what all businesses are trying to do—make a profit.

Business owners try to produce goods and services that consumers will buy. If consumers buy enough and the business's expenses are not too great, the business will make a profit. Economists describe the reason for businesses' doing business as the profit motive.

Businesses continue to operate as long as they can make a profit. Some businesses survive for hundreds of years. Others last only a short time. Several factors, many of which you will read about later, determine whether or not a company will make a profit.

The Marketplace   To satisfy their needs and wants, consumers must buy goods and services from producers. To make a profit and stay in business, producers must sell the goods and services to consumers. The place where producers and consumers get together to buy and sell goods and services is called the marketplace.

The word *market* and several words made from it, such as *marketplace,* are very important in our economy. In fact, our free enterprise system is also known as a market system or free market system.

The use of these words comes from the days when the market, or farmer's market, was a place in the center of town where people would get together to buy, sell, and trade their products. People would set up their stands or park their carts in a big, open area where everyone could shop.

The stockmarket is a modern version of the old farmer's market. At certain places in the world, such as the New York Stock Exchange, many people gather together in one place to buy and sell. Instead of buying and selling fruits, vegetables, cows, and pigs, however, these people are buying and selling ownership shares in companies.

Consumers and producers do not actually come together in one place as much as they used to. Today, people drive from one store to the next to buy what they need. They also do much of their buying and selling by telephone and mail. Although the buying and selling no longer occur in one place, there still is a marketplace. The word *marketplace* is used to describe all of this economic activity that goes on all over the world.

Another *market* word that you will hear often is *marketing.* **Marketing** is the process of getting goods and services to the consumers who want them. Recall from the beginning of this chapter that it is an important function of an economic system to distribute goods and services. There is no reason to produce goods and services if you have no way to get them to consumers who will pay for them. Activities such as packaging, shipping, advertising, and selling all go together to make up marketing.

As the marketplace has expanded, so has the importance of marketing. Marketing used to be as simple as carrying your goods a few miles to the village market. Today marketing involves national advertising, trucking goods from California to New York, and worldwide distribution. Because the marketplace has expanded, marketing has become more important in our economic system.

Prices   In our system of free enterprise, the prices of goods and services are constantly going up and down. Several factors determine how much goods and services cost at any particular time.

The first is supply and demand. Supply is the amount of goods and services available for sale. Demand is the amount of goods and services consumers want to buy. The relationship between the two and its effect on prices is spelled out in an economic principle called the law of supply and demand. The law states that when the supply of a product is greater than the demand, prices will fall. When the demand is greater than supply, prices will rise.

For example, suppose all your friends wanted to buy a car just like yours, but no others were available. If you decided to sell your car, you could command a very high price. The potential buyers would compete with each other, offering higher and higher prices. Finally, only one buyer would be left—the one who was willing to pay the highest price. All that demand chasing your limited supply would drive the price up.

Suppose, however, that just before you were to close the deal a local auto center brought in a shipment of 1,000 cars just like yours. Suddenly supply would exceed demand. You and the center's salespeople would have to compete for buyers by lowering your prices. The person who offered the lowest price would make the sale. The glut of similar cars would force prices down.

Marketing involves getting products to consumers. One of the most important functions of business, it's everywhere along the street shown here. Explain.

Production costs are another key factor in determining prices. The more it costs to make a good or provide a service, the higher its price must be. Remember the profit motive. To make a profit, businesses must sell their goods and services for more than they cost to produce. It is because of the profit motive that business people talk so much about productivity, or high production. They want to produce the greatest amount of goods and services at the lowest possible cost. This will allow them to set lower prices, which will in turn result in more sales and higher profits.

Competition is the final factor that affects prices. Our economy is based on competition among businesses. Generally speaking, the more competition there is, the lower prices are. When two or more companies produce the same goods or services, all must keep their prices as low as possible. Recall that consumers will try to get the best value for their money. If quality is about equal, they will buy the lower-priced item. Therefore, to compete successfully, businesses must keep their prices close to or lower than their competitors' prices.

Of course, a lack of competition among producers means higher prices. If you produce a new item that everyone wants but no one else makes, you can charge whatever you think consumers will pay. Later you will read how the government prevents businesses from taking unfair advantage of consumers when there is no competition.

Measures of Economic Growth

As mentioned earlier, economists study our free enterprise system. Their purpose is to understand it better and predict how it will perform. To help them do this, economists have a number of measurements that they use as indicators of economic health or weakness. In this section we'll discuss two of them—GNP and balance of trade.

Gross National Product   Economists call the value of all the goods and services we produce in one year the **Gross National Product (GNP)**. Most economists believe that the Gross National Product is one of the most effective ways of evaluating the economy. You will often read about the GNP in newspaper articles and hear about it on television when people discuss the productivity of the national economy.

Our economy has grown at a remarkable rate over the years. In 1989 our GNP exceeded $4 trillion.

Case Study 1

Mary Demski bought a small restaurant in Rossville, a city of 40,000 people. Soon Bill Rogers opened a similar restaurant nearby. When Mary's restaurant began to offer a salad bar, Bill noticed a real drop in business; so he added a salad bar, too, plus a Tuesday special. His business increased. Three months later Mary started to offer special prices during the lunch hour. Then last month she offered Rossville a first. Her restaurant sponsored a bus to take fans 200 miles to see the Pittsburgh Steelers play. Bill wasn't sure what he'd do next, but he knew he had to do something.

There have been times, though, when the economy has not done well. You have probably heard and read about the Great Depression in the 1930s. During this depression our economy was at a near standstill, and millions of people had no money or jobs. There have been other depressions since, but none has been as severe as this one.

There are many reasons why the economy expands and contracts so frequently. New technologies, the amount of capital available, wars, crop failures, and public confidence in our economic future are some of the factors involved.

Consider, for example, public confidence. When economic times are good, consumers have jobs and money, and they feel confident about the future. This causes them to spend more of their money. They buy new cars and build new homes. They don't bother to save their money because it seems that there will always be more coming in.

When consumers spend a great deal of money, businesses start producing more to meet the demand. They hire more workers and build new plants. This creates more jobs and puts more money in the hands of the consumers. The cycle goes on and on—much of it due to public confidence. Unfortunately the cycle works in reverse when public confidence is low.

Balance of Trade   When economists and business people talk about trade, they are talking about buying and selling, not swapping. Trade can refer to any activity in the marketplace, but it is

The law of supply and demand spells out the relationship between the price of a product and its availability. What does the situation shown here suggest about the prices these people will have to pay once they reach the ticket window?

most frequently used to discuss business dealings with other countries.

Trade with other nations is essential to our economic well-being. International trade allows us to apply more of our work and resources to activities where we can do a better job than other nations. It also allows other nations to be successful where they can do a better job than we can.

A company can have a production advantage because of the availability of certain raw materials, a favorable climate, lower wages, or more advanced manufacturing processes. Products of our agriculture, aerospace, machine tool, and computer industries are examples of goods that we export (sell to other countries). We export these goods because we have long had superior technology and resources for producing them.

Through international trade we import (buy from other countries) raw materials and foods that are not available in sufficient supply here. One obvious example is petroleum. Others are tin, chrome, bananas, and coffee.

When the value of our exports is less than the value of our imports, we have a trade deficit. A **deficit** is a shortage. Thus, a trade deficit is a shortage of money that results when we compare the amount spent on imports to the amount received from exports. Huge trade deficits have a negative impact on our economy.

The United States has run large trade deficits in recent years. This has been especially true in our trade with Japan.

✓ *CHECKING UP*

1. Of all economic systems, why is free enterprise so unpredictable and confusing to many people?

2. Assume you are setting up a building supply business. Name three general categories of resources you will need and give a specific example of each.

3. How do supply and demand affect prices?

2 *Exploring Economic Roles*

From the first lesson in this chapter, it should be obvious that people and organizations play multiple roles in our economy. The department store salesperson who is a producer by day becomes a consumer by night when he or she shops at other stores. The company that is a producer of tractors becomes a consumer when it purchases parts from its suppliers. Both individuals and businesses, then, are consumers as well as producers.

The roles of consumer and producer, however, are not the only ones in our economy. Businesses are also not the only organizations that influence how our economy operates. In this lesson you will learn about some of the other important participants in our free enterprise system.

Management and Labor

An important factor in our free enterprise system is the bargaining that goes on between labor and management. You've read how entrepreneurs and workers join together to work as producers. Within a company, though, there is often a division, with the owners and top managers on one side and the majority of the employees on the other side. The two sides are called management and labor.

History of the Labor Movement   In the early days of industry in the United States, people worked long hours. Men, women, and even children worked 12 or more hours a day. Working conditions were often dangerous, and workers were paid only enough to buy the bare necessities. If they complained, they were often fired.

Why did employers treat workers like this? Like all employers, they wanted to keep expenses down so that they could increase their profits. There were many more workers than there were jobs, so employers could always find someone willing to work for the low wages.

Eventually the workers began to join together to help one another improve their situation. They formed labor unions. Labor unions are organizations of workers who join together for the purpose of obtaining higher pay and better working conditions.

The strength and power of unions grew throughout the first part of this century. As a result, Americans are now paid higher wages than at any time in the country's history. They also work shorter hours and receive more benefits. It is estimated that for every $100 paid in wages, employers pay another $20 in fringe benefits for employees. Much of the credit for obtaining these higher wages and increased benefits belongs to unions.

In 1950, 30 percent of all workers in the United States belonged to a union. Union membership has dropped, though, and now less than 20 percent of all workers belong to unions. Much of this drop in union membership was caused by the decline in industrial jobs in the past decade. As a result of this drop, unions do not have quite as much power as they did in the 1950s and 1960s.

The Negotiation Process   As you know, employers are in business to make a profit. An important part of making a profit is keeping expenses low. Since employees' wages are usually an employer's biggest expense, management wants to keep wages from going up and reducing profits.

Unions, on the other hand, want to get the highest possible wages and benefits for all workers. Unions also want management to spend money to improve working conditions.

Obviously, what unions want is in direct conflict with what management wants. This is why unions and management must get together and settle their differences. They go through a process of give-and-take to arrive at a compromise agreeable to both sides. When an agreement is reached, it is written down in the form of a labor contract.

A labor contract is signed by representatives of both labor and management. Such contracts usually last for periods of from one to five years. When the contract expires, a new one is negotiated. The labor contract states how much workers will be paid, what fringe benefits they will receive, and how disagreements will be handled.

In negotiations between labor and management, both sides must be willing to give a little. If one side refuses to compromise, agreement is impossible. Sometimes a union may try to force management to give in by going on strike. A strike is a refusal by employees to work. It causes a loss in production and, therefore, a loss of profit for the company.

Employees on strike receive no wages from their employer, but they may receive some pay from their union. This money is built up through membership dues.

Strikers forego wages for the duration of a strike and increasingly today risk losing their jobs to replacement workers. How do you think this affects the effectiveness of a strike as a union tactic? What other alternatives do you think union members have?

In some states you must join a union if you want to work for a certain company. When you have no choice but to join a union, the company is said to have a closed shop. When you have a choice of joining or not joining a union, the company is said to have an open shop.

The Role of Government

In our free enterprise system people do not have total economic freedom at all times. Our governments—federal, state, and local—are involved in economic matters.

In early America government had little control over business activities. The people involved in business made most of the economic decisions. Even then, though, there was an ongoing debate about how much government should be involved in economic life.

Today our economy is much more complicated. Government at all levels is much bigger, and it does control and regulate many different parts of the economy. For this reason, our economic system is often called a mixed free enterprise system. Whatever the system is called, however, the debate on government involvement in it continues. Depending on which political figures are in office, the government takes a more active or less active role in the economy.

Today federal, state, and local governments employ millions of people, many of whom are involved in activities that somehow affect the economy. Their involvement can be divided into three areas—business regulation, public services, and economic control.

Regulating Business   People have come to expect government to pass and enforce laws to regulate business activities. In many different ways, federal, state, and local laws protect consumers and businesses from unfair practices. Some of the more important areas of regulation are listed below.

- *Antitrust.* These laws prevent one or more companies from developing a monopoly. Having a monopoly means having complete control of a particular market. A monopoly prevents competition and thus goes against an important principle of free enterprise. Antitrust laws give the government the power to break up companies that have too much control over a market. The government's involvement in the breakup of AT&T in 1984 was an attempt to make the telephone service industry more competitive.
- *Public utilities.* There are a few areas in which people have decided that competition would do more harm than good. In the utility service areas (electrical power, telephone, and water), local residents do not usually have a choice of companies to buy from. Since there is no competition among

utility companies, government regulates them to prevent their taking unfair advantage of consumers. Government agencies must approve all rate increases before they can go into effect.

- *Consumer protection.* The government has established agencies and passed laws that require inspection and testing of certain goods and services. You will read much more about these laws in Chapter 16.
- *Fair employment.* Federal and state laws make it illegal for employers to discriminate against job applicants because of race, sex, creed, or age. Laws have also been passed that require employers to maintain safe working conditions and pay a minimum wage.

Providing Public Services Governments provide services such as defense, police protection, education, and transportation that make up a big part of our economy. Some people argue that private companies could not provide these services. Other people believe that governments should take a less active role in many of these areas. It takes a great deal of tax money to pay for all these services. This tax money is money that consumers could spend on goods and services if they didn't have to pay taxes. Thus, the more services governments provide, the more potential profits they take away from businesses.

A very serious problem has resulted from government's increased role in providing services. The federal government is spending a great deal more money than it is taking in (see Figure 13-1). In

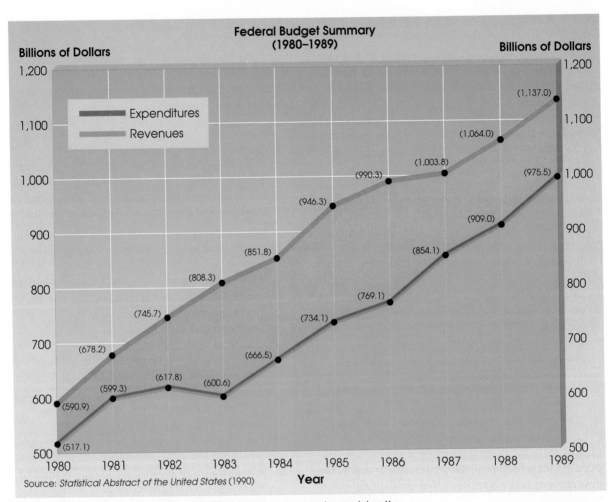

Figure 13-1   During the 1980s, the federal government consistently spent more than it collected in taxes. In what year was this difference greatest? How do you know?

1989, for example, federal spending exceeded income by $161.5 billion. (Even this figure, large as it is, was considered low at the time by many lawmakers and economists. Critics of government accounting practices pointed out that the figure used money collected for social security benefits to offset some of the excess spending. It also did not reflect the full cost of bailing out the nation's ailing savings and loan industry. The real amount by which spending exceeded tax receipts in 1989 was, critics argued, somewhere in excess of $240 billion!)

The difference between what government spends and what it takes in is called a budget deficit. As would be necessary for any business, the government must borrow money when it can't meet expenses. The government must also pay interest (see Chapter 19) on the money it borrows. As a result of the deficit, a great deal of the money we pay in taxes (about 20 percent in 1989) goes toward paying interest to banks and other lenders.

Many people believe in a balanced budget, which means that the government should spend no more money than it takes in. To balance the budget, government would need either to raise taxes or cut spending. The people who argue for a balanced budget believe that the huge deficits are dangerous to the growth and well-being of our economy. Economists have different views on the seriousness of this problem.

Controlling the Economy   You read earlier that our free enterprise system is not a perfect economic system. Many people believe that the system works better if the government helps to control it. It was during the Great Depression of the 1930s, when the economy was doing so poorly, that the federal government began to take a more active part in helping the economy grow and prosper.

The two major problems that occur in our free enterprise system are unemployment and inflation. These are examples of the types of problems that government tries to solve.

Unemployment refers to the number of workers who want jobs but can't find them. Unemployment rises when the economy slows down. Ideally everyone who wants a job should be able to find one. This ideal condition, called full employment, almost never occurs. In recent years unemployment has risen as high as 20 percent in many industrial areas where large factories are closing or cutting back on production. High unemployment

rates like this create a serious problem for the entire economic system.

Inflation is an economic condition in which prices rise sharply. During the 1970s, our country suffered through periods of tremendous inflation. Prices were rising at the rate of 10 to 12 percent a year. This is a serious problem since it lessens the value of the dollar. If wages don't go up, people must lower their standard of living.

Governments can do several things to combat these problems. When unemployment is high, they can spend more money, which creates jobs. They can also reduce taxes, which gives consumers more money to spend, which in turn stimulates the economy and creates jobs.

During periods of inflation, governments can do just the opposite—spend less money and raise taxes. The effect is to slow down the economy and stop the increase in prices.

The federal government's use of the Federal Reserve System also has a great effect on the economy. The **Federal Reserve** is a government agency responsible for controlling our nation's money supply. The money supply is the total of all money in circulation. By changing the monetary policy of the "Fed," as it's often called, the government can lessen the effects of economic ups and downs.

The primary factor in the Fed's monetary policy is interest rates. By raising or lowering interest rates, the Fed affects the amount of money that banks can loan. Generally, the Federal Reserve lowers interest rates and makes money more available when total spending is considered too low. It raises interest rates and makes money less available when total spending is too high.

Your Role in the System

You will play several different roles in our economic system. Like everyone else, you will be involved as a consumer who needs and wants certain goods and services. You will also be involved as a producer, either as an entrepreneur or an employee. Finally, you will be involved as a citizen and a voter. In each of these roles you will have to make decisions that will affect your future and the future of our country.

Consumer   You are already affecting our economy as a consumer. When you move away from home and get a full-time job, you'll have even more money to spend. Your impact on the

Strive for Success

An Economist with a Conscience

Over 200 years ago Adam Smith, who is hailed as the founder of economics, stated that if people and businesses were allowed to act in their own interests, they would naturally do what was best for society as a whole. Since then, few Western economists have argued with this theory. One who did was Joan Robinson.

Robinson was a British economist. She is considered one of the world's most important modern economic theorists.

Robinson criticized economists in general because they have ignored social and moral issues. She disagreed with Smith and those who accept his theories. To her, the Great Depression of the 1930s provided ample proof that self-interest does not necessarily make everyone better off, that morality does not take care of itself. Robinson also believed that economists have a duty to enlighten the public about the economic aspects of social and moral problems, such as the nuclear arms race and the destruction of the environment.

In teaching circles, Robinson is best known for developing the theory of monopolistic competition. The theory tries to make sense of the marketplace in an age when many large industries are dominated by relatively few companies. Robinson found that a firm could obtain a partial monopoly simply by advertising a particular brand name. When enough consumers came to associate the product with the name, the company would have a partial monopoly. That would mean that the firm could raise its prices a little and not lose its customers. They would remain loyal to the brand.

Robinson taught for more than 40 years and was professor of economics at Cambridge University. She wrote and lectured widely on economic subjects. Among her books are *Introduction to the Theory of Employment, The Accumulation of Capital, Economic Philosophy,* and *Freedom and Necessity: An Introduction to the Study of Society.*

economy will increase as your income and spending increase.

If you are like most consumers, you will not have all the money you want. You will buy those goods and services that you need and want the most. In doing this you will help some businesses make a profit.

If you are a wise consumer, you will help those businesses that provide the best values. If you are not careful with your spending, you may help companies that are not producing quality products stay in business. Unit Four of this book will help you learn how to make wise consumer decisions.

Producer   If you have already made a career decision, then you should have a good idea what your role as a producer will be. After reading about our free enterprise system, you should realize more than ever before that you can choose your own role. Whether it's the risk-taking and challenging role of entrepreneurship or the more secure but potentially less profitable role of employee, you decide.

Whatever type of producer you choose to be, be a productive one. Even if you are an employee with a fixed wage or salary, it's important that you work hard and put in a full day's work. Businesses can't make a profit unless their workers are productive, and you know now what happens if a business fails to make a profit.

With the economy changing so rapidly, it's also important that you be able to adapt to change. Do not limit yourself to developing one particular skill that may not be needed someday.

This is where the basic skills that you read about in earlier chapters become important. Employers want to hire workers who have good communication, math, and—more and more—computer skills. They feel they can train workers to do the specific tasks that need to be done in their companies. Employers are not as capable, though, of teaching these basic skills.

You've already done some career research. Continue to read newspapers, magazines, and current books on our economy. Keep up with changes. By doing this, you will be one of the first to know about new career opportunities. You may be able to take classes or receive training that will qualify you for jobs that few people are qualified to do. Who knows—you might even see a change coming before it happens and turn your idea into a new and prosperous company of your own.

Voter   You've read about the many ways in which government is involved in our free enterprise system. Many people believe that government should take an even more active role in the economy. These people believe that unemployment and poverty could be eliminated with more government help.

Others believe the opposite is true. They believe our economy would provide a higher standard of living for more people if government would stop interfering with the free enterprise system. They believe that a big, expensive government creates more problems than it solves.

As a voter, you will have countless opportunities to voice your opinion about government's role in our economy. Most candidates have definite opinions about economic policy. It is your job as a responsible voter to learn which candidates' opinions are closest to your own.

As you know, our economic system is very complex. Millions of people and countless situations and events affect what happens to the economy. This makes it difficult for most of us to understand economic issues. It's important, however, that we all make an effort to understand and vote according to what we believe will be best for ourselves and the country as a whole.

MAKE A DECISION

You are about to vote for U.S. senator. You've read about the candidates and know their views. One is a liberal candidate who advocates raising taxes to provide more services for everyone, especially the needy. The other candidate is a conservative who wants to cut back on all federal spending, which could mean lower taxes. What's your decision—do you vote for the liberal or the conservative? Give the reasons for your decision.

✓ CHECKING UP

1. Describe at least three ways in which government regulates business.
2. Where do budget deficits come from?
3. Every person has one principal role in our economic system—true or false? Explain.

Review Your Learning

CHAPTER SUMMARY

Every country needs an economic system to satisfy the basic needs and wants of its citizens. The economic system used in the United States is called the free enterprise system. This system is based on the idea that people should have the freedom to make their own economic decisions. Other key factors at work in our system are the profit motive, competition, and the law of supply and demand.

Briefly, the operation of the system begins with consumers' needs and wants. The producers organize themselves into businesses, started by entrepreneurs, and produce the goods and services that consumers want. The businesses succeed or fail depending on how successful they are at satisfying consumers.

Our economic system is constantly changing. It goes through alternating periods of growth and decline. Some industries die out, and others take their places. Economists study these changes and evaluate them in terms of standard economic measurements, such as GNP and deficits (trade and budget).

Although ours is a free enterprise system, government (federal, state, and local) does have a big impact on the economy. The role of government has increased over the years, and the debate goes on as to how much government involvement is desirable. Government affects the economy through three major types of activity—regulating business, providing public services, and controlling the money supply.

You will have three roles in our economic system—consumer, producer, and voter. Admittedly, the system is confusing and difficult to understand, but you should do your best to keep up with the changes occurring in it. Doing so will increase your chances—and your country's chances—for success.

TERMS TO KNOW

On a separate sheet of paper, write sentences for each of the following terms:

economic system
free enterprise
consumer
entrepreneurs
capital
profit
marketing
Gross National Product
deficit
inflation
Federal Reserve

STUDY QUESTIONS

1. How do producers decide which goods and services and how much of each to produce?
2. What are three major resources that entrepreneurs bring together when starting a business?
3. What is the main reason people start businesses?
4. Why has marketing become a more important part of our economic system?
5. What are three factors affecting the rise and fall of prices?
6. If the demand for a product goes up, what usually happens to its price.
7. If U.S. companies exported $200 million of products in a given year while importing $350 million of products, would the United States have a trade surplus or deficit?
8. What is the difference between an open shop and a closed shop?
9. Name three basic ways that government is involved in our economy.
10. What two things could the federal government do to balance the budget?

1. Describe a completely free enterprise system. Would it work? Why or why not?
2. You and a friend observe a long line outside a local tire store. The cartoon below shows what all the fuss is about. "What a rip-off," says your friend. "There oughta be a law against that sort of thing." Do you agree? Why or why not?

DISCUSSION STARTERS

1. If you were to become an entrepreneur, what sort of business would you start? Explain the reasons for your choice.
2. Our economy is constantly changing. How has the economic situation changed in your area during the past two years? What companies have gone out of business? What new companies have started?

BUILDING BASIC SKILLS

Math
1. You have read that a high school graduate earns twice as much as someone with an eighth grade education and that a college graduate earns 1½ times as much as a high school graduate. Assume that someone with an eighth grade education averages $14,000 per year.
   - How much more will a high school graduate earn in 40 years of working than the eighth grade graduate?
   - How much more will a college graduate earn in 40 years than the high school graduate?

Citizenship
2. In recent national elections only about 50 percent of those registered to vote cast ballots. Your father is getting ready to join their ranks. He says he doesn't like any of the candidates the major parties are offering, that there's no real difference between them, and that they don't stand for the things he supports. How would you persuade your father that his course of action is unwise? What alternatives would you suggest?

Problem Solving
3. Assume you're the manager of a card and gift shop, and you're having a cash flow problem. It's six weeks before Mother's Day, the biggest card-buying holiday of the year, and you don't have enough cash on hand to buy inventory. Your suppliers won't send you cards unless you pay up front. What are your alternatives?

SUGGESTED ACTIVITY

Interview someone who has lived and worked in an economic system other than free enterprise. Ask him or her to describe the differences in the two systems. Take notes and report your findings to the class.

Becoming an Entrepreneur

*T*here are about 14 million businesses in the United States—all of them started by entrepreneurs. With their new ideas and their willingness to take risks, entrepreneurs create the businesses that give millions of Americans a place to work.

There are both advantages and disadvantages to being an entrepreneur. All entrepreneurs have the satisfaction of being their own boss, and many earn a great deal of money. On the other hand, entrepreneurs must take great financial risks, and they must work long, hard hours to keep their businesses profitable. Almost two out of every three new businesses fail within four years of their opening.

In this chapter you will get a better idea of what it's like to be an entrepreneur. You will learn about the importance of planning and the many different ways you could go about starting your own business. You will also learn about the record keeping and financial planning that must take place once you have your business started.

1 *Ways to Enter Business*

Nearly a half million businesses are started each year in the United States. Not all of these are entirely new enterprises. Some are established businesses transferred into the hands of new owners. Others are new branches of existing businesses that are expanding.

To become an entrepreneur, then, you do not always need to start from scratch. There are other possibilities.

Buying an Existing Business

If you are interested in owning a retail or wholesale business, you may find it easier and safer to buy an existing business than to start a new one. This arrangement has several advantages.

First, it's cheaper. The main reason for this is that you avoid costly start-up expenses. You can also benefit from the current owner's business agreements, such as a lease signed when rents were lower. Finally, if the owner is retiring or anxious to sell for a similar reason, you may be able to get a lower purchase price. The owner may even be willing to finance the transaction. Such arrangements usually carry lower interest rates than those offered by banks.

The second advantage to buying an existing business is goodwill. If the business has been successful, it will already have a solid customer base and a good reputation in the community. It will also likely have good employees who will remain with the business and continue to provide valuable assistance.

There are some possible disadvantages to buying an existing business, however. The business may be for sale because it is *not* successful. The neighborhood in which it is located may be changing. (It may be in decline, or perhaps new and aggressive competitors have recently entered the area.) The business may have a decaying building or obsolete equipment that must be replaced if the firm is to operate efficiently. Finally, the business may have a reputation for providing poor service or poor quality products. Individually or together, these things could mean low or nonexistent profits with little or no prospect for improvement.

Buying a Franchise Business

A **franchise** is the legal right to sell a company's goods and services in a particular area. In recent

Case Study 1

Tom Combs studied auto body repair in a high school vocational class. After graduation, he worked in the Kimmons Body Shop and attended the university at night. After six years of experience, Tom had become a skilled auto body mechanic. He had also earned a degree in automotive technology.

Mr. Kimmons had established the auto body business 35 years ago and was now planning to retire. He was proud of his highly successful business, and, if at all possible, he wanted it to continue under his name.

Tom was offered a number of good positions, but he liked Mr. Kimmons' offer best. Mr. Kimmons agreed to sell Tom the business and finance the debt. Tom would pay the debt over a ten-year period.

Tom was pleased to get this "once in a lifetime" opportunity to buy a well-established business under such favorable terms.

years franchise businesses, especially in the food service industry, have grown rapidly. A number of entrepreneurs who started food service businesses and sold franchises have become very wealthy.

When you buy a franchise, you buy an established business concept and the right to operate the business. Your local business becomes a member of the parent company's chain of franchises. In return for a portion of your revenues, the parent company gives you use of its name, advertising, and other services.

There are about 2,000 different chains of franchise businesses in operation in the United States. These businesses offer nationwide service and account for about 35 percent of all retail sales in this country.

There is usually less risk involved in opening a franchise than in opening a totally new business. You would probably receive training and consultation services, thus reducing the possibility of failure. Your franchise would also be identified with a national name (such as Pizza Hut or McDonald's), which usually means more customers and easier-to-obtain loans.

Still, you must be cautious. There are some possible problems. The expense of buying the

The owner of a franchise business benefits from the support services provided by the franchisor—here, McDonald's. How does the franchisor benefit from the arrangement?

franchise and continuing its operation will greatly reduce your profits. Franchise contracts are complex, and it is sometimes difficult to meet all the requirements imposed by the company. Increases in the fees could drive you out of the business. Another disadvantage is that you get little personal recognition as a franchise owner.

Taking Over the Family Business

For those who have relatives who are entrepreneurs, taking over or expanding the family business may be an option. Such an arrangement has major advantages. Costs are lower (family members usually don't have to buy their way into a family business). If the family and the business are well known in the community, the firm's reputation is probably already established, thus ensuring a firm customer base. Finally, transfer of the business will likely be aided by advice and training from family members familiar with the firm's operation. Such an arrangement amounts to hav-

ing all the benefits of a franchise and none of the burdens (namely, the excessive fees).

Still, family businesses do have some of the pitfalls of other business arrangements. Where multiple family members are involved, conflict may arise over the proper way to run the business. At the other extreme, reluctant family members may find themselves pressured to take over a failing business "for the sake of the family."

✓ CHECKING UP

1. Even if you don't have an idea for a new business, you can still become an entrepreneur. Explain how.

2. What is a franchise, and how does it operate?

3. How does taking over a family business compare with buying a franchise business?

2 *Planning a Business*

What is the most important factor in determining the success or failure of a new business? One expert answered this question by saying, "They've got to have a plan—they've got to know where they're going." He was talking, of course, about entrepreneurs.

If you become an entrepreneur, *you* will be the one who plans the business. This will require knowledge and motivation. The same expert mentioned above also said that "starting a business is not a 9 to 5 job, five days a week—it's 24 hours, 365 days a year." If you enjoy the work and receive satisfaction from it, those factors will be your motivation to do the necessary work and planning.

Gathering Information

Vocational programs often include courses in entrepreneurship. In these programs you can gain knowledge and experience with the products or service that you would be offering in your business. You would study business trends that may affect your business. You would learn to analyze a geographical area to estimate the number of customers or clients and the competition that you can expect.

An important part of entrepreneurship is learning what types of assistance you will need and can expect to find from experts. For example, you will probably need an accountant. An accountant can help you devise a bookkeeping system. An accountant can also make sure you file the required forms, such as the many different tax and insurance forms.

You will almost certainly need to borrow money. A banker can give you financial advice and information on obtaining loans. An insurance agent can help you choose the kinds and amounts of insurance you will need for your business.

In many cases you can get free information from knowledgeable people. Many of the people who work in the same business or industry as you will answer your questions. For example, the salespeople who would be supplying you with materials can be valuable sources of information.

There are several other sources of information. Contact the small-business institute at the nearest university. The local Chamber of Commerce and the public library are also good sources of information. You will, of course, want to contact state and federal agencies to make sure you fulfill all your licensing requirements.

A good beginning source of information is the Small Business Administration. You can contact the national office in Washington, D.C., or the regional office closest to you. The SBA will send you a great deal of information about various problems and questions related to starting a new business.

Making Key Decisions

You shouldn't start a business unless it involves work that you like and know something about. For example, if you are a good welder and like the work, that may be a good business for you.

Before you make a decision, consider several things. First of all, look at what you want the business to do for you. Think about the following questions:

- Will I have time for this business?
- What will be the start-up cost?
- How much competition will I have?
- Will sales be great enough for me to make a profit?
- Can I find competent employees to help me?
- Should I do it alone or have partners?
- Will this business keep me away from my friends and family?
- What growth potential does the business have?
- Will the business give me the status I want?
- What will be my interest in this business after 5, 10, or 15 years?

Your answers to these questions will help you decide whether or not you should go into business for yourself. So will the entrepreneurial checklist (Figure 14-1) on the next page. The more questions you can answer before you begin your business, the better. Remember what you've been reading throughout this book—planning is the key to success. Good planning, more than any other factor, will contribute to a successful new business.

Form of Ownership   One of the planning decisions to be made is the choice of legal ownership. There are three basic kinds of ownership. A business may be operated as a sole proprietorship, partnership, or corporation.

Small businesses usually start as **sole proprietorships.** This means that the business is completely

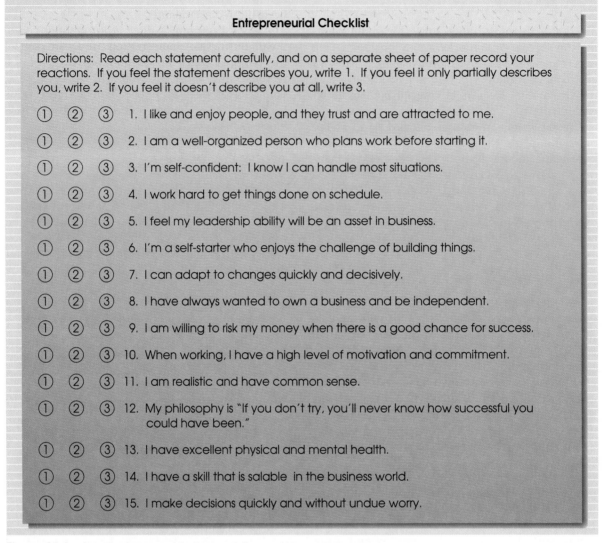

Entrepreneurial Checklist

Directions: Read each statement carefully, and on a separate sheet of paper record your reactions. If you feel the statement describes you, write 1. If you feel it only partially describes you, write 2. If you feel it doesn't describe you at all, write 3.

① ② ③   1. I like and enjoy people, and they trust and are attracted to me.

① ② ③   2. I am a well-organized person who plans work before starting it.

① ② ③   3. I'm self-confident: I know I can handle most situations.

① ② ③   4. I work hard to get things done on schedule.

① ② ③   5. I feel my leadership ability will be an asset in business.

① ② ③   6. I'm a self-starter who enjoys the challenge of building things.

① ② ③   7. I can adapt to changes quickly and decisively.

① ② ③   8. I have always wanted to own a business and be independent.

① ② ③   9. I am willing to risk my money when there is a good chance for success.

① ② ③   10. When working, I have a high level of motivation and commitment.

① ② ③   11. I am realistic and have common sense.

① ② ③   12. My philosophy is "If you don't try, you'll never know how successful you could have been."

① ② ③   13. I have excellent physical and mental health.

① ② ③   14. I have a skill that is salable in the business world.

① ② ③   15. I make decisions quickly and without undue worry.

Figure 14-1   Is entrepreneurship for you? Personal inventories like the one shown here can help you decide. To score yourself, multiply each figure (1, 2, or 3) by the number of times you selected it and add the results. For example, if your answers included two 3s, four 2s, and nine 1s, your score would be calculated as follows: $(2 \times 3) + (4 \times 2) + (9 \times 1) = 6 + 8 + 9 = 23$. The closer your score is to 20 (or below), the more "entrepreneurial" you are.

owned by one person. About 75 percent of all businesses in this country are sole proprietorships.

In a sole proprietorship business, the owner keeps all the profits. This is the major advantage to this type of ownership. The major disadvantage is that the owner has complete financial responsibility. If the business loses money, the owner must pay all the debts.

A **partnership** is a business owned by two or more persons. These people pool their money,

time, skill, and knowledge to operate the business. They share both the profits and the risks.

Partnership agreements should be prepared by an attorney who knows the relevant state and federal laws. Operating a business with a partner can be beneficial, but a poor or dissatisfied partner is a great disadvantage. The partnership agreement should cover all phases of decision making, responsibility, division of profits, and the means for ending the partnership if that becomes advisable.

Strive for Success

Nice Guys Finish First

They began their training with a five-dollar correspondence course. They started their business with only $12,000. Today they drive around in a modified motorhome called the Cowmobile and give away samples of their products. They also place community, employee, and ecological concerns above their interest in the bottom line. Does anyone *really* take Ben Cohen and Jerry Greenfield seriously?

Time does: in 1981 the magazine hailed their product as "the best in the world." The White House does: in 1988 President Ronald Reagan named them the U.S. Small-Business Persons of the Year. The financial community does: what was started for $12,000 has become a multimillion dollar business recognized as one of the best in its field.

Ice cream eaters also take Ben and Jerry seriously, and that may be most important of all. The two founded Ben and Jerry's, Vermont's Finest All-Natural Ice Cream, in 1978 and have been busy winning converts to their chunky, flavorful concoctions ever since.

Ben and Jerry, however, have done more than just make and sell great ice cream. They have also shown a deep commitment to their employees and their community. As a part of this commitment, they established the Ben and Jerry's Foundation, a nonprofit institution that awards funds to charitable and community service organizations. Ben and Jerry donate 7.5 percent of their company's pretax earnings to this foundation each year.

Ben and Jerry have also demonstrated a commitment to their employees. As a part of the corporate structure, there is a Joy Committee whose job it is to create and implement programs to put more joy in the workplace. During one particularly hectic week, the committee called in a masseuse to give workers massages during their breaks.

From the start, Ben and Jerry's threefold commitment—to a quality product, to their community, and to their employees—has proved to be a recipe for success. The company has

grown rapidly and has made a great many people take Ben and Jerry very seriously.

That's not to say, however, that this growth has come without its setbacks. The first Cowmobile driven by Ben and Jerry burned up outside Cleveland, Ohio, during its maiden trip across the country—a tragedy, said Ben, that looked like "the world's biggest baked Alaska."

One of the principal benefits of a partnership is that each person brings his or her particular talents to the business. How does this help the enterprise?

Would a Partner Help?

You are the owner and principal carpenter of Custom Cabinetry. Despite the high quality of your work, you have done little more than break even for three years. You attribute this fact to not being "a people person." (You would rather let your work speak for itself than "chat up" the customers.) You also have little liking for the management side of the business—coordinating schedules, workers, and supplier deliveries so that jobs get done on time.

Your accountant says you'll never be successful if you continue this way. He recommends that you take on a partner and has offered two candidates. Angela is extremely personable and articulate. She has a good ability to visualize and a working familiarity with carpentry (it's her father's hobby). Bill isn't as personable as Angela, but he's an experienced building contractor and has a thorough knowledge of the building trades. For a share of the business, both Angela and Bill offer minimal cash payments—and their substantial skills.

1. Who would you choose for a partner—Angela or Bill? neither or both? Why?

2. What, if any, special provisions would you require to be included in the partnership agreement?

3. What other solutions might there be to your problem? What advantages or disadvantages would they have compared to partnership?

MAKE A DECISION

You are good at what you do, and everyone says you have a real knack for getting along with people. The idea of starting your own business has crossed your mind several times. You have some money saved up—probably enough to get someone else to loan you the rest of what you'd need. However, you would have to give up your job and the steady, reliable income it provides. You like your job, but if you stay you know you will never do more than just get by. With your own business you'd have a chance to get ahead. What's your decision —do you take a chance with your own business or play it safe at your present job? Give the reasons for your decision.

A **corporation** is a business owned by a number of people who buy shares in the firm. These people are called stockholders. The stockholders vote to elect a board of directors, which is responsible for making general policies and hiring people to manage the business. Stockholders share the profits, which are called dividends.

Forming a corporation protects the personal savings of the owners. Any legal judgment against the corporation is limited to the value of the business. Corporations may pay a lower tax rate than sole proprietorships and partnerships. They may also find it easier to borrow money to expand

Case Study 2

Frank studied plastics technology at City Vocational School. After graduation he was employed by Capital Plastic Container Company. He became very skilled in design and fabrication.

After work Frank enjoyed his hobby of building small fiberglass boats. He used his garage as a workshop. The boats were of high quality, and many of Frank's friends bought them. In fact, so many people wanted boats that Frank started a small factory in a barn. He worked evenings and weekends to fill orders for the boats.

Business increased rapidly, and soon Frank had more orders than he could fill. His wife, Lisa, and his friends urged him to devote all of his time to his boat business, which he decided to do. Lisa, an accountant, managed all the financial records. With her help and that of his friends and some of his suppliers, Frank established the City Boat Company.

To raise the money he needed to expand the business, Frank incorporated and sold stock. Within five years, City Boat Company had 20 employees and over $2 million in sales. Frank, Lisa, and all the stockholders were very pleased with the success of the new business. Frank and Lisa became quite wealthy.

For any kind of retail or service business, a good location is essential. Would you want to open a fast-food take-out business in this mall? Why or why not?

- The cost of renting or buying property
- The location of competition
- The area residents—how many and their potential as customers

Financing   Getting money to start a new business is a major problem for entrepreneurs. This is especially true when credit is tight or interest rates are high. The potential owner of a new business has only a few sources of capital available.

Before setting out to get a loan, determine the financial requirements of starting and operating your business. Include detailed plans and expectations for the enterprise. You will also want to include information about yourself and a statement of your total financial need.

The business description should clearly and precisely present the following information:

- Description of the goods or services you will offer
- Operation plan, including location, size, and lease for the business site

the business. Strict legal requirements must be followed to form a corporation.

Location   If an entrepreneur needs to work outside his or her home, the choice of a good business location will be essential for success. This is especially true of retail businesses and businesses that provide services, such as laundromats, beauty shops, and car washes. The convenience of the customers is of major importance. If the location is wrong—if it's too far from most customers or in an undesirable area—people will go somewhere else.

Careful research is needed before a decision is made. For each potential site, the following factors should be considered:

- The type of business area
- The condition of streets and buildings in the area

Case Study 3

Linda started working in pizza restaurants when she was a sophomore in high school. She is now assistant manager of Vanetti's Pizza. Linda knows that pizza restaurants have been very successful and wants to start her own in a neighboring town. She has found three possible locations.

The first site is in a mall on the south side of the town. The mall has a small theater, a deli, and a video rental store. The space is adequate, and the rent is $1,200 a month (including utilities). The nearest fast-food restaurant is a half mile away. Most of the area is residential, and there's a state university campus within walking distance.

The second site is an unused service station just south of the business district. This location has a dozen parking spaces and all the utilities needed for a pizza restaurant. It is 15 blocks from the university and 10 blocks from two other pizza restaurants. The area is combined residential and small business. The building will require remodeling, but the rent with a six-month lease is only $400 per month.

The third site is on a highway at the north end of the town. There are seven fast-food establishments within a half mile. The building is new, with 30 parking spaces, and was recently used as a pizza restaurant. (That business failed.) The facility is still equipped, however, and ready for use. The rent is $750 per month.

Linda made her decision—she chose the second site. The rent for the first location, she felt, was more than she could afford to pay. The location of the third site was too crowded with competitors. The second site was affordable with a good potential customer base and little nearby competition. True, the building would have to be remodeled; but the lower rent for the first six months would make that factor manageable.

- Financial plan, including start-up capital, expected profit and sales, and loan payment plans

- Personnel plan, including needed staff, salaries, and benefits
- Competition, including the number of competitors and their strengths and weaknesses
- Timetable and schedule for starting the business

The amount of information included in your business description will depend on the size of the loan you are seeking. The larger the loan, the more information you will need.

The third item above, the financial plan, is necessary to determine your financial need. This type of plan will help the lending company better understand your actual needs. Your financial plan should include the following:

- Start-up expenses for the first few months (including remodeling, equipment, supplies, and advertising expenses)
- Operating expenses to cover the months the business is becoming established and may operate at a loss
- Total expenses for the first few months of operation

When you apply for a loan, you will have to supply personal information. The credit businesses, banks, and loan companies use standard forms to list personal information. These forms usually ask for the following:

- Your education and experience in the business you want to start
- Your credit rating
- Your assets (cash and property) and liabilities (money you owe)
- Your collateral, or security (See Chapter 19 for more information.)

It can take a great deal of money to start a new business. Where will you get this money? There are several possible sources.

- Your own savings (Unless you put some of your own money into the business, it will be difficult to convince others to share the risk.)
- Banks and credit unions
- Small Business Administration
- Family and friends (a good source of loans with low interest rates)
- Suppliers and distributors
- Leasing companies

New small business owners often find it difficult to get financing from banks. Why?

Obtaining a loan from a bank or savings and loan is difficult. These institutions prefer making less risky loans to businesses that are already established. Once you achieve success as an entrepreneur, though, getting financial help becomes much easier.

Since most loan agencies hesitate to finance start-up businesses, entrepreneurs usually risk mostly their own money. If you borrow money from a friend or family member, do so in a legal way. The statement of the loan should be written in legal form. The terms should be clearly stated. This will help prevent financial matters from getting in the way of a friendship.

The more of your own money you can put into your new business, the less finance expense you will have. Saving to start a business may take several years. You can find more information on money matters in Chapters 17, 18, and 19.

Permits   All businesses must meet federal, state, county, and city operating requirements. Even entrepreneurs working out of their own homes (like inventors, artists, and consultants) usually need some official documents. At a minimum, these would include a permit or license to operate and an assignment of tax number.

Application for such items should be made early in the planning process. By the time the business is ready to operate, the new owner's applications should have been approved and the necessary documents issued.

✓ CHECKING UP

1. What are the three major forms of business ownership, and how do they differ from each other?
2. What factors are most important in selecting a potential business site?
3. You are a new business owner. To get a start-up loan, you will have to provide potential lenders with a detailed description of your enterprise. What general categories of information will you include?

3 *Operating a Business*

In a manufacturing business, the primary goal is to produce a salable product. The cost and quality of the product are of prime importance. The cost must be competitive and the quality acceptable, or the product will not sell.

Manufacturing requires a much greater start-up investment than some other types of businesses. Special machines, which can be very expensive, are often needed. In addition, once it is operating, a manufacturing business may have to keep large quantities of raw materials in stock.

Service businesses (such as restaurants, motels, and trucking firms) do not sell goods. They provide a service. Operating costs for these businesses include salaries, equipment, rent, utilities, and buildings. Operating expenses vary and depend on the type of business.

In a retail business, everything centers on selling goods, such as groceries, shoes, and clothing. A big part of a retailer's expense goes toward buying inventory. **Inventory** consists of the total amount of goods in stock, or available at any given time.

An important part of being a successful retailer is regulating the size of the inventory. It should be large enough so that most customers can find what they want. It should not be so large, however, that it limits the owner's ability to spend on other necessary business expenses. Remember, a retailer must buy inventory with his or her *own* funds before it can be sold to make a profit. Thus, a reasonable balance must always be maintained between sales and inventory.

The use of modern, computerized bookkeeping makes inventory control much more efficient. Small retail businesses, however, do not need large or especially complex computer systems. Many personal computers can run versions of the same software large enterprises use to keep track of their inventories.

Setting Prices

The selling price of a product is determined by the following factors:

- Cost of goods to be sold
- Total operating expenses of the business, including start-up costs
- Amount of customer demand
- Competition
- Percentage of profit desired

All retailers struggle to maintain just the right size inventory for the amount of business they do. What would be the consequences of guessing wrong and ending up with too much inventory on hand?

The cost of goods is the actual cost the business owner must pay to the supplier. Some suppliers give discounts to owners who buy regularly in large quantities.

Setting prices is critical to the success of a business. Only an enterprise that has a monopoly on a product can afford to charge whatever the market will bear. Others must price with an eye to their competitors. The business owner who sets prices higher than the competition's risks losing customers. Most shoppers will go where the prices for the same or similar items are lower.

Keeping Financial Records

Keeping accurate business records is a legal requirement. It is also essential to making a profit. Every business owner keeps records of all transactions. These records must be kept for daily, monthly, and annual reports. The size and type of business will determine the extent of records needed, but every business needs the following records:

- *Revenues—money taken in from sales.* Records of sales and services must be recorded each day in a ledger. Cash register receipts and sales slips are used as records of revenue. These records give the owner a base to determine if the break-even point is being reached.

- *Expenses—includes purchases, utilities, rent, salaries, depreciation, and taxes.* Separate accounts must be kept for all of these.

- *Business reports—special forms for reporting sales taxes, payroll tax, and income tax.* Reports on worker's compensation and unemployment insurance must also be sent to government agencies on the local, state, and federal levels.

The bookkeeping system used to keep these records should be established before a business is in operation. A beginning entrepreneur should become familiar with bookkeeping procedures. A few courses in bookkeeping and computer operation would be helpful in this regard. Assistance from an accountant may also be needed to select and set up a bookkeeping system.

Using Sales Slips   Sales slips provide a good way to record sales. They can also be used for inventory control. Sales slips are numbered and printed to make two or more carbon copies. Most of the slips have places to write the following information:

- Date of sale and salesperson's number
- Name, address, and telephone number of customer
- The quantity, stock number, and name of item sold
- Unit price, amount of sale, sales tax, and total amount charged the customer

Businesses offering credit or credit card sales may also use sales slips for the above information.

Using Business Checking Accounts   Sales slips are useful in recording revenues and managing inventory, but an expense record is of equal importance. A business checkbook is typically used for this purpose. It provides a record of income from the daily deposits of sales receipts. It also provides a record of expenses if all bills are paid by check. The records from your checking account will help you decide if your business is profitable. Chapter 18 provides additional information on the use of payroll checks and checking accounts.

Figuring Profit   Making a profit is the major goal of any business owner. To determine if a business has been profitable, an owner must prepare an **income statement** at the end of each year. This document clearly shows how much the business earned or lost. (An income statement is also sometimes called a profit and loss statement.)

Income statements are used to make many key business decisions, such as whether to expand into new product areas or to hire additional help. They are also required to compute state and federal income taxes. Entrepreneurs should therefore be familiar with both the format and the wording of such documents.

Figure 14-2 shows a simplified income statement for a small business. It contains two terms you will encounter frequently in business records —operating expenses and net profit. **Operating expenses** include all the expenses that must be paid to keep a business going. **Net profit** is the amount of money remaining after all expenses have been paid from revenues.

The contents of an income statement are often used to evaluate the progress and potential of a business. For example, two of the entries, net profit and total revenue, can be used to compute a percentage called a **profit ratio**. Owners and financial analysts employ this figure to compare profits

**Mountain-Air Bikes
Income Statement**

Year Ended December 31, 19—

Revenue:

Sales	$212,015	
Cost of goods sold	109,614	
Gross profit		$102,401

Operating expenses:

Salaries	$ 24,019	
Rent	11,211	
Utilities	4,514	
Advertising	2,422	
Total operating expenses		42,166
Net profit (before taxes)		$ 60,235

Figure 14-2   An income statement shows the profit status of a company for the preceding business year. If Mountain-Air Bikes had lost money, how would their statement look different from the one shown here?

and expenses from year to year. The higher the profit ratio, the healthier the business.

Here is the formula for profit ratio:

$$\text{Profit ratio} = \frac{\text{net profit}}{\text{total revenue}}$$

If a business had $15,500 in revenues and a net profit of $13,500, its profit ratio would be computed as follows:

$$\text{Profit ratio} = \frac{\$13,500}{\$15,500} = .87 = 87\%$$

If the following year revenues increased by $10,000 and net profits by $1,000, the new computation would show the following results:

$$\text{Profit ratio} = \frac{\$14,500}{\$25,500} = .57 = 57\%$$

The lower second year figure is an indication of possible problems. Revenues are up sharply but not net profits. To business people, this is often a sign that expenses should be cut.

Case Study 4

Les Mason, a community college student, needed summer work. Since he was studying selling, he decided to get some practical experience.

First, Les bought a used concession trailer for $600 at an auction. (He knew he could pull the trailer easily with his jeep.) He spent an additional $400 painting and equipping his purchase for use. Next he paid the city $400 for a concession license to sell food in the city park and spent $100 for insurance. His total start-up expenses were $1,500.

The Pittsfield Ice Cream Company agreed to sell Les soft drinks at 40 cents per can, ice cream bars at $30 per hundred in containers packed with dry ice, and cakes at $3 per dozen. Les decided on a 100 percent markup. That meant he would charge 60 cents for ice cream, 50 cents for cakes, and 80 cents for soft drinks.

The first day Les sold 100 ice cream bars, 90 cakes, and 100 soft drinks. Sales totaled $185. Expenses were $92.50 for food plus napkins, straws, and gas for the jeep.

Les knew he had spent $1,500 and had expenses every day. When would he begin to make a profit? To find out, he made a break-even chart for his costs and his sales. Based on present sales and operating expenses, he made estimates for 12 weeks, working 7 days each week. That would mean a total of 84 days, so he estimated sales at $15,540. With start-up costs of $1,500 and operating expenses of $8,590, his estimated net profit would be $5,450.

✓ CHECKING UP

1. How do the operating expenses of manufacturing, service, and retail businesses differ?
2. Why is accurate record keeping important to any business?
3. What is the profit ratio of a business that has (a) $335,000 in revenues and $150,000 of net profit? (b) the same revenues and twice the net profit?

CHAPTER SUMMARY

People who start new businesses are called entrepreneurs. Entrepreneurs have new ideas, a desire to be their own boss, and a willingness to take risks. The rewards of being a successful entrepreneur are money, independence, and the satisfaction of doing something well.

The most important factor in becoming a successful entrepreneur is planning. There are several things you need to do before starting a business. First, you'll have to look at yourself. Do you have the personal qualifications to operate a business? Next, you'll have to gather information and make key decisions. Do you want to start an entirely new business or take over one that already exists? Are you interested in a franchise? What form of ownership do you want for your business? Where do you want it to be located? How do you plan to finance the enterprise?

Your primary concerns in operating a business will depend on the type of business you have—manufacturing, service, or retail sales. You will need to keep your prices competitive. You will also need to keep extensive financial records if your business is to be profitable. Unless you have accounting experience, you will probably want to obtain bookkeeping advice and assistance from an accountant.

TERMS TO KNOW

On a separate sheet of paper, write definitions for each of the following terms:

franchise
sole proprietorship
partnership
corporation
inventory
income statement
operating expenses
net profit
profit ratio

STUDY QUESTIONS

1. What is the failure rate for new businesses in the United States?
2. What are the advantages of taking over an existing business rather than starting an entirely new enterprise?
3. How does buying a franchise business reduce an entrepreneur's risk of failure?
4. Name at least five sources of information for someone who is starting a business.
5. What are the main advantages of the corporate form of business ownership?
6. What factors are especially important in locating a retail business and why?
7. What is the retailer's major dilemma regarding inventory?
8. List five factors that determine the selling price of an item.
9. Write a word equation that describes the content of an income statement for a retail business.

CRITICAL THINKING

1. Compile a chalkboard listing of franchises in your community. In what, if any, businesses do they appear to be concentrated?
2. A large display of canned goods topples over in a food store, seriously injuring a mother and her two-year old son. The case goes to court, where a jury awards the injured $1.5 million. The store's insurance policy pays only a third of that amount. Who pays the rest if the store is
   a. Dan's Deli?
   b. Dan & Andy's Quick Stop?
   c. Dandy Markets, Inc.?

3. The cartoon below is a comment on the importance of planning to entrepreneurship. What specifically is the artist saying?

1. If the failure rate for new businesses is so high, why do people keep starting them?

2. Under what circumstances do you think an entrepreneur might knowingly buy an unsuccessful enterprise?

Math

1. Patrick builds planter boxes after school. Last year he spent $340 on materials, $75 on advertising circulars, and $120 for delivery services. He sold 90 planters at $15 apiece. Prepare an income statement for Patrick's Planters. Then compute the business's profit ratio.

Decision Making

2. You and your family own a motel an hour's drive from a major midwestern city. The motel does a good business, but you have always wanted to be part of a national chain. One such chain has agreed to accept the motel as a franchise, but the change will be expensive. What factors would you consider in making the decision?

Citizenship

3. Your community is suffering through its second year of drought. Business owners have been asked to reduce their water consumption by 30 percent on a voluntary basis. If you were the owner of one of the businesses listed below, how would you do this?

- May-Belle's Family Restaurant
- Sam's Drive-Thru Car Wash
- Central Gardening & Landscape

Imagine that your class is going to open a shoe store in your community. Scout around for possible locations. Identify two, three, or four sites, depending on how many are available. Obtain information on rents, inspect the facilities, and analyze the potential markets surrounding each location. Each person should then pick what he or she believes is the best location and give the reasons why.

Leadership in the World of Work

After studying this chapter and doing the activities, you will be able to:

- list the personal qualities effective leaders display;
- name the communication skills leaders must have;
- use a checklist to evaluate your own leadership potential;
- specify the order of business commonly used for formal meetings; and
- explain the purpose of at least six parliamentary motions.

TERMS TO KNOW
extemporaneous
parliamentary
  procedure
acclamation
motion
point of order
quorum
second
table

*T*he world of work needs leaders—many leaders. Without leadership, workers are unproductive and resources are wasted. Without leadership, problems remain unsolved and millions of dollars are lost.

Good leaders are needed to organize, motivate, and provide direction. Leaders at all levels—company presidents, division managers, department supervisors—are necessary if workers are to achieve their maximum potential. Good leaders provide that extra push or pull that's needed to reach peak efficiency and excellence. Good leaders help people make decisions and then follow a plan of action.

You can be one of these leaders. In Chapter 7 you learned about the things you must do to receive promotions. Many of the same qualities are needed for leadership. Here you will learn about some of the skills a person needs to be a good leader. You will learn how to conduct meetings, which leaders must often do. Perhaps most important, you will learn to think of yourself as the successful leader you can be.

257

1 *What Makes a Leader?*

Some people believe that leadership ability is inherited. They believe that only a small number of people are born with a gift for leadership. All other people are destined to be followers.

Certain people do have greater natural leadership ability than others, but many who are not "born" leaders can and do learn to be good leaders. Many people who become successful leaders make mistakes in their first leadership roles. They learn from those mistakes, however, and gradually become more effective. They are the proof that hard work and intelligence are more important than inherited traits when it comes to making great leaders.

Authority

Many people believe that authority makes a leader. In every organization—whether it's a business, government, school, or social organization—there is a system of authority. In the past especially, leaders used their position of authority to control those under them. All orders came "from the top." These leaders paid little attention to whether the workers approved or disapproved of the orders they were given.

Today authority is much less effective than it used to be as a leadership tool. The concept of teamwork at all levels of operation is becoming a more common practice. The key to success with this approach is increased worker participation in

The characteristics of great leaders are as varied as leaders themselves. From your knowledge of American history, what were the most outstanding attributes of these U.S. presidents?

Participation in school organizations is an ideal way to develop your leadership skills. How many of these organizations are represented on your campus?

decision making. Groups of workers take on more leadership responsibility. The good leader guides and assists workers rather than giving unchallenged orders.

Personal Qualities

If not authority, then what do good leaders have that makes others follow them? Most are mentally alert, vigorous, and energetic. They are very enthusiastic and have positive attitudes. Studies also show that they have the ability to make quick and accurate decisions. Other leadership traits include intelligence, imagination, honesty, integrity,

knowledge, and good health. Beyond these characteristics, it is difficult to generalize because there are so many different kinds of leaders.

Leadership Style

There is no one best way to lead. Different leaders have different styles—what works for one may not work for another. Some lead quietly, preferring to lead by example. Others are more vocal, constantly giving pep talks and encouragement. Some leaders get involved in every part of the job. Others prefer to delegate authority and stay in the background until they are needed.

You have probably noticed that some people who are not leaders seem to have more leadership ability than some people who *are* leaders. Why do you think this happens? Some people simply don't want to be leaders. It's their choice, and this is perfectly all right. Only in critical situations, when there is no one else to lead, would we want these people to step forward and take charge. Other people have the ability and desire but lack the self-confidence they need to take charge. Many of these people don't give themselves enough credit. They don't think themselves worthy of leadership. Are you one of these people?

Image

How do people become leaders? Why are some selected for leadership roles while others are not? The images that people project and the images they have of themselves have a great deal to do with this.

Your image is how others see you. If most people have a favorable impression of you, you have a good image. If you appear to be intelligent, honest, well-organized, respected by others, and someone who gets things done, people will see you as a potential leader. They will trust you and award you with leadership opportunities.

Some students are recognized early for their athletic performance. Others are identified with artistic or academic excellence. Still others are noted for their outstanding personalities, which make them instantly popular wherever they go. As a result of their superior accomplishments, these students often become well known and are given leadership roles. To maintain a leadership image, though, these students need qualities other than the talents that won them recognition.

Leaders have positive self-concepts. They are self-motivated—they don't need someone else to push them along. They are also knowledgeable about the organizations they are leading.

It is possible to overcome a negative self-concept. You can learn to like yourself and develop self-confidence. Psychologists tell people who lack confidence that they should participate in activities at which they can excel. "Find something you're good at and do it," they say.

Vocational education clubs, such as the Vocational Industrial Club of America and the Future Homemakers of America, provide numerous opportunities to build confidence. Club members

MAKE A DECISION

You belong to a group of employees who are choosing someone to represent them in negotiations with the company you work for. You are trying to decide between two people—an intelligent, knowledgeable person who seems quiet and insecure and a very confident, forceful person who probably doesn't understand the issues as well as the other person. You want to vote for the one who is more likely to represent your group successfully. What's your decision—the more knowledgeable, meeker person or the less knowledgeable but more forceful person? Give the reasons for your decision.

work on projects in areas in which they have an interest and a talent. Other clubs, such as the Circle K Clubs of Kiwanis International, concentrate on developing good self-concepts and high self-esteem.

Communication Skills

Because communication skills (speaking, listening, reading, and writing) are so important to on-the-job success, a whole chapter of this book, Chapter 10, has been devoted to them. As important as such skills are to the average worker, however, they are even more important to leaders. Almost all successful leaders are outstanding communicators.

The communication skills of listening and reading are important because they are learning skills. Leaders must know many things—they can never stop learning.

Writing is also an important skill for most leaders. In the business world leaders write memos and reports describing their ideas and plans to workers and investors. The success of the company can depend on how clearly and persuasively the leader writes these messages.

The ability to use correct English and speak fluently is essential to leadership. Many leaders must make formal speeches from time to time, and almost all leaders must be skilled at **extemporaneous** speaking. Extemporaneous means spontaneous and unprepared.

For their formal speeches, leaders carefully write out and practice what they are going to say. In conducting meetings, though, they do not have an opportunity to prepare and practice. They must be able to react quickly to what other people are saying. Speaking effectively in these situations is a very valuable skill.

If you are like most people, you get nervous, even scared, at the idea of speaking in public. The only way to conquer this fear is to force yourself to speak in front of others. Remember, many of the world's most successful business and political leaders had to struggle to overcome this fear. The following suggestions may help you.

- If you have any grammatical weaknesses, learn to correct them. Use good grammar in your everyday speech.
- Write as often as possible. Concentrate on saying what you want to say clearly and precisely.
- Work at increasing your vocabulary. (It also helps to learn famous quotations and funny stories to fit different occasions.)
- Use a tape recorder to evaluate and improve your oral delivery.
- If possible, videotape your speeches in private to improve your facial expressions and gestures.
- Get suggestions from teachers and friends.
- Look for opportunities to speak in public.
- Be realistic. Don't expect to become one of the world's great speakers in just a few weeks. It takes time and effort.

A Leadership Checklist

Right now you may have no desire to be a leader. If that is the case, why, you ask, should you concern yourself with developing leadership skills? There are two reasons. First, you may one day be forced into a position of leadership. Workers who had no leadership aspirations often accept promotions into management, where they must lead. Second, there are many leadership roles in our economy other than those at the very top. Big companies are organized into departments, each of which needs a leader. These departments, in turn, are broken into divisions, and the divisions into offices, and the offices into groups—all of which need managers. Thus, there can be hundreds or even thousands of leaders between the

Case Study **1**

When he was a junior in high school, Harry was very shy and self-conscious. He was the tallest person in school but too slow-moving to play basketball. Other students teased him about his height and his lack of speed. Harry thought his hair was ugly and that his ears and nose were too big. His self-concept was low, and he felt his chances for success were limited.

One day his English teacher had Harry write a report on the life of Abraham Lincoln. Harry discovered that President Lincoln had many of the same problems Harry had. Harry read that Lincoln was a very homely man who had had many disappointments. Despite his physical defects and lowly beginnings, Lincoln became one of the most famous men in American history.

The story of Lincoln inspired Harry. Perhaps he, too, could overcome his homely appearance and low self-esteem. Harry set goals to improve his appearance. He had his hair cut by a cosmetologist so that it covered the top of his ears. He thought he looked better. Then he joined the debate club to improve his communication skills. Next he joined VICA, and that motivated him to work even harder on his self-improvement goals. It was hard to participate in club meetings, but it became easier each time he spoke before the group.

In his senior year, Harry was elected treasurer of his VICA club. Harry felt that his image had changed as he worked hard for his club and school.

CEO at the top and newly hired, entry-level workers.

You can use the following checklist to evaluate your leadership potential. Your goal in considering each item is to be able to answer, "Yes, I do that." Each positive answer indicates a key attribute of leadership that you have. The more positive answers, the more likely that you will someday make an effective leader. Try to be honest about yourself, however. Remember, the checklist is for your own evaluation. You should use any negative answers for self-improvement. Consider them areas in which you have work to do.

- I enjoy working with all people.
- I respect the rights of others.
- I enjoy helping people in need.
- I try never to embarrass people.
- I try to avoid arguments.
- I never take unfair advantage of others.
- I try to avoid becoming angry.
- I try not to show off my knowledge.
- I am dependable and responsible.
- I am friendly to all and smile often.
- I am a good listener.
- I admit my mistakes.
- I try to remember other people's names.
- I try not to talk loudly, swear, or gossip.
- I dress neatly and appropriately for the occasion.
- I do my best at home, in school, and at work.
- I have enthusiasm and a sense of humor.
- I congratulate others on their achievements.
- I make good, quick decisions.
- I try to profit from constructive criticism.
- I practice to improve my grammar, speech, and voice.
- I strive to develop positive attitudes.
- I accept honors and awards graciously.
- I try not to brag about my own achievements.
- I hold no ethnic prejudices.
- I try not to be sarcastic and arrogant.
- I am courteous, polite, and sincere.
- I follow the golden rule—"Do unto others as you would have others do unto you."
- I am slow to criticize others.
- I accept assignments cheerfully from supervisors.
- I obey all local, state, and national laws.

SITUATION
SOLUTION

Lead—or Play It Safe?

You are the head of a local union whose members are hired on a daily basis. The union's seniority policy, which says that those with the longest service get first chance at any available jobs, is causing a great deal of bad feeling within the membership. The group's older members are enjoying long hours and generous paid overtime. The younger members are losing medical benefits and even voting privileges because they are not working enough. Many are thinking of leaving the union.

The dilemma for you is that you are facing re-election in the fall. If you go along with the current system, you will surely win—only the older members will be voting—but the union will lose power in the long run as its younger members drift away. If you advocate a change in the system, it will strengthen the union in the long run but prove unpopular with the older members. As a result, you may not be re-elected.

1. What would you do—support the existing seniority system or try to change it? Why?
2. Assume you decide to try to change the system. How would you convince the older members to go along?
3. Assume you decide to uphold the seniority system. How would you get the younger members to stay with the union?

✓ CHECKING UP

1. What personal qualities make a good leader?
2. Why are communication skills so important to effective leadership?
3. According to the leadership checklist, which attributes of leadership do you already have? In which areas do you need work?

2 *Using Parliamentary Procedure*

Leaders are frequently responsible for conducting meetings. This is an important responsibility. Meetings are usually held to make business decisions and plans for the future. How the meetings are conducted has a lot to do with whether or not the meeting results in good decisions and plans.

Long ago, members of democratic gatherings found that they needed rules for group discussions. Without rules, some people did all the talking, while others never got to speak. Gradually people developed rules that helped keep meetings running fairly and smoothly.

Some of the first crude rules were used in England's Parliament (England's version of our Congress) in 1580. These rules were revised and published in 1583. As more and more people began using the rules, they became known as **parliamentary procedure.**

Parliamentary procedure is a democratic method of conducting meetings. It is as important today as it ever was. Today's leaders may not follow the rules as strictly as leaders used to, but the principles are still there. It is through these principles that leaders can give everyone an opportunity to express their opinions and then reach a majority decision.

Parliamentary procedure is based on the following principles:

- During a debate, group members must be fair and polite.
- Any member of the group may debate under the established rules.
- The majority decides the issues.
- The minority is free to express its opinion.
- Minority members must go along with the decision made by the majority.

Everyone who belongs to a club or organization should learn parliamentary procedure. Knowing parliamentary rules can help you become a leader in your school and at work. Many of today's local, state, and national leaders are still using the parliamentary skills they learned in school clubs and organizations.

Legislative bodies usually have their own rules modeled on parliamentary procedure. Why are such rules especially necessary in a body like the U.S. House of Representatives, shown here?

Parliamentary Terminology

Figure 15-1 lists some terms commonly used in meetings conducted under the rules of parliamentary procedure. You will need to know the meanings of these terms if you wish to participate in any meetings using the procedure.

Not all of the terms or rules used in parliamentary procedure are listed here. If you are elected to office or want to learn more about parliamentary procedure, study any edition of *Robert's Rules of Order Revised* by Henry M. Robert.

Order of Business

The president of an organization or club is usually responsible for planning meetings. Careful planning is very important. It will keep the meetings interesting and productive. This, in turn, will keep attendance high and help to build a spirit of cooperation and pride within the group.

Many school clubs and organizations, such as the Future Farmers of America and the Future Homemakers of America, have established procedures for conducting their meetings. These include the following order of business:

- Call to order
- Reading and approval of the minutes
- Treasurer's report
- Officers' reports
- Standing committee reports
- Special committee reports
- Unfinished business
- New business
- Announcements
- Adjournment

Glossary of Parliamentary Terms

acclamation Method of voting to approve a motion without a ballot.

adjourn Motion to close a meeting.

agenda List of items to be covered in a meeting.

amend To change a motion by another motion.

aye Formal way of saying yes (pronounced I).

ballot Written vote, usually secret.

bylaws Rules and regulations that govern an organization's operation, including such things as the election of officers, membership qualifications, and meeting times.

call to question Statement made by a member when he or she believes it is time to vote on a motion.

Chair Chairperson; one who is in charge of a meeting.

constitution Document stating an organization's name, objectives, and purposes and describing its organization.

convene To gather for a meeting; to call a meeting to order.

debatable Describes a motion that may be discussed by the members.

gavel Mallet used by the Chair to bring a meeting to order.

have the floor Permission to speak to the group.

majority Number greater than one-half of the voting members at a meeting.

minority Number less than one-half of the voting members at a meeting.

minutes Written record kept by the Secretary of what is said and done during a meeting.

motion A formal proposal for action.

nay Formal way of saying no.

new business Topic brought before the group for the first time.

point of order Statement made by a member to question a ruling by the Chair or to enforce the regular rules.

quorum Minimum number of members that must be present at a meeting for the group to conduct official business.

second Statement made to show approval of a motion made by another member of the group. At least one member must second a motion before it can be discussed.

standing vote Voting method in which members stand to signify their position for or against a motion.

table To postpone making a decision on an issue under discussion.

unfinished business Topic brought before the members for at least the second time.

Figure 15-1   By studying the terminology of parliamentary procedure, you can get a feel for the formality with which meetings are conducted and the options that are open to participants. For example, how many different forms of voting are possible according to the glossary above? Name and distinguish them from each other.

Several people besides the president have definite duties concerning meetings. Committee chairpersons are responsible for having reports ready for the meeting. There may be an arrangement committee which would be responsible for obtaining a meeting room and any needed equipment.

Model Meeting

If you have never attended a meeting conducted according to the rules of parliamentary procedure, now is your chance. The following passages represent an imaginary meeting of a local Vocational Industrial Club of America. See if this meeting is conducted in the way you thought a properly conducted meeting would be.

To start, no business can be officially conducted unless a quorum is present. The number of members making up a quorum is usually a majority. The number can vary, however, depending on the organization's bylaws.

The meeting begins as the club President taps his gavel.

PRES.: The meeting of the Pittsburg VICA Club will come to order. The Secretary will now read the minutes of our last meeting.

(The Secretary reads the minutes.)

Are there any corrections to the minutes? (Pause.) The minutes stand approved as read. We will hear the Treasurer's report.

(The Treasurer reports on receipts, expenses, and the club's account balance, and the report is approved.)

The next order of business is officers' reports.

Officers' reports and reports of any special or standing committees are given and approved in the same fashion as the Treasurer's report. Standing committees are permanent bodies. They might include committees for membership, finance, and operations. Special committees are temporary. They are usually set up to handle upcoming events, such as competitions, workshops, or social gatherings like parties and picnics.

After all the reports have been given, the meeting moves on to business proper.

PRES.: Is there any unfinished business to be considered? (Pause.) If there is no unfinished business, the meeting is now open for new business.

At this point in the meeting, anyone who wants the club to take some action stands up and makes a motion. Any member can make a motion to introduce a new item of business. Consider this example from Kim.

KIM: Mr. President.

PRES.: Kim.

KIM: I move that the club buy a new ceremonial emblem before the state contest in April.

Another club member, Anne, agrees.

ANNE: I second the motion.

PRES.: It has been moved and seconded that the club buy a new ceremonial emblem before the state contest this April. Is there any discussion?

(Members who have something to say stand and address the Chair. They are recognized and state their opinions.)

Often during discussion someone will want to change a motion in some way. Assume, for example, that Juan has this suggestion:

JUAN: I wish to amend the motion by adding the words *and new ceremonial flags* after the words *new ceremonial emblem*.

ANNE: I second the motion.

PRES.: It has been moved and seconded that the pending motion be amended to say that the club should buy a new ceremonial emblem and ceremonial flags before the state contest in April. Is there any discussion?

As before, the members would discuss the motion. When the time for discussion was over (or if there were no discussion), the President would call for a vote.

Meeting participants should stand and address the Chair when offering motions. Under the rules of parliamentary procedure, what actions would precede this? What actions would follow?

PRES.: All in favor of the amendment to the motion signify by saying aye. (Pause.) All opposed to the amendment signify by saying no. (Pause.) The ayes have it. The amendment is passed.

At this point discussion would resume on the now amended motion.

After all new business and any announcements have been taken care of, the President will usually bring the meeting to a close.

PRES.: Is there a motion to adjourn?

KIM: I move that this meeting be adjourned.

JUAN: I second the motion.

PRES.: All those in favor say aye. (Pause.) All those opposed say no. (Pause.) The meeting is adjourned.

Types of Motions

As you read about the VICA meeting, you learned the following:

- Business is introduced at a meeting through the use of motions.

- A motion is a proposal made by a member requesting some action by the group. At most meetings any member may make a motion.
- After a motion is made, it must receive a second from another member before it can be discussed by the members.
- Before a member can make a motion, he or she must stand and be recognized by the Chair.

Only one main motion at a time can be discussed by the group. Secondary motions to amend a main motion must be voted on before the main motion comes to a vote.

Only the most basic types of motions were included in the imaginary VICA meeting. There are many others. Reading about them will help you participate more fully in future meetings.

Motion to Reconsider   A motion to reconsider allows the results of a vote to be put aside. The motion in question is discussed and voted on again later. Only a member who voted with the majority can move to reconsider. For a reconsider motion to pass, it must be seconded and receive a majority vote.

Motion to Postpone   A motion to postpone —either indefinitely or for a definite period of time—stops consideration of a motion. A motion to postpone cannot be made when someone has the floor. It must have a second, is debatable, and requires a majority vote.

An indefinite postponement can be reconsidered only if the majority votes to do so. A postponement to a definite time can be amended only to change the amount of time. A definite postponement is debatable only in regard to the reasons for postponement.

Motion to Limit/Extend Debate

A motion to limit or extend debate is used to set the amount of time allowed for discussion of an issue. This type of motion requires a two-thirds vote of those present. The person making this motion cannot interrupt while someone else has the floor. The motion must be seconded, is not debatable, and cannot be reconsidered. The time limit may be amended.

Motion to Table

A motion to table (or, more formally, to lay on the table) is used to delay action until a more favorable time or until more facts are available. This motion must be seconded and cannot be debated, amended, or reconsidered. It can be taken from the table later in the same meeting or during the next meeting. The question cannot be considered at a special meeting unless members are notified in advance. If the business is not taken up at one of these three possible times, the question dies.

Motion to Appeal

A motion to appeal is used by a member to challenge a decision by the Chair. The appeal is stated immediately after the Chair's decision and is in order even if someone else has the floor. A motion to appeal must have a second. A majority vote in the negative is required to reverse the Chair's decision.

Point-of-Order Motion

A member makes a point-of-order motion when he or she thinks someone else has violated a rule. To make this motion the person says, "I rise to a point of order." A point of order does not require a second and is not debatable or amendable. The motion is decided by the Chair, often on the advice of the Parliamentarian (an expert on the rules), and no vote is taken.

Before making a point of order, a member should carefully consider its importance. It can be a source of disruption to the meeting if made without good reason.

Motion to Divide a Question

A motion to request a division of a question is sometimes used when there are two or more ideas in one motion. The ideas can then be considered and voted on separately. This motion cannot interrupt a speaker or be reconsidered. It requires a second and is amendable, but is not debatable. A majority vote decides.

Division-of-Assembly Motion

A motion for division of assembly is made if there is doubt about the vote count. In a small group a show of hands may be adequate for voting. In larger groups a standing vote counted by appointed members is required.

The member making the division-of-assembly motion may interrupt. No second is needed, and the motion is not debatable, amendable, or able to be reconsidered. The motion is decided by the Chair who may request another vote.

Question-of-Privilege Motion

A question of privilege is used to call attention to physical problems or distractions in the meeting room. As an example, this motion might be stated by saying, "I rise to a point of personal privilege. This is a cold room. Can someone turn up the heat?" Such a motion requires no second and is not debatable or amendable. It does not require a vote—the Chair makes a ruling on the question.

Motion to Suspend Rules

A motion to suspend the rules is used to propose a deviation from the standard rules of procedure. This motion may be used to consider a question out of its proper order on the agenda. The motion must have a second, but it cannot interrupt a speaker or be reconsidered, debated, or amended. A two-thirds vote is required to pass the motion.

Motion to Withdraw

A motion to withdraw allows the person who offered a motion to remove it from the floor. This is done when discussion and debate show that there is no need for the motion. It is not debatable or amendable, and only a negative vote can be reconsidered. It cannot interrupt a speaker and requires a second. The decision to withdraw the motion is made by the Chair when there is no objection from the group.

Request for Parliamentary Inquiry

A request for parliamentary inquiry is a motion directed to the Chair by a member who wants more information on a parliamentary question.

Strive for Success

An Electrifying Leader

The term *leader* usually calls to mind great generals like Dwight D. Eisenhower or George Washington or powerful political leaders like Franklin D. Roosevelt or Britain's Margaret Thatcher. Electricians do not normally pop up at the top of the list. However, when historians look at the most influential leaders of the twentieth century, an electrician from the shipyards of Gdansk, Poland, will certainly be among those remembered.

Lech Walesa began his career as an electrician working in the busy shipyards of Gdansk in 1967. The workers in the shipyard and throughout much of Poland were beginning a movement to ensure more equitable treatment. Walesa soon became involved in the workers' rights movement and joined the trade union.

By 1980 over 50 Polish trade unions had banded together to form an organization called Solidarity. In the summer of that year, thousands of workers in Gdansk and throughout Poland went on strike. Their demands included higher pay, free trade unions, and political reform. The strike was successful, and the Communist Party leaders of Poland agreed to many of the demands of the striking Solidarity members.

Walesa was a strong, courageous part of Solidarity and was named chairman of the organization in 1981. Later that year government opposition to Solidarity grew. The government suspended the organization's activities and arrested Walesa as well as other Solidarity leaders. Walesa remained imprisoned until November 1982.

While he was out of jail, however, Walesa was not free. The government maintained tight restrictions on his activities as well as Solidarity's—to no avail. Walesa's efforts had already achieved worldwide recognition. In 1983 he was given the Nobel Peace Prize for his work with Solidarity.

By the end of the decade, Walesa was riding the crest of a wave of political change sweeping through Poland and the rest of Eastern Europe. On December 9, 1990, he was elected president of Poland. The electrician from the shipyards of Gdansk, who had once been imprisoned, was now the preeminent political leader of his country and one of the most influential leaders of his time.

If the results of a voice vote are in doubt, a member of the group may move for a more formal count. What is such a motion called?

The motion is decided by the Chair, and no vote is required. It is not seconded, debatable, or amendable. It can interrupt a speaker but not be reconsidered.

Election of Officers

The democratic process requires leaders to be nominated and elected by the members of the club or organization. Nominations are made from the floor by the members, by a committee, or by ballot.

In many clubs, new officers are nominated by a committee. The members of the committee are either appointed by the President or elected by the members. The committee should be given enough time to make selections and contact persons to be nominated. Some clubs instruct the nominating committee to select two persons for each office. Other clubs require that the nominating committee choose only one person for each office.

On the date set for the election, the President asks for a report from the chairperson of the nominating committee.

JUAN: For President, Anne Davis; for Vice-President, Tim Beal; for Secretary, Larry Weigel; and for Treasurer, Sophie Fong.

PRES.:   For the office of President, Anne Davis has been nominated by the committee. Are there further nominations for President?

(There are none.)

Are there further nominations for President? (Pause.) Without objection (pause) nominations are closed.

The Chair will repeat this procedure for each office, saying the position and the name of the person nominated by the committee, asking twice for further nominations, and declaring nominations for that office closed. (After nominations are closed, a majority vote is required to reopen them.)

When only one person is nominated for each office, those individuals are considered unofficially elected. Formal election by acclamation usually follows.

✓ CHECKING UP

1. What is the standard order of business for meetings conducted under the rules of parliamentary procedure?

2. How do the rules of parliamentary procedure ensure that meetings will be conducted in a democratic fashion?

3. How would you make a motion to have your school's VICA chapter sponsor a participant in a local charity walk? How would you amend the motion to sponsor two walkers?

CHAPTER SUMMARY

The world of work needs many good leaders, especially now, as our economy is going through a period of great change. Authority itself no longer makes a leader. Leaders must earn the respect and the support of those who follow them by being mentally alert, positive, and good decision makers. Leaders must also be intelligent, honest, knowledgeable, and in good health.

You can make yourself into a leader with hard work and desire. Participation in school clubs, such as the Vocational Industrial Club of America and the Future Homemakers of America, will help you build self-confidence and develop leadership skills. The communication skills—reading, writing, listening, and speaking—are especially important skills for leaders.

Leaders in school clubs and in the world of work must frequently conduct meetings. It is very important that the meetings go smoothly and that all business is accomplished. This is why leaders must plan their meetings and know the basic rules of parliamentary procedure. Leaders must know the proper order of business as well as the types of various motions and the conditions under which they can be made.

TERMS TO KNOW

On a separate sheet of paper, write a paragraph using all of the following terms:

extemporaneous
parliamentary procedure
acclamation
motion
point of order
quorum
second
table a motion

STUDY QUESTIONS

1. Is authority more or less effective than it used to be as a leadership tool? Why?
2. List at least five personal qualities most good leaders have.
3. Give at least two reasons why the people who would make the best leaders do not always have the leadership positions.
4. How can participation in a school club help you develop your leadership skills?
5. Why are the communication skills of listening and reading important for leaders?
6. How can you improve your speaking skills?
7. Why were the rules of parliamentary procedure developed?
8. On what principles is parliamentary procedure based?
9. Your club is in the middle of discussing a difficult issue when the janitor appears and announces that he must lock up the meeting room for the day. What are your parliamentary options to close out discussion quickly?

CRITICAL THINKING

1. Consider the four leadership styles described on page 259. Name at least one public figure who in your opinion typifies each style and explain the reasons behind your choices.
2. You and other members of a school club are considering the use of parliamentary procedure for the organization's bimonthly meetings. One member in particular is very much opposed. He says the rules of parliamentary procedure are needlessly complex, will slow things down, and make meetings boring. How would you change his mind?
3. Your text cautions you about resorting too quickly to a point-of-order motion, calling it

"a source of disruption" (page 267). How could such a motion disrupt a meeting? What alternatives might you consider instead?

DISCUSSION STARTERS

1. Think of some class, club, church, or athletic leaders you have known. Do any stand out as being especially effective? What made these leaders superior to the others?
2. You show the leadership checklist on page 262 to a friend, who has this reaction: "A person who does all that isn't a leader—he's a saint." Do you agree? Why or why not?
3. To some people, nomination of officers by committee seems elitist—or at least somewhat less democratic than taking nominations from the floor. Do you agree? Why or why not?
4. Do you think that men and women have different leadership styles? In what respects, if any? Use examples from current events or your personal experience to support your opinions.
5. Your text describes a number of leadership styles—quiet vs. vocal, hands-on vs. delegator. In which situations might one of these styles be more effective than another? Explain your choices.

BUILDING BASIC SKILLS

Math
1. Your FHA chapter has 40 voting members. How many must be present for a meeting if the group's bylaws state that a quorum shall be
   a. two-fifths of the membership?
   b. a simple majority?
   c. 10 percent of voting members, but in no event fewer than ten people?

Communication
2. Assume the city council in your community is debating one of the following proposals:

   - A ban on smoking in all restaurants

   - An increase in taxes to support local public schools (specifically, to reduce class size)
   - An ordinance making it a crime to burn the flag

   Write a one-page letter to your councilperson explaining your position for or against the measure.

Human Relations
3. Your sister recently had what for her was a devastating experience in one of her classes. At your instigation, she chose to do an oral presentation for a class project. (You told her that the experience speaking would be a good way to develop her leadership potential.) A visitor to the class asked a number of questions that she could not answer. The whole experience left your sister feeling embarrassed and a failure, so much so that she has vowed never again to speak in front of a group. What would you tell her to put the experience in perspective?

SUGGESTED ACTIVITIES

1. Assume you want to run for class office your senior year. Draw up a plan for your candidacy. Include as part of your campaign strategy a description of the kind of image and leadership style you want to develop. List the steps or actions you will take to achieve this end.
2. Research leadership style and management as practiced within Japanese companies doing business in the United States. Compare their approach with the one presented in your text on pages 261 to 262. Write a report summarizing your findings.
3. Watch a televised session of a legislature, school board, or similar body. Compare the procedures they use with the parliamentary practices presented in this chapter. List the similarities and differences. Then comment briefly on the effectiveness of the rules used by the televised body.

UNIT
Four

Becoming a Wise Consumer

You, the Consumer

*Y*ou read earlier that people have basic human needs. All people must have food, water, and shelter to survive. You also read that few people are satisfied with the necessities. Most people also want the luxuries that make life enjoyable.

If you are like most people, you will buy the things you need and want. When you do this buying, you are a consumer. Whether you knew it or not, you've been a consumer ever since you made your first purchase in a supermarket or department store.

As a consumer, you want to get the most value possible for your money. This chapter will help you do this by making you more aware of why you spend your money. In this chapter you will also learn how to recognize and avoid some of the more common practices people use to cheat consumers. Finally, you will learn what the federal government, consumer groups, and others are doing to protect consumers.

1 *Responsible Buying*

In our society we have many chances to spend our money. With so many goods and services available, how do we decide which ones to buy?

Influences on Consumers

Many factors will affect your buying choices in the years to come. Being aware of these factors will help you get the most for your money. Understanding how and by whom you are being influenced will help you become a wise consumer.

Income   Your income, more than any other factor, will influence your buying. You can't spend more than you earn—not for long anyway. If you have a well-paid job, you will be able to buy most of the things you want. If you do not, you will have to be more careful how you spend your money.

Job   The type of work you do will also affect your buying. If, for example, you do a great deal of physical work, you will have a greater appetite than someone who sits at a desk all day. This means that you will probably eat more than an office worker and, therefore, will spend more money on food. The office worker, on the other hand, might be expected to dress in a more formal

manner. He or she would buy more expensive clothing than, say, a construction worker.

Interests   What are your interests? What do you like to do in your leisure time? Whatever your interests may be, they will greatly affect your buying.

If you are interested in sports, you will probably buy such things as golf clubs, tennis racquets, and tickets to ball games. If you like to travel, you will spend a good deal of your money on gasoline or plane tickets. However, if your idea of a good time is making and repairing things, you might buy tools and equipment for a home workshop.

Environment   The climate and customs of the place where you live will affect your buying. If you live in Maine, for example, you will likely spend money on heavy coats, snow tires, and heating bills. If you live in Southern California, however, you probably won't even own snow tires or a winter coat. You'll have one fairly lightweight wardrobe and pay your largest utility bills for air-conditioning.

Peer Pressure   Do you have a certain group of close friends? If so, the people in your group will probably affect your buying. For example, if someone in your group buys a new style of shoe, you may want to buy a similar pair of shoes. Can you

All attire makes a statement. What does the dress of these students say about them and their relationship with each other?

remember any occasion when you bought something just to be like your friends?

The people in your group are your peers, and the influence they have on you is called **peer pressure.** Don't let peer pressure make your decisions for you. Ask yourself, "Do I buy things because *I* want them or because I want to be part of the crowd?" Don't try to keep up with the crowd, especially if you have less money than most of your friends.

Advertising   Another big influence on your buying is advertising. Advertising is so much a part of our lives that most of us don't realize how much it affects us. Television, radio, billboards, newspapers, magazines—advertising is everywhere.

Advertising can help you be a better-informed and more efficient consumer. For example, you can find out about new or improved products through advertising. You can also find the best buys by comparing advertised prices. Shopping this way can save you time as well as money.

However, advertising can also cost you money. Most companies raise their prices to pay for their advertising. This means that heavily advertised products usually cost more than similar products that are not widely advertised. Don't refuse to buy a product just because you have never heard of it. In many cases products carrying less familiar names offer equal quality.

Advertising can also cost you money if you don't think carefully about the advertised message. Advertising companies spend billions of dollars to study human behavior and to hire talented writers, artists, and salespeople. Their goal in doing these things is to convince you to buy a certain product. They use persuasive techniques that are so clever and indirect you may not even realize you're being influenced. You may think you're just being informed.

Here are a few techniques to watch for.

- *Association—linking a product with a popular idea or person.* The most common example of this technique is an ad showing a celebrity using a product. When we see such an ad, we link the popularity of the person with the product.
- *Group appeal—suggesting that use of a product will make the consumer part of the crowd.* We are told that more people take a certain cold medicine than any other. We see a large

group of people enjoying the same soft drink. If everyone else uses a product, we reason, it must be good—and we want to try it, too. We want to be part of the group.
- *Snob appeal—suggesting that use of a product will raise the consumer above the crowd.* We are told that we will be more popular, respected, or admired if we drive a certain car, serve a certain food, or use a certain shampoo.

Buying Skills

In this section, we'll discuss some of the special skills that will help you make the right buying decisions for yourself and your family. The more you know about such things as supply and demand, planned spending, and mail-order buying, the better your chances of making the best possible purchases.

Understanding Supply and Demand   You read about the law of supply and demand in Chapter 13. You will remember that when the supply of a product is greater than the demand, prices go down. When the demand is greater than the supply, prices go up.

An understanding of the law of supply and demand can make you a more effective consumer. Consider an example. People who buy Christmas cards and wrapping paper right *after* the holiday pay at least 50 percent less. Why? Demand before the holiday is at its peak—and so are prices. Right after the holiday, though, demand is much lower. Most people don't want to buy cards and wrap a year in advance and store them for that period of time. The owners of most gift shops and retail businesses feel the same way. They don't want to hold inventory for a whole year. They would rather sell it at a reduced price and invest in new merchandise.

You can probably think of many other similar examples. There's the homemaker who buys local fresh fruit and vegetables in the summer when they're plentiful and priced low. In the winter when only small quantities of such produce can be brought in from other states, prices rise sharply. The homemaker then switches to cheaper canned or frozen products. There's the music outlet that sells tapes and CDs for top dollar when they are first released and demand for them is high. Six months to a year later, when popular interest has slackened, the tapes are marked down. The same

Advertisers use images designed to appeal to our emotions—to our desires to belong, to experience, to achieve, and to be like those we admire. Which of the three persuasive techniques discussed in this lesson does each of these ads employ?

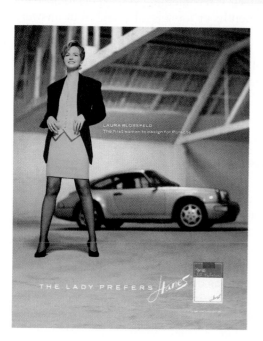

can be said for books, cars, and many other items. Consumers who are aware of these shifts in availability and demand can save substantial amounts of money.

Planning Purchases You will be able to pay less for many of the things you buy if you make a long-range buying plan. To make such a plan work, you will need to save a little money each payday for things you will buy in the future. You can then buy each item at the best possible buying time—when the prices are lowest.

The first step in long-range planning is to **inventory,** or make a list, of the items you now have. In your inventory, note the condition of each item. This will help you determine how long the items will last and when they will need to be replaced.

The second step is to determine what you will need to buy during the upcoming year. For example, after doing your clothing inventory, consider your needs for school, work, sports, and dress clothes—as well as clothes for different seasons. If the clothes you already have won't meet these needs, you can plan to buy the clothes you do need.

Wise consumers use this two-step procedure to avoid being without a necessary item at a time when the item is priced high. Long-range planning ensures that people can buy what they want when they want it—and at the lowest possible price.

Shopping for Value   After completing your inventory and doing long-range planning, you are ready to do your shopping. A wise consumer knows the following things about shopping:

- How to judge quality
- Which items receive heavy use and need to be of better quality
- What makes one item wear longer than another
- What the difference in cost should be for different levels of quality

Think about how you will use your purchase. Will you use it every day or just two or three times

Volume bookstores usually have large displays of remainders. These are books whose prices are lowered once their sales slow. What basic law of economics does this practice reflect?

MAKE A DECISION

The battery in your car is dead. You learn that for $100 you can buy a well-known, brand-name battery with a five-year warranty. You can buy another battery with a three-year warranty for only $50. The salesperson hasn't had much experience selling batteries, but he thinks the cheaper battery is a good one. What's your decision —do you buy the cheaper battery or the more expensive one? Give the reasons for your decision.

a month? Is it something that will get worn from use (like shoes), or will it only be looked at (like a wall poster)? Is it something you expect to have for several months or for several years? Your answers to these questions will help you know which items need to be of better quality.

Usually the most important factor in shopping for value is judging the quality of products. It is especially important that purchases you will use often or for a long time should be of good quality. You can determine quality by checking what the product is made of and how it is put together. Here are some examples:

- Tightly woven cloth usually wears longer than open weaves.
- Leather usually wears longer than plastic.
- Heavy, thick plastic lasts longer than light-weight plastic.
- Stainless steel outlasts aluminum.

A list such as this could go on and on. There's a great deal to learn about various materials and the quality of those materials. If you know someone who uses a product similar to the one you want to buy, ask that person about its quality.

How an item is made also affects how long it will last. The seams in clothing should be made with small, even stitches. Check the strength of all fasteners. Rough edges usually mean the item was made quickly and perhaps even poorly. From experience you will learn what makes one item last longer than another. Learn from both your good and bad purchases.

Usually things of better quality cost more than things of lesser quality. However, this is not a hard-and-fast rule. Sometimes a less expensive product is just as good as a more costly one.

It is always difficult to judge the quality of an item without handling it. Still, from what you have read here and what you know about garment materials and construction from your own experience, how would you rate these five pairs of gloves in terms of quality? Rank them from 1 (lowest quality) to 5 (highest quality) and explain your reasons for doing so.

There are several reasons why items of the same quality would have different prices. One reason is supply and demand, which you read about earlier. If one item is in demand while another is not, the item in demand will cost more, regardless of quality.

Different prices for equal quality also result from the different quantities companies buy. Large companies buy in large amounts. When they do this, they can buy at a low price. A small company buying smaller amounts has to pay a higher price. Thus, the small company must charge its customers more for the same item.

Another reason for different prices for the same quality has to do with brand names. Many people buy well-known brands thinking they are of better quality. Sometimes they are—and sometimes they are not.

Many products sold under house, or store, brands are identical to the higher-priced, nationally known brands. For example, household appliances made by a large company are sometimes sold to smaller companies, who then put their own brand name on the appliances. Food canning companies do this, too. Different labels are wrapped around cans with identical contents. The smart shopper learns that it is possible to get the same high-quality items much more cheaply under a less familiar name.

Can you see how much there is to know about price and quality? If you feel you need help in making wise purchases, you might check some consumer magazines. These magazines offer much information on the quality of products.

Case Study 1

Lee paid $55 for some brown Neet-Fit boots at Monroe's Shoe Store in downtown Carlisle. He had worn Neet-Fit shoes before and knew they were a good brand. The next day, however, Lee and his friend Pat were in the Valley Discount Store. Lee saw brown Neet-Fit boots exactly like his—except the price was $45. Lee was angry. He felt cheated.

Pat tried to explain that Monroe's had to charge more. They bought only a few pairs of each size and style, so they didn't get the quantity discount that Valley received. Pat also explained that Monroe's paid higher rent because their store was downtown. Valley was outside the city limits. Finally, Pat pointed out that Monroe's paid salespeople to measure Lee's feet, get the right size for him, and make sure that the boots fit. At Valley Lee would have to get the boots from the shelf and check the fit without help. No wonder he paid more at Monroe's.

Buying by Mail   Being a wise consumer is harder than ever when you shop by mail. In such cases you must depend on ads or catalog copy for your information. You cannot actually see what you are buying.

Here are some tips to help you buy wisely through the mail.

- *Have a good reason for shopping by mail.* Is the item something you can't find locally? Is the price lower by mail?
- *Read the catalog or advertisement carefully.* What sizes does the product come in? What colors are available? What is it made of? Is it ready to use, or must it be assembled?
- *Print your order carefully.* Give your name, address, and zip code. Copy the item number, color, and size that you want.
- *Never send cash.* Send a check for the exact amount and keep the canceled check as a receipt. If you don't have a checking account, send a bank check or money order.
- *Make a photocopy of your order.* If you are sending payment, lay the check or money order beside the order form on the photocopy machine. You will then have a record of your payment as well.
- *If you don't receive your order within 30 days, write to the company.* Verify that the firm received your order, and ask for a delivery date.
- *If you receive your order and don't like the item, return it to the company's customer service de-*

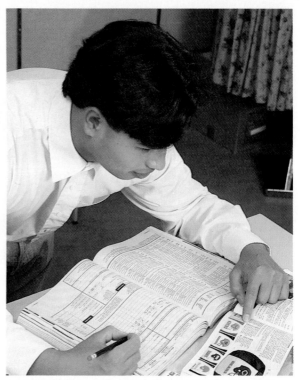

Mail-order buying is convenient, but it also puts more of the burden on the customer. What errors might creep into the transaction at the point shown here? What would the result be?

partment. Include a letter in the package telling what is wrong. Be sure to insure the package and keep the receipt.

Large mail-order houses depend on repeat business. They try to correct all errors and please customers. A few smaller companies, however, may not be so careful about correcting errors. Later in this chapter, you will learn how to report such problems.

✓ *CHECKING UP*

1. What is the most important influence on a consumer's buying habits?
2. Suggest a series of ad ideas for an electric pencil sharpener. Provide one ad for each of the persuasive techniques described in this lesson—association, group appeal, and snob appeal.
3. How could two items of equal quality end up priced very differently?

MAKE A DECISION

You have decided that you are going to buy a new stereo CD system. A local store has some top-rated brands, but all the prices seem too high. A mail-order catalog lists some of the same systems at lower prices, but you are worried about buying something that would be shipped halfway across the country. You have heard that a new discount appliance center will be opening in your neighborhood in three months, so you could wait and see what the new store has to offer. What's your decision —buy locally now, buy through the mail, or wait and hope for a better deal? Give the reasons for your decision.

2 *Consumer Fraud*

Most business people believe that being honest and providing quality products will lead to success. These people usually give the best possible service and produce the best possible goods.

Some business people, however, try to trick or cheat consumers. This practice is known as **consumer fraud.** Being aware of some of the more common types of consumer fraud will help you detect and avoid dishonest business people.

Auto Service and Repair

Millions of drivers nationwide must have their cars and trucks serviced regularly and, on occasion, repaired. Most of these people are not very knowledgeable about vehicles. This has led some individuals in the car repair business to engage in fraudulent practices.

One of the most common forms of auto repair fraud is the replacement of parts that do not need replacing. For example, a service-station attendant might remove a vehicle's air filter and replace it with one that is used. The car's owner would then be shown the dirty filter and told that a new one was badly needed. The same trick might also be used to sell car batteries and other parts.

Another common form of fraud is padding the bill—specifically, that portion of the bill that labor charges account for. The customer is charged for work that wasn't done or for more hours than were actually devoted to the repair.

Some service-station owners have been known to mix regular gasoline with premium and sell the mixture at the premium price. This practice gives the station a higher profit. Another tactic is to install a less-expensive oil in place of a better oil. The owner doesn't notice, and again the station owner makes a higher profit.

It is important to protect yourself against dishonest automobile service and repair people, especially if you do not know much about cars. The following suggestions will help you avoid fraud.

- *Be a regular customer.* Try to use one service station rather than going to different stations. Once the people at that station get to know you, they will probably give you better service than they would a stranger. They will also be less likely to take advantage of you.
- *Keep your car serviced.* This can avoid breakdowns on the road. It is very important to have tires, batteries, hoses, and belts checked often. You should also have your car checked and serviced before long trips. (A great many incidents of auto repair fraud occur when people are away from home.)
- *Don't leave your car unattended when you stop at unfamiliar service stations.* Watch the attendant while the car is being serviced. If he or she starts to do something unexpected, such as take off the air filter, ask the reason. Also, be careful if the attendant checks the battery with a tester or inspects other parts of the car without your asking. Don't be

There are limits to how closely owners can observe auto service or repairs in progress on their cars. In circumstances like these, what is the vehicle owner's best protection?

talked into buying parts for your car if the attendant has done any of these things.

- *Use a reliable service station.* For major repairs and tune-ups, take your car to a place with a reputation for providing good service.
- *Discuss the work you want done before signing the work order.* Don't let additional work be done until you understand the problem and know the cost.
- *Use praise.* Everyone likes to be told they are doing a good job. A little praise and courtesy for the people who take care of your car may help you get the best service.

Bargains and Contests

Sometimes consumers are cheated by retail stores. One frequently used trick is called **bait and switch.** An advertised bargain is used to lure people to a store—this is the bait. When the people get there, however, they find that the store is out of the bargain item. Instead, a salesperson tries to interest them in a similar item that is much more expensive—this is the switch. The store makes money from all the extra customers who came in for the nonexistent bargain and ended up buying full-priced merchandise.

The contest winner is another trick used to cheat the consumers. It works like this. You are called on the telephone and asked a simple question anyone could answer. After you answer the question, you are told you are a winner. Your "prize" is a discount on one of the store's products. Unless the discount is really a big one, the prize may not be a prize at all. You may end up paying what the item is actually worth. In such a case the store tries to make you think you are a winner when you are not.

Door-to-Door Sales

Some door-to-door salespeople are dishonest. One of the oldest door-to-door frauds is the phony magazine subscription. You should be suspicious if you are told any of the following:

- "I'm working my way through college."
- "I'm selling for a charity group."
- "I'm earning points for a promotion."

Not all door-to-door magazine salespeople are dishonest, but it can't hurt to be careful.

SITUATION
SOLUTION

Admitting a Mistake

You're in charge of product promotion for the General Grits Cereal Company. A promotion you ran in a dozen states is turning into a disaster.

Coupons were placed inside boxes of several varieties of General Grits cereals. Purchasers were asked to match the numbers on their coupons with winning numbers printed in this past weekend's Sunday newspapers. The grand prize was a one-week, expense-paid vacation in Hawaii.

There was supposed to be a single winner. Because of a printing error on the coupons, however, there are 56.

1. The company publicly acknowledges its mistake and invalidates the contest results. The angry winners scream, "Fraud!" How would you answer this charge?
2. The company's president is furious at all the adverse publicity. "Tell me why I shouldn't fire you," he yells. Tell him.
3. The company cannot afford to honor 56 winning tickets. What alternatives are there that might both satisfy the winners and repair the company's damaged image?

Encyclopedia salespeople have also been known to trick consumers. The salesperson might offer you a big discount on the new edition if you let the company use your name to promote the books. To accept this offer, you are asked to pay $50 down on the books you will get. Many times the salesperson and your $50 are never seen again.

Door-to-door salespeople must register with local officials and, in many cases, buy permits. If a door-to-door salesperson seems dishonest to you, ask to see his or her identification or city permit. If you have any questions about salespeople or their companies, call your local police station. Someone there may be able to help you.

Home Inspections

Beware of people who come to your home uninvited, offering free inspections. Some of these people will check your roof, furnace, or insulation and tell you that repairs are badly needed. Some pest-control companies also do a free, unsolicited inspection and then tell you that your home has termites or some other type of pest.

The wise homeowner questions free inspections. To protect yourself, deal only with established local firms. Check on all inspectors as you would door-to-door salespeople.

Job and Educational Opportunities

Young people sometimes learn about fraud when they try to get jobs or more education. High school and college graduates must be careful about offers to sell insurance, start their own business, or get extra education.

To attract students, correspondence schools often make false promises. Sometimes they are dishonest about the real chances for jobs.

Beware of high school diplomas and college degrees offered by **nonaccredited** (not officially approved) schools. Unless the school is accredited, the diploma or degree is worthless.

Case Study 2

While she was in the work experience program during her senior year, Dorothy worked in a law office. Last month she graduated from high school and went to work full time for the law firm.

Recently Dorothy received a letter from an out-of-state school urging her to enroll in a "preparalegal" correspondence course. When she finished the course, the letter said, she would get a promotion.

Dorothy showed the letter to Mrs. Lynn, her supervisor. Mrs. Lynn said schools and businesses sometimes get lists of graduates. These graduates are then contacted about job and educational opportunities. In many cases the jobs and opportunities aren't real.

Mrs. Lynn also said that the school writing to Dorothy was nonaccredited and that being one of its graduates wouldn't earn her a promotion. Mrs. Lynn suggested instead that Dorothy consider the local community college. Not only did it cost less, but credits earned there could eventually help Dorothy advance on her job.

Foods

Have you ever bought a can of peaches that contained more juice than peaches or a meat sauce that seemed to contain little or no meat? How can you tell if a packaged food product actually contains what it's supposed to? The answer is "Read the label."

Ingredient Labeling   The law requires that the contents of food packages be listed on their labels. The law also says that the ingredients must be listed in order of weight. In other words, the ingredient making up the largest part of the product by weight must be listed first. Next would come the ingredient making up the second largest part by weight, and so on.

Fraud in this area often consists of mixing fillers in food products to stretch expensive ingredients. For example, meat processors have been caught adding soybean product to ground beef. Since soybeans were not listed as an ingredient on the package labels, the processors were guilty of fraud.

Nutrition Labeling   Including nutritional information on food packages is voluntary—it is not required by law. However, if a food product contains ingredients added to improve its nutritional value, the label must say so. Also, if a food product is advertised as having greater nutritional value, the label must provide the information to support the claim.

Today, for example, some of the most frequently made nutritional claims deal with fat content. Ads proclaim that products contain no cholesterol, or saturated fat. To many consumers, this means the products are low fat or fat-free. This is not true. Many margarines, for example, are cholesterol-free since they are made with vegetable oil. However, they are still 100 percent fat. Some consumer groups think tighter controls should be placed on the use of cholesterol claims because they tend to mislead people.

Natural Foods   Artificial flavoring is another item that must be listed on labels. The word *imitation* must be used when the food product doesn't come from natural sources. For example, a lemon pie made without real lemons must say on its label, "Imitation lemon flavor." Its taste must also compare well with the taste of real lemons.

Today the whole question of what is and is not a natural food is much debated. Our laws do not provide a definition of natural foods, but most

Product labeling can help you shop smarter—but only if you know how to use it.

a. Is the product at the right real or not? Only an educated consumer knows for sure. How?

b. If the jars of spaghetti sauce whose labels are shown above were priced the same, which would be the better buy? Why?

authorities agree that they should not contain artificial or imitation ingredients. Natural foods should also not contain preservatives (chemicals added to prevent spoilage) or coloring.

Some authorities would go further and say that natural foods should be grown without commercial fertilizers or pesticides. Such foods are said to be organically grown. In reality, however, much organically grown produce has traces of insect spray and commercial fertilizer. Apparently, these chemicals are so common in our environment (in the soil, air, and water) that they cannot be escaped. Future definitions of natural or organic foods may have to take this into consideration.

In any event, it is difficult if not impossible to tell natural foods just by looking at them or tasting them. You should check labels carefully. If necessary, question the store owner or product supplier about his or her produce sources.

Drugs

In watching old movies on television, you've probably seen traveling medicine shows. These were common around the turn of the century in rural areas of this country. Between the music and entertainment, fast-talking salespeople pitched their cure-alls. Most of these products were worthless as medicines. They often consisted of little

more than herbs and alcohol. Occasionally, however, they were poisonous. (Perhaps this was to be expected, since the people mixing them had no knowledge of chemistry.)

Traveling medicine shows no longer exist, but today many drugs are advertised on radio, on television, and in newspapers. Some of the claims made for these products have been challenged by government agencies and proved false.

Case Study 3

Rosa's consumer education class was studying fraud in advertising. One evening she heard a television commercial that sounded like a fraud. Fast Action aspirin was being advertised as "twice as strong as EZ aspirin."

The following day Rosa found both brands of aspirin at a discount drug store. She was surprised when she read the list of ingredients on each label. Each Fast Action tablet contained ten grains of aspirin, while EZ tablets had only five grains each.

Rosa decided that not all commercials that sound dishonest really were. She realized the importance of reading labels on food and drug products.

Government agencies have a great deal of control over what drug companies can make and sell. As a result, some companies have been forced to change their advertisements. They have had to eliminate health claims for their products because they could not support them with scientific evidence. Failure to do so would have meant large fines.

Health Care

Many people are uncertain about whether or not they are getting the best health care for their money. They don't know how to judge the ability of doctors or the quality of service provided by hospitals.

Fraud in health care is even harder to identify. How can you prove that expensive tests or treatments were not needed? How can you establish that they were done only so the doctor and/or hospital could collect a fee?

Some of the most publicized cases of health care fraud have involved services provided under federal programs like Medicare and Medicaid. In these cases, doctors have charged the government for services that were never performed. They did this by claiming they performed multiple procedures on individual patients (two appendectomies, for example). They also claimed that they handled impossible numbers of office visits daily.

The following suggestions will help you protect yourself from health care fraud.

- *Choose a doctor carefully.* Ask your friends and family for suggestions. Learn as much as you can about the doctor you select. Be especially sure to find out where he or she has hospital privileges.
- *To get the most from a visit to the doctor, make a list of questions you want to ask.* In particular, inquire about any drugs you are prescribed. Also, ask about fees.
- *Select a hospital before you need one.* Don't wait until there is an emergency. The hospital should be accredited (approved by the state health department). Find out if it is a teaching hospital. (Such hospitals usually have more doctors on their staffs.) Also, inquire about its charges. How do they compare with the charges of other area hospitals?
- *Do not rush into surgery or tests.* Find out the reasons and the risks. A good doctor usually tells you these things without being asked.
- *Before any surgery, get a second opinion.* A good doctor won't object if you consult someone else, and your insurance company may require it.
- *If health insurance pays your bill, check to see that the charges are correct.* Excessive charges or mistakes are fairly common. Both, if they occur on a large scale, can increase insurance rates for everyone.

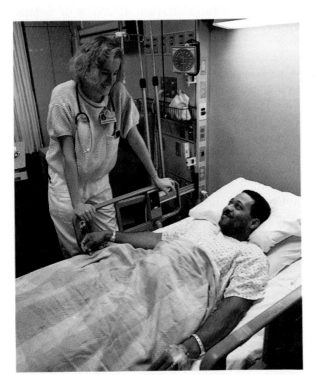

The time to select a doctor and a hospital is before a health emergency occurs. Why?

✓ CHECKING UP

1. Consumer fraud is dishonesty practiced by consumers—true or false? Explain.
2. Briefly describe the most common form of consumer fraud in each of the following areas: auto repair, retail sales, and health care.
3. What officially are natural foods?

3 *Consumer Protection*

The first two lessons in this chapter have described the buying environment in which U.S. consumers must operate. That environment is dynamic, confusing, and occasionally even threatening. To cope, consumers need skills. They must know how to take advantage of basic economics, plan purchases, and shop for value. They must know how to protect themselves from dishonesty and fraud. Finally, should a problem arise, they must know how to go about solving it.

Consumer Responsibility

If you feel you've been cheated, call or visit the business involved. Present all the relevant facts calmly and simply. Then give the company a chance to settle your claim.

If you have a problem with an out-of-town firm, you might phone in your complaint. Many companies have numbers that customers can call free of charge. (Such numbers usually have an 800 area code.)

If these informal approaches don't get results, make your complaint in writing. Look for the firm's mailing address somewhere on its products, packaging, order forms, or receipts. If you cannot find the address, visit your local library. There you can look up the firm in Standard and Poor's *Register of Corporations, Directors, and Executives.* If you use this reference, also note the name of the company's president. This is the person to whom you will write.

Use standard business letter format for your complaint. (See Chapter 5 for a review.) You should organize the body of your letter in three paragraphs (see Figure 16-1).

In the first paragraph, give the purchase (or order) details. Specify the date and place of purchase and the name and model number of the product. If you have already paid, include the number of your check or money order and/or a photocopy of your sales receipt.

In the second paragraph of your letter, give the details of your complaint. As briefly as possible, state what is wrong. Describe when and how it happened, and tell what (if any) actions you have already taken to correct the situation. (These might include service or repairs, return and exchange, or previous phone calls or letters.)

In the third paragraph, state the remedy you are seeking. Do you want a full or partial refund? Would you accept a repair of the item, or will only replacement do? Be specific.

If you have contacted the business before without results, you might add a final paragraph setting a deadline for action. State, for example, that if you have not heard from the firm in three weeks, you will take the matter up with a government consumer agency. Once you have made this statement, however, you should be prepared to act on it. If the company does not respond in the specified time, it is your responsibility as a consumer to make good your word.

Federal Agencies

Consumer agencies exist at all levels of government. For most consumer problems, state and local agencies offer the best chance for a quick response.

Sometimes, however, a problem is too big for such agencies to handle. For example, it may affect consumers in different states or the public in general. It is at times like these that federal consumer protection agencies can help. We shall discuss three of these agencies in this section.

Food and Drug Administration   The **Food and Drug Administration (FDA)** is a federal agency that regulates the production and sale of foods and drugs. The FDA sets standards for these products and does tests to make sure that those standards are met. FDA technicians also verify the safety of new drugs and medical devices. FDA inspectors visit workplaces such as bakeries and canneries to make sure that they are not producing contaminated products.

The FDA also checks product labels. The Fair Packaging and Labeling Act makes it illegal to put misleading information on a label. The label must not give the consumer the wrong idea about what is in a product or what the product can do. The FDA can take action against false and misleading labeling on products it regulates.

Federal Trade Commission   The **Federal Trade Commission (FTC)** is a federal agency that administers laws ensuring fair trade. The FTC prevents unfair competition and enforces rules that define unfair or deceptive practices in certain industries. Consumers are probably most familiar with the agency through its activities in three main areas—warranties, labeling, and advertising.

1111 Otsego Street
Glenoaks, CA 91423
May 10, 1991

Craig Wilner, President
Summit Home Appliances
400 Fernando Drive
Phoenix, AZ 85014

Dear Mr. Wilner:

On January 12 of this year I purchased a Summit hot-air corn popper (Model No. 1330-23D9) from the Sellco Department Store in Glenoaks. A copy of my receipt is enclosed with this letter.

The corn popper operated perfectly for about one month. Then it began to heat erratically, and finally it failed to heat at all. On February 20 I took the appliance to an authorized service center (see work order enclosed). There, after two weeks, the problem was diagnosed as a defective heat transfer element. The service center ordered the part, but one month later it had still not arrived. Hoping to speed things up, on April 11 I wrote a letter of inquiry to your customer relations department. To date, I have received no response.

When am I going to get my corn popper back? If Summit cannot provide a replacement part in 2 1/2 months, then I think the company should provide a replacement appliance.

I would hope that with your help this matter can be quickly resolved. I shall wait another two weeks--that's more than three months since my appliance went in for repairs. If I don't hear from you by then, I shall refer the matter to the California Consumer Affairs Department.

Sincerely,

David Retsmacher

David Retsmacher

Enclosures

Figure 16-1   A letter of complaint should be brief (no more than one page long), clearly written, and well organized. Measure this letter against this standard. Take two minutes to read it and quickly note the main idea of each paragraph.

Strive for Success

Fighting on the Side of Safety

Most people would probably be intimidated at the thought of taking on a large corporation in a fight over how it does business. Even more intimidating would be the thought of taking on an entire industry. You can imagine, then, what it must be like for one man to carry on a crusade against many industries—including one of our nation's largest, the automobile industry.

In his role as a consumer advocate, Ralph Nader has waged legal and public battles against some of the most powerful corporations in our country. He has fought these companies to protect American consumers. In the process he has become known as one of the most effective consumer advocates of all time.

Nader, who was born in 1934 in Winsted, Connecticut, is the son of Lebanese immigrants. He is a graduate of Princeton University and Harvard Law School.

Nader first became interested in auto safety while he was at Harvard. His research into auto injury cases led in 1965 to the publication of *Unsafe at Any Speed*. The book attacked automobile manufacturers for producing unsafe cars. In 1970 one of Nader's environmental groups wrote a report on air pollution called *Vanishing Air*. The report blamed the auto industry for greatly contributing to air pollution problems in the United States.

Nader's studies were very effective. Directly or indirectly, they led to such milestones as the Clean Air Act of 1963, the Air Quality Act of 1967, and the current trend toward air bag restraint systems in all cars.

Nader hasn't confined his activities to the auto industry, however. He founded Public Citizen, Inc., to investigate energy problems, health care, tax reform, and other consumer issues. He has even turned his investigative eye on Congress. His study of that body led to the book *Who Runs Congress?* which was published in 1982. More recently, Nader has been active in the area of insurance reform.

Like the FDA, the FTC gets some of its authority from the Fair Packaging and Labeling Act. It is the FTC, for example, that requires clothing manufacturers to put care labels on all their products. These labels give directions for proper washing or dry cleaning of clothing items. The FTC also exercises some control over product advertising. It requires, for example, that product descriptions in ads be factual and clearly stated. Again, to use clothing as an example, a clothing manufacturer cannot say in an ad that a garment is wash-and-wear if it isn't.

The FTC enforces similar restrictions on warranties. A **warranty** is a guarantee of a product's quality. It usually contains the manufacturer's promise to correct by repair or replacement any failure caused by defective parts, materials, or workmanship. Companies are not required to provide warranties, but if they choose to do so they must meet FTC standards. This means providing warranties that are clearly worded and printed, conveniently placed, and accurately labeled as either full or limited.

Consumer Product Safety Commission   In 1972 Congress passed a law to protect consumers from equipment that could harm the user. This law, which is part of the Consumer Product Safety Act, tries to

- protect people from injuries caused by consumer products,
- help consumers judge the safety of products, and
- encourage companies to develop products that meet safety standards.

As part of the law, a government agency called the **Consumer Product Safety Commission (CPSC)** was established. The CPSC determines safety standards for equipment and makes sure those standards are met. The agency can take a product off the market if it finds that product dangerous to users.

Consumer Groups

Consumer groups work at local, state, and national levels. These groups investigate consumer complaints and keep the public informed about them. They also lobby (or try to influence) lawmakers to pass legislation that protects consumers.

In some areas consumer groups have been quite successful. One of these is highway safety. Thanks to the efforts of consumer advocates, auto manu-

facturers must recall cars with faulty parts and repair or replace those parts free of charge. Tires also are recalled if they do not meet safety standards.

Business Organizations

If a company doesn't respond to your complaint after a reasonable amount of time, you might call the Better Business Bureau. The bureau is a private organization financed by business and made up of local Better Business Bureaus. The organization's goals are to improve local business service, eliminate false advertising, and settle consumer complaints. You will find a telephone number for the local Better Business Bureau in your Yellow Pages.

Other Sources of Help

You may also get help with consumer problems by writing to a local radio or television station. Such stations often have employees who work on consumer problems. Some newspapers also offer this service. In your letter, describe your problem and tell what you have done to try to solve it. Keep a copy of your letter.

In some areas the police department handles cases of fraud. If you feel you've been cheated, talk to your local police. Even if they don't handle problems like yours, they can tell you who does.

In many states the attorney general checks into cases of fraud. If you cannot get help locally, write to the state attorney general's office. You will find the address and telephone number in the government listings of the Yellow Pages.

✓ CHECKING UP

1. Briefly summarize the contents of a consumer complaint letter.
2. The FDA and FTC both enforce rules regarding labeling. How are their functions in this area similar? How are they different?
3. Comment on this comment: "Warranties are useless. Even if you could find them, you can't read them. The print's too small and the language is hard to understand."

16 *Review Your Learning*

CHAPTER SUMMARY

As a consumer, you will buy many things. Which things you buy will be influenced by your job and income, your interests, your environment, your peers, and the advertising to which you are subjected.

If you practice responsible buying, you will get the most for your money. To do this, you must know how to take advantage of basic economics (like the law of supply and demand), how to plan purchases, and how to shop for value. You must also know how to protect yourself against consumer fraud. Examples of fraud include deceptive sales practices like bait and switch; phony contests; unsolicited home inspections; and misleading labels on food, drugs, and other products.

If you do have a problem with a business, first try to settle it informally, in person or by phone. If this approach doesn't work, write a letter of complaint. Include three main elements in your letter —the details of the purchase, the details of the problem, and the remedy you desire. If you do not get a satisfactory response, consider seeking the help of a consumer group or advocate or a government agency.

TERMS TO KNOW

Write a serious or tongue-in-cheek essay, two or three paragraphs long, entitled "Why I Work for the Government." Use all of the following terms:

peer pressure
inventory
consumer fraud
bait and switch
nonaccredited
Food and Drug Administration (FDA)
Federal Trade Commission (FTC)
warranty
Consumer Product Safety Commission (CPSC)

STUDY QUESTIONS

1. Name six factors that influence consumer buying decisions.
2. How can advertising save you money? How can it cost you money?
3. Describe three techniques advertisers commonly use to persuade people to buy.
4. If half of the Florida orange crop freezes this year, will the price of oranges go up or down? Explain.
5. What are the two steps in a long-range buying plan?
6. What is usually the most important factor in shopping for value?
7. Suggest three reasons why two similar products might be priced very differently.
8. You should have a good reason for buying by mail. Suggest two possibilities.
9. Name three federal consumer agencies.
10. List at least five things you can do to protect yourself from auto service and repair fraud.
11. How can you tell which ingredient makes up the largest part of a packaged food?
12. What's the first thing you should do if you feel you've been cheated by a local company? If that doesn't work, what's the second thing you should do?

CRITICAL THINKING

1. Murray lives in Nome, Alaska. Alvin lives in Miami, Florida. How do you think their different environments would affect their purchase decisions?
2. Recall that the advertising technique of association can be used to link a product with an idea as well as a celebrity. If most people think rodeos are exciting, for example, and an advertiser wants people to think a certain car is exciting, what might he or she suggest as an ad?

3. What's going on in the cartoon below? Is there any way the customer could have avoided the situation? Explain why or why not.

DISCUSSION STARTERS

1. Consider your spending for the last month. In what ways did your peers influence your buying decisions?
2. In an economic system where individualism, independence, and self-reliance are valued, why should the government get involved in consumer protection? Shouldn't every consumer protect himself or herself? Why or why not?

BUILDING BASIC SKILLS

Math

1. Assume that all forms of promotion (including advertising) add 27 percent to the cost of the average grocery item. If a nationally advertised brand of paper towel sells for $1.03 a roll, how much should a generic (or no-name) brand sell for?
2. Assume you order the following items from a catalog house: woolen scarf ($15), cotton turtlenecks (three at $18 each), and rain boots ($27). What is the total cost of your order including 6¼ percent sales tax and shipping charges of $4.50?

Communication

3. When the order that you placed in the previous problem arrives, you find that you like only one of the turtlenecks. The second doesn't fit quite as well as the first. The third fits fine, but the color is all wrong. Write a short letter to the customer service department of the catalog house, explaining what's wrong and what you want to do about it (refund, exchange, or a combination of both —you decide). Make up any dates or item numbers you might need.

Decision Making

4. In March you placed an order with ABC, Inc. Two months later you had still neither heard nor received anything. You tried to contact the sales rep who helped you, but he was at lunch and never returned your call. Two weeks later you phoned customer relations to complain about the poor service and request a refund. The phone calls were long distance and cost you about $15. Finally your order arrived, but it was incomplete. A refund check was enclosed to cover the missing items. It covered more than that, however— $50 more. What will you do—return the money or return the portion of the order you were sent? Explain your choice.

SUGGESTED ACTIVITIES

1. Working with three or four other students, gather ads for a bulletin board display on persuasive techniques in advertising. Group the ads by technique—association, snob appeal, or group appeal. Place any ads that don't seem to fit in these categories off to one side. Then, working with the rest of the class, try to devise some new categories to account for these ads.
2. Working with others in your class, stage a quality comparison demonstration. For each item included, have two samples—one representing the high end of the quality scale, the other representing the low end. Have the presenter of each pair of items point out the features that make the high-end item superior.

Managing Your Money

OBJECTIVES

After studying this chapter and doing the activities, you will be able to:

- list the steps involved in drawing up a budget;
- suggest some ways to stick to a budget;
- describe the personal and economic factors that influence financial responsibility; and
- name several sources of help for people who are having problems managing their money.

TERMS TO KNOW

budget
financial responsibility
deflation
liquid assets

*D*o you have enough money to buy all the things you would like to have? If your answer is no, you may feel better knowing you aren't alone. Very few people have all the money they want.

You may have noticed, though, that some of your friends have more cash than you do. This may be true even though some of them don't earn as much money as you. Why do you think these people have money whenever they need it?

It could be that some of your friends have learned how to manage their money. Learning money management isn't easy, however. It's like learning to drive a car—you get better with practice.

In this chapter you'll learn how to set up and stick to a budget. You'll also learn how to anticipate and deal with changes in your financial situation. This type of good money management will help you get the most out of your money.

1 *Budgeting*

To be successful in managing your money, you must accept responsibility. You need to set your own goals and make a plan that will help you meet them. This process is called planned spending. The actual plan that you use to manage your money is called a **budget.** To practice planned spending you must know how to make and keep a budget.

You might think that while you are in school you don't need to make a budget. Even if you have very little money and few expenses, you can benefit from making a budget. You can gain valuable budgeting experience that will help you later in life. Making a budget will also help you avoid wasting your money.

Setting Goals

The first step in preparing a budget is to make a list of all your goals. Include things you want to do and to buy. If the list is very long, underline the things that are most important to you. Copy these items onto another sheet of paper.

Put the first list in your personal file for safe keeping. Someday you will enjoy looking at this list. Your goals may be the same in the future, or you may have new interests and new goals. Regardless, it will be interesting to see how many of your goals you achieve.

Estimating Expenses and Income

Now look at your second list. Cross out anything on this list that isn't essential. You must first take care of your needs. After you have budgeted money for your needs, you can plan to spend for things you simply want.

Group your needs under such headings as food, housing, education, and clothing. Use these headings to set up an expense record like the one in Figure 17-1. You will use this record for a few weeks to keep track of what you spend. This will tell you just where your money is going. Once you know this, you will be able to make an informed estimate of how much your weekly expenses are likely to be.

Of course, your expenses will probably not be exactly the same each week. For example, your first week's expenses may be unusually heavy compared to what your average week's expenses eventually turn out to be. This is why it's a good idea to track your expenses for a few weeks before doing an initial budget.

You should also track your income for a few weeks using a similar form. Be sure to include all

| | | | | | | Medical/ | | Gifts and |
Date	Food	Housing	Education	Clothing	Transportation	Dental Care	Recreation	Contribution
1/6							$3.50	$1.00
1/7	$3.00				$5.00			
1/8	.50			$13.29				
1/9	1.50							
1/10	1.50							
1/11	.50							
1/12	4.00				1.50		6.50	
Total	$11.00			$13.29	$6.50		$10.00	$1.00

Expense Record

Figure 17-1 An expense record can give you a clear picture of exactly where your money is going. Assume that on January 14 you had to make the following payments: car insurance installment ($35), phone bill contribution ($10), and dry-cleaning bill ($8.35). In which columns would you enter them?

money that will be available to you for spending or saving. This means counting not only wages but also tips, allowances, bank interest, and monetary gifts.

Once you have a few weeks' data to work from, you can estimate what your average weekly income and expenses will be. You can then multiply these figures by four to get monthly estimates.

Drawing Up a Budget

You should format your personal budget so that it looks similar to the one shown in Figure 17-2. You will notice that this form is a little more complicated than the expense record discussed earlier. To start, the form is divided into two parts—income (at the top) and expenses (at the bottom). If you are not spending more than you earn, these two amounts should be equal.

The expenses portion of the budget statement is itself divided into parts. First, there are day-to-day expenses, which are sometimes called flexible ex-

penses because they vary from one budget period to another. Next, there are monthly expenses, which are sometimes called fixed expenses because they do not vary from month to month. Fixed expenses include predictable amounts such as rent, car payments, and insurance premiums. Finally, there is a section for savings. This is one of the most important parts of a budget. Saving contributes to good money management in two ways. Long-term saving helps you meet your career and life-style goals. The building up of an emergency fund helps you cope with unexpected situations that might otherwise cause you to go "over budget."

Revising a Budget

At the end of each month, you should check to see if your income and expenses balance. If they don't, you will have to find a way to bring them into line with each other. If you can't increase your income in some way, you will have to cut back on

Figure 17-2 A personal budget can show you at a glance whether or not you are living within your means. Is the person who filled out this form staying within budget? How do you know?

Personal Budget	
Income, Expenses, and Savings	**Amount per Month**
Total income	$ 200
Savings	$ 30
Regular monthly expenses:	
Rent or mortgage payment . . . . $	—
Utilities	10
Installment payments	—
Other	—
Total	10
Day-to-day expenses:	
Food . . . . $	45
Household operation	
and maintenance	—
Education	—
Clothing	30
Transportation	50
Medical/dental care	—
Recreation	30
Gifts and contributions	5
Total	160
Total savings and expenses	$ 200

Checking and revising your spending plan is an essential part of the budgeting process. Why?

your spending. For example, you may have to forgo some clothing purchases or reduce the amount you spend on recreation.

Remember, a budget is something you keep working and reworking until it fits you. Don't expect your expenses and income to balance on your first try. They'll come closer as you gain skill in managing your money.

MAKE A DECISION

You don't spend much money on yourself for extras, but you've gotten in the habit of buying a couple of doughnuts for your coffee break in the morning and a 40-cent candy bar in the afternoon. You figure that by doing without these snacks you could save over $200 a year—enough money to buy several things you want. What's your decision—a few small pleasures daily or one or two large, lasting purchases at the end of the year? Give the reasons for your decision.

Sticking to a Budget

Making and using a budget is hard, especially at first. If you can stick to it, however, your budget will be an excellent tool for managing your money. It will show you where you spend too much. It will help you match your expenses to your income.

Here are some tips that will help you stick to your budget and keep it working well.

- *Keep it simple.* The easier your budget is to use, the easier it will be to stick to.
- *Be realistic.* If your income is less than your complete list of expenses, your budget will show that. Don't try to spend money you don't have.
- *Keep day-to-day records.* It's easy to forget what you spend unless you record your daily expenses.
- *Keep your budget, incoming bills, receipts, and canceled checks all in one place.* This will help you organize your budgeting efforts.
- *Choose a definite time to pay bills and review your budget.* This will prevent your budget from "getting away from you." It will also increase the likelihood that your payments will be made on time.

✓ CHECKING UP

1. To budget, you need to estimate your expenses. If you have no records, how do you know how much you spend each month?
2. If you have to revise your budget, it means you're a poor money manager —true or false? Explain.
3. Suggest three things you can do to stick to a budget.

2 *Coping with Financial Responsibility*

Managing your money is not something you do once or twice, and then it's over. As you grow older and move into the adult world, you will have more income and more expenses. Even if you don't take on new expenses, many of your present costs will probably go up. You must constantly be alert to changes in your personal financial situation and in the economy as a whole.

Adjusting to Personal Change

Responsibility where money is concerned is called **financial responsibility.** Some people have more financial responsibility than others. While you are in school, for example, you probably earn only a small amount of money from an allowance or a part-time job. This means that you can be responsible for only a small part of your expenses.

When you get a full-time job, however, you will probably help pay more of the household expenses. You will take on greater financial responsibility. If you move away from home, you will have even greater financial responsibility.

For the first time you will be entirely responsible for paying for such things as groceries, utilities, and insurance as well as rent. Most likely, you will be surprised at how much these things cost. It will be a genuine challenge for you to manage these payments on the salary from an entry-level job.

If you get married and have children, you will have a still different level of financial responsibility. If you are the only spouse who works, you will have to pay for food, clothing, transportation, housing, and a host of other items for others as well as yourself. If both you and your spouse work, however, you will probably share financial responsibility. This arrangement is often necessary today when housing and education costs for families exceed the ability of most individuals to pay them.

You can see that different people have different levels of financial responsibility. You probably know that responsibilities usually grow as you get older, but many young people have them, too. To better understand some of the problems of young consumers, look at the case studies beginning on this page.

Case Study 1

Joe Thompson is 18 years old and a senior at Sandusky High School. He has two brothers and three younger sisters. Even though Joe's parents shop wisely, it's hard to meet the expenses of such a large family.

Last summer Joe decided he would help the family by going to work. His father is a sales representative for the Microdyne Supply Company. Joe's father gets a salary and commissions. Joe thought he, too, might like sales work, so he got a job selling aluminum cooking utensils.

To travel from town to town, Joe knew he would need a car. He also needed expense money until he made some sales. Joe's father cosigned a bank loan for $1,500, and Joe bought a used car. It cost $1,200. That left $300 for travel expenses.

Joe worked very hard during June, July, and August. His earnings were high, but so were his expenses. He was unable to repay the loan completely. Now he works evenings and Saturdays so he can make payments on his loan. Joe is determined to prove that he is financially responsible and trustworthy.

Case Study 2

Marta Lu is 17 years old and a junior at Washington High School. She lives with her father, two brothers, and a sister. Her mother died three years ago.

Marta's father is a carpenter. Bad weather and a scarcity of construction jobs in the area have kept him unemployed for much of the last three years. The family has had to cut back on its spending.

Marta works part-time at the public library. She knows that she will be responsible for herself after finishing high school.

Marta has studied available occupations and found television repair very interesting. Her friend Jane has an older sister who owns a television repair service. Marta enjoys visiting her shop.

Marta discussed her goals with her school counselor. She then decided to take the television repair course at the community college after graduating from high school. The cost of the course is $900.

Marta has been saving one-fourth of the money she earns. She works two hours each day after school and three hours on Saturdays. She's paid minimum wage. Marta expects to have the $900 saved before graduation.

Case Study 3

Helen Lane has always wanted to be a bookkeeper. Her family encouraged her to take bookkeeping courses at Northern Regional Vocational School.

To be closer to the school, Helen needed to leave the farm where she had lived all her life. She rented a furnished apartment five blocks from the school. She chose this apartment because there was a shopping center nearby. She wanted to live near the school and a shopping center because she didn't have a car. The shopping center had a bank, several stores, and a supermarket.

Helen's family sent her an allowance each month, and Helen managed this money wisely. She always had enough to pay the rent and buy groceries.

After four months of living on her own, Helen felt she had learned a great deal. She was able to keep accounts and manage a budget. She knew about buying food and clothing and caring for an apartment. She had become a wise consumer.

Helen's family was very proud of her. She had proved that she could handle financial responsibility.

Case Study 4

Felipe and Maria Luna have been married six years. They live in an apartment close to the factory where Felipe works and the hospital where Maria is a nurse. Since their son, Armando, was born two years ago, the Lunas have been thinking about buying a house.

Felipe and Maria began saving for a down payment. Six months ago they found a house they liked—small, three bedrooms, and a yard for Armando. Because it was older, the house cost less than most they had seen. Felipe and Maria thought their savings would cover the down payment. With Felipe's latest raise, they were sure they could meet the monthly payments.

Felipe and Maria studied their budget. Then they talked with a loan officer at the First National Bank. She asked about their finances and suggested they spend no more than $650 per month on house payments. She gave them a list of things to look for when checking the house.

According to this checklist, the house Felipe and Maria found was perfect for them. Both the inside and outside were in good condition. The house also had a good location for their needs. The school was only five blocks away. The neighborhood seemed quiet, and there were only a few busy streets. Most of the houses on the block were well cared for and were owned by young families.

The Lunas thought the house met their needs, so they called the bank. A bank employee looked at the house and decided the bank would lend the money for it. The loan was approved.

The Lunas have now lived in their new house for four months. They like it more than ever, but the $610 monthly payments have not been easy to make. Felipe and Maria have had to give up some things to make ends meet. They now spend less on recreation, watch television instead of going to the movies, and eat out less. They also save money by participating in a car pool instead of driving to work by themselves. They feel that buying a home is worth these changes in their life-style.

Adjusting to Economic Change

Added financial responsibilities are not the only reasons for reviewing your spending. You may need to change your budget from time to time because of higher prices. You probably don't remember a time when a soda or a candy bar cost a nickel or a dime. Today both cost more—and they will probably cost still more in the future.

Inflation   As you know from reading Chapter 13, when prices are constantly rising, we have an economic condition known as inflation. In a time of inflation workers want higher wages, and they buy more with credit. This causes prices in general and the cost of credit to go up even higher. Thus, inflation causes more inflation. It is sometimes very difficult to break this cycle.

During inflation, as prices go up, your dollar buys less. It loses some of its value, or purchasing power. It's still a dollar, but it takes more and more dollars to buy the same things.

Inflation can help some people, hard as that is to believe. People who borrowed money before the inflation started can repay their loans with dollars that are worth less. Obviously, this is to the advantage of borrowers.

People who saved their money, however, are hurt by inflation. The dollars that they put in the bank years ago are worth much less when they withdraw them from their savings.

Deflation   Just as prices in general can rise, so they can fall. This is called **deflation.** In a deflationary period the value of your money increases. In other words, a dollar stretches further. It buys more.

As with inflation, there are winners and losers in this situation. People who have their money invested in **liquid assets** (those that can easily be turned into cash) benefit. They can sell their assets and buy relatively more with the money they receive. People whose money is invested in assets that are more difficult to convert to cash—assets like real estate—suffer. The value of such assets falls, making them unattractive to many buyers— at least until their prices hit bottom.

There has been no general deflation since the Great Depression. Rather, inflation has been the more common problem.

It is likely that a certain amount of inflation will always be with us. We must therefore learn to live with it. This means learning to review and adjust our budgets from time to time.

In a period of deflation, people with dollars to spend—like these home buyers—get more for their money. How specifically do they benefit? How do you think the same economic condition affects the sellers of the home? the real estate broker?

When this man was the age of the teenager at the next pump, gasoline cost about 20 cents a gallon. Today it costs over a dollar more. What is the name of the economic condition characterized by such price increases?

Finding Help for Money Management Problems

Most people could manage their money better than they do. If you're having trouble managing your money, try to find out why. Did you have to pay any large, unexpected bills? These bills are often the major cause of money management problems.

Sometimes people find themselves in economic trouble because of the way they respond to problems. For example, Anita felt angry when she broke up with her boyfriend, so she went on a buying spree. She did the same thing when her boss criticized her work last week. If she isn't in debt already, Anita soon will be.

Here is another example. Loren is shy and has no close friends. He tries to buy friends by taking them to expensive restaurants. He also buys costly sports equipment that he lets others use. Loren owes a lot of money. Chances are that his poor money management will continue. Loren is sure that no one could like him for himself. His low self-esteem leads to economic problems.

Both Anita and Loren fail to see the cause of their trouble. Do you sometimes act as they acted? If you want to avoid these problems and improve your money management, help is available.

Strive for Success

No Hiding His Success

His work was known and loved throughout the world, yet he was hardly a well-recognized figure. People from all over the world knew his voices, but few knew his real voice. He was the star of the world's most watched television show (235 million viewers in more than 100 countries), yet he was hidden from the camera. He was Jim Henson, the magic behind the Muppets.

Born in 1936, Henson grew up in Hyattsville, Maryland. In high school, he joined (with only casual interest) the puppet club. Puppetry, however, soon became a hobby—and the hobby became an enormously successful career.

"It was in the early 1950s, and I was between high school and college and needed a job," he said. "There was this job available for a puppeteer on a local NBC station in Washington (D.C.). I figured it would be a pretty good job, so I applied for it and got it."

He kept the job while he attended the University of Maryland, where he studied art, staging, and scenic design. During his freshman year, the station gave him his own show. It aired five nights a week and was only five minutes long. Still, it was enough to earn Henson a local Emmy award.

It was for this show that Henson created Kermit the Frog. (Kermit would later become one of the most famous Muppets.) However, it was a series of appearances on ABC's "Jimmy Dean Show" that first brought national attention to the Muppets.

Soon there were Muppets appearing on many popular television shows. Then came "Sesame Street," which made the Muppets household words. From there Muppetmania was born. By 1976 "The Muppet Show" was being produced in England and shown in over 100 different countries. Muppet movies and Muppet merchandise soon followed. The Muppets were stars.

Jim Henson died suddenly and unexpectedly on May 16, 1990. He had become a success as both a business person and an entertainer, but he

still saw himself as primarily a puppeteer. He once explained that he enjoyed puppetry because it allowed him full creative control. "Also," he added, "puppetry is a good way of hiding."

SITUATION
SOLUTION

When Layoffs Are Threatened

Times are hard in the restaurant business—and getting harder. The state economy has taken a nosedive, and business is way off. People seem to be cutting back on meals out.

You've been waiting tables for two years at Taft's, a downtown eatery near the garment district. It's the lunchtime rush, and you stop in the kitchen to talk with Phil, a fellow employee. He's muttering under his breath.

"Gees, I hate waiting on women. They demand all this extra service—water with ice, water without ice, extra napkins, extra silverware, reheat this. All this nonsense, and they tip half what a bunch of guys would."

You're a little surprised at the tone of Phil's remarks. It's the financial pressure talking, you tell yourself. You're all feeling it.

1. Your tips are off, too. You know that working more hours is not a possibility. What might you do instead to get your tips up again, given the economic situation?

2. What, if anything, would you say to Phil to dampen his hostility toward the restaurant's female patrons?

3. Taft's has to cut costs. Management gives the staff a choice—everyone stays but works fewer hours, or four people lose their jobs so that ten can work full shifts. How would you vote? What questions might you want to ask before making your decision?

Schools Many high schools have consumer education courses. In these classes, students learn the best ways to buy and use goods and services. Other courses, such as social studies, often include a unit on consumer education. Many high schools and community colleges also offer adult education classes that help people learn money management.

Don't forget that your teachers can help you with your problems. Most teachers in agriculture, business, homemaking, and industrial arts have studied consumer education. Your school counselor is another possible source of help.

Newspapers and Magazines You can find a great deal of information about money matters in newspapers and magazines. Most newspapers print daily or weekly columns by writers who are experts on handling money. Several magazines, such as *Business Week, Forbes,* and *Fortune,* are devoted entirely to financial matters.

Government Agencies Many government agencies publish free or inexpensive booklets that will help you get the most for your money. These booklets are available at federal and county offices and in many local libraries. County agricultural agents and extension services also provide consumer information for individuals and groups.

Banks Many banks employ people to give free financial information to customers. Information is given on savings plans and bank loans. As a public service, some banks sponsor courses, called seminars, in money management. The seminars may be at the bank in the evening or on Saturday, but more often they're held at a high school or college. If you have money problems, ask at your bank if such a seminar is planned.

Lawyers Sometimes money problems require professional help. A lawyer should be consulted when a legal opinion is needed. This is necessary when making contracts, selling property, and collecting money. It may also be necessary when the payment of funds is in dispute or a person finds himself or herself unable to pay money owed. You can find more information on legal help in Chapter 21.

Other Sources Check the Yellow Pages of your telephone book. Look under the name of your city or town. You may find agencies that can help you. In some areas, for example, a Department of Family Services may have counselors available to help you.

✓ CHECKING UP

1. Why does financial responsibility generally increase for young people as they get older?

2. What is the difference between inflation and deflation?

3. You're either born able to manage money responsibly or you're not—there's no help for it. Is this statement true or false? Explain.

CHAPTER SUMMARY

To get the most for your money, you must plan your spending. The actual plan that you use is called a budget.

Budgeting involves four main steps—setting your goals, estimating your expenses and income, drawing up your actual budget (or spending plan), and revising your budget as necessary. You should review your budget regularly to allow for changing personal responsibilities and economic conditions.

As your financial responsibilities increase and you continue to budget your money, you will improve your money management skills. If you need help, however, plenty is available. School courses, newspaper and magazine articles, government agencies, lawyers, and banks are just a few of the organizations and individuals you can turn to for help.

TERMS TO KNOW

On a separate sheet of paper, write a brief description of a situation that illustrates each of the following terms:

budget
financial responsibility
deflation
liquid assets

STUDY QUESTIONS

1. What are the main steps in the budgeting process?
2. What are two reasons why you should begin budgeting while you are still in school?
3. What is an expense record, and how is it used?
4. Briefly describe the major parts of a personal budget form.
5. List at least five day-to-day expenses you might find in a typical budget.
6. What is the purpose of revising a budget?
7. Suggest five things you can do to help yourself stick to a budget.
8. What two major factors make it necessary to review and change a budget on a regular basis?
9. Which condition has been more common in our economy recently—inflation or deflation?
10. Where can you get help in managing your money? List at least four sources.

CRITICAL THINKING

1. What economic concept do you think the fine print in this ad discusses? What do you think it says?

Want to retire someday? Here's food for thought:

"That'll be $131.20, please."

Inflation can eat into your savings *fast*. That's why it's wise to prepare for retirement *now*... by investing in a fund with proven ability to grow *faster* than inflation.

Today thousands and thousands of Americans are saving for retirement by investing in the Franklin Income Fund. It's easy to understand why.

If you had invested $10,000 in the Franklin Income Fund on April 2, 1975, your investment would have been worth $70,034 on March 31, 1990 — a growth in value of 600% over 15 years.† During the same

period the Consumer Price Index increased just 143%.

Set the table for your retirement *today* — by investing in the Franklin Income Fund!

Franklin Distributors, Inc.
777 Mariners Island Blvd.
San Mateo, CA 94404-1585

YES! I would like to improve my ability to save for my retirement. Please send me a free prospectus containing more complete information on the Franklin Income Fund, including charges and expenses. I will read it carefully before I invest or send money.

☐ I am currently a Franklin shareholder.

Name _____
Address _____
City/State/Zip _____

†Dividends totalling $51,469 were reinvested at the offering price. Capital gains distributions of $9,326 were reinvested at net asset value. No adjustment has been made for taxes. The total investment cost was $61,469. The average annual total returns for the 1, 5, and 10 year periods ended March 31, 1990, were 1.96%, 9.70%, and 14.63%, respectively. Investment return and principal value will fluctuate so that your shares, when redeemed, may be worth more or less than their original cost. Past performance cannot guarantee future results.

1-800-342-FUND Ext.415
FRANKLIN
Member $42 Billion Franklin Group of Funds

2. Your friend Warren is doing his first budget. When he gets to the step where he must estimate his income, he exclaims, "That's simple—I remember that from my tax form. I made $5,000 last year, so I just divide that by 12." Is he right? Why or why not?

3. Do a word equation that describes what's going on in a personal budget form.

4. Speculate about the pitfalls of budgeting. You know how the process is supposed to work. You know how your own mind does work. You also know something about human nature. Where is the process most likely to break down? Summarize your conclusions in the form of a list titled "The Ten Biggest Mistakes that Budgeters Make."

DISCUSSION STARTERS

1. Why do you think that so many people spend so much more than they can afford to?

2. You know the value of budgeting and feel you need to develop more skill in the area. One of your friends recommends that you get a free government or similar publication and learn on your own. Your other alternative is to enroll in an evening class at the high school, for which there is a fee of $30. What factors would influence you to choose one method of learning over the other?

3. How has inflation affected you personally?

4. The federal government in recent years has had an extremely difficult time doing its budget. Explain the nation's problem using the terminology of personal money management. Give examples of fixed and flexible expenses and income sources. Decide where the national debt would fit in Uncle Sam's personal budget form.

BUILDING BASIC SKILLS

Math

1. If inflation continues at 5 percent for the next ten years and your present salary is $15,000 a year, what should your salary be in ten years just for you to keep up with inflation (that is, just to maintain your purchasing power)?

Computer Literacy

2. Try using the spreadsheet application of an integrated software package like Appleworks or PFS:First Choice to do your budgeting. Use the program's tutorial disk and/or manual to learn the basics of setting up a budget form. Once you have made your entries, explore the predictive functions of the software. Try some "What if" analysis by adding or subtracting different amounts of income, expenses, or savings.

Problem Solving

3. Consider the personal budget form in Figure 17-2 (page 294) to be your own. Assume further that you are now going to be laid off from work one day a week for the foreseeable future because of a slowdown in the economy. How would you go about cutting your budget the necessary 20 percent?

SUGGESTED ACTIVITIES

1. Write a short paper describing your financial responsibilities. If you have no responsibilities, describe those of someone you know.

2. Imagine you and your friends are discussing budgets. Your friend thinks making a budget is just too much trouble. Try to convince your friend that a budget will really help. Explain why it is worth the time and trouble. Also, tell why it's important to keep within the estimated budget.

3. Make a daily record of all your expenses for one week. Use this record to plan a budget for yourself for one month. Try to follow this budget. At the end of the month, revise the budget wherever necessary.

4. Find out what money management services are available in your community. Check the sources below and report to your class on the instruction offered.

- Banks
- County extension services
- Credit unions
- Finance companies
- Savings and loans

Banking Services: Savings and Checking

OBJECTIVES

After studying this chapter and doing the activities, you will be able to:

- describe the various ways of saving that banks offer to customers;
- complete a deposit slip;
- write a personal check;
- fill out a check register; and
- explain how electronic fund transfer works.

TERMS TO KNOW

interest
compounding
certificate of deposit (CD)
canceled checks
balance
endorse
overdrawn
bank statement
electronic fund transfer (EFT)

*Y*ou may not have thought about it, but a bank is a business much like any other. Just as grocery stores, insurance companies, and hardware stores are in business to make a profit, so are banks. What makes banks seem different is that the products they handle are money and credit, not groceries and hardware.

Banks provide many services. They manage personal checking accounts for thousands of customers at a time. They help people save their money. Banks also lend money to people for a variety of needs such as purchasing cars or houses, paying college tuition, or starting a business.

In this chapter you will learn about the many different ways banks can help you manage your money. Specifically, you will learn about the various savings plans that banks offer. You will also learn how to use a checking account and how to take advantage of electronic fund transfers.

1 Saving Money

Most people who want to save put their money in financial institutions. These include banks, credit unions, and savings and loan associations. In this lesson, we will focus on the use of banks for saving money and on the various methods of saving they offer their customers.

Advantages of Banks

There are two main reasons why people save with banks. Banks are very safe places to keep money—and they pay interest.

Safety You probably won't spend all the money you make as soon as you get paid. After paying your bills and buying what you need, you will probably have some money left over.

Where will you keep your extra money? Perhaps you'll carry it with you or put it in a drawer in your room or apartment. However, what would happen if you lost your wallet or if there were a fire at home? Given these possibilities, it would be far safer to deposit your money in a bank.

Banks do not simply hold the money deposited with them. They invest it. That's how they make a profit. Suppose, however, a bank makes bad investments and fails (or goes out of business). To protect their depositors in such an event, most banks have deposit insurance.

Deposit insurance is commonly provided by the Federal Deposit Insurance Corporation (FDIC). The FDIC guarantees individual accounts up to $100,000. For example, if the bank in which you have a savings account of $6,000 fails, the FDIC would pay you $6,000 to replace the money the bank lost. If your account contains $106,000, however, you could count on receiving only $100,000. (You might lose all or part of the remaining $6,000.) Note, though, if you had *two* savings accounts, each containing $53,000, you would be paid in full.

Interest Payments Another reason to keep your savings in a bank is the interest it will earn. **Interest** is money that banks pay their depositors for the privilege of investing their money. Interest makes it possible for your savings to grow even if you don't add to your account.

Interest is calculated as a percentage of the money you deposit. For example, if you deposit $100 at 5 percent interest, the bank will pay you $5 in interest at the end of the year (.05 × $100). The next year (if you deposit nothing to the account), the bank will pay you 5 percent interest on $105. This paying of interest on interest (as well as on the amount deposited) is called **compounding.**

How much interest you earn will depend on the interest rate paid, how much money you deposit, and how often interest is calculated. The higher the interest rate, the more money you will make. For

The availability of deposit insurance is one of the main reasons people feel that banks are safe places to save money. In the case of this bank, who is doing the insuring?

example, suppose there is a second bank in town. Instead of paying 5 percent interest, it pays 8 percent. In one year in this bank, your $100 would earn $8. The difference this can make over an extended period of time is shown in Figure 18-1. Clearly, given the choice, you would probably deposit your money in the second bank.

How much interest you make also depends on the amount of money you deposit. Suppose you deposit $500 instead of $100 at 5 percent interest. After a year, $25 in interest (.05 × $500) would be added to your account. Five times more money will earn you five times more interest.

A final factor determining how much interest you earn is the frequency with which it is calculated. In all of the examples given thus far, interest was calculated once, at the end of each year. Interest calculated this way is called simple interest. Banks may also calculate interest every few months or even daily. For example, when interest is calculated every three months, it is said to be compounded quarterly.

Ways to Save

How much money, if any, should you save? Some experts say that to handle emergencies you should have three to six months' pay in a savings

There are many savings alternatives to choose from. What are some ways to find out about them?

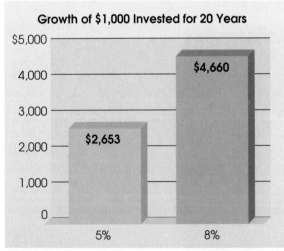

Figure 18-1   A relatively small increase in interest rate can mean a large increase in earnings. According to the graph, by how much will $1,000 increase in 20 years at 5 percent? at 8 percent? How much more would a depositor earn at the higher interest rate?

account. You, however, are the only person who knows how much you can and should save.

Banks offer their customers many different ways to save. Three of the more commonly used ones are discussed in this section. Which method is best for you will probably depend on how much money you have and when you might need to withdraw it. Discuss your situation with someone at your bank. That person can help you pick the method best suited to your needs.

Savings Accounts   For most people just starting out in the world of work, a savings account is the best way to save. Such accounts are also called passbook accounts. The name comes from the booklet, called a passbook, that the bank gives you to help you keep track of how much money is in your account.

You don't need a great deal of money to open a savings account. A few dollars will probably be enough to get you started. If you live in a large city, however, you may find that some banks require a minimum deposit to open and maintain a savings account. Small accounts, such banks assert, cost

Strive for Success

His Bank Holiday Was No Picnic

No president since Abraham Lincoln was so bitterly hated or so deeply loved by the American people. No president since Lincoln served during more trying times—and no president ever served longer.

Franklin Delano Roosevelt, the 32d president of the United States, served more than 12 years as the chief executive officer of the United States. He was elected to the office four times, dying only 83 days into his fourth term. His years of service, from 1933–1945, included the worst years of the Great Depression and all but the final months of World War II.

During these years, FDR, as he came to be known, faced many crises. His actions in these crises led many people to hate him and fear that he was leading the country down the road to socialism. Many more Americans, however, saw Roosevelt as someone who was on the side of the common man. It was this popularity that led him to be elected president four times.

One of the crises Roosevelt faced came to be known as the banking crisis. About three weeks before Roosevelt first took office in 1933, a banking panic began. This panic had its roots in the stock market crash of 1929. As a result of the crash, business firms failed, workers lost their jobs, and farmers lost their farms. Banks had made loans to thousands of people who had lost their money and could not now repay what they owed. Many depositors, now jobless, were also forced to withdraw their savings. As a result, many banks were having difficulty keeping enough money on hand to cover all the withdrawals. Soon, depositors throughout the country were demanding all their money from banks. These "runs," as they were called, ruined many financial institutions.

Roosevelt saw this crisis as a demand for drastic action. On March 6, 1933, he declared a bank holiday. This meant that all banks had to close for business until federal officials could examine their books. No bank was allowed to reopen until it was determined to be financially sound.

Many never reopened. Those that did, however, faced little threat of a run by their deposi-

tors. Roosevelt's action had renewed public confidence in banks and ended the panic. Legislation passed later that same year set up strict guidelines limiting risky banking practices and providing federal insurance for each depositor's funds.

more to service than they make. If you encounter this situation, just look elsewhere. Medium-sized or small banks will probably welcome your business.

Usually, you can withdraw your money from a savings account at any time without penalty. (You can't always do this with other methods of saving.) For example, if you need a large amount of money for an emergency auto repair, you can take the funds out of your savings account. There is a price, however, for this kind of convenience. The interest your account earns will be relatively low—usually no more than 5 or 6 percent.

Certificates of Deposit Another way to save your money is to buy a certificate of deposit (CD). A **certificate of deposit** is a piece of paper that says the bank will pay your money back to you, plus interest, on a certain day.

You can buy a CD for different lengths of time—six months, one year, two years, for example. Usually the longer the time period, the higher the interest rate. Interest rates on CDs are often several percentage points higher than they are on savings accounts.

To buy a CD, you usually need a large amount of money—$500, $1,000, $2,000, or more. Usually, the more you invest, the higher the interest rate.

You can see that there are some disadvantages to CDs. One is that you need to have a certain amount of money to buy one. Another disadvantage is that you can't withdraw your money as quickly and easily as you can from a savings account. Some banks require a 30-day notice. In most cases there is a penalty for withdrawing your money before the payment date. The penalty is usually the loss of some or all of your interest.

If you have a large amount of money that you won't need for a long time, you may want to buy a CD. Talk to someone at your bank about the amounts, time periods, and interest rates available.

Savings Bonds Another way to save is by buying U.S. Savings Bonds. You can buy these bonds at your bank. Because they are issued by the U.S. government, savings bonds are one of the safest ways to save money.

You can buy savings bonds in different denominations—$50, $75, $100, $200, $500, and higher, up to $10,000. You pay half the face value (this is the amount printed on the bonds). The remaining half is the interest you earn and is paid when you cash the bond in. At the current minimum interest rate of 6 percent, bonds should double in value in 12 years. If you cash them in before that, you receive less than the full face value.

U.S. Savings Bonds have several advantages compared to other ways of saving.

- Bonds are available for smaller amounts than CDs.

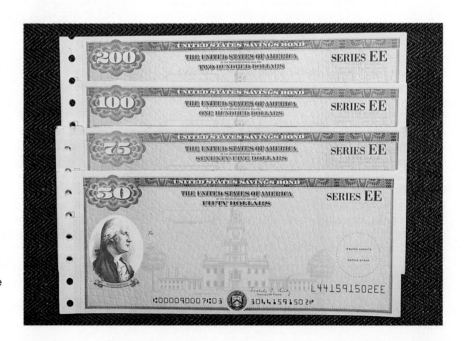

The relatively small denominations of savings bonds and their competitive interest rates make them an attractive savings vehicle. Given the face values of these bonds, how much did each cost?

- Bonds can earn a higher rate of interest than savings accounts.
- Bonds are safer because the money goes into the federal treasury. (In effect, you are making a loan to the U.S. government rather than a private institution that could fail.)
- The interest earned on bonds, unlike the interest paid by banks, is not taxable by state and local governments. (You must, however, still pay federal income tax on it, unless you use the proceeds for certain educational purposes.)

Retirement Plans

In addition to saving money for more immediate needs, such as a house or a car, people save money for their retirement. Two commonly used retirement plans are IRAs and Keoghs. Both plans have tax advantages.

Individual Retirement Accounts In 1981 Congress enacted legislation authorizing individual retirement accounts, or IRAs. To open an IRA, an employee must be under the age of $71\frac{1}{2}$. If single, he or she can put up to $2,000 each year in such an account. If married and the sole working spouse, he or she can invest up to $2,250.

All or some of the money you put in an IRA is tax deferred. This means that you pay no taxes on it until you withdraw it from the account after age $59\frac{1}{2}$. If you withdraw it before that time, you have to pay a penalty.

How much of your contribution to an IRA is tax deferred depends on two factors:

- Whether or not you are covered by a retirement plan at work
- How much you earn

If you are not covered by a retirement plan at work, you can deduct the full amount from your taxable income. If you are covered at work, however, the amount you may deduct decreases as your income rises. For example, if you make $30,000, you can deduct only $1,000, half of the maximum contribution.

Keogh Accounts What IRAs are to people who work for others, Keogh accounts are to the self-employed. Keoghs differ from IRAs in that much more income can be tax deferred—20 percent of annual earnings or $30,000, whichever is less. Also, withdrawal must start by age $70\frac{1}{2}$. As

Many people who fail to save adequately for their retirement are forced to economize on necessities like food. Name two kinds of accounts people can use to supplement their social security benefits later in life.

with IRAs, there is a penalty for withdrawal before age $59\frac{1}{2}$.

Laws regulating tax-deferred investments change. Before considering an IRA or a Keogh, check with the Internal Revenue Service, your bank, or a financial advisor such as an accountant. They will be familiar with the current rules governing such accounts.

✓ CHECKING UP

1. Name three ways to save that banks commonly offer their customers.
2. What are some advantages of buying U.S. Savings Bonds?
3. How are IRAs and Keogh accounts alike? How are they different?

2 *Using a Checking Account*

Most people have a personal checking account at a bank near their home or place of work. People use their checking accounts to pay most of their bills and make many of their major purchases. In this section you will learn about the many different types of checking accounts—why people use them and how you can open your own account.

There are many reasons for using checks instead of cash. The main reason is that using checks is safer than using cash for paying bills. If you paid all of your bills with cash instead of checks, you would need to have large amounts of cash on hand at all times. It is not a good idea to keep large sums of money in your home or to carry them with you. It is also not safe to send cash through the mail.

Another reason for using checks is that you receive **canceled checks** (checks that have been cashed and processed by the bank). At the end of each month, your bank will send you your canceled checks. These checks serve as receipts, proving that you paid your bills. They also help you with your budgeting and bookkeeping.

A third reason for using checks is that they save time for everyone. For example, without checks, companies would need to pay their employees with cash. For the employees this would mean standing in line to receive their pay. They would

also need to sign a payroll book to show that they had received their money. All of this would take a great deal of time.

Choosing the Type of Account You Need

As with savings accounts, there are several kinds of checking accounts from which to choose. Some checking accounts require the payment of a service charge while others do not. Some pay interest, and some do not. Some are intended for individual use while others are shared accounts. You'll have to decide which type of checking account best meets your needs. You'll then want to shop around to determine which bank offers you the best terms on such an account. (See Figure 18-2 for other factors that might be involved.)

Most banks usually impose a fee, or service charge, for managing a checking account. They calculate service charges in different ways, depending on the type of account.

With many checking accounts, the amount of the service charge depends on the account balance. (The **balance** is the amount of money in an account.) Service charges are usually paid monthly. The bank can base these charges on either a minimum balance or an average balance. The minimum balance required is typically $500. As long as there is at least this amount in your account, you do not have to pay the service charge.

Many people write personal checks for large purchases. List the steps that would be involved if this consumer paid for his purchase with cash. What risks would be involved in such a transaction?

Factors to Consider in Choosing a Bank

- **Location**—Is the bank close to your home or place of work? Will you have to go a long way out of your way?
- **Hours**—Will the bank be open when you need to do your banking? What are the bank's hours?
- **Drive-up window**—Most, but not all, banks have them. Will you use the drive-up window? Is it important to you?
- **ATMs**—Does the bank have a large number of conveniently located ATMs? What are the charges, if any, for using them?
- **Service**—Do the people working in the bank seem friendly and helpful?
- **Interest rates**—What are the bank's interest rates? How is interest calculated on savings? on checking?
- **Service charges**—What are the charges for checking accounts? Is free checking available?
- **Check charges**—Banks charge different amounts for checks. Compare prices. If you write many checks, this could be a key factor.
- **Charges for overdrafts**—Some banks charge more than others for overdrafts. You shouldn't overdraw your account, but if you do make a mistake, what will it cost?
- **Gifts for opening accounts**—Some banks offer incentives for opening accounts. This shouldn't be a major factor in your choice, but if all other things are equal, you might as well get the bonus.

Figure 18-2   This checklist will help you compare banking services so that you can choose the financial institution that best meets your needs. Which factors would be most important to you?

If the balance falls below that amount, however, then you do. Service charges usually range from $3 to $6.

Some banks offer special checking accounts for people who write only a few checks a month. The service charge for these special accounts is based on the number of checks you write. The cost may be 15 cents to 25 cents per check. If you write many checks, this type of service charge would be more expensive than the typical monthly charge. If you write only two or three checks a month, though, this type of account would save you a great deal of money over the course of a year.

Interest-bearing Accounts   More and more banks are offering checking accounts that pay interest. These accounts work much like the savings accounts that you read about earlier. The amount of interest you receive depends on how much money you keep in your account.

Most banks that offer interest-bearing checking accounts require that you maintain a minimum balance in that or some other account. This minimum balance can be $500, $2,500, or more. If your balance drops below this amount, the interest payments stop.

Individual and Joint Accounts   Depending on your situation, you may want to open either an individual or a joint checking account. An individual account is just what you would expect—an account for one person. If you have an individual account, you are the only person who can write checks on it.

A joint checking account is one in which two or more people can use the same account. Each person involved can deposit money and write checks. Husbands and wives often share a joint checking account.

Some banks require that you be at least 18 years old to open a checking account. These banks may, however, let you open a joint account with a parent or guardian if you are under that age.

Many banks offer special checking accounts from time to time. They may have discounts for senior citizens or recent high school graduates. In some cases a bank may even offer free checking.

MAKE A DECISION

Lucky you! You won $1,000 in a drawing at the local supermarket. There are several things you'd like to buy, but your parents insist that you save the money, at least for a while. At the bank, you learn there are basically two options. You either put the money away for a year or two at a high interest rate or keep the money available at a lower interest rate. What's your decision—high interest and untouchable or lower interest and available? Give the reasons for your decision.

Opening an Account

Opening a checking account is easy. Visit the bank of your choice and ask to talk with the person in charge of new checking accounts. Someone will interview you and help you decide which type of account best meets your needs.

You will have to sign a signature card when you open an account. Write your name on this card in the same way that you will write your name on your checks. The bank can then compare the signatures on your checks with the signature on the card. In this way the bank can prevent other people from forging, or copying, your name in order to get money from your account.

When you open a checking account, the bank will assign you an account number. This number will be written on your signature card and all other documents and forms you use for the account. For example, all of your checks will have your account number printed on them.

The bank will let you choose from the various styles of checks available. They will then have your name and address printed on the checks you choose. The bank will probably give you a few temporary checks to use until your personal checks are ready.

You won't have to pay for your checks when you open the account, but you will be charged for them later. The cost is minimal (usually two or three cents a check), but the prices can vary from bank to bank. Choosing a special style of check and having extra personal information printed on your checks can raise the price. You might want to compare check costs at a couple of banks in your area.

Writing Checks

As soon as you open an account, you can begin writing checks on it. If you have never written a check, don't worry—it's easy. First, remember to write clearly and use a pen. This will make it more difficult for someone else to change your checks for their benefit. The check number should be printed on your check. If it is not, write it in the upper right-hand corner. Then follow the steps listed below.

- *Date the check.* Fill in the current month, day, and year.
- *Fill in the payee.* This is the name of the person or company to whom the check is to be paid. The name should closely follow the words *Pay to the order of.*
- *Fill in the amount of the check in figures.* Notice in Figure 18-3 that the numbers begin as far to the left as possible. This will keep anyone else from slipping in a digit and increasing the amount of the check.
- *Fill in the amount a second time, in words.* Again, begin as far to the left as possible. Show cents as a fraction. In Figure 18-3, for

Personal Check

BILL SMITH OR NANCY SMITH		**225**
4623 W. WILDWOOD		
PITTSBURG, KS 66762		
(316) 693-3478	February 1, 19 91	83-24/1011

Pay to the Order of *Crossroads Auto Service* _____ $ 13.50

Thirteen and 50/100 ~~~~~~~~~~~~~~~~ Dollars

BANK IV PITTSBURG, N.A.
Pittsburg, Kansas   *   STATUS 55

Memo *Fan belt* _____   *Bill Smith*

⑆1011002491⑈15811⑆443601⑈

Figure 18-3   This sample check was written to pay for a minor auto repair. How could the check be used to help the account holders, the Smiths, with their budgeting?

example, 50 cents is $\frac{50}{100}$. If the check is for an even dollar amount, show no cents as $\frac{xx}{100}$ or $\frac{00}{100}$. Any space that remains between the fraction and the word *Dollars* should be filled with a line. (Again, see Figure 18-3.)

- *Note the purpose of the check.* Most checks provide a line for this at the lower left. It is usually labeled *Memo* or simply *For.*
- *Sign your name.* Be sure to use the form of your name that appears on the bank's signature card for your account.

When you have finished, look the check over carefully to be sure that everything is correct and that nothing has been left out.

Making Deposits and Withdrawals

Each time you put money in your checking account you will fill out a deposit slip. Most deposit slips look much like the one shown in Figure 18-4. Usually several such slips, with your name and account number printed on them, are located at the back of each packet of checks you receive. Blank deposit slips are available at the bank. You can use these slips by filling in your name and account number.

To fill out a deposit slip, follow these steps:

- *Write in the amount of cash, if any, being deposited.* Cash includes both currency (paper money) and coins.
- *List each check being deposited.* These would be checks written to you. List each check separately, continuing on the back of the deposit slip if there are more than two or

three. Identify each check by amount and bank number. (The bank number is the hyphenated portion of the "fraction" that appears to the right of the date line. In Figure 18-3 it is 83-24.)

- *Total the cash and checks.* This will give you the total amount of the items included in the deposit.
- *Subtract the amount of any cash you want back from the teller.* This situation is likely to occur when you are depositing a large check, such as your paycheck. You will probably want something back, perhaps spending money to carry with you. Fill in this amount next to the words *Less cash received.* Then subtract it from the total of cash and checks to get your net deposit. This is the actual amount that goes into your account.
- *Sign your deposit slip.* This step is usually necessary only if you want cash back from the teller.

Before you can deposit a check written to you, you must **endorse** it. This means that you must write your name on the back of the check. When you do this, you are transferring your rights to the check to someone else—in this case, the bank. The bank then adds the amount of the check to your account.

If you deposit checks by mail, you should write the phrase *For deposit only* above or below your signature on the back of the check. (See Figure 18-5.) You should also use this phrase if you endorse a check before you get to the bank, when there is a chance you could lose the check. Doing this

Checking Account Deposit Slip

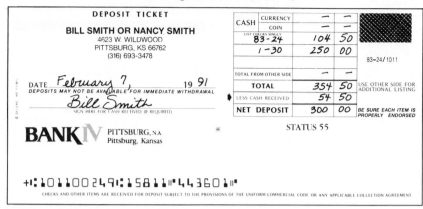

Figure 18-4   Suppose Bill Smith had had three more checks to deposit. Where and how would he have listed them on this sample deposit slip?

prevents anyone who finds the check from using it for their own purposes.

After endorsing your checks and filling in the deposit slip, give your cash, checks, and slip to the bank teller. The teller will give you back a transaction slip that shows how much you deposited. This is a valuable record that you should keep. If the bank makes an error, you can use the transaction slip to prove that you made the deposit.

You can, of course, also withdraw cash from your checking account. The easiest way to do this is by using an ATM, a procedure that you will read about a little later in this chapter. You can also write yourself a check. To do this, you fill in your own name or the word *Cash* on the line indicating to whom the check is to be paid.

It is probably a good idea to wait until you are at the bank to write a check to Cash. If you lose such a check, the person who finds it could cash it. All

Endorsed Check

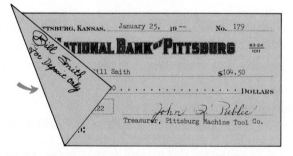

Figure 18-5   This sample check has been endorsed by Bill Smith. Why might he have written the words *For deposit only* under his name?

Case Study 1

On her way to work this morning, Sharon drove past one of her favorite stores, the Flower Basket. In front of the shop was a hanging basket that Sharon thought her mother would love. She decided she would stop on her way home and buy the basket for her mother.

At lunch Sharon counted the money in her wallet. Buying lunch had taken all her cash. She knew the Flower Basket wouldn't take a check, so she wrote a $10 check to Cash. She'd get the money at the bank's drive-in window after work.

That evening at the bank Sharon opened her wallet to take out the check. It wasn't there. She was sure she had put the check in her wallet. She looked everywhere, but there was no check to be found.

Sharon knew that anyone who found the check could cash it. She had learned a valuable lesson the hard way. She knew she would always wait until she was at the bank to write a check to Cash.

that it would take would be a careless teller who did not check identification.

Keeping Track of Your Account

You probably know that you can't write checks for more money than you have in your account. If you do, your account will be **overdrawn.** In other words, you will have drawn from your account an amount over your balance. Since banks charge a fee (usually $10–$20) for each overdrawn check, this could be a costly mistake.

Keeping track of how much money you have in your account at all times will help you avoid overdrawing it. Your bank will help you keep track by including a check register in each box of checks it sends you. A check register is a small pad that fits in your checkbook. It is used to record your checks and deposits. It is important to get in the habit of filling out your check register as you write checks and make deposits.

Figure 18-6 shows a carefully filled out check register. The account holder began the page shown with a balance of $394.50 brought forward from the previous register page. Then, for each check written or deposit made, he or she entered the following information:

- Check number (none for a deposit)
- Date (month and day)
- Description of transaction (usually the payee's name on the first line and the purpose on the line below)
- Amount of payment or deposit (in the appropriate column and in the balance column as well)

Once this information was entered, the account holder added or subtracted the transaction amount from the last figure in the balance column.

Whenever you write a check or make a deposit, record it in your register. If you do this, the correct balance will always be shown in the tinted space. You will always know if you have enough money to write another check.

SITUATION
SOLUTION

Managing Your Money

You have a checking account with First State Bank. You have always been careful with your account and have never been overdrawn.

Sunday, on the way home from a weekend trip, you wrote a check for an emergency car repair. You knew there wasn't enough money in your account to cover the check, but you thought it would take the bank a few days to process the check.

1. You get paid on Tuesday. Will you wait until then to make a deposit? Why or why not?

2. If you do not feel comfortable waiting until Tuesday to make a deposit, would you choose to borrow money from a friend, borrow money from your credit union and pay interest, or take money from your savings account? Explain your reasons.

3. What might you do to see that this type of emergency doesn't threaten to overdraw your checking account again?

Check Register

NUMBER	DATE	DESCRIPTION OF TRANSACTION	PAYMENT/DEBIT (-)	√T	FEE (IF ANY) (-)	DEPOSIT/CREDIT (+)	BALANCE
							$ 394 50
225	2/1	Crossroads Auto Service (Fan belt)	$ 13 50	$	$		13 50
							381 00
—	2/7	Deposit —				300 00	300 00
							681 00
226	2/12	Wilderness Store (Jacket)	42 79				42 79
							638 21
ATM	2/16	Cash (Pocket money)	20 00				20 00
							618 21
227	2/20	Midwest Water and Power (Electric bill)	52 14				52 14
							566 07

Figure 18-6 It's February 26, and Bill Smith knows that at the very end of the month he will have to write his two biggest checks—the rent ($425) and a car payment ($236). What do you think he'll decide to do when he looks at his check register, shown here?

Balancing Your Checkbook

You read earlier that most banks return canceled checks to account holders on a regular schedule, usually once a month. Along with these checks, banks will also send a **bank statement** (Figure 18-7). This is a record of account activity during the previous month. The statement lists all the deposits, ATM withdrawals, canceled checks, and charges that were handled during that time. The statement also shows the account balance as of the statement date.

When you get your statement and canceled checks, you should balance your checkbook. This is the process of making sure that the checks, withdrawals, deposits, and balance in your check register agree with those shown on your bank statement. You need to balance your checkbook to make sure your register is correct and that the bank hasn't made any mistakes. Do this as soon as possible after receiving your statement. If there are any errors in your statement, notify the bank immediately.

You will find instructions on how to balance your checkbook on the back of your statement (Figure 18-8). When you are finished, the balance in your checkbook should match the ending balance shown on your statement.

Checking Account Statement

BANK IV
BANK IV Pittsburg, N.A.
E.F.T. Department
Pittsburg, Kansas 66762-0599

Account Statement

Bill Smith or Nancy Smith
4623 W. Wildwood
Pittsburg, KS 66792

0009

Statement Date   3/1/91   Page Number   1

Account Number   443-601

SUMMARY				
Previous Balance	404.50	Minimum balance	381.00
Deposits	550.00 +	Average balance	546.50
Interest paid	1.82 +	Average rate	4.000%
Withdrawals	799.43 –		
Service charges	.00 –	Interest paid in 1991	3.33
New balance	156.89		

CHECKS AND WITHDRAWALS	Check	Date paid	Amount	Check	Date paid	Account
	222	2/6	426.00	225	2/5	13.50
	223	2/5	236.00	226	2/15	42.79
	224	2/12	10.00	227	2/22	52.14

ELECTRONIC BANKING	Withdrawal #0382 at U018 on 2/16		2/16	20.00

DEPOSITS		Date posted	Amount
	Customer deposit	2/7	300.00
	Customer deposit	2/27	250.00
	Interest payment this period	2/28	1.82

INTEREST INFORMATION	From	To	Rate	Annual Yield
	2/1	2/28	4.000%	4.081%

ATM LOCATIONS USED   U018: 401 Main Street, Pittsburg, KS

Thank you for banking with Bank IV

Member FDIC

Figure 18-7 This sample bank statement shows all activity in the Smiths' checking account for the month of February. How does the statement reflect the entries in Bill's check register?

Checking Account Worksheet

THIS WORKSHEET IS PROVIDED TO HELP YOU BALANCE YOUR ACCOUNT

1. Go through your register and mark each check, withdrawal, ATM transaction, payment, deposit, or other credit listed on this statement. Be sure that your register shows any interest paid into your account and any service charges, automatic payments, or EFTs withdrawn from your account during this statement period.

2. Using the chart below, list any outstanding checks, ATM withdrawals, payments, or any other withdrawals (including any from previous months) which are listed in your register but are not shown on this statement.

3. Balance your account by filling in the spaces below.

ITEMS OUTSTANDING		
NUMBER	AMOUNT	
218	51	82
TOTAL	$ 51	82

ENTER

The NEW BALANCE shown on this statement _____ $ 156.89

ADD

Any deposits listed in your register or transfers into your account which are not shown on this statement.
$ 215.00
$ _____
$ _____
+ $ _____

TOTAL _____ + $ 215.00

CALCULATE THE SUBTOTAL _____ $ 371.89

SUBTRACT

The total outstanding checks and withdrawals from the chart at left _____ − $ 51.82

CALCULATE THE ENDING BALANCE

This amount should be the same as the current balance shown in your check register _____ $ 320.07

Figure 18-8 The reverse side of a checking account statement provides account holders with a place and a procedure to balance their checkbooks. Suppose the Smiths, on whose account this sample form is based, had been assessed a $20 service charge for overdrawing their account. Where would this entry go on the form? Suppose they had made an additional $40 withdrawal from an ATM. Where would this item go? Finally, suppose they had received and deposited an IRS refund check that does not appear on their statement. Where would they record its amount ($173)? After all of these additions, what would their ending balance be?

✓ **CHECKING UP**

1. List the steps you must follow to write a personal check.
2. What steps must you take to fill out a deposit slip?
3. Why is it important to keep track of the amount in your checking account?

3 *Using Other Banking Services*

In addition to providing safe ways to save your money and checking account management, banks offer some other services that can make your life a little easier. They include electronic fund transfer and some special payment methods.

Electronic Fund Transfer

You may recall from Chapter 12 that **electronic fund transfer (EFT)** allows you to deposit or withdraw money from an automated teller machine (ATM). If a bank offers this service and you sign up for it, you can use the bank's ATMs 24 hours a day, seven days a week.

To operate an ATM, you need a plastic EFT card with your name and number embossed on it. Your bank will furnish you with the card and also give you a personal identification number, or PIN. The PIN is needed to activate the machine. You should therefore not carry it with you or write it down. Rather you should commit it to memory and give it to no one. That way, if your card is lost or stolen, no one can use it.

Some banks also offer point-of-sale (POS) transaction service. The EFT card is then used at a merchant's place of business rather than at an ATM. For example, grocery stores and gas stations are accepting EFT cards for payment. In these transactions money is taken out of your account and credited to the merchant's account.

When using either an ATM or a POS terminal, you will get a receipt. It is important to keep these receipts and record all EFT transactions in your check register or savings passbook. All EFT transactions will appear on your bank statement, so you should check your EFT receipts against it. If you find an error, contact your bank as soon as possible.

The Electronic Fund Transfer Act establishes the rights and responsibilities of those providing EFT services and their customers. For example, the act establishes the time you have to report an EFT error and the time the bank has to correct it. When you sign up for EFT service, your bank will give you information regarding your rights and responsibilities.

You should also be aware of the potential risk in using EFT. If your card is stolen or lost, you must notify the bank within two business days after learning of the theft or loss. The risk limit is $50 per card. This means that once your card's loss is reported, you are liable for only $50 of the total amount taken by someone using your card without your permission. You could lose all the money in your account if you fail to notify the bank within the specified time.

Checks offered people a cashless payment system. Now POS terminals, such as the one this shopper is using, offer people a different sort of payment system. How would you describe it?

Special Payment Methods

Another service provided by most banks is the issuing of cashier's checks, traveler's checks, and money orders. You will occasionally have need of these special forms of payment. For example, there will be times when a retailer or other payee will not accept a personal check. This section explains your options in such situations.

Cashier's Checks   Some people write personal checks without the money to back them up. When this happens, the business that took the check does not get paid. This is why all businesses are very careful about whose personal checks they accept—especially when the check is for a large amount. Some businesses simply refuse to take any personal checks at all.

If you must pay someone who won't take your personal check, you may want to get a cashier's check at your bank. A cashier's check is a check written by a bank employee and guaranteed by the bank to be a good check.

To get a cashier's check, you pay the bank the amount of the check plus a small fee. A bank employee then writes the check to the person or business you want to pay.

Traveler's Checks   Traveling with large amounts of money is not very safe. It's too easy to lose the money or have it stolen. This is why many people use traveler's checks when they are away from home. You can usually buy $10, $20, $50, or $100 checks. The cost of these checks is quite low or even free to customers with certain kinds of accounts.

When you buy traveler's checks, you sign your name on each check. Then, when you use a check, you sign it again. The signatures must be identical before the check will be accepted in place of cash.

If you lose traveler's checks, go to the nearest bank. The bank will help you stop payment on the lost checks and issue you new ones. This is what makes traveler's checks a safe way to handle your money away from home.

Money Orders   Most money orders are used to buy and pay through the mail. Sending a money order is a safe way to mail money.

When you buy a money order, you will write your name and address on it. You will also write in the name and address of the person or business receiving the money. The purpose of the money

People go on vacations to relax and have a good time. If this little girl's family were carrying large amounts of cash to pay for their vacation expenses, how might it affect their trip?

order should also be included to make a complete record of the payment on the order itself.

You will be charged a fee for a money order. The amount of the fee will depend on the amount of the money order. The larger the amount, the higher the fee.

✓ CHECKING UP

1. In what ways can a bank customer use electronic fund transfer?
2. What two things do you need to operate an ATM?
3. What are the advantages of using traveler's checks?

Review Your Learning

CHAPTER SUMMARY

Banks provide many services in money management, such as savings plans. Most people keep their savings in banks because banks are safe and they pay interest. Banks also offer several ways to save money, such as savings accounts, certificates of deposit, and U.S. Savings Bonds.

Banks provide management for personal checking accounts as well. You can choose from several different kinds of accounts—some that require payment of a service charge, some that do not, and some that pay interest. You can also choose between an individual and a joint account. If you have your own checking account, you will need to know how to write a check, how to fill out a deposit slip, and how to use your check register so that you do not overdraw your account.

Banks provide other services such as electronic fund transfer. EFT allows you to withdraw money at automated teller machines (ATMs) and to use point-of-sale (POS) terminals. If you have signed up for EFT service, you will need to know your rights and responsibilities as described by the Electronic Fund Transfer Act. Banks also provide special payment methods—cashier's checks, traveler's checks, and money orders.

TERMS TO KNOW

On a separate sheet of paper, write one or two paragraphs describing common banking services. Use all of the following terms:

interest
compounding
certificate of deposit (CD)
canceled checks
balance
endorse
overdrawn
bank statement
electronic fund transfer (EFT)

STUDY QUESTIONS

1. What is the function of the Federal Deposit Insurance Corporation?
2. What three factors determine how much interest you can earn on money you deposit in a bank?
3. What is an advantage of putting your money in a savings account rather than buying a CD that pays higher interest?
4. What is the tax advantage to saving money in a retirement plan such as an IRA or a Keogh account?
5. Name three reasons for using checks instead of cash.
6. When should you write the words *For deposit only* on the back of a check?
7. What is the purpose of a check register?
8. What does it mean to balance your checkbook?
9. Why is it so important to inform the bank immediately if your EFT card is lost or stolen?
10. Name three ways to make payments when you cannot use cash or personal checks.

CRITICAL THINKING

1. After paying your expenses each month, you will have $75 you would like to save. You plan to use this money in about two years to help pay your college tuition. You visit your local bank and discover that you have three savings alternatives. First, you can put your money in a savings account that earns $5\frac{1}{4}$ percent interest. Second, you can save for a $500 CD that earns 10 percent interest. Third, you can buy a U.S. Savings Bond each month, which will increase in value in two years even though it will not double. What factors will you consider before choosing one of these options?

2. Now that you're working, you decide to open both checking and savings accounts at a nearby bank. A bank service representative suggests the two plans below. What factors will you consider before choosing one or the other?

- *Interest-bearing checking account.* You must maintain a minimum balance of $1,500. The interest rate is 6 percent, and there are no service charges.
- *Noninterest-bearing checking account.* A minimum balance of $500 would mean no service charges. The account would be used in combination with a savings account that pays 5 percent interest.

3. A bank customer is overheard protesting, "My account can't be overdrawn. I've got records!" The "records" consist of a register featuring missing check numbers, missing dates, and no running balances. Write two or three paragraphs explaining why the customer could (or could not) be overdrawn. Conclude with a brief comment on the limits of recordkeeping.

DISCUSSION STARTERS

1. What makes saving money harder for some people and easier for others?
2. How should a person determine how much money to save?
3. When should a person decide to open a checking account?

BUILDING BASIC SKILLS

Math

1. Your bank offers savings accounts with an interest rate of $6\frac{1}{2}$ percent compounded yearly. If you deposited $400, how much interest would you earn in one year?
2. You have $1,000 to put into a savings plan for one year. You can deposit it in a savings account that pays $5\frac{3}{4}$ percent interest compounded annually or a one-year CD that pays 8 percent interest. Which savings plan pays more and by how much?

Human Relations

3. When you balance your checkbook for the month, you find the bank has made a $68.50 error. You believe that the error was made by a particular teller and that this is the second time it's happened in two months. You are upset because you must take time off from work to get the error corrected. What do you say and to whom to make certain that these mistakes do not occur again?

Leadership

4. You are the personnel director for a medium-sized company that does not provide a retirement plan for its employees. You would like to set up an awareness program for your mostly young work force. You don't feel they truly understand that social security alone is not enough for retired people to live on. You want to impress upon them the need to start early to provide for themselves. List the elements you would include in your program and briefly explain why you think each is

SUGGESTED ACTIVITIES

1. As part of a small group, survey selected banks or other financial institutions in your community to find out about checking account charges, interest paid on various savings plans, and other services provided. Design a table to show the results of your survey and report to your class.
2. Research newspaper advertisements of savings plans offered by banks, savings and loan associations, credit unions, and private investment firms. Compare the amounts required for each interest rate. Answer the following questions:

- Which savings plan pays the highest rate for the lowest minimum balance?
- How do interest rates compare with the length of time the money must remain on deposit?
- Which financial institutions advertise insurance for savings? Does this make a difference in the interest rates offered?

Using Credit

When making a purchase, have you ever been asked, "Cash or credit?" Have you ever noticed ads that say, "No money down," "Easy financing," "Buy now, pay later," or "Your job means instant credit"? Have you ever wondered why so many businesses seem to make it easy for people to buy on credit? Do you know what credit is?

If you have ever used a credit card, purchased a stereo by paying for it over several months, or bought a car, you have already had some experience with credit. In this chapter you will learn exactly how credit works and how to use it responsibly. You will also learn about the different types of credit and how to compare credit costs. Once you understand the advantages and disadvantages of credit, you will be able to get the greatest benefit from buying with it.

1 *What Is Credit?*

Credit is a method of buying that involves trust. When you buy on credit, a business trusts you to pay later for a good or service that they give you today. The business accepts your promise that you will make regular payments until you have paid all that you owe.

Businesses that Offer Credit

Most businesses, especially those that sell expensive items, let their customers buy on credit. Department stores, furniture stores, and car dealers are just a few of the businesses that offer their customers credit.

Banks and other financial institutions are another type of business that offers credit. They are a little different, however, since what they provide on credit is money. When you need a very large amount of money (to start a business or buy a house, for example), the bank will lend you the money you need. You will then pay back the money in monthly payments.

Businesses that offer credit know that most people do not have large sums of money to pay for expensive purchases all at once. To sell their goods and services, these businesses must trust their customers to pay a little at a time until the product is completely paid for.

Types of Credit

There are many different kinds of credit. Some kinds are so commonly used that we don't even think of them as credit at all. Reading about the different kinds of credit will help you decide how you will want to use credit.

Credit Cards   Most people use credit cards at one time or another. **Credit cards** are plastic cards embossed with your name and an assigned account number. They allow you to use a certain amount of credit. The amount of credit a person has with each card is the total amount of money he or she can spend using the card. For example, if your credit amount (or limit) is $500, you can spend up to $500 with that card.

There are many different kinds of credit cards. You can use some of the nationally known cards, such as American Express, VISA, and MasterCard, all across the country. You can buy many different kinds of products from many different businesses with these cards.

Many large companies issue their own credit cards for their customers. Many of the oil companies, for example, have credit cards that you can use at any of the service stations selling that company's gasoline. Department stores and clothing stores also issue their own credit cards.

Many people have several different kinds of credit cards. They might have a gasoline credit card

When offering credit, a business is trusting the customer to pay for a good or service later. How does the business benefit from doing this?

Case Study 1

Jim loved baseball—it was his favorite sport. He never missed his favorite team, the Yankees, when they played on TV. Now he was especially excited because the Yankees would be playing in the World Series.

Then, just two days before the series was to start, Jim's TV went completely blank. He took the set to a local TV shop to see if he could get it fixed. He almost fainted when the store owner told him that the repair would cost $200. The owner suggested Jim might as well spend a little more and buy a new set.

Jim could only think about the World Series two days away. He had about $50 in his savings account, which wasn't nearly enough to buy a new TV.

When Jim said he didn't have enough money for either the repair or the purchase, the store manager suggested he buy on credit. As long as his credit rating was good and he could pay a little money now, he could actually have a new TV the next day—just in time for the series. Jim couldn't have been happier.

---

to buy gasoline and other goods and services offered by a particular oil company. They might have a credit card at their favorite local department stores. They might also have one of the nationally known cards to use for meals and motel expenses when they travel.

Charge Accounts   Many local businesses that do not issue their own credit cards do offer charge accounts. Charge accounts work just like credit cards but without the cards. A **charge account** is the privilege of being able to buy on credit.

Businesses that sell goods to other businesses often offer charge accounts to their customers. For example, a carpenter may have an account with a lumber yard, or a secretarial service may have an account with a business supplies store.

Businesses that offer charge accounts keep individual records for each customer who has an account. These records show the amount of each purchase and each payment. Many businesses send each charge account customer a statement at the end of the month.

Each business has its own payment policy for its charge accounts. Some businesses require that you pay the full amount at the end of each month. Others let you carry your balance over into the next month.

Installment Plans   Many businesses will let you buy on an installment plan. An **installment plan** is a form of credit in which you agree to make regular payments on a good while using it. You don't own the good until you have paid the full purchase price, however.

People usually use installment plans to buy expensive products. For example, furniture stores that offer credit may use installment plans. Most businesses require a down payment at the time of purchase. A **down payment** is a certain percentage, usually 10 or 20 percent, of the total price.

When you buy on the installment plan, you must make your payments on time. If you fall behind in your payments, the company may repossess the good you were purchasing. This means the company will take it back. In such a case you would *not* get your money back.

Loans   A loan is another form of credit. You probably know what a loan is. It is something, usually money, that someone gives you with the understanding that you will give it back. When someone lends you money, you agree to pay it back.

Most people need cash loans from time to time. Very few people have enough money to pay for expensive goods, such as cars and houses, or services, such as home remodeling. When they want these things, most people go to a bank or other financial institution to borrow the money.

Advantages and Disadvantages of Using Credit

Almost everyone uses credit at one time or another. When you borrow a dollar from a friend, you are using credit. Even large companies and governments use credit. Most companies must borrow money to operate their businesses, and governments usually need to spend more than they collect in taxes. You may remember from Chapter 18 that the U.S. government sells U.S. Savings Bonds. In effect, the government is borrowing money from those people who buy bonds.

Strive for Success

Where Credit Is Due

Over the next 10 to 15 years, many of you will visit a jewelry store with your fiancé to select an engagement ring. Like many other couples, you will probably choose a ring that costs more than you had expected. However, you will probably be able to buy the ring that you want—on credit. You can thank Morris Zale for giving you—and others—that affordable way to buy jewelry.

Morris B. Zalefsky came from a small Jewish ghetto in Russia. He and his family immigrated to the United States when Zale was seven years old. Like so many others, they made the Atlantic crossing in an overcrowded ship. However, unlike the many thousands of immigrants who simply settled in New York upon landing, the Zalefsky family moved on to Fort Worth, Texas.

Zale did not spend many years in school there. In fact, he left school in the seventh grade to go to work, as many children did then. Also, as was common then, he went to work for his family, finding a job in his uncle's jewelry store.

Zale learned the business well, and by the time he was 21 he was ready to go out on his own. He opened his first store in Graham, a small town about 60 miles northeast of Fort Worth.

From the beginning, Morris Zale was a merchandising revolutionary. To get his fledgling business off the ground, he knew he had to attract as many customers as possible. One method he used to draw people into his store was to play a Victrola outside the front door.

Zale also advertised heavily and aggressively in the newspapers. He and his stores became controversial when he introduced the policy of letting customers pay for jewelry in installments. In a Zale's store, you could buy almost anything for a penny down and a dollar a week.

His advertising ideas worked. By the Great Depression, the young entrepreneur had three stores in his chain. By initiating serious belt-tightening measures, he managed to help his company ride out the hard times. When things began to turn up afterwards, Morris Zale was ready to forge ahead.

To choose the sites for his new stores, Zale used to take long, thoughtful walks around the cities he

visited. His insight and intuition in choosing locations boosted the number of stores in the chain to 13 by 1945 and to 1,223 by 1971. Their success was in no small part due to Zale's continued aggressive advertising.

As times changed, so did Zale's advertising techniques. In 1969 the company bought a 434.60 carat rough diamond and had it cut into a 130.27 carat stone called the Zale Light of Peace. The stone received wide publicity—and so did the company.

By giving credit where credit was due (and needed), Morris Zale opened up the world of jewelry to people who could not otherwise afford it. He also set an example for other retailers to follow.

This young man was unable to make the monthly payments on this sofa, and so it is being repossessed. Right now he feels bad, but how might he benefit from this experience?

The advantage of using credit is probably obvious. When you buy or borrow on credit, you can have what you want when you want it. You don't have to wait until you save the full amount. This is especially helpful when you need something expensive, like a car or house, or when you have an emergency, like a car repair.

The disadvantage of using credit should be just as obvious. Using credit costs money. We will discuss the costs of credit a bit later, but you need to remember that paying for something using credit almost always costs more than paying for it in cash.

Many people lose control of their credit buying. They buy more and more on credit until they reach a point where they can't afford to make all their monthly payments. Make sure that your credit payments are no more than you can afford.

Do you know how much credit you can afford each month? To find out, first determine your monthly expenses. In addition to your regular monthly expenses, consider any special payments you make throughout the year, such as tuition, insurance, vacation, and taxes. Find the total of these special payments and divide that by 12. Add this amount to your regular monthly expenses. This gives you your estimated monthly expenses.

Next, subtract your estimated monthly expenses from your monthly income. One-half of the money you have left after deducting expenses is the most you should spend on credit payments. The other half should be kept for savings and emergencies.

Before you buy something on credit, you should weigh the advantages against the disadvantages. Ask yourself if you need the good or service right away. Will it be worth the extra cost of buying on credit to have this item now instead of later? Could you do without it until you save enough to pay the full price at the time of purchase?

MAKE A DECISION

Once you are 18 years old, you can apply for almost any credit card you want. As you know, there are several advantages to having your own credit cards. There are no major disadvantages as long as you exercise good judgment and pay what you owe on time. Credit cards, however, can lead to serious problems for those unable to control their spending. What's your decision —will you apply for credit cards or continue to use cash? Give the reasons for your decision.

✓ CHECKING UP

1. What is credit?
2. What kind of businesses usually offer credit?
3. Name the different types of credit available.

2 *The Cost of Credit*

As you read earlier, you almost always have to pay for the privilege of buying on credit. How much you will pay depends on

- the credit policy of the company giving your credit,
- the amount of money you owe, and
- the length of time you take to pay back the full amount.

Credit policies vary depending on the type of credit being offered and the company's policies. As you may remember, companies that offer charge accounts may require the full amount charged be paid each month, or they may allow the balance to be carried over to the next month.

Some credit card companies require card holders to pay a fee in order to receive and use their card. Most of these companies will send you a monthly statement showing how much you owe. You may be expected to pay all or part of what you owe each month.

In some cases whether or not you have any collateral will affect how much you pay. **Collateral** is something of value that you own that you promise to give up if you can't make your payments. Collateral is most often asked for by banks as security that you will pay back the money you owe.

Each company will have its own rules and regulations regarding credit payments. In most cases the costs will be based on a certain interest rate. Make sure each time you buy on credit that you understand how charges will be calculated.

Interest

Interest is money paid to borrow money. In Chapter 18 you read about the interest that banks pay you. The interest you are charged for credit works the same way. It is based on the interest rate, the amount of credit given, and the length of time it takes to repay that amount. Two common methods used by businesses to calculate interest on credit are simple interest and finance charges.

If you don't understand the credit charges offered by a business, ask questions until you do. A reputable company or financial institution that offers credit will be willing to explain all charges.

Simple Interest Simple interest was explained in Chapter 18. To review, here is the way you would calculate 5 percent interest on $100:

$$\$100 \times .05 = \$5.00$$

Whether you are borrowing or lending money, the interest paid is $5. This is called simple interest because it is based on the interest's being calculated for one year.

This couple pays their bills monthly and uses a budget as a guideline for their spending. How would using this method to pay bills help them decide whether to buy something with cash or on credit?

When simple interest is used, you pay a single lump sum within a certain period of time, usually one year. If you repay what you owe before the set time, you pay less than the full amount. For example, if you borrowed $100 for one year at an interest rate of 10 percent, at the end of one year you would owe $110. If you paid the amount borrowed in half the time, or six months, you would only owe $105 ($5 is one-half of $10).

Finance Charges   Interest can also be based on the unpaid portion of the amount owed each month. This type of interest is often called a **finance charge.**

Here is an example of how interest on unpaid balance works. Barbara wanted to buy a bicycle that cost $200. Payments of $20 plus 1.8 percent interest on the unpaid balance were due each month. Barbara divided $200 by $20 and knew she would need to make ten payments. Because the interest was on the unpaid balance, the amount to be paid would be less each month. Barbara made the following calculations:

- Interest on $200 at 1.8% is $3.60. The first payment is $20 + $3.60 = $23.60.
- Interest on $180 at 1.8% is $3.24. The second payment would be $20 + $3.24 = $23.24.

Each month, Barbara subtracted the payment of $20 and calculated the interest on the unpaid balance. She figured out that the total interest paid was $19.80.

Although Barbara figured that her interest charge would change slightly from month to month, she made payments of $21.98 every month. Can you see why this happened? What do you get if you add the total interest—$19.80—to $200 and then divide by ten?

Most banks and companies offering credit figure the total cost of what you owe, including the interest charges. They then divide the total by the number of payments. Using this method allows the customer to pay equal amounts each month, which is much easier than paying a different amount each month.

Finance charges may also include other charges, such as service charges or credit-related insurance premiums. (Some lending institutions offer insurance that pays the balance of an amount owed if the borrower becomes disabled or dies.) Make sure you understand how the company or financial institution figures its finance charges.

This businesswoman received a simple-interest loan of $2,000 to be paid in full in one year with 10 percent interest. She's paying back the loan in six months instead of one year. How much money does she save by doing this?

Calculating the Cost of Credit

Before buying anything on credit, you should consider the cost of credit in dollars and cents. This is often called the total finance charge (TFC). It is important to be able to calculate the difference in cost that various interest rates can make.

To calculate the cost of credit, follow these steps:

- Multiply the amount of the monthly payment (this includes finance charges, if any) by the number of months to pay.
- Add the down payment, if there is one.
- Subtract the cash price from the sum of the first two steps.

Example:

Monthly payment	$ 65
Number of months to pay	× 24
	$1,560
Down payment	+ 1,000
Total cost	$2,560
Cash price	− 2,200
Cost of credit	$ 240

You can see from the example that it would cost $240 more to buy this item with credit instead of cash. Using this information, you can make an informed decision about how to buy something.

Case Study *2*

Sally was relieved when she finally found the right sofa for her new apartment. The only problem was the cost—$450. Sally had the money. In fact, she had exactly $459.24 in her savings account, but she didn't want to spend her entire savings on the sofa. That would leave her with no money to take care of any unexpected bills. It looked as though she would have to find a less expensive sofa or wait until she saved some more money.

When Sally said she couldn't afford the sofa right now, Ron, the salesperson who had helped her, told Sally about the store's credit plan. Ron said that if Sally could pay just $45 now, she could have the sofa delivered tomorrow. She could take up to three years to pay. This sounded great to Sally, and she said okay. Much later, Sally learned about the cost of credit. She figured up how much the sofa had really cost her. Instead of $450, she had paid $540. Sally realized that she could have saved $90 by paying cash for the sofa.

Comparing the Cost of Credit

The Federal Truth in Lending Act requires that all creditors must state the cost of their credit (their interest rates) in terms of the **annual percentage rate (APR).** This is the percentage cost of credit on a yearly basis and is used to compare credit costs regardless of the amount of credit or how many payments you have to make. The law doesn't set interest rates but allows the consumer to compare credit costs among creditors. For example, if you were shopping for a new car, you could compare the interest costs among car dealers because they all must calculate their interest in this manner. You wouldn't have to worry about comparing apples to oranges.

For example, Josh is buying a car for $7,500. He plans to make a down payment of $1,500 and finance the remaining $6,000. Using the APR, he is able to compare the interest rates available from three different financial institutions (Figure 19-1) and, therefore, the cost to buy the car. He can decide on where to borrow based on the lowest total cost or lowest monthly charge.

You will find that the companies and financial institutions that offer credit charge different rates for it. You should therefore shop for credit when you can. Try to get it at the lowest possible cost to fit your purpose.

Hidden Costs

In many cases, there are costs for the use of credit that may not be obvious. These are called hidden costs. For example, when you buy gasoline with a credit card, it costs the company money to keep a record of what you owe and mail you a monthly statement. This added expense causes the company to raise the price of gasoline for credit card users. This is why people who use cash may sometimes pay less than those who use credit.

Another hidden cost consists of losses that occur when credit customers do not pay their bills. When this happens, the lost income takes away from the company's profits. To make up for this loss, the company may raise prices. This is why stores that sell on a cash-only basis can sometimes sell at lower prices than stores that offer credit.

Credit Cost Comparisons					
	APR	Length of Loan	Monthly Payment	TFC	Total Cost of Car
ABC Credit Union	14%	3 years	$205.07	$1,382.52	$7,382.52
America Bank	14%	4 years	$163.96	$1,870.08	$7,807.08
City Bank	15%	4 years	$166.98	$2,015.04	$8,015.00

Figure 19–1 The Truth in Lending Act requires firms extending credit to tell their customers the annual percentage rate and the total finance charge. Of the credit sources listed here, which offers the lowest APR? the lowest TFC? What accounts for the difference?

With a walletful of credit cards, it's easy to spend beyond your ability to repay. If these were your cards and you wanted to reduce their numbers in order to reduce your reliance on credit, what standard would you use to select the cards you would keep?

SITUATION
SOLUTION

Charged to the Limit

After graduation from high school, you found a job you really enjoy that pays you more than you ever thought you'd earn. You had no trouble getting a VISA card through your bank. In that first year after graduation, you also received credit cards from three department stores and two oil companies. Because your income was so high, you didn't stop to think about how much you were spending on credit.

Now your monthly credit card payments are out of hand. Your annual review is coming up, and you're hoping to get a raise big enough to help you cover them.

1. You receive an application for another VISA card in the mail. This card is being offered by another bank. Would you consider applying for it and (assuming your application is accepted) using it to help you make your other monthly payments? Explain why or why not.

2. The raise comes through, but you decide to make some changes in your spending habits. What financial plan might you come up with to manage your credit better?

3. A friend tells you about his VISA card rate, and it sounds somewhat less expensive than yours. However, your VISA card is part of a package arrangement with your bank. What might you consider in the future before choosing a national credit card? If you decide to shop for a new credit card plan, what features would you look for?

MAKE A DECISION

You are going to buy a used car for $3,000. You have $2,500 in a savings account that pays 5½ percent interest. If you put $500 down, the bank will loan you $2,500 at 12 percent interest. You were thinking you might use your entire savings and just borrow $500. Of course, you could pay anything between $500 and $2,500 and borrow the rest. What's your decision— keep your savings and borrow most of the money, use your entire savings and borrow just a little, or something in between? Give the reasons for your decision.

✓ CHECKING UP

1. What three factors determine the cost of credit?

2. Describe how finance charges are a kind of interest payment.

3. List the steps to calculate the cost of credit.

3 *Applying for Credit*

After deciding you need credit, you must apply for it. You must also make sure you understand your rights concerning credit. Regardless of the credit plan you choose, you will need to give a creditor information about yourself and your financial background so that the creditor has a basis on which to trust you with the loan or credit. This information is personal, and the federal government has taken steps to protect it for you.

Credit Contracts

To apply for credit you will fill out an application form, listing your name, address, place of employment, length of time employed at your present job, and much more. A creditor will use this information to determine how long you live in one place or stay at one job. Most creditors believe that people who live in many places or work at many jobs in short periods of time are poor credit risks.

In many cases the application you fill out to apply for credit is the credit contract. In some cases, it is not. The credit contract is the paper you sign that spells out the responsibilities of both the creditor and the borrower regarding a purchase on credit. When you sign the contract, you are agreeing to everything it says. This is why it is very important for you to read and understand every word of the document before signing it.

Most credit contracts will include statements about the following items:

- Purchase price or amount borrowed
- Interest and extra charges in dollars
- Down payment
- Trade-in allowance
- Insurance charges or other special charges
- Total amount due
- Amount of each payment
- Number of payments
- Date each payment is due

Be sure all the information is correct before you sign the contract. Ask questions about anything you don't agree with or understand. By signing you are saying that the contract is accurate. Be sure to get a copy of the contract for your own records.

Some contracts, such as home mortgages, are very long and detailed. You should probably have a lawyer read such a contract to make sure every-thing is in order. You will read more about contracts in Chapter 21.

Remember, the costs of your credit are explained in the contract. Read the contract very carefully. Make sure you understand how much and when you must pay. A form like the one shown in Figure 19-2 is often included with the contract papers to help you.

Credit Rating

After you have applied for credit, the company will check with a credit bureau to find out your credit history. A **credit bureau** is an agency that keeps track of how people pay their bills.

Most businesses belong to a credit bureau. Each business reports the names of people to whom it has extended credit. The businesses inform the bureau about which people are paying on time and which people have failed to make their payments.

With the information it receives, the credit bureau can give each person a credit rating. A **credit rating** is an estimate of how likely a person is to pay his or her bills on time. A person who always pays on time gets a good credit rating. Someone who is always late or who fails completely to make payments gets a poor credit rating.

You can see how important it is to maintain a good credit rating. When you apply for credit, the company will check with the credit bureau. If its records show that you have a poor credit rating, the company may refuse to give you credit.

Federal Laws that Apply to Credit

You may remember from Chapter 18 that the federal government helps to protect people who keep their money in banks. In the same way the government helps protect people who borrow from financial institutions and companies that offer credit. When you apply for credit, you should also know your rights as a credit consumer.

You have already read that the Truth in Lending Act requires all creditors to state their credit terms as an annual percentage rate. Another act, the Fair Credit Reporting Act, sets up a procedure for correcting mistakes in your credit record, or credit rating. This act establishes your rights in the event that a credit institution refuses you credit because of unfavorable information in your credit record. You must be given the name and address of the

Disclosure Form

ANNUAL PERCENTAGE RATE The cost of your credit as a yearly rate.	FINANCE CHARGE The dollar amount the credit will cost you.	Amount Financed The amount of credit provided to you or on your behalf.	Total of Payments The amount you will have paid after you have made all payments as scheduled.	
13.50%	$ 1,178.06	$ 5,314.90	$ 6,492.96	

Your payment schedule will be:

Number of Payments	Amount of Payments	When Payments Are Due
36	$ 180.36	Commencing monthly 8-27-91
	$	

Insurance
Credit life insurance and credit disability insurance are not required to obtain credit, and will not be provided unless you sign and agree to pay the additional cost.

Type	Premium	Signature
Credit Life for Term of Credit	$ 97.39	I/we want credit life insurance _____ Signature _____ Signature
Credit Disability for Term of Credit	$ 217.51	I want credit disability insurance _____ Signature
Credit Life and Disability for Term of Credit	$ N/A	I want credit life and disability insurance _____ Signature

Security: ☒ right of set-off against any moneys, credits or other property of yours in the possession of the Holder, on deposit or otherwise.
Late Charge: If a payment is late, for more than 10 days, you will be charged $5.00 or 5% of the payment, whichever is less.
Prepayment: If you pay off early, you will be entitled to a refund of part of the finance charge.
See your contract terms for any additional information about nonpayment, default, any required repayment in full before the scheduled date, and prepayment refunds and penalties.

Figure 19-2   Merchants extending installment credit to their customers often provide a disclosure form like this one to summarize the transaction. What APR is the customer paying and over what period of time? What is the total finance charge, and how was it arrived at?

agency furnishing the negative information so you can clear it from your record if it is untrue.

The Equal Credit Opportunity Act assures that all credit applications will be considered using standard criteria for all applicants. Loans and credit may not be made on the basis of age, sex, religion, race, or marital status. The act also stipulates that you must be notified within 30 days after your application has been completed, whether or not your loan or credit has been approved. The notice must be in writing, and, if credit is denied, the notice must include the reasons for denial.

✓ **CHECKING UP**

1. What is a credit contract?
2. Why is it important to have a good credit rating?
3. What is the difference between the Fair Credit Reporting Act and the Equal Credit Opportunity Act?

CHAPTER SUMMARY

Credit is a method of buying in which a business trusts the buyer to pay later for a good or service received now. Most businesses, including banks and other financial institutions, offer credit. In fact, they may offer several different types, such as credit cards, charge accounts, installment plans, and loans.

There are advantages and disadvantages to using any kind of credit. The most obvious advantage is that you don't have to wait to make a purchase until you've saved enough to pay for it in full. The most obvious disadvantage of using credit is that it costs money. Therefore, you should understand how businesses and lending institutions determine the cost of credit. The cost of credit depends on credit policies, the amount owed, and the length of time you take to pay back the full amount.

Interest is the money paid to use credit. Two common methods used by businesses to calculate interest are simple interest and finance charges. The Federal Truth in Lending Act requires that all creditors state the cost of their credit as an annual percentage rate (APR). This enables consumers more easily to compare credit costs among competing sources.

Knowing how to calculate the cost of credit will help you decide if you can afford or want to spend the extra money necessary to use credit. Also, there may be additional hidden costs when using credit. With this information, you can make more informed decisions about whether or not to buy on credit.

Once you decide you want credit, you will need to sign a credit contract. The contract should explain all the credit terms. You should sign the contract only if you have read and understood it.

Once you have obtained credit, it is important to maintain a good credit rating by paying your creditors the amount you owe in the length of time to which you agreed. You will also need to know your rights regarding credit as provided by several federal laws, such as the Truth in Lending Act, the Fair Credit Reporting Act, and the Equal Credit Opportunity Act.

TERMS TO KNOW

On a separate sheet of paper, write sentences for each of the following terms:

credit
credit cards
charge account
installment plan
down payment
collateral
finance charge
annual percentage rate (APR)
credit bureau
credit rating

STUDY QUESTIONS

1. Why do businesses offer credit?
2. What is the difference between a charge account and an installment plan?
3. What is the most obvious advantage of using credit?
4. What is a good guideline to help you determine how much of your income you can afford to spend on credit payments?
5. Define collateral.
6. What are two common methods used by business to calculate interest on credit?
7. You buy a CD player on credit. The cash price is $360; the monthly payments, $35 for 12 months. How much are you paying for credit?
8. Describe a hidden cost that might make using credit more expensive.

9. Give some reasons why people are denied credit.
10. What information should be included in a credit contract?
11. How does a credit bureau get its information about borrowers?
12. In what ways does the federal government help to protect credit consumers?

CRITICAL THINKING

1. If your monthly income is $1,200, and your estimated monthly expenses are $1,000, how much credit can you afford each month?
2. Compare the interest a bank pays you for the money kept in a savings account with the interest you pay a bank for borrowing money.

DISCUSSION STARTERS

1. Do you think using credit encourages people to live beyond their means? Explain why or why not.
2. Some credit bureaus have a great deal of personal information about people. How might this information be used unscrupulously? What can consumers do to protect themselves? What should the government do to protect consumers?

BUILDING BASIC SKILLS

Math

1. You would like to buy a new coat that costs $145 with cash or six monthly payments of $30. Your monthly income is $200, and your estimated monthly expenses are $160. If you have no other credit expenses, can you afford to buy the coat on credit? How do you know?
2. You have applied for a $1,200 loan. It's to be repaid in one year at an interest rate of 1.5 percent per month on the unpaid balance. You are to repay the loan in 12 equal installments. What will be your monthly payments (including finance charges) and your total finance charge for the loan?

Communication

3. A credit card company has refused to issue you a credit card on the basis of a poor credit rating. You believe the credit bureau has made an error with your credit record. You are going to call the credit bureau to recheck the accuracy of their report. Write the notes you would follow to make such a phone call.

Human Relations

4. Your brother has asked you to cosign a loan to buy a small business he would like to operate. By cosigning you are stating that if he can't repay the loan, you will. You don't have much faith in his ability to manage a small business or his ability to repay the loan. How do you handle this matter without damaging your relationship with your brother?

SUGGESTED ACTIVITIES

1. Obtain the credit applications for three credit cards. Choose cards used for similar purposes. Make a chart that shows the charges of each credit card company and the APR on the unpaid balance. List any other differences, such as the number of days to pay or places each card can be used. Based on your analysis, determine which card is the best deal. Present your findings to the class.
2. Write a one-page report on one of the federal acts that apply to credit. Your report should include information on why the act was introduced, when the act was introduced, by whom, and so forth.

Buying Insurance

OBJECTIVES
After studying this chapter and doing the activities, you will be able to:

- define some terms commonly used in insurance;
- describe five types of auto insurance coverage;
- explain the factors that influence the cost of automobile insurance;
- distinguish between basic medical coverage and major medical coverage; and
- describe term, whole, and universal life insurance.

TERMS TO KNOW
insurance
policy
premium
deductible
liability
health maintenance organizations (HMOs)
preferred provider organizations (PPOs)
face value
cash value

*I*magine that you've just bought a new car for $12,000. As you drive home from the dealer, you're hit by a truck. The damage estimate on your car is over $2,000. Who will pay for the repairs?

Imagine that you are married and have young children. Both you and your spouse work just to make ends meet, and there is little money left over to put into savings. If you were seriously injured on the job or in a car accident, how would you continue to pay your bills? How would you afford the additional medical expenses?

While you can't do anything to guarantee that you will never have an accident, you can help protect yourself from the financial ruin an accident can cause. Like most people, you can buy insurance.

In this chapter you will learn about insurance—what it is and what it can do for you. You will read about the different kinds of insurance that are available to you and what you need to know to buy it.

1 *Understanding Insurance*

Insurance is a financial precaution against injury, loss, or damage. It is a way of protecting yourself against enormous bills that you could never pay without help. When you buy insurance, you pay relatively small amounts of money at regular intervals to guarantee that you will receive a large sum of money when and if you ever need it.

It is important to understand how insurance works because a great deal of money will be at stake. You will want to be sure you have the right protection and that you do everything necessary to keep your coverage up-to-date.

To understand insurance better, you need to understand terms that are used frequently and the different kinds of insurance that are available. In this lesson we will look at both.

The Language of Insurance

People buy different kinds of insurance for different needs, and different kinds of insurance cost different amounts of money. However, many of the terms used when talking about insurance are the same regardless of the kind of insurance being discussed.

Policy and Policyholder   An insurance **policy** is a contract between a person buying insurance and the insurance company that sells it. The person who buys the policy is called the policyholder.

An insurance policy states how much the insurance company will pay if an event causing a financial loss occurs. Such events include automobile accidents, illnesses, fires, and deaths. The policy also states the conditions under which such events must happen for payment to be made. For example, you are not entitled to payment under your fire insurance policy if you set fire to your own house.

Coverage   Your insurance coverage is limited to those events listed in your policy as occurrences for which you are entitled to receive payment. For example, if you have auto insurance, you'll probably have coverage for theft. In discussions with your insurance agent, the language you'll hear is "You're covered for theft" or "You're covered if your car is stolen."

Benefit and Beneficiary   If an event specified in the policy does occur, and it occurs under the conditions of the policy, the insurance company pays the policyholder a certain amount of money. This amount is often called the benefit or cash benefit. The person who receives this payment is called the beneficiary. In most cases, the policyholder and the beneficiary are the same. However, in the case of life insurance, which we will discuss later, the beneficiary is the person who receives the payment in the event the policyholder dies.

Premium   The insurance **premium** is the amount of money the policyholder agrees to pay the insurance company at regular intervals for his or her insurance coverage. Premiums can be paid monthly, quarterly (four times a year), semiannually (twice a year), or annually (once a year). It is important to pay your premiums on time, or your insurance coverage may not take effect.

The amount of the premium is usually determined by the amount of coverage you have. The greater the coverage, the larger the premium. Like anything else you buy, the more you buy, the more it costs.

Deductible   When buying most kinds of insurance, you will be asked to specify the amount of the deductible. The **deductible** is the amount of a loss the policyholder must pay. For example, if you have a $100 deductible and you wreck your car, you pay the first $100 toward the cost of the repairs. The insurance company then pays the rest or whatever amount is specified in your policy.

The amount of the deductible can vary and can affect the amount of the premium you pay. The more you pay toward the cost of a loss, the less the insurance company will have to pay. Therefore, the higher your deductible is, the lower your premiums will be.

Filing a Claim   When an accident, death, or loss occurs, the policyholder reports it to the insurance company. Reporting a loss to collect payment is called filing a claim. After you file a claim, the insurance company often investigates to find out what happened and why. The company then decides if your claim meets policy conditions and, if so, how much money you should receive.

Kinds of Insurance

People buy insurance to protect themselves against all kinds of losses. The most common kinds of insurance policies protect against losses of prop-

MAKE A DECISION

The premium will soon be due on your car insurance. Since gasoline costs have been going up, you're looking for a way to cut other costs. Your insurance agent tells you that you can lower your premium $40 every six months ($80 a year) by raising your deductible from $100 to $250. An unexpected repair bill of $150 would be difficult for you to manage, but you think you might take a chance. What's your decision —higher deductible and lower premium or lower deductible and higher premium? Give the reasons for your answer.

Personal Property Inventory

Item	Date Purchased	Purchase Price
Television		
VCR		
Stereo		
CD player		
Radio		
Tape player		
Camera		
Typewriter		
Calculator		
Computer		
Printer		
Software		
Jewelry		
Watch		
Collections		
Stamps		
Coins		
CDs		
Video tapes		
Cassette tapes		
Albums		
Sports equipment		
Bicycle		
Motorcycle		
Boat and motor		
Power tools		
Musical instruments		
Clothing		
Family heirlooms		

Figure 20-1 Using this form as a guide, do your own personal property inventory. What would be on your list? Can you see why you might want these things insured?

erty, health, and life. These are the areas in which people suffer the greatest financial hardship when something bad happens. Of course, the money received from insurance does not make up for the loss of personal mementos or the death of a loved one. Still, by helping people cope financially, the insurance does make it easier for them to adjust to personal losses.

Property insurance helps to protect against damage to your personal property. It also protects you if someone is injured while on your property. Property insurance includes renter's, homeowner's, and automobile insurance.

Renter's Insurance When you first move away from home, you will probably rent rather than buy. If you have many valuable personal possessions, consider buying renter's insurance.

Your landlord will probably have insurance on the building in which you live. However, that insurance will not pay to replace the personal belongings of the renters. If you own any expensive items, such as a stereo, CD player, television, computer, or large pieces of furniture, check into the cost of insuring them. Estimate how much it would cost to replace everything in your apartment. (A personal property inventory, like the one shown in Figure 20-1, can help you do this.) A small monthly premium compared to the total replacement cost might be a bargain.

Homeowner's Insurance If you someday buy your own home, you will want to have homeowner's insurance to protect it against damage or loss. If you borrow money from a bank or other financial institution to buy your home, you will probably be required to buy homeowner's insurance. The people lending you the money will want to make sure that their investment is protected against fire, storm, and other damage.

Case Study 1

Because of the part-time job he had while in high school, George was able to buy an expensive stereo and many albums and CDs. For graduation he received a personal computer and software.

Last fall George and his friend, Mario, both began working for the Homes Construction Company. They rented a mobile home near the job site. George moved his stereo equipment, computer, and kitchen items into the new place. Mario moved in a couch, a refrigerator, and a dining set.

George had learned in high school that renters need property insurance. He figured that all the things he owned were worth about $5,000, so he insured his personal property against fire, storm, and theft.

A few months later George was glad he had bought the insurance policy. While he was away one weekend, the mobile home burned to the ground. Mario was able to get their clothing out of the closet, but that was all. George used the insurance payment to replace his stereo and computer.

When people buy homeowner's insurance, they usually buy a policy that pays enough to replace the home. For example, if you bought a house that would cost $80,000 to build, you would probably buy an $80,000 homeowner's policy. If the costs of building a home went up, you would want to buy more insurance.

Automobile Insurance   Automobile insurance is also property insurance because your automobile is your personal property. It is insurance to protect you against the loss, damage, or injury that may happen to or because of your car. Auto insurance will most likely be the first kind of insurance you will purchase. We will cover it in greater depth in the next lesson.

Health and Life Insurance   As you enter the work force, you will be hearing more about health insurance and life insurance. As you may recall from Chapter 3, many companies offer these forms of coverage as fringe benefits. Health insurance

helps protect you against financial loss in the event of illness or injury. Life insurance offers financial protection in the event of death. These will also be covered in greater depth, in Lessons 3 and 4.

Other Kinds of Insurance   Do you know of any other kinds of losses for which people buy insurance? What insurance people buy depends primarily on their circumstances. Farmers buy hail insurance, home buyers buy title insurance, and banks buy deposit insurance.

To determine the kinds of insurance you may need, contact an insurance agent. An agent may work exclusively for one company or may represent several companies. In either case, remember that an agent is in business to sell insurance. It may be necessary to talk to several agents to obtain the best coverage and lowest premiums.

The owners of this house paid $50,000 to buy it 15 years ago. They bought a homeowner's insurance policy at the same time. If the value of the house increased to $90,000 and the homeowners have not updated their coverage, what will happen?

✓ CHECKING UP

1. Why do people buy insurance?
2. What is an insurance premium?
3. What are the most common kinds of insurance?

2 *Automobile Insurance*

The first kind of insurance many people buy is automobile insurance. If you own your own car, you most likely have automobile insurance. In many states drivers are required to have it by law.

Types of Coverage

When you buy a standard automobile insurance policy, you are usually buying several different kinds of coverage. Each type of coverage insures your car and you for a different kind of loss, damage, or injury. Insurance companies will give you some choices about which types of coverage you want in your particular policy.

Liability   The most important part of any automobile insurance policy is the liability coverage. **Liability** means responsibility. Liability insurance covers your responsibility to others. If you cause an accident—if you are at fault—you are responsible for any injury, loss, or damage that other people suffer because of your mistake. Your liability insurance would pay the other people's expenses.

No one has to tell you that automobiles can be very dangerous. Everyone who drives a car runs the risk of causing serious injury to other people. When accidents do happen, people suffering permanent disabilities often file lawsuits for large sums of money against the person responsible for the accident. Very few people have enough money to pay these sums of money. That is why most people buy liability insurance.

Liability insurance can be divided into two types—bodily injury and property damage. You should have both. In fact, many states require that you have both.

If you are injured or your car is damaged in an accident caused by someone else, that person's liability insurance should pay for your injury or damage. You should not use your own insurance to pay for expenses that someone else has created.

You might think it doesn't matter whose insurance company pays. However, you shouldn't look at it that way. There are several reasons why it's to your advantage that the other person's company pays.

First, if you have a deductible, you would have to pay it before your company would pay the remaining costs. Whatever the deductible, however small, that is money you shouldn't have to

Case Study 2

Mike, Jean, and Tom were on their way to a party. They were all in a good mood and ready for a good time. Tom, who was in the back seat, was telling a funny story about something that had happened that day at school. Mike, who was driving, became so absorbed in the story that he momentarily forgot what he was doing and turned to look at Tom. At that same instant, Tom yelled, "Watch out!" It was too late, though. Mike had let his car drift over the center line where he hit an oncoming car. Mike, Jean, and Tom were all right, but the driver of the other car was seriously injured. He was taken away in an ambulance.

Two weeks later, Mike learned from his insurance agent that the other driver was just out of the hospital. He was also suing Mike for all damages and medical expenses.

Mike was relieved to have liability coverage. Even though his rates would go up as a result of the accident, his liability coverage would pay for almost all of the damages and expenses.

pay. Second, insurance companies keep track of the driving records and claims of their policyholders. The more violations and claims a person has, the higher that person's premiums will be. This means that by filing a claim for an accident that wasn't your fault, you may be adding to the cost of your future premiums.

Medical   Many automobile insurance policies include medical coverage. This coverage helps pay medical expenses for you and your passengers should your car be involved in an accident. The policy usually states a maximum amount of money that will be paid per person per accident.

Collision   If you have a new car or a valuable older car, you will certainly want your automobile insurance policy to include collision coverage. Collision covers damage to your car, whether the accident is your fault or someone else's. The coverage pays to repair your vehicle or replace it.

Not everyone needs collision insurance. Your car may be old and worth very little. In this case

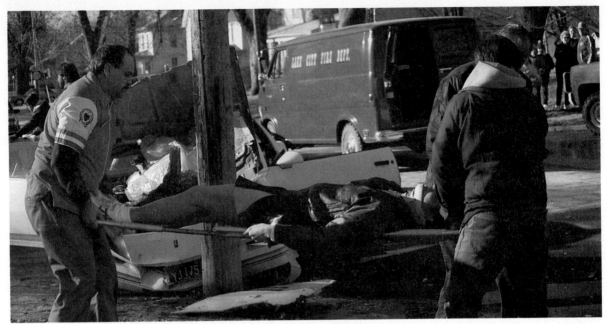

The driver who forced this young woman's car into the pole was uninsured. How will both he and she be affected by this fact?

the cost of your insurance might be more than the value of your car. You would be wise not to buy any collision coverage for such a car.

Comprehensive   Comprehensive automobile insurance covers most kinds of damage other than that caused by collisions. Damage resulting from fire, lightning, wind, flood, and hail is covered. Your coverage may also include losses from glass breakage, theft, vandalism, and falling objects.

Uninsured Motorist   Although most people have liability insurance, some don't. You could be injured and your car damaged in an accident caused by a driver without liability insurance. Insurance companies have special coverages for just such an event.

You can buy two kinds of uninsured motorist insurance. One kind insures you for bodily injury. Your medical expenses are paid if you are injured and someone else was at fault. Some states require people to have a certain amount of this coverage.

The other kind of uninsured motorist insurance covers property damage. This coverage pays for repairs on your car if the responsible person cannot pay. If you have collision coverage, you probably

Case Study 3

One day while Judith was waiting for the traffic light to change, a pickup truck hit the side of her van. When she saw the damage, she knew repairs would cost a great deal. However, since the accident wasn't her fault, she thought the other driver would pay her repair costs.

The police soon arrived on the scene. While writing the report, the police officer asked the other driver for the name of his insurance company. Judith was shocked to hear the driver say he didn't have any insurance. The officer told the driver that state law required liability coverage and that legal action would be brought against him. The officer also told the pickup driver that he would be responsible for the cost of repairing Judith's van.

Judith never heard from the other driver again, and she never received any money. She had to take care of the costs herself even though the accident was not her fault.

Strive for Success

Getting the United States Rolling

We think nothing of getting in our cars today to go across town for a bottle of milk or across the country for relaxation. People have even been known to drive around the world for publicity. However, this four-wheeled, forward motion we take for granted might not have been possible without the father of the auto industry, Henry Ford.

Ford was born on a farm near Dearborn, Michigan, during the latter part of the Civil War. His father wanted him to become a farmer, but Ford was fascinated by anything mechanical. His fate was sealed when he was 12. That year he received a watch as a gift and saw his first "horseless carriage," a road engine being used near his home. Soon, Ford could take the watch apart and put it back together. A few years later, he had built a working model of the road engine.

At 17, Ford left home and went to work as a mechanic in Detroit. His wages were low—$2.50 a week. He made extra money cleaning and repairing watches at night. A friend gave him an article about the internal combustion engine, and fate received another nudge. Ford became convinced that the gas engine was the engine of the future, not the steam engine.

Now a skilled machinist and mechanic, Ford began to design a gasoline engine. He finished his first working model in 1893. In 1896 he hooked up a two-cylinder, four-horsepower engine to four bicycle wheels, a three-gallon tank, and a bicycle seat and created the first Ford. A few days later, he exchanged the bicycle seat for a buggy seat, and he and his wife chugged the nine miles to Dearborn in triumph. He sold the car for $200. There was no turning back.

Ford established and dissolved several automobile companies in the next few years. The companies did not survive long because Ford wanted to build an inexpensive car and plow all the profits back into the company. His backers were more interested in the dividends they would be paid. Finally, the Ford Motor Company was established in 1903.

The first car produced was the Model A, which sold for $850. This no-frills vehicle was a tough, simple, well-made automobile designed to get

the owner where he (women rarely drove) wanted to go. Customers had a simple choice of color—the car could be painted any color they wanted as long as it was black.

The Model T, however, was the car that made the company—and the future of the auto industry. The demand for this popular model forced Ford to find a way to speed up production. He began experimenting with an assembly line, which called for "the reduction of the necessity for thought on the part of the worker." The change in production pattern led to a high turnover of employees dissatisfied with the repetitive work. Even today, the assembly line is criticized for the unchallenging nature of the work.

It produced large numbers of cars, however—cars that most of us could not afford to buy without this kind of production. With those cars came one of the largest insurance industries—auto insurance. The fact that almost everyone owns a car makes car insurance the one kind of insurance almost everyone has.

won't need much property coverage for uninsured motorists. Some states do require this coverage for people who do not have collision coverage.

Systems of Automobile Insurance

Up to this point we've been discussing a system of insurance based on fault. Most people believe that the person who causes an accident should pay for the damages.

There are usually disagreements about who was at fault in an automobile accident. Someone other than the people involved must decide which driver, if either, caused the accident. This is why the police should be called to the scene of an accident.

To reduce the delays and costs that result from disagreements about who was at fault, many states have passed laws to establish another system of insurance. This system is known as no-fault insurance.

A no-fault insurance system requires insurance companies to pay for their own policyholder's damages, regardless of who is at fault. With this type of system, there are no guilty parties. The main advantage of no-fault is that it reduces the lawsuits and delayed payment of benefits caused by insurance companies' disputing fault.

Buying Automobile Insurance

Automobile insurance can be very expensive. Obviously you don't want to pay any more than you have to. Still, you want to be sure you have enough insurance to cover any losses, damage, or injuries you might suffer.

Costs for automobile insurance vary considerably. Some people pay much more than others for the same coverage. Insurance companies take several factors into account in determining how much your premiums will be. Understanding these factors may help you get the coverage you need and want for the lowest possible cost.

Driving Record   The most important factor in determining the amount of your premiums is your driving record. In fact, if you have a history of violations and accidents, you may not be able to get insurance at all. In states that require liability insurance, this means you can't drive.

Insurance companies also base their rates on the number of claims. If you are involved in several accidents, your rates will go up.

Insurance companies usually go back three years in checking your records. Driving safely is the surest way to save money on premiums.

The Company   Rates vary from company to company. Some companies are very selective about which people they sell automobile insurance to. They do not sell policies to drivers with bad driving records. Because they are selective, they have fewer claims. This means that they can charge lower rates. If you have a good driving record, you may be able to get lower rates from a selective company.

Age   Insurance companies have found that male drivers under the age of 25 file more automobile claims than any other group. Since these people have more accidents, they pay a higher rate for insurance. You'll find that when you get older, your rates will go down.

Where You Live   If everything else were the same—same car, same driving record, same company—your premiums would still vary from place to place. Urban areas have a higher rate of accidents than rural areas. For this reason, the premiums are higher in cities. Some cities have more accidents than others. If you move, your rates may go up or down.

Other Factors   There are some additional factors in determining rates. Some companies give special discounts to students who have good grades. People who have taken driver education classes sometimes get lower rates than those who haven't. Ask your insurance agent about any special factors that might affect your rate.

Other Vehicles   Vehicles other than cars, such as motorcycles or motorboats, should also be insured. The same kinds of coverage are usually available. The same factors—number of claims, age, company, and location—will determine premium rates.

✓ CHECKING UP

1. What is the most important coverage in an auto insurance policy? Why?
2. What types of coverage can you buy as part of your automobile insurance?
3. What factors determine the cost of automobile insurance?

3 *Health Insurance*

Now, while you are young and healthy, you probably don't think much about hospitals and doctors. As you get older, though, you will become concerned about health and health care. If you have a family to support, you will need medical attention for your children. All this medical care can cost a great deal of money.

For example, a routine visit to the family doctor can cost anywhere from $25 to $100. One day in a hospital can run well over $400. Charges for even common surgeries can be hundreds or even thousands of dollars. Health insurance is the method that most people use to pay for these medical expenses. Your parents or guardians are probably taking care of your health care costs at the present time. They almost certainly have a health insurance policy for this purpose.

Case Study 4

Adam and a group of his friends from work liked to play football. On Saturdays they often met in the city park, divided into teams, and had a great game.

Last month things changed. Adam made a fast tackle and then didn't get up. His friends had to call an ambulance to take him to the hospital.

Adam was told he would be kept in the hospital in a body cast for several weeks. He knew it would cost thousands of dollars, and he wondered how he would pay. He had decided not to enroll in the group medical plan at work. Why? His reason seemed rather feeble now. He thought that young people didn't need health insurance.

Types of Coverage

Most insurance companies offer several kinds of health insurance coverage. They explain and organize their coverages differently. The most common breakdown, however, is basic coverage and major medical coverage.

Basic Coverage Basic medical covers two areas—hospital-surgical expenses and other medi-

cal expenses. Hospital-surgical expenses include room and board in the hospital, medicines given and lab tests taken while in the hospital, operating room fees, and surgeon's fees. Other medical expenses are nonhospital expenses, such as doctor's appointments, prescription drugs, and tests performed on an out-patient basis.

Basic coverage is just that—basic. There are limits to what services are covered and how much will be paid for them. The benefits paid out under such coverage are based on what the insurance company feels is "reasonable" regardless of what is charged by the doctor or hospital.

Major Medical Coverage In addition to basic coverage, most insurance companies offer major medical coverage. Major medical pays for hospital-surgical and medical expenses beyond those covered by a basic plan. It helps pay for long-term hospital stays and catastrophic illnesses, such as intensive care for a heart-attack patient.

Major medical takes up where basic coverage leaves off in two ways. First, it covers more services than the basic plan. For example, major medical would pay for the services of a nurse to come to a patient's home after he or she left the hospital. The basic plan would not.

Second, major medical pays most of the medical expenses that remain after the basic plan has paid its share. Remember, basic coverage will pay only a certain amount for an expense, regardless of how much is charged. For example, if a surgeon's fee is $2,000 and basic coverage pays only $1,000 for surgeon's fees, the remaining $1,000 will be covered by major medical.

Major medical payments are based on a percentage of the remaining expenses and require a deductible. Let's look at an example that shows how major medical coverage works with a basic plan and $17,500 in hospital expenses.

$17,500	Total expenses
− 7,000	Amount paid by basic plan
$10,500	
− 500	Deductible (paid by patient)
$10,000	
× .80	Percentage paid by major medical
$ 8,000	Amount paid by major medical
$10,000	
− 8,000	
$ 2,000	Amount paid by patient

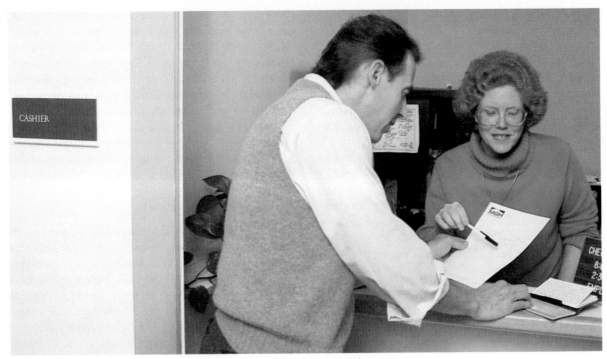

This man's hospital expenses were as follows: total expenses, $21,700; basic plan pays $10,000; major medical pays 85 percent of the remainder, minus a $1,000 deductible. What is the exact amount paid by major medical? How much does the patient actually pay?

It costs more to have major medical in addition to a basic plan. You can, however, get greater or smaller amounts of major medical coverage. As with other forms of insurance, the amount of coverage you want and the size of the deductible you can afford will affect how much your insurance will cost.

Disability Disability coverage provides money for people unable to work. This money takes the place of the worker's regular paychecks. The amount of the payments could be equal to or a percentage of the employee's regular pay.

Disability coverage is often of two types—short-term and long-term. Short-term disability pays for just a few months; long-term disability can pay for a lifetime. Many policies include short-term disability in the overall coverage but charge an additional amount for long-term disability. In other plans, both short- and long-term disability coverage cost extra.

Buying Health Insurance

There is growing concern today about the cost of health care. Because the cost of health care is rising, the cost of health insurance is rising as well. Insurance companies, in an effort to make some level of health insurance available to most people, offer a variety of health insurance packages. Coverage, premiums, and deductibles can vary greatly from one package to another.

For many years most people got their insurance through the companies they worked for. This is changing, however, as more companies cut back on expenses by limiting employee benefits and more people work independently. Traditionally people have received health insurance from either group plans or individual plans. However, alternative forms of health insurance are now being offered.

Group Insurance Plans Most people today get their health insurance through a group insurance plan at work. The main advantage of group insurance is that the insurance company can offer better rates to a large group of people than it can to an individual. Another advantage of group plans is that the employer usually pays part or all of the premium for each employee. As a result of these advantages, employees can obtain much more coverage for much less money.

When you belong to a group insurance plan at work, you have less say in the kinds and amounts of coverage you get than you would if you bought your own policy. In most cases, though, the group plan will offer the kinds and amounts of coverage you want. Getting more insurance for less money is usually far more important than having the exact policy you want.

If you belong to a group plan, your employer will either pay your premium for you or deduct a certain amount from your paychecks at regular intervals. This amount is usually considerably less than you would have to pay if you were buying the same coverage for yourself.

In most plans, employees can add their spouse and children to the policy. This means that more money will be deducted from the employee's paychecks. Plans differ as to how much extra it costs to add family members. Again, it is usually much less expensive to insure family members through a group plan rather than an individual policy.

When you check into the high costs of health care and health insurance, you will better appreciate the value of a group plan at work. Not all employers provide group health insurance for their employees. The group plans offered by some companies are much better than those offered by other companies. Some include dental and eye care, for example, although most do not. If you are deciding between two or more job offers with similar pay and working conditions, the health plans should be an important factor in your decision.

Individual Insurance Plans   If you work for a company that does not offer health insurance, if you are self-employed, or if you don't work, you should consider buying individual health insurance. You can purchase such coverage through an insurance company, much as you would purchase automobile insurance. Some companies specialize in health insurance, while others offer it in addition to other kinds of policies.

It is important to have health insurance. If you have a serious illness or accident, the cost of the health care that you'll need could impose a financial hardship on you and/or your family. You could find yourself in debt for years to come.

When you buy health insurance, you'll want to consider the coverage you need and how much you can afford to pay for it. Remember that different companies offer different health insurance packages, so consider carefully before you buy.

Health   Maintenance   Organizations
Health maintenance organizations (HMOs) are one of the alternative forms of health insurance. They are made up of members who pay for medical services in advance, usually by making regular monthly payments. Members can visit the HMO facility when they need health care. These facilities provide a full range of medical services, including a staff of doctors and other medical personnel.

HMOs are based on the idea that health care costs can be kept down if people are treated for minor health problems before they become major health problems. With traditional forms of health insurance, you must be ill, injured, or hospitalized to receive benefits. HMOs encourage members to come in for routine checkups, immunizations, and other forms of early treatment. In this way people are less likely to require more expensive kinds of health care.

HMOs are sponsored by many different kinds of organizations. Doctors, community groups, insurance companies, labor unions, and corporations have organized HMOs throughout the country.

Preferred   Provider   Organizations **Preferred provider organizations (PPOs)** are another alternative form of health insurance. They are usually operated in conjunction with employer-sponsored group health plans. A PPO is a group of health care providers, such as doctors or hospitals, who provide health care for groups of employees at reduced rates. The employees have the option of choosing one of the doctors or hospitals on the PPO list, or they may choose another doctor or hospital. An employee who chooses a provider on the list will pay much less for health care than an employee who chooses a non-PPO provider.

✓ *CHECKING UP*

1. Describe basic medical coverage.
2. How does major medical differ from basic coverage?
3. How do you go about buying health insurance? Suggest two basic ways.

4 *Life Insurance*

Chances are good that as you grow older, you will marry and raise a family. You will probably help to support your family. If you die, however, your family may have a difficult time paying bills and buying food without your income. Life insurance can provide enough money for your family to continue its usual life-style after you've gone.

Types of Life Insurance

People buy life insurance to provide future financial security for their families. Life insurance can accomplish this in a number of ways. If you have life insurance when you die, your policy will pay a benefit to your family to help them cover the expenses associated with your death. It may also provide them with additional funds to help them cope with the loss of your income. Buying life insurance can also provide an investment to be borrowed against or cashed in.

There are two terms you should know when talking about life insurance—face value and cash value. The **face value** is the amount of protection stated on the policy. This is the amount of money your beneficiary would be paid if you died. It is also called the death benefit. All life insurance policies have a face value. The **cash value** is the amount of money the policyholder can take by either borrowing against or cashing in the policy. Only certain kinds of life insurance policies have a cash value.

Term Life Insurance   This life insurance covers the insured for a specified period of time, or a term. The period of time could be five, ten, or more years. If the insured person dies within that period of time, the beneficiary is paid the face value of the policy. When the term ends, so does the insurance protection. Term life insurance has face value only.

Term life insurance is the least expensive type of life insurance, but it must be renewed at the end of the specified period of time. At the time of renewal, the premium will most likely go up.

If you buy term life insurance, you will want to know if the insurance is convertible at the end of the term. This means that the term life insurance can be converted to whole life insurance without a physical examination. This can be very important if the term ends when you are quite a bit older and your health may be more questionable.

Whole Life Insurance   Whole life is also called ordinary or straight life insurance. Like term insurance, whole life pays a face value to the beneficiary when the insured person dies.

Whole life differs from term insurance in several important ways. First, whole life coverage does not end after a certain period of time, as does term insurance. Whole life coverage continues for the insured person's whole life or until the policyholder stops making payments.

Second, the premiums for term insurance go up as the insured person gets older. This usually means that term insurance is less expensive in the early years but more expensive later. Whole life premiums stay constant throughout the policy.

The third difference is that whole life builds up cash value. When you buy term insurance, your premiums pay for the death benefit and nothing more. If you don't die during the term of the insurance, you get no money back. If you buy a whole life policy, your premiums are invested for you, and your policy will increase in value.

Traditionally people have used whole life insurance policies as a type of savings plan or investment. Insurance companies have offered this as an

This woman is considering buying a life insurance policy. Give some reasons why she might be doing this.

incentive to buy whole life insurance. The fixed premiums you pay earn interest or dividends for you. This is how whole life insurance builds up a cash value.

SITUATION
SOLUTION

What Is Fair?

You work for Western Construction Company. Recently, the company decided to pay one-half of the premium cost for a $100,000 term life insurance policy for each of its employees. You, however, already have such a policy. You feel that if the other employees are getting half of their premiums paid, half of yours should be paid, too.

1. You discuss this situation with your boss who says nothing can be done. What would you do next?
2. You discuss this situation with your boss who offers to go with you to see the personnel officer. What should you say to the personnel officer?
3. You talk to other employees and find that several of them are in the same situation. How should you approach the company's representatives about premium sharing for this group?

People use their cash value in different ways. Some people wait until they are older, and then use the money from their policy as retirement income. They can take the money in one lump sum or in monthly installments. Others cash in their policies to obtain the money they need for an emergency. When you cash in a policy, you lose the death benefit of the policy. With most policies you must pay premiums for at least two or three years before the policy has any cash value.

One special kind of whole life insurance is called limited-pay life. With this type of policy the policyholder pays higher premiums but for a shorter period of time, usually from 10 to 30 years. People who have enough money to pay the high premiums often prefer this type of policy.

Universal Life Insurance   Universal life insurance is a form of whole life insurance. It pays a death benefit and builds cash value based on premiums paid and interest rates. However, the premiums are variable rather than fixed.

Buying Life Insurance

The amount of your life insurance premiums will depend on several factors—the coverage you feel you need, your age, your health, and the type of policy you choose. For example, it is less expensive to buy life insurance when you are young. The rate of death for young people is much lower than for older people. This means that young people pay less in premiums. It is also less expensive to buy life insurance when you are young because your health is probably at its peak. You will probably be required to have a physical exam when you buy life insurance. If you have a serious medical problem, the insurance company will consider you a high risk. This will mean very high premiums or perhaps no life insurance at all.

Before you buy life insurance, ask yourself the following questions.

- How much money do I want to leave my beneficiaries if I die this year? Do I need more insurance to provide for them in the way I want to?
- What are my retirement plans? Will I need income from an insurance policy?
- How much can I afford to pay for insurance? How much life insurance will my employer provide?
- Do I want just the death benefit, or do I want to build up some cash value?

After answering the questions above, you will have a better idea of what you need from an insurance program. When you know what you need, talk to an experienced insurance agent. Try to balance your insurance needs with your ability to pay.

From time to time, you should analyze your insurance situation. Ask yourself if anything has changed since you bought your policy. If the answer is yes, you may need more or less insurance.

✓ CHECKING UP

1. Describe term life insurance.
2. What do whole life and universal life insurance have that term life insurance does not?
3. What are some differences between term life insurance and whole life insurance?

CHAPTER SUMMARY

Most people buy insurance policies to protect themselves against the tremendous financial cost of accidents and death. The most common kinds of insurance are property, health, and life. Property insurance includes renter's, homeowner's, and automobile. Automobile insurance is the first kind of insurance most people buy.

Automobile insurance includes several kinds of coverage. They are liability, medical, collision, comprehensive, and uninsured motorist. Benefits paid under these kinds of coverage often depend on who is determined to be at fault. This determination can cause delays in benefits and increase insurance expenses. To avoid this, some states have opted instead for a no-fault system. In this system, all victims are paid by their insurance company, regardless of who is at fault.

Health insurance coverage includes basic medical coverage, major medical coverage, and disability. Major medical coverage goes beyond the basic coverage, and disability coverage provides money for people who have become unable to work. Health insurance plans include group plans, individual plans, HMOs, and PPOs.

Life insurance pays a death benefit to the beneficiary of the policy. Some life insurance policies also offer a means of investment or savings. As with all kinds of insurance, the cost of life insurance depends on balancing the coverage you need with what you can afford to pay.

TERMS TO KNOW

On a separate sheet of paper, write a sentence for each term listed below. Your sentences should show that you understand how each term relates to insurance.

insurance
policy
premium
deductible
liability
health maintenance
    organizations (HMOs)
face value
cash value

STUDY QUESTIONS

1. What might happen if a policyholder fails to pay an insurance premium on time?
2. How would changing the deductible on your automobile insurance from $100 to $250 affect the amount of your premium?
3. What factors should you consider before buying renter's insurance?
4. How would you decide how much homeowner's insurance to buy?
5. Why should you talk to several insurance agents before you decide to buy any insurance?
6. Why shouldn't you use your own insurance to pay for damages to your car when someone else was at fault?
7. What is the difference between collision and comprehensive coverage?
8. Describe how a no-fault system of insurance works.
9. How is health insurance most commonly organized by insurance companies?
10. How are hospital-surgical expenses different from medical expenses?
11. Major medical does not pay all remaining medical expenses after basic coverage has paid its share—true or false? Explain.
12. Describe what it means to be a member of an HMO.
13. What are some of the benefits of receiving health insurance through a group plan?

14. What are some advantages of buying life insurance when you are young?
15. How do some types of life insurance build a cash value?

CRITICAL THINKING

1. Study the cartoon below. Do you think the car owner's indignation is justified? Why or why not?

"BUT I PAY TEN TIMES THAT MUCH IN INSURANCE PREMIUMS EVERY YEAR!"

2. Sean has started his own business as a computer software designer. He is the only employee. He has begun to look into health insurance and believes that because he is young and healthy, basic medical is all the insurance he needs. What reasons would you give Sean for considering major medical in addition to basic coverage?

DISCUSSION STARTERS

1. Suppose you have just finished high school and have started your first job. Your new employer does not offer life insurance as a benefit. Would you buy term life insurance, whole life insurance, or no life insurance at all? Defend your decision.
2. Should every state require drivers to carry liability insurance? Is this fair? Why or why not?

BUILDING BASIC SKILLS

Math
1. Your gross earnings for the year were $16,000, and your insurance costs for the year were as follows: automobile insurance, $400; health insurance, $480; and renter's insurance, $120. What percentage of your annual income goes to pay insurance?

Human Relations
2. A good friend, who is also a very poor driver, wants to borrow your car for the weekend. Your insurance rates are low because you have never needed to file a claim, and you want it to stay that way. How can you refuse to let him borrow your car without damaging your friendship?

Citizenship
3. While leaving work one afternoon, you see the driver of a jeep back into a parked car and damage the car's side. The jeep driver leaves the scene of the accident without reporting it. You do not know who owns the parked car, but you get the jeep's license number. What will you do?

SUGGESTED ACTIVITIES

1. Create a class file of insurance advertisements. Sources should include newspapers, magazines, and mail received by students, their families, and teachers. Classify the advertisements under automobile, other property, health, and life. Compare the types of coverage offered.
2. Working with one or two other students, investigate the cost of insurance in your community. Select one of the types of insurance discussed in this chapter. Talk with insurance agents and policyholders to develop information on premium ranges. Prepare a report and a graphic summarizing your findings.

UNIT
Five

Meeting Your Adult Responsibilities

Handling Legal Matters

*F*or people to live together and get along, they must have rules. Without rules there are no guidelines to follow when problems occur.

You are probably very familiar with rules—most families have their own. Parents make rules to protect their children's health and safety. Family members agree on rules for doing chores around the house.

Laws are rules, not for a family, but for a city, state, or country. Laws are rules that our governments enforce through the courts and other government agencies. You've heard people say, "It's against the law." This means that to do a certain act is to break the rules established by the people of our country or by the residents of a certain community.

In this chapter you will learn some basic facts about the law and how it affects you. As you become more responsible for your own actions, you will have more dealings with the law.

1 Contracts

The word *legal* refers to anything having to do with the law. In our country the legal system is the combination of laws, processes, and people that go together to protect our rights and safety. Elected officials, judges, the courts, lawyers, and police officers are all part of the legal system.

There are two major classifications of laws within our legal system—public laws and private laws. Public laws are those that regulate the relationships between individuals and the government. Public law includes constitutional, international, administrative, and criminal law. Private laws, also called civil laws, are the laws that regulate the relationships among people. This section will help you learn about contracts, which will be an important part of your dealings with civil law.

A **contract** is a legal agreement between two or more people. The legal term for a person who enters into a contract is **party.** Each party in a contract agrees to do or pay something in return for something from the other party or parties. As you become more independent, you will become involved in many contracts.

It is important that you understand how contracts work. You must know your rights and responsibilities concerning contracts. Contracts contain many legal terms that are difficult to understand. The most important terms are explained in this lesson.

What kinds of contracts will you be involved with? You've already read brief discussions of credit contracts, insurance policies (a type of contract), and union contracts. You will enter into contracts when you buy things and when you agree to do work for a certain amount of money. For example, a professional actor may agree to perform a stage play at a certain time and place. The theater company agrees to pay him a certain amount of money for acting in the play. Both the actor and theater company agree and sign a contract.

Contracts may be informal (spoken) or formal (written). Informal contracts are made when you buy clothing at the local store. The store agrees to turn over a shirt to you, and you promise to pay some money. No papers are signed. You also enter into an informal contract when you have your shoes repaired or your clothing cleaned.

Spoken agreements are legally enforceable only when they deal with relatively small amounts of

Formal, or written, contracts usually involve large amounts of money. They must be prepared carefully and read closely by everyone involved. What sort of contract is shown here? Read what you can of it, and note any unfamiliar terms.

money. For example, a contract for building materials may be informal if the price is less than $500. A contract for buying an expensive piece of property, however, must be a formal agreement. Help from a lawyer will be needed in drawing up this type of contract.

Required Elements

When you enter into a contract, you want the contract to be binding. A binding contract is one that is legally valid and cannot be broken. Five elements are essential if a contract is to be binding. Each of these essential elements is discussed here.

Mutual Agreement In every contract one party offers something, and another party accepts it. Mutual agreement takes place when both parties are in agreement on the terms of the contract. This means that both parties understand and are willing to enter into the agreement.

To be considered legal and binding, a contract must be clear and definite. Both parties must understand completely what the other party is offering to sell, pay, or do.

Case Study 1

Mr. Jones, a farmer, had 50 riding horses for sale. The horses were priced from $300 to $600. Mr. Jones told Mr. Smith that he would sell him a horse for $300. Mr. Smith thought he could take any one of the horses for $300.

Mr. Jones' offer was not clearly stated, and Mr. Smith did not understand it. As a result, there was no legal contract to sell a certain horse.

Competent Parties   According to civil law, **competent parties** are people who are responsible for their actions. No contract is binding and valid unless the parties involved are competent parties.

Competent parties are those who are able to understand their rights and obligations. These people can be considered responsible for what they do. Various state laws define who is competent to make contracts. Certain persons are prevented by law from making enforceable contracts.

People who don't have the ability to understand a contract may be declared incompetent in a court of law. They may be mentally handicapped, or they may have been mentally unfit when the contract was made. People who have been drinking heavily and people who are declared temporarily insane are examples of people who can be considered incompetent parties. Contracts made with such persons are not enforceable.

Other people considered legally incompetent are minors. A minor is someone who is not yet old enough to receive certain legal rights and responsibilities. In most states and for most laws, anyone under the age of 18 is considered a minor. The legal definitions for who is and who is not a minor vary considerably. Even in the same state a 19 year old might be considered a minor with regard to one law but not another.

Contracts made by minors can be voided, or broken, by the minor. If an adult makes a legal contract with a minor, though, the adult must carry out his or her part of the contract. Only minors may void the contracts on the basis of the competent party requirement.

Although minors may cancel many kinds of contracts, they must honor others. When minors agree to pay for necessities, such as food, clothing, shelter, and medical attention, they must honor the contracts. Minors cannot use the excuse of being minors to avoid necessary obligations. If, however, the item in question is not a necessity, the contract can be voided.

Because of problems with voidable contracts, store owners often ask parents to countersign contracts involving minors. To **countersign** means to sign a contract in support of someone else. If someone else countersigns a contract with you, that person is agreeing to make good your obligation if you fail to do so. Knowing that minors are not always considered competent parties, you can see why business people often want parents to countersign agreements made by their children.

Other contract problems are caused by minors who do not tell the truth about their ages. In such cases, the purchase price and money for damages can usually be collected from the minor. Most store owners protect themselves from these problems by asking for identification.

Case Study 2

Rachel, a 15 year old, bought an expensive leather jacket from a local clothing store. Since Rachel's family had already bought her several jackets, she didn't really need the purchase. When her parents refused to pay for it, Rachel had no choice but to return the jacket. The store was forced to accept it and refund the full purchase price. Since Rachel didn't need the jacket for protective clothing, she was able to void the contract as a minor.

Legal Purpose   The purpose of a contract must be legal for the contract to be binding. No agreement that is illegal or harmful to public health is a binding contract. Such agreements are not enforceable.

Agreements dealing with gambling or betting are illegal in most states. Suppose gambling is illegal in your state, but you made a bet with

Minors can enter into binding contracts if a parent or guardian countersigns for them. In this case, what is the young woman's mother promising to do?

someone anyway—and won. If that person refused to pay you, you couldn't take legal action to collect the money. Your agreement wasn't binding. You might be able, however, to take legal action to collect your winnings if you lived in a state where gambling was legal.

Obviously a contract to steal or commit murder would not be binding. You may not be aware, though, of some other types of unlawful acts that can void a contract. For example, in many cities and states, people who do certain kinds of work must be licensed. Contracts involving people without the necessary licenses are not valid.

Consideration   For a contract to be binding, something, such as money or property, must be exchanged between the parties. One party may agree to do something, while the other party agrees to give the first party something in return. Whatever one party gives the other in return for the promise is known as **consideration.**

For example, Mr. South agreed to let the electrical company run an electrical line across part of his farm. In return, the company gave him $1 as consideration when he signed the contract. Although Mr. South did not really want any money, the $1 consideration was necessary to make the contract legal.

Consideration is not always in the form of money. It can be services, goods, or a promise to not do something one has the legal right to do.

Legal Form   The law requires that certain contracts be in writing. Among those that must be in writing are the ones listed on the following page.

Case Study 3

Tom Woods built a small house for his family. He had no trouble doing the carpentry work, but he knew nothing about electrical work. Tom's neighbor, Joe Johnson, had done some electrical repair work on his own house, so Tom asked Joe to help him.

Joe agreed to furnish the materials and wire the house for $1,000. Joe wrote a contract stating what he would do and how much payment he would receive. Then he and Tom signed it.

When Joe went to buy the electrical material, he told the dealer about his contract with Tom. The electrical dealer advised Joe not to buy the materials. The city wouldn't provide service to Tom's house until the job was approved by an inspector. The dealer said that the inspector wouldn't approve work done by an unlicensed electrician. Since Joe didn't have a license, Tom and Joe's contract didn't have a legal purpose. The contract could be voided.

You shouldn't be embarrassed to ask for an explanation if you don't understand some portion of a contract. Why?

- Installment contracts
- Contracts to buy or sell real estate, including buildings, land, trees, and mineral rights
- Contracts to pay the debt of another person if that person doesn't pay it
- Contracts to sell personal property valued at over $500 (the amount varies from state to state)
- Contracts not to be carried out until one year from the date of signing

Written contracts must be in proper legal form. This means that the contract must contain certain pieces of information. To be legal and binding, a written contract must contain the following:

- Date and place of the agreement
- Names and addresses of the parties entering into the agreement
- Statement of the purpose of the contract
- Statement of the amount of money, goods, or services given in consideration of the agreement
- Signatures of both parties or their legal agents
- Signatures of witnesses (when required by law)

Precautions When Signing

Many people have trouble understanding contracts. If you are going to sign a contract, be extremely careful. Below are some suggestions for making sure that in signing a contract you are agreeing only to what you want to agree to.

- *Read the contract carefully before signing.* Be sure the terms and amounts of money are accurate.
- *If part of the contract is in small print, be sure to read that part.* If you don't understand, ask someone to explain. Be sure you understand everything before you sign.
- *Always keep a copy of the signed contract for yourself.* The copy should be signed by both parties. Keep your copy in a safe place.

You may not want to sign a contract until you've had a lawyer examine it. This is your right, so feel free to have a lawyer check any contract. Complex contracts that involve large amounts of money should be prepared by a lawyer.

A contract is defective if it lacks any of the five elements mentioned above. Under certain conditions, either party may break a defective contract. One or both parties may have been pressured to enter the agreement under threats of violence. The terms of the contract may have been fraudulent, or a mistake may have been made. In any of these cases, the contract can be voided.

✓ CHECKING UP

1. Under what circumstances can a minor be a party to a binding legal contract?
2. In legal terms, what is consideration?
3. To be in proper legal form, what elements must a written contract contain?

2 *Criminal Law*

Criminal law is one of several kinds of public law. Criminal laws are passed to protect your safety and legal rights. These laws are the basis for punishing people who commit crimes.

In our legal system a person is considered innocent until proven guilty. This protects innocent people.

Criminal laws differ from state to state. The maximum and minimum punishments also vary from state to state.

Two groups of people—those considered mentally incompetent and minors—are treated differently from other people who break the law. Mentally incompetent people cannot tell right from wrong. If there is any doubt about someone's mental abilities, an expert will examine the person. The expert will then state whether or not the person is mentally competent. If experts decide that someone being charged with a crime is mentally incompetent, that person will not have to go to trial.

As you know, minors are not legally responsible for their actions in the same way that adults are. When minors are charged with a crime, their cases are usually tried in a special court called juvenile court. A juvenile court is a court that handles only those cases involving minors.

Laws do not call for the same punishments for minors and adults. Punishments are less severe for minors—they don't include death or life imprisonment. In a few special cases, though, a judge may order that a minor be tried as an adult. This can happen when the crime is very serious.

Types of Crimes

A serious crime is called a **felony.** Felonies include such crimes as murder, rape, armed robbery, and arson (setting fires). Felonies may be punished by large fines, prison terms, and even death in some states.

Less serious crimes are called **misdemeanors.** Misdemeanors include petty theft (stealing something of minimal value), traffic violations, and disturbing the peace. Punishments for misdemeanors are usually smaller fines, short jail terms, and community service. Misdemeanors often result in an evaluation period, called probation. During this period the guilty party is given an opportunity to show that he or she will not commit further crimes.

Corporate crimes (crimes that take place in businesses) are sometimes called white-collar crimes. These crimes include forgery and fraud. Forgery is the dishonest changing of forms and records. Fraud was discussed in Chapter 16.

Arrest Procedures

If you are ever stopped by the police, what will you do? Suppose you decide to jog home after getting off work at 11:30 p.m. You're four blocks from home when you are stopped by two officers.

If you are arrested, even if it's a mistake, you should avoid getting angry or trying to argue with the officers. Why?

Strive for Success

The Lady and the Law

Riding with cowboys, mending fences, shooting straight, driving a truck across an Arizona ranch—it's the dream of many young boys. It was reality for Sandra Day—and she was only eight.

The first woman to sit on the U.S. Supreme Court, Sandra Day O'Connor was raised in a four-room adobe house, the Southwest's equivalent of a log cabin. She learned early how to work hard, be independent, and think for herself. She has never been one to go along with the herd. While in the Arizona State Senate, O'Connor voted for bills she thought were good for the state regardless of which party had proposed them. Her issue-oriented attitude did not make her popular with "clubhouse politicians," those who tended to vote blindly with their party.

Even today O'Connor goes her own way. When she agrees with the majority decision of the Court, she has been known to write a clear, concise concurring opinion giving her thoughts on an issue. Observers are often surprised that her perspective is very different from the majority opinion.

When O'Connor graduated from Stanford Law School in 1952, she discovered that no law firm in California would hire a woman. She had to go to work in the district attorney's office in San Mateo County. She quit for five years in 1960 to raise her children. When she went back to work, it was as assistant attorney general in Arizona. She became a member of the State Senate in 1969 and majority leader in 1973, the first woman in the United States to hold that position.

O'Connor left office to become a judge in Maricopa County Superior Court. Despite repeated requests by the Republican party to run for governor, she chose to remain in law, accepting a place on the Arizona Court of Appeals in 1979. Two years later, President Ronald Reagan nominated her for the post on the Supreme Court.

O'Connor is known for her self-control. She needed all of it and a generous dose of determination to face a diagnosis of breast cancer in 1988. The night before surgery she delivered a talk she had scheduled. Within a few weeks, she was golfing, playing tennis, and working. Once during her chemotherapy treatments she remarked to her husband that she felt a little tired. He hugged her and said, "Welcome to the human race."

Justice O'Connor is considered a shrewd attorney and judge. Generally mild, she can be ruthless with lawyers who show up before the high court unprepared. By contrast, she has been known to bake birthday cakes for her law clerks.

Because O'Connor focuses on issues and does not allow political arguments to sway her, hers is often the pivotal voice heard in the Court's decisions. She will be a strong influence on the law of the land for years to come.

Don't panic! The officers will ask you for identification, and they may ask other questions. Answer as completely as possible. You may ask, "Am I under arrest?" or "Why are you arresting me?"

If you are under arrest, don't resist in any way. You could be charged with resisting arrest. Tell the police that you will have nothing to say until you see a lawyer. You have the right to remain silent.

The officer has the right to search for concealed weapons. A legal paper called a search warrant permits a police officer to search your home. Police officers cannot obtain search warrants whenever they want. They must convince a judge that there is good cause to expect that stolen goods or unlawful possessions (such as drugs) will be found.

Booking   If you are arrested, the police officer will take you to a police station to be booked. This means formal charges will be filed against you.

The time and place of the arrest may affect the procedure. If you are arrested after midnight, you may not be booked right away. You would probably be kept in jail until morning.

Legal experts advise people to remain silent after they are arrested. Don't discuss your case with others in the jail. Don't sign any forms except the list of personal belongings taken from you. These things will be placed in the police safe until you are released.

Setting Bail   Anyone arrested must be charged with a crime or be released. If formal charges are made, the court will set bail. **Bail** is money deposited with the court so that an accused person can be freed from jail until the trial. The amount of bail varies with the crime.

Bail money is held by the court until the case is over. If the accused person does not appear at the trial, the money is not returned.

If you have no money for bail, you may contact a bail bondsman. For a fee, the bondsman will give you money to pay your bail. The fee, which is set by law, is often 10 percent of the amount borrowed. The bail money is returned to the bondsman when the case is over.

Appearing in Court   Some people choose to defend themselves in court, but this is usually not a good idea. If you are like most people, you do not know enough about the law to defend yourself properly. If at all possible, hire a lawyer. The lawyer will gather all the facts about the case and then advise you to plead either guilty or not guilty. If you plead not guilty, you will have a trial.

MAKE A DECISION

You have gotten yourself into some minor trouble with the law. A police officer suggests that you get a lawyer. You know you are guilty, and you have already decided to plead guilty. You think you can handle the problem yourself, without a lawyer, and save some money. At best the lawyer might get you off with a smaller fine. What's your decision—defend yourself or hire a lawyer? Give the reasons for your decision.

In our court system, every effort is made to protect the innocent. If you are arrested, you will be given a fair chance to prove your innocence. Few innocent people are ever punished for crimes.

You should have an attorney represent you in any criminal matter. Why?

✓ CHECKING UP

1. How are minors treated differently from adults under our criminal laws?
2. What is the difference between a felony and a misdemeanor?
3. List three things you shouldn't do if you are arrested.

3 *Using Legal Services*

Most people need a lawyer's help at some time during their adult life. Some of these times include the following:

- When you plan to sign a contract with major financial consequences
- If you are arrested or served legal papers
- When you are involved in an accident that results in injury or property damage
- If you need help in collecting money owed to you or when another party is seeking to collect money from you that you feel you do not owe
- If you have a tax problem involving a substantial amount of money
- When you organize or dissolve a business
- When filing for divorce
- When adopting a child

Many lawyers specialize in one kind of law. Some specialize in criminal cases; others specialize in civil cases. You should think about the type of case you have when seeking legal help. If you need help with a contract, a small firm or legal clinic can help you. For a serious criminal case, you should put a great deal of attention into finding a lawyer.

Finding a Lawyer

You can find a lawyer in several ways. Your friends or family members can sometimes suggest a lawyer they know. If you are in a new area, look in the Yellow Pages of the telephone directory. You may find a toll-free number for a state legal association. When you call this number, be ready to describe the service you need. You will then be told the names of lawyers in your area who might help with your problem.

You can also use the Yellow Pages to find the names and phone numbers of lawyers in your area. You might call several firms and ask about fees. With this method, though, you won't learn much about the experience or legal ability of the lawyers you call.

Legal services obtained through a private attorney are often very expensive. A less costly alternative is a legal clinic. This is a group of lawyers who offer legal services at reduced rates. They can afford to do so because they hire law students and paralegals to handle routine legal problems and research.

Finally, for those who cannot afford even a clinic's minimal fees, there are special free legal services. Help with civil matters is provided by the Legal Aid Society. Help with criminal matters is provided by public defenders. (Public defenders are lawyers appointed by the court to give legal help to those who cannot pay for it.)

Paying Legal Fees

You should know a lawyer's fees before requesting services. Your first meeting with a lawyer is the time to get definite information on fees. Don't be afraid to ask. You should learn how fees are determined and get an estimated cost for your case.

Lawyers may charge a flat fee, an hourly rate, or a contingency fee. Rates per hour may start at $40 and can go as high as several hundred dollars.

Lawyers specializing in personal injury or malpractice claims may take a case on a **contingency basis.** What this means is that the attorney is paid only if he or she wins the case. Normally, payment consists of a certain percentage of the money awarded by the court. For example, if the person winning the suit gets $100,000 and has a 25 percent contingency arrangement with his or her attorney, the attorney collects $25,000 as a fee. This sort of arrangement is usually made when the

One of the easiest ways to find a lawyer is to look in the phone book. What are the advantages and disadvantages of this approach?

You should always discuss fees with an attorney *before* engaging his or her services. At least three fee arrangements are possible —flat fee, hourly rate, and contingency basis. Give an example of each.

person bringing the suit has a good case but no money to pay a lawyer. Contingency fee arrangements are not permitted in divorce or criminal cases.

SITUATION
SOLUTION

To Sue or Not to Sue?

You've worked for the last four months as a parking attendant for a valet parking service. The service handles parking for clubs and restaurants that have limited parking space in downtown areas. Two weeks before returning to school, you tell your supervisor of your intention to quit. On August 30, your last work day, you leave your school address so that the service can send you your final paycheck.

The check never arrives. The owner of the service refuses to pay you, saying that you did not give notice of your intention to quit.

1. How could you have avoided this problem?
2. Since you didn't avoid the problem, what do you think is the best way to handle it? Should you get an attorney? Why or why not? What are your other alternatives?
3. Assume you're planning to argue your own case. How would you go about making the strongest possible presentation? What evidence would you use?

Going to Small-Claims Court

In cases that do not involve large amounts of money, the lawyer's fee may exceed the amount a person can hope to win. For cases like these there is a special court—the small-claims court.

Typically small-claims cases involve no more than $1,000. The types of cases most often heard include bill collections, consumer cases, and land-lord/tenant disputes. Individuals appear without attorneys. Instead they present their own cases. Costs are minimal—usually only a small filing fee (sometimes no more than $5). Court sessions are usually held at night for the convenience of the parties involved.

Parties appearing in small-claims court should be prepared to present their cases using any documentary evidence they have. They can also call witnesses. Parties should try to present their cases in as clear and concise a manner as possible. Immediately after the two sides have been heard, the judge will give his or her decision. Usually there is no delay.

✔ CHECKING UP

1. Suggest five situations in which you should consult a lawyer.
2. Name the factors that determine which lawyer a person will hire.
3. What kinds of cases are usually heard in small-claims court?

CHAPTER SUMMARY

Our laws are the rules that our society has decided we need to protect the safety and rights of all people. As citizens we all have a legal responsibility to obey all the laws, both public and civil.

Everyone enters into contracts. There are many different kinds of contracts, but to be legal and binding a contract must have five essential elements. These are mutual agreement, competent parties, legal purpose, consideration, and legal form. Read and understand every part of a contract before you sign it. If you are confused or uncertain, have a lawyer examine the contract for you.

Criminal law is the type of public law with which people are most familiar. Crimes are divided into two major types—felonies and misdemeanors. If you are arrested, do not discuss your case with anyone except your lawyer. He or she will gather the facts of the case and advise you on the best way to proceed.

Most people will need a lawyer at some time in their lives—to review a contract, represent them in court, collect a debt, solve a tax problem, organize a business, or adopt a child. To find an attorney, ask relatives or friends to suggest someone. If you receive no recommendations, call the state or local legal association or check the Yellow Pages.

In some cases (usually those that involve less than $1,000), you may have to represent yourself. For a small fee, you can file a case in small-claims court. There you can appear without an attorney, present your evidence, and get a decision from a judge immediately.

TERMS TO KNOW

On a separate sheet of paper, write a definition for each of the following terms:

contract
party
competent parties
countersign
consideration
felony
misdemeanors
bail
contingency basis

STUDY QUESTIONS

1. What are the two major types of laws?
2. What is the difference between a formal and an informal contract?
3. When is an informal contract enforceable?
4. What are the five essential elements of a binding contract?
5. Name two groups of people who may not be held to the terms of a contract.
6. A store wants to protect itself against voidable contracts made by minors. How can it do this?
7. Why do many contracts call for one party to pay another party $1?
8. Name five kinds of contracts that must be written to be binding.
9. What are the two major types of crimes?
10. Why is it not a good idea to try to defend yourself in a criminal case?
11. If you need a lawyer, what is the least expensive alternative? the most expensive? Are there any options in between?
12. How does a small-claims court work?

CRITICAL THINKING

1. Work with the class to compile two chalkboard listings—one of public laws, the other of civil laws. For example, a law that says you must have auto insurance before the state will register your car is a public law. A law that allows you to sue someone who prints a lie about you is a civil law.

2. Give some examples of contracts in which the consideration is *not* in the form of money.
3. Explain how bail works and what you think is the reasoning behind it.
4. One of the criticisms of contingency fee arrangements is that too much money intended for, say, an accident victim goes to the victim's lawyer. Do you agree? Explain.

DISCUSSION STARTERS

1. Should minors convicted of murder be exempt from the death penalty? Why or why not? Would the age of the minor in any way change your response? For example, would it be the same if the minor were 9 years old as opposed to 16? Explain.
2. Think about any ads you've seen or heard for lawyers, law firms, or legal clinics. If you suddenly found yourself in need of a lawyer, would you patronize any of these individuals or organizations? Why or why not? What does this say about the effectiveness of advertising by the legal profession?

BUILDING BASIC SKILLS

Math
1. Sammie Smalltime was arrested and jailed. Bail was initially set at $50,000. Sammie couldn't come up with the 10 percent fee he needed to get a bail bondsman to put up the money. As a result, he stayed in jail for a month, until the judge lowered his bail to $15,000. That was an amount he could cope with. How much less did Sammie have to raise for a bail bondsman after the judge lowered his bail?
2. Vivian Victim is awarded $2.5 million in a medical malpractice case (the doctor removed the wrong organ). Victim's contingency fee arrangement calls for her lawyer to get 35 percent of any amount she is awarded by a jury. How much will Victim's attorney get? How much will Victim eventually collect?

Communication
3. Working with a partner, draw up a formal contract for the performance of some simple task—washing someone's car every Saturday for a month, making an article of clothing to order, tutoring a fellow student in math or some other school subject. Include all the elements necessary to make the contract legal and binding. When you have finished, exchange contracts with another pair of students in the class and critique each other's work. Give special attention to any feature or omission that might void the contract.

Problem Solving
4. Assume that you have just been elected governor of your state. You campaigned hard on a law-and-order platform, urging the prosecution, conviction, and jailing of lawbreakers in greater numbers. Now you are told that there isn't enough jail space to hold the people who are currently being convicted. In fact, you'll have to let current inmates out early to make room for the newcomers. Given these realities, how will you keep your campaign pledge? (*Note:* You also promised during your campaign not to raise taxes.)

SUGGESTED ACTIVITIES

1. Read a local newspaper for two weeks. Give special attention to stories dealing with arrests, prosecutions, and trials of individuals. Note the crimes they are being accused of and compile them into two lists—felonies and misdemeanors.
2. Interview a law enforcement officer from your community. Inquire about training and procedures in three areas—making arrests, obtaining search warrants, and testifying in court.
3. Attend a session of the local small-claims court. Report to the class on one case that came before the court. Describe the nature of the case, the evidence presented, and the judge's decision.

Paying Taxes

*Y*ou are going to earn a great deal of money in your lifetime. At the very least, you will probably make close to $1,000,000. There's a very good chance you will make much, much more. Most of the money you earn will be yours to spend as you please—most of it but not all.

What happens to the part of your earnings that isn't yours to spend? The answer is taxes. **Taxes** are the payments people must make to maintain their government and provide government services. Most people pay between 15 and 28 percent of their income in federal taxes. That means that if you make a million dollars in your lifetime, you will pay between $150,000 and $280,000 in federal taxes.

This being the case, you will surely want to know all there is to know about taxes. This chapter will help you learn about your taxpayer responsibilities and how the tax system works.

1 *Understanding Taxes*

All governments must have some kind of tax system. It costs money to run a government, and the tax system is the government's way of obtaining this money.

In our country there are three levels of government—federal, state, and local. Since the government at each level needs money to operate, each government must levy, or require people to pay, taxes. Some of the taxes you pay go to the federal government, other taxes go to the state government, and still others go to your local government.

At the federal level, Congress has the power to levy and collect taxes. Congress was given this power by the Constitution of the United States.

The Constitution also gave Congress the authority it needed to establish the Department of the Treasury. One branch of the Treasury Department is the **Internal Revenue Service,** commonly referred to as the **IRS.** The IRS is the federal agency responsible for collecting taxes. Congress passes the laws that say what kinds of taxes will be levied, who must pay, and how much. The IRS then enforces these laws and collects the taxes. All the tax money collected goes into the U.S. Treasury.

Each state and local government has its own version of the IRS. Although much smaller and less complex, these state and local agencies have authority to levy and collect taxes from their citizens. The money then goes into the state or local treasury.

How Tax Dollars Are Spent

The federal, state, and local governments collect taxes because they need money to maintain the government. It costs money to run any government. It costs a great deal of money to run a government as large as your state government, and even more to maintain the federal government. In 1989, for example, our federal government collected $964.7 billion in taxes. Even with this tremendous amount of money, the government still had much less than it needed to pay all of its bills, as you learned in Chapter 13.

Why do governments need so much money? One part of the answer is salaries for government employees. The president of the United States, the governor of your state, legislators, judges—all of these people are government employees. More than 6 million people, including civilians and military personnel, work for the federal government alone. All of these people must be paid, and the money to pay them must come from taxes.

In addition to the salaries of the government workers, taxes must provide the money to pay the cost of all the facilities and equipment government

The IRS is the federal government's tax collector. You will be a taxpayer (if you are not one already). What role does Congress play in our system of taxation?

workers need to do their jobs. Office buildings must be built, and these buildings must have light, heat, telephones, and all the other necessities. The armed services must spend tremendous amounts of money to buy airplanes, ships, weapons, uniforms, and countless other items. Because it needs so much, the federal government spends millions of dollars just for small, inexpensive items, such as pencils, paper, screwdrivers, and hammers.

What is the result of spending all this money? In exchange for the tax dollars you pay to the federal, state, and local governments, these governments provide you with valuable services. It would be impossible for you to go about your normal routine were it not for the things that governments do for you.

Probably the most important services governments provide are protection and enforcement of the law. The armed services have stationed military personnel all over the world to maintain our national defense. The Federal Bureau of Investigation, the National Guard, your state police, and your local police—all work to make life safe for everyone. Judges, prison guards, and lawyers then work to see that criminals are punished.

Governments also use our tax dollars to build airports, interstate highways, bridges, dams, canals, state roads, city streets, and sidewalks. All of these are needed to help us get from place to place. It takes a great deal of money to pay for the workers and materials needed to build and maintain these facilities from year to year.

Governments spend your tax dollars on education and research, too. Governments pay for the buildings, teachers, and books that make "free" public education possible. Governments also pay to maintain libraries and research centers that promote learning and new technology. A great deal of medical research and all the work that has gone into our exploration of space have been paid for with tax dollars.

You are probably beginning to see what governments do with the tax money they collect. It would be impossible to list all the services either fully or partially provided by governments using your tax money. Just a few more of the many services are listed below.

- Health services (hospitals, community and public health centers, Medicare programs, health inspections)
- Welfare (payments and help for the needy)
- Social services (payments to veterans, legal services, social security, and employment services)
- Protective agencies (environmental and conservation departments)
- Postal services (mail delivery)
- Emergency services (fire department, paramedics)

MAKE A DECISION

Once again you find yourself in the voting booth. This time you're voting on a tax referendum. Voting yes means you are in favor of paying higher property taxes next year so that your community can build a new school. Voting no means you're against paying higher taxes for a new school building. What's your decision—yes or no? Give the reasons for your decision.

Your Tax Responsibility

It is the responsibility of every able citizen to pay his or her fair share of taxes. Since we all share in the benefits of taxes (the protection and services you just read about), it's only fair that we all contribute. Later in this chapter, you will learn about the different types of taxes and how you go about fulfilling your responsibilities.

Although few people would want to give up the services provided by taxes, few people enjoy paying taxes. Some people have a serious problem accepting their responsibility for paying taxes. There are several reasons for this.

Very few people have all the money they need and want. Many people like to keep all of their money for themselves. There is a tendency to say, "Let someone else pay for that. I worked hard for my money, and I don't want to give it away."

People are also reluctant to pay their taxes because they often disagree with the way the government spends their tax money. They feel that it is spent for things that aren't necessary or for things that they personally don't need.

Unmarried men and women without children, for example, may not feel that they should have to pay taxes that pay for public education. Many people feel that it's wrong to spend so much money on space exploration and military weapons when people are hungry and homeless. Other

Taxes are the price we pay for government services. Assume you want to reduce taxes. Which of the government services shown here would you be willing to cut? Explain the reasoning behind your choice.

people feel that it's wrong for the government to take tax dollars from hard-working people and give it to people who don't have jobs, no matter how needy they may be. In other words, people have many different opinions—sometimes very strong opinions—about how tax money should be spent.

There is another reason why people sometimes complain about their taxpayer responsibilities. Some people feel they are paying more than their fair share of the taxes. They think that wealthy people have ways to avoid paying taxes. They also believe that others simply don't pay their taxes and aren't penalized. The idea that those more able to pay are not paying at all makes it difficult for many people to live up to their responsibilities.

There is one answer for all of these complaints—vote. It will be your duty as a taxpayer to vote and express your opinion about how the tax laws should be written and the dollars spent.

Voting is one way to influence tax policy. Think about a recent election in your own state or community. What specific opportunities were voters given to voice their opinions on taxes?

The United States Congress, your state legislature, and your local city council pass the laws and ordinances that determine what taxes you must pay. The legislators and council members who vote on these tax laws are all elected to their positions. It is your responsibility to know each political candidate's opinions and to vote for the candidate who will represent your beliefs. In this way you will have just as much say on how taxes are collected and spent as any other American citizen.

Learning about the candidates and voting for the candidate of your choice does not guarantee that the tax system will be managed in the way you

want. In our system of government, the majority rules. You may not always hold the majority opinion. Fulfilling your responsibility as an informed voter, however, will give you a great deal of satisfaction. You will know that you did your part to see that everyone paid a fair share and that your money is being spent wisely.

A Good Tax System

Governments have tried using all sorts of tax systems to obtain the money they need. Because people feel strongly about how much they must pay and how their money is spent, it has been difficult to develop a system that satisfies everyone.

If you are going to exercise your responsibilities as a taxpayer, you will need to have some basic ideas about what makes a good tax system. Here are some basic principles that people often cite.

- *Fairness.* Almost everyone believes that taxes should be fair and just. Everyone should have to pay his or her fair share. No one who is able to pay should be allowed to avoid this responsibility.
- *Simplicity.* The tax system should not be so complicated that most people can't understand it. This is a criticism many people make of our present system. If you believe the system should be simpler, it's your responsibility to vote for a legislator who believes as you do.
- *Convenience.* Taxes should be levied at a convenient time, when most people are able to pay.
- *Stability.* People need to know how much they will have to pay so that they can plan how to make their payments. This means that the tax laws cannot be changing constantly, demanding payments that people weren't expecting.
- *Flexibility.* At certain times (during a war, for example), governments need more money than during other times. The government should have the ability to adjust the tax system to bring in more or less income, as needed.
- *Minimal payment.* Many people believe taxes should be kept at the absolute minimum. They believe that governments should reduce spending so that they don't need as much money. This sounds good to taxpay-

ers, but the problem is in deciding which government services to reduce or eliminate.

• *Expanded payment.* Many people believe just the opposite of those who would minimize taxes. These people would have everyone pay the maximum amount they can afford so that governments can provide more services and help for the needy. These people believe that a strong, central government can accomplish a great deal for the country as a whole. To accomplish these things, though, the government needs more tax dollars.

Notice that some of these ideas are directly opposed to each other. In these cases, you must decide which principle is more important to you. You can then vote for candidates who will represent your views when it comes time to develop and change the tax laws.

Types of Taxes

There are many different kinds of taxes. You are probably already familiar with some of them. If you bought something at the grocery store or ate in a restaurant this week, you paid some taxes. If you have a part-time job, your employer probably takes some money for taxes out of your paycheck.

You may never have to pay some of the special kinds of taxes. In your lifetime, though, you will pay several different taxes—some to the federal, some to the state, and some to the local governments. In some cases you will make your payments yourself directly to the government. In other cases employers and business people will take your money and then turn it over to the government.

As the tax needs of the government and the ability of the people to pay taxes change, so do the tax laws. This section will explain in general the most common types of taxes. If you need the most

Tax fairness has always been a major feature of the ongoing national debate on government spending. In the late 1970s, for example, people resented the fact that major corporations could use tax loopholes to avoid paying any taxes at all. How is the fairness issue being expressed today?

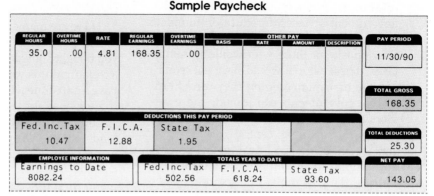

Sample Paycheck

Figure 22-1   Employers make a whole series of paycheck deductions so that you can pay your taxes as you earn rather than all at once. What figure here is most nearly equivalent to disposable income?

current, detailed information, contact the closest IRS or state revenue office.

Income Taxes   An income tax is just what you would expect it to be—a tax on income. The income people receive from all sources is called **personal income.** Among other things, it includes wages, interest on savings, and (if people own shares in a business) profits. Personal income also includes payments, such as social security or unemployment benefits.

Income tax is figured as a percentage of the money you make in a given year. Your employer will deduct money from your paychecks to pay your income tax for you (see Figure 22-1). The money you have left after paying income and other taxes is called **disposable income.**

Personal income tax is by far the federal government's biggest source of income. For example, in 1989 the government collected $964.7 billion in taxes. About $412 billion of that amount, or almost half, came from personal income taxes.

The federal income tax is, for the most part, a progressive tax. A **progressive tax** is one in which the tax rate goes up as taxable income rises. There are currently three tax brackets, or levels, for four income ranges. These are shown in Figure 22-2.

As you can see, the very highest wage earners actually pay a lower rate than those with moderately high earnings. This third bracket, where the rate rises before falling again for those who earn more, has been called the "bubble." The existence of the bubble has led to criticism that our income tax system is not really progressive and therefore not fair. As Congress struggles to reduce the federal deficit, it is likely that the bubble will be eliminated. A single tax rate of between 31 and 33 percent will probably be imposed on all people in these two brackets.

Most states also levy income taxes (see Figure 22-3). About 4,000 cities in the United States have income taxes as well. The rates of these state and local taxes vary, but on the whole they are much lower than federal rates. Like the federal income

Figure 22-2   In 1986 the number of federal income tax brackets was reduced from 16 to the 3 shown here. This was done in the name of tax simplification. What other principle of a good tax system may this change have violated, however?

Individual Tax Rates (1989)

Tax Rate	Taxable Income	
	Single	Married/Filing Jointly
15%	$ 0–$ 18,550	$ 0–$ 30,950
28	18,551– 44,900	30,951– 74,850
33	44,901– 104,330	74,851– 177,720
28	over 104,330	over 177,720

State Income Tax Rates for Individuals

State	Rate	State	Rate
Alabama	From 2% on first $1,000 to 5% on income over $6,000	Mississippi	From 3% on first $3,000 to 5% on income over $10,000
Arizona	From 2% on first $1,229 to 8% on income over $7,374	Missouri	From 1.5% on first $1,000 to 6% on income over $9,000
Arkansas	From 1% on first $2,999 to 7% on income over $25,000	Montana	From 2% on first $1,400 to 11% on income over $50,000
California	From 1% on first $7,636 to 9.3% on income over $50,104	Nebraska	From 2% on first $3,000 to 5.9% on income over $45,000
Colorado	5% of modified federal income tax liability	New Hampshire	5% on dividends and interest
Connecticut	Dividends and interest: from 1% on first $54,000 to 14% on amounts over $100,000. Capital gains: 7% on adjusted amount.	New Jersey	From 2% on first $20,000 to 3.5% on income over $50,000
Delaware	From 3.2% on amounts between $2,000 and $5,000 to 7.7% on income over $40,000	New Mexico	From 2.4% on first $8,000 to 8.5% on income over $65,000
District of Columbia	From 6% on first $10,000 to 9.5% on income over $20,000	New York	From 4% on first $11,000 to 7.87% on income over $26,000
Georgia	From 1% on first $1,000 to 6% on income over $10,000	North Carolina	From 3% on first $2,000 to 7% on income over $10,000
Hawaii	From 2% on first $2,000 to 10% on income over $40,000	North Dakota	From 3.24% on first $3,000 to 14.57% on income over $50,000
Idaho	From 2% on first $999 to 8.2% on income over $20,000	Ohio	From .743% on first $5,000 to 6.9% on income over $100,000
Illinois	3% on taxable net income	Oklahoma	From .2% on first $2,000 to 6% on income over $15,000
Indiana	3.4% on adjusted gross income	Oregon	From 5% on first $2,000 to 9% on income over $5,000
Iowa	From .4% on first $1,000 to 9.98% on income over $45,000	Pennsylvania	2.1% on specific classes of taxable income
Kansas	From 3.65% on first $35,000 to 5.15% on income over that amount	Rhode Island	22.96% of modified federal income tax liability
Kentucky	From 2% on first $3,000 to 6% on income over $8,000	South Carolina	From 2.5% on first $2,000 to 7% of income over $10,000
Louisiana	From 2% on first $10,000 to 6% on income over $50,000	Tennessee	6% on dividends and interest
Maine	From 2% on first $7,999 to 8.5% on income over $32,000	Utah	From 2.6% on first $1,500 to 7.35% on income over $7,500
Maryland	From 2% on first $1,000 to 5% on income over $3,000	Vermont	25% of modified federal income tax liability
Massachusetts	Dividends, interest, and net income from capital gains: 5% on amounts over $8,000	Virginia	From 2% on first $3,000 to 5.75% on income over $16,000
Michigan	4.6% on all taxable income	West Virginia	From 3% on first $10,000 to 6.5% on income over $60,000
Minnesota	From 6% on first $19,000 to 8% on income over $165,000	Wisconsin	From 4.9% on first $10,000 to 6.93% on income over $20,000

Figure 22-3 As of 1989, all states except Alaska, Florida, Nevada, South Dakota, Texas, Washington, and Wyoming levied a state tax on personal income. Shown here are the tax rates for each of the other 43 states and the District of Columbia. In the table, how can you tell a progressive income tax from one that isn't?

tax, state and local income taxes tend to be progressive in form.

Social Security Taxes Social security taxes are federal taxes that people pay while they are working so that they can receive monthly checks after they retire. Like income taxes, social security taxes are based on earnings. Almost every worker in the United States participates in the social security program. (An entire chapter, Chapter 23, is devoted to social security, its many programs, and the tax that finances them.)

Your employer will deduct social security taxes from your paycheck. This deduction is separate from your income tax deduction. Your check stubs may show your social security withholding in a box or space labeled FICA. This abbreviation stands for Federal Insurance Contribution Act.

The FICA deduction is calculated as a percentage of your earnings—7.65 percent as of 1990. The base, or maximum, amount on which the tax is imposed is $50,400. This means that any amount above that figure will not be subject to FICA withholding. For example, if one worker earns $50,400 and another earns $55,000, both would pay the same amount in social security taxes— $3,856 ($50,400 × .0765). Since (like most beginning workers) you will earn much less, you will always have social security taxes withheld from your paychecks.

Many people don't realize that their employer matches their tax contributions to social security. For example, if in one week you earn $100, your employer would deduct $7.65 for social security taxes ($100 × .0765). Your employer would also set aside another $7.65, making the total contribution in your name $15.30. Your employer is responsible for sending this money to the IRS.

Sales Taxes   You are probably more familiar with sales taxes than any of the other kinds of taxes. Sales taxes are paid on goods and services that people buy. Almost every state levies a sales tax. Many local governments also levy sales taxes.

Sales tax is calculated as a percentage of price. For example, if a department store purchase comes to $50 and the sales tax rate in the state is 5 percent, the salesclerk will add $2.50 ($50 × .05) to the bill. This will bring the total to $52.50.

Sales tax rates vary from state to state. Some states charge as little as 3 percent, while others charge 6 percent or more. In most states the rate is 4 or 5 percent (see Figure 22-4).

The rate you are actually charged is usually higher than the state rate. This is because local governments often add 1 or 2 percent to the state rate. If, for example, your state has a 4 percent sales tax and your city adds 1 percent, a store owner will add 5 percent to your bill.

Many states have different sales tax rates for different kinds of goods and services. Food and drug items, for example, may not be taxed at all, or they may be taxed at a lower rate. In some states packaged food (such as you buy in the grocery store) is not taxed, but prepared food (which you get in a restaurant) is.

Property Taxes   Property taxes are taxes levied on the value of property. Property usually means real estate (land and buildings). Business equipment and inventory, and even stocks and bonds, are sometimes considered property. Only people who own property have to pay property tax.

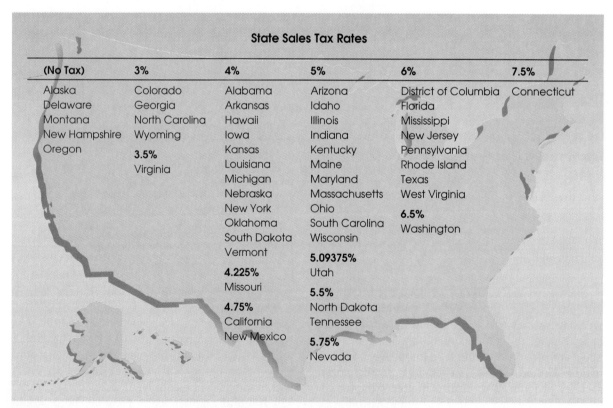

State Sales Tax Rates

(No Tax)	3%	4%	5%	6%	7.5%
Alaska	Colorado	Alabama	Arizona	District of Columbia	Connecticut
Delaware	Georgia	Arkansas	Idaho	Florida	
Montana	North Carolina	Hawaii	Illinois	Mississippi	
New Hampshire	Wyoming	Iowa	Indiana	New Jersey	
Oregon	**3.5%**	Kansas	Kentucky	Pennsylvania	
	Virginia	Louisiana	Maine	Rhode Island	
		Michigan	Maryland	Texas	
		Nebraska	Massachusetts	West Virginia	
		New York	Ohio	**6.5%**	
		Oklahoma	South Carolina	Washington	
		South Dakota	Wisconsin		
		Vermont	**5.09375%**		
		4.225%	Utah		
		Missouri	**5.5%**		
		4.75%	North Dakota		
		California	Tennessee		
		New Mexico	**5.75%**		
			Nevada		

Figure 22-4   The sales tax rates shown here were based on a 1988 report on state taxation. How does your state's sales tax rank with those of other states—high, low, or average?

Like sales taxes, property taxes are levied by state and local governments. In some states the money that funds public schools is primarily property tax money. Property taxes are also used to pay for police and fire departments, street repair, and other state and local services.

If you are like many people, your first encounter with property taxes won't occur until you buy your first house. A tax assessor will assess your home and the land on which it's built. To assess property is to estimate its value. A tax assessor is someone who estimates the value of property for the purpose of levying taxes.

Property tax is often expressed in terms of dollars per hundred or thousand of assessed value. The assessed value, in turn, is given as a percentage of the market value, or the amount for which the property could be sold. Suppose, for example, that the property tax rate in a community is $10 per $1,000 of assessed value. Suppose further that the assessed value is 50 percent of market value. If your home were worth $120,000, here is the way your tax would be figured:

- Find the assessed value.
  $120,000 × .50 = $60,000
- Find the number of thousands in the assessed value.
  $60,000 ÷ $1,000 = 60
- Apply the tax rate to the number of thousands.
  $10 × 60 = $600

The yearly tax bill for this particular homeowner would be $600.

Other Taxes   Most of the taxes you pay in your lifetime will consist of those types you've just read about—income tax, social security tax, sales tax, and property tax. There are a great many other taxes that you may pay at one time or another. Brief explanations of these taxes appear below.

- *Excise tax.* This is a federal or state tax on certain goods and services, such as liquor, tobacco, and gasoline, produced within this country. The manufacturers and distributors of the products pay the tax. Since they usually add the amount of the tax to the selling price, the consumer indirectly pays.
- *Estate (or inheritance) tax.* This is a tax on the value of the money and property a person leaves behind after dying. The federal government and almost all states levy estate

taxes. The tax rate for estate tax is progressive, like the income tax, and ranges from 18 percent up to 50 percent.
- *Gift tax.* This is a tax on gifts to individuals that exceed a certain value. This tax prevents older people from giving all their money to their heirs before they die as a way to avoid estate taxes.
- *Licenses.* The licenses you buy that allow you to do certain things, such as drive a car and go fishing or hunting, are also a form of tax. The money you pay for license plates or license stickers for your car is money the state uses to maintain the state roads and highways.

To most drivers, renewing license plates for a vehicle is just something they must do in order to drive. What is it to government officials?

✓ CHECKING UP

1. What in general terms does government do with all the tax money it collects? Give some specific examples.
2. What does it take for a tax system to be regarded as fair?
3. Name two kinds of taxes that are levied on income. Name two kinds of taxes that are levied on purchases.

2 *Filing Federal Income Tax Returns*

In our country everyone is responsible for figuring and paying his or her own federal income taxes. This is done by filing an income tax return. An income **tax return** is a formal statement of a person's income and taxes. Filing is the process of turning in (usually by mail) the completed return to the IRS.

Unless you live in one of the few states that does not levy an income tax, you will have to file a state income tax return as well. The laws for filing state returns are usually similar to those for filing federal returns. State returns are filed at the same time as the federal returns.

In this section you will be given some general information about filing tax returns. The returns themselves will provide more detailed instructions. You can also get assistance from the IRS office in your area and your state's revenue office.

Should You File?

What determines whether or not you need to file an income tax return? The IRS has very specific guidelines as to who must file a return. Whether or not you are required to file depends on several factors. The most important factor is how much money you earn.

In general, if you earn $4,950 or more in a calendar year (January 1 to December 31), you must file a return. This minimum was in effect in 1989. You should check the figure each year, however, because the IRS does change it from time to time.

Even if you earn less than $4,950, you may still want to file a return. Your employer probably deducted federal and state income taxes from each paycheck. To get this money back, you will have to file.

When Should You File?

If you earn $4,950 in a calendar year, you must file your return no later than April 15 of the following year. For example, if you earned $6,000 in 1990, you would have to file your income tax return for that year on or before April 15 of 1991.

The IRS will penalize you for filing your return after April 15. The penalty is usually a late charge

---

Case Study *1*

It was the evening of April 15. Ron could put off doing his taxes no longer.

He sat down at the kitchen table with his wage and interest statements and his tax booklet. He tore out the 1040EZ, the form he had used last year.

Almost immediately, Ron had a problem. He had received a modest inheritance following his grandmother's death last May. It had boosted his bank account. It also boosted his annual interest $12 beyond the limit for using Form 1040EZ. Ron had to switch to the longer 1040A. Still, it could have been worse. At least the new form was also in his tax booklet.

When he got to the end of the 1040A's income entries, however, Ron realized he had another problem. There was no place to include the $200 he had won in a bowling competition. He checked the instruction booklet again. Because of this "other income," he would have to use a Form 1040. That form was *not* in his tax booklet.

Ron panicked. Then he remembered that tax forms were available at the local library. If he rushed, he could make it before closing time.

The 1040 form was even longer and more complicated than the 1040A. Still, Ron was able to struggle through it (and his state tax form) by 10:45 p.m. He put stamps on both envelopes and headed out the door.

At the corner, Ron checked the pickup schedule for the mailbox and got yet another surprise. The last pickup for the day had been two hours earlier. Ron raced back to his apartment. It was now 11 p.m. He grabbed his car keys and again headed out the door with his tax returns.

Ron was still two blocks from the post office when he got stuck in traffic. It was the crush of last-minute tax filers crawling toward the post office. There postal workers waited at curbside to accept returns for the needed midnight postmark. Ron beat the deadline by 11 minutes—time to spare, the postal employee who accepted his return told him. Ron smiled his agreement, but he promised himself that next year he really would have time to spare.

based on how late your payment is and how much tax you owe the IRS. The IRS will give you more time to file your return in certain cases.

How Do You File?

Filing an income tax return can be a quick and easy process, or a long and difficult one. It depends on how much money you made, how you made your money, and many other factors. When you are just starting out in the world of work, your income tax returns are usually fairly simple to do.

Using Tax Forms   Employers deduct money from their employees' checks on the basis of the employees' W-4 forms. A W-4 is a legal statement allowing an employer to deduct pay from an employee's check. If you have a job now, you filled out and signed a W-4 when you started. The information that you supplied told the employer how much to deduct from your checks.

Each January, employers are required to send each employee a W-2 form (Figure 22-5). A W-2 is a statement of how much money was earned and how much was deducted for taxes during the preceding year. You must have this form to prepare your tax return. If you worked for more than one employer during that year, you should receive a W-2 from each employer. Employers must send a W-2 to every employee, even if the employee worked only one day during the year.

In most cases the IRS will send you an income tax return to fill out. The IRS has three different forms—the 1040EZ, the 1040A, and the 1040. The 1040EZ is the easiest form to fill out. If you can use it, you should.

If you do not receive a form in the mail, you can write or call the nearest IRS office and ask for the form you need. You may also get tax forms at your local library.

How do you know which form to ask for? Before you can decide, you must first know the meanings of three important income tax terms—exemption, dependent, and deduction.

An **exemption** is a set amount of money that is not taxed. The IRS lets you set aside $2,000 (the 1989 figure) for each of several possible exemptions. You are allowed an exemption for yourself. Under certain conditions you are also allowed exemptions for your spouse, blindness, deafness, and each dependent.

A **dependent** is a person who is supported by a taxpayer. If you live at home and your parents pay most of your bills, you are a dependent. Your parents will list you as a dependent on their tax form. Since each dependent qualifies as one exemption, your parents will also be able to subtract $2,000 from their income because you are their dependent.

A **deduction** is a personal expense that can be subtracted from income before figuring tax. The IRS will let you subtract certain expenses, such as

Federal Income Tax Form W-2

Figure 22-5   A W-2 form tells you how much you paid in federal and state income taxes. If your city imposed a local wage tax, where would its withholding be noted on the form?

SITUATION
SOLUTION

Pay Now—or Pay Later?

You just filed your federal income tax return, and you had what you regard as a close call. You came within $80 of having to pay a penalty for not having enough tax withheld from your paychecks.

At first you were stunned and a little angry. You don't feel you earn that much, and you take only the one exemption to which you are entitled on your W-4. You can't imagine cutting back to zero just to make sure you don't underpay.

As nearly as you can figure, your problem is the result of two circumstances. First, the tax law changed. The tax instructions say that you may have to pay a penalty if "the amount you owe the IRS . . . is $500 or more *and* the amount of your federal income tax withheld is less than 90 percent of your total tax." That 90 percent used to be 80 percent.

The second circumstance has to do with how much you save—close to 15 percent of your take-home pay. That mounts up, and no income tax is withheld from the interest it accumulates. That extra money (now about $800 a year) added to your salary without any withholding is pushing up your tax due.

1. You project that your tax withholding at the end of the year will be $4,106 and that you will owe $510. Will you have to pay a penalty?

2. You decide to have extra money withheld from your paychecks. How much? Why did you choose this amount?

3. You opt for an alternative. You decide to "spend down" your savings so that you don't earn quite so much interest. Is this a good strategy? Why or why not?

some medical costs, business expenses, real estate taxes, and interest on home mortgages, from your income. There are far too many deductions to list here. You will need to read your tax form booklet to learn about all the possibilities.

Now that you understand these terms, you can probably determine which tax return you should file. Remember, Form 1040EZ (Figure 22-6) is the easiest to fill out. You can probably file Form 1040EZ if you

- are single,
- do not claim exemptions for age or blindness,
- have no dependents, and
- earned less than $50,000 during the year.

There are some additional requirements for using the 1040EZ, but they will probably not apply to you. Most people can use the 1040EZ, at least in their first few years of filing tax returns.

If you get married and start raising a family, you will need to use Form 1040A or Form 1040. Most people who do not itemize, or list, their deductions, use Form 1040A. The IRS has looked at the deductions claimed by thousands of people to determine a standard deduction. The people who use 1040A are given the standard deduction for people in their filing category.

People who believe they have more deductions than the average use Form 1040 and itemize their deductions. If their deductions add up to more than the standard deduction, they can subtract the higher total. However, these people must be able to prove that they paid each expense listed as a deduction. They must keep receipts, canceled checks, and any other legal records necessary to prove their deduction amounts are correct.

Figuring Your Tax   If you can use Form 1040EZ, figuring your tax is not that difficult. It is essentially a three-step procedure:

- *Step 1—Total your income from all sources.* Include wages, salaries, tips, and bank interest (provided it's under $400).
- *Step 2—Subtract the standard deduction and your personal exemption.* This amount is provided for you on the form, right next to the line where it must be entered. The result is your taxable income.
- *Step 3—Look up the tax on your income in the tax table, and compare it to the amount of your withholding.* If more money has been withheld than you owe, you have a refund coming. If less money has been withheld, you will have to enclose a check or money order with your return.

None of these steps is complicated, especially with the form guiding you. Still, if you are not sure how to go about filing your return, don't worry. There is plenty of help available. There

Simplified Tax Return

Department of the Treasury - Internal Revenue Service

**Form
1040EZ**

**Income Tax Return for
Single Filers With No Dependents** (P) **1990**

**Name &
address**

Use IRS label (see page 9). If you don't have one, please print.

Please print your numbers like this:

| 9 | 8 | 7 | 6 | 5 | 4 | 3 | 2 | 1 | 0 |

L
A
B
E
L

Print your name (first, initial, last)

Carol A. Wallis

Home address (number and street). (If you have a P.O. box, see page 9.)   Apt. no.

201 East Arminta Way

H
E
R
E

City, town or post office, state, and ZIP code. (If you have a foreign address, see page 9.)

Tucson, AZ   85718

Your social security number

| 1 | 2 | 3 | 4 | 5 | 6 | 7 | 8 | 9 |

**Please see instructions on the back. Also, see the
Form 1040EZ booklet.**

Presidential Election Campaign (see page 9)
Do you want $1 to go to this fund?   Note: *Checking "Yes" will not change your tax or reduce your refund.* ▶

Yes No
[✓] [ ]

Dollars   Cents

**Report
your
income**

Attach
Copy B of
Form(s)
W-2 here.
Attach tax
payment on
top of
Form(s) W-2.

*Note: You
must check
Yes or No.*

1   Total wages, salaries, and tips. This should be shown in Box 10
    of your W-2 form(s). (Attach your W-2 form(s).)   **1**

8 , 7 5 5 . 6 0

2   Taxable interest income of $400 or less. If the total is more
    than $400, you cannot use Form 1040EZ.   **2**

6 2 . 1 9

3   Add line 1 and line 2. This is your **adjusted gross income.**   **3**

8 , 8 1 7 . 7 9

4   Can your parents (or someone else) claim you on their return?
    [ ] **Yes.** Do worksheet on back; enter amount from line E here.
    [✓] **No.** Enter 5,300.00. This is the total of your standard
    deduction and personal exemption.   **4**

5 , 3 0 0 . 0 0

5   Subtract line 4 from line 3. If line 4 is larger than line 3,
    enter 0. This is your **taxable income.**   **5**

3 , 5 1 7 . 7 9

**Figure
your
tax**

6   Enter your Federal income tax withheld from Box 9 of your
    W-2 form(s).   **6**

5 4 4 . 6 7

7   **Tax.** Use the amount on **line 5** to find your tax in the tax table
    on pages 14–16 of the booklet. Enter the tax from the table on
    this line.   **7**

5 2 9 . 0 0

**Refund
or
amount
you owe**

8   If line 6 is larger than line 7, subtract line 7 from line 6.
    This is your **refund.**   **8**

1 5 . 6 7

9   If line 7 is larger than line 6, subtract line 6 from line 7. This is the
    amount you owe. Attach your payment for full amount payable to
    "Internal Revenue Service." Write your name, address, social security
    number, daytime phone number, and "1990 Form 1040EZ" on it.   **9**

**Sign
your
return**

Keep a copy
of this form
for your
records.

I have read this return. Under penalties of perjury, I declare
that to the best of my knowledge and belief, the return is true,
correct, and complete.

Your signature   Date

X *Carol A. Wallis*   2-17-91

For IRS Use Only - Please
do not write in boxes below.

For Privacy Act and Paperwork Reduction Act Notice, see page 4 in the booklet.   Form 1040EZ (1990)

Figure 22-6   Study the sample tax return shown here. What evidence
can you find of the three steps involved in figuring your income tax?
What evidence can you find that you're required to have a W-2 in order
to file a return?

Strive for Success

A Taxing Business

Henry Bloch and his brother, Richard, were trying to get out of doing income taxes for their accounting clients. They had begun to tell clients to go somewhere else for that service. One client finally asked, "Where?"

Today the answer to that question for thousands of people is H & R Block (the brothers changed the spelling of the family name to prevent mispronunciation). Thirty-two years ago, however, there were no firms specializing in income tax preparation. That is when the Blochs realized such a service might earn additional income for them and give their accounting business a boost.

They took out an ad for $100 and charged $5 for both the state and federal returns. They even made house calls. They hoped at least to be able to pay for the ad.

Things didn't go quite the way they expected. From the first day there were long lines of people waiting for the service. They became so involved in tax preparation, their accounting clients began to go to other firms. They finally sold that business to concentrate on the new one. To say that their venture was an unqualified success would be an understatement.

Almost from the beginning, the Blochs franchised their idea. Although there were some problems with quality control at first, today almost all offices are run independently. However, Henry Bloch (Richard is now retired) controls the offices thoroughly. Managers operate according to a detailed policies and procedures manual. They are given a plan-ahead calendar that tells them when to rent offices, when to put in the furniture, when to hire their employees, and so forth. They are also given extensive manuals on the H & R Block method of tax preparation.

There are only 2,800 full-time employees at H & R Block. The 40,000 tax preparers are hired only for the four-month season from January to April. The company trains all its preparers in special classes offered each fall. Approximately 100,000 people a year take the training. Most come to learn how to do their own taxes. Those

who score the highest on the final test are offered work in H & R Block offices.

Most of the preparers are housewives and retired people who do not want to work full time. Seventy-five percent of them come back to the company each year. That pleases Bloch. Every year an employee comes back, he or she becomes faster, more accurate, more knowledgeable, and more valuable to the company. Experienced preparers also develop their own following, clients who ask for them year after year. By staying loyal to the preparer, the client stays loyal to H & R Block. They have a return rate of 80 percent.

Part-timers who aspire to greater things can work their way up through the ranks. The company promotes almost exclusively from within. Office managers have virtually all started as tax preparers.

Helping people get through a taxing time of year has been profitable. What started out as Henry and Richard Bloch's moonlighting venture is now a $700 million a year business.

For taxpayers with no dependents and few or no specific deductions, figuring their income tax is relatively simple. Express the procedure in two word equations.

are instructions for every form and additional booklets and instructions for every part of the filing procedure.

Toll-free numbers are listed under the IRS in the telephone book. By calling these numbers you can talk to someone who can answer your questions.

You can also hire an accountant to do your tax return for you. Millions of people do this every year. For a modest fee, you can also hire someone who works for a tax preparation service to do your return for you. You can find these companies listed under Taxes in the Yellow Pages of your telephone book.

MAKE A DECISION

Several friends have told you that for only $35 they had their taxes done for them by an accountant. They say you are silly for doing your own taxes. At first glance, the form does look complicated, but you think that if you take your time you can figure it out—maybe. What's your decision—do your own taxes or have someone else do them for you? Give the reasons for your answer.

Filing by Computer If you expect a large income tax refund, you may want to consider filing your federal return by computer. Returns filed in this manner are given priority for processing.

Presently only authorized tax preparers can file returns electronically. It is more expensive, but it may be worth the extra cost if you need your refund money immediately.

Electronic income tax filing was begun in 1986 on an experimental basis. Its use has increased each year. Many think the system will continue to grow and revolutionize the way income taxes are filed. Much depends on how quickly the IRS can convert to more modern equipment—and on how many taxpayers take advantage of the system.

Electronic filing will reduce the work load of IRS personnel and save time and money. It will also lead in other promising directions. Large companies may eventually be able to use it for all of the filings they must make for each of their employees. Individuals might eventually be able to file their tax returns from personal computers in their own homes.

✓ CHECKING UP

1. What is the deadline for filing federal income tax returns?
2. What is the difference between a W-2 and a W-4? between a 1040A and a 1040?
3. What are the three steps involved in filling out a 1040EZ tax form?

Review Your Learning

CHAPTER SUMMARY

Since all levels of government—federal, state, and local—levy several different types of taxes, you will pay a great deal of money in taxes during your lifetime. Governments need your tax dollars to maintain operations and to provide needed services. National defense, law enforcement, transportation, and social services for individuals are some of the services we've come to expect. People who disagree with the ways in which taxes are collected and spent can voice their opinions by voting for legislators sympathetic to their position.

There are many different kinds of taxes. Income, social security, sales, and property taxes are the major kinds. The federal government and most state governments levy income taxes. Social security taxes are paid by people while they are working so they can receive payments after they retire. Most states levy a sales tax, which is a percentage of what people pay for the goods and services they buy. Local and state governments levy property taxes on the assessed value of property.

Every citizen is responsible for paying his or her own income tax. A federal income tax return showing the amount of tax owed for the previous calendar year must be filed by April 15. During your first years in the world of work, you will probably be able to file Form 1040EZ, which is fairly simple to complete.

TERMS TO KNOW

On a separate sheet of paper, write definitions for each of the following terms:

taxes
Internal Revenue Service (IRS)
personal income
disposable income
progressive tax
income tax return
exemption
dependent
deduction

STUDY QUESTIONS

1. What agency of the federal government is responsible for collecting taxes?
2. List ten services we receive in return for paying taxes.
3. What can you do if you disagree with the way your tax dollars are being spent?
4. List five principles generally thought necessary for a tax system to be a good one.
5. List eight different types of taxes.
6. Why do we have a progressive income tax?
7. Your employer withholds $140 from your paychecks for social security. How much was contributed to the program in your name?
8. On what two items are sales taxes frequently *not* levied?
9. What tax provides most of the money for public education?
10. Why might you file a federal income tax return even if you earned only $1,200 in a given year?
11. What form must you receive from your employer before you can prepare your tax return?
12. What is the simplest federal income tax return to fill out?

CRITICAL THINKING

1. There has been a great deal of discussion lately about imposing limits on the number of terms members of Congress and state legislatures can serve. Assume your Congress-

person takes the following stand: "What do we need term limits for? If you don't like the way I vote on spending and taxes, you already have the only tool you need to get me out of office. It's called a vote." Do you agree or disagree? Explain why.

2. How does the current federal income tax measure up against the standards of a good tax system presented in this chapter? Based on what you've heard on the news and your own personal experiences, is the federal system fair, simple, convenient, etc.?

DISCUSSION STARTERS

1. You have the opportunity to question a Congressional candidate who visits your workplace. What questions would you ask about taxes?

2. Most states have increased their sales tax rates in recent years. What do you think should be the maximum rate in any state? Give the reasons behind your position.

BUILDING BASIC SKILLS

Math

1. Using Figure 22-6 (page 377) as a guide, prepare a tax return for yourself based on the following information: wages—$9,450; interest—$160; and income tax withholding—$656. To find your tax, refer to the portion of the tax table below. Do you owe money, or do you have a refund coming?

If line 5 is at least—	But less than—	Your tax is—
4,200	4,250	634
4,250	4,300	641
4,300	4,350	649
4,350	4,400	656
4,400	4,450	664
4,450	4,500	671
4,500	4,550	679
4,550	4,600	686

2. Assume that the property tax rate in your community is $17.50 per $1,000 of assessed value. If homes are assessed at 60 percent of their market value and your home's market value is $79,000, what will your property taxes be?

Citizenship

3. You know someone who is part of the underground economy. In other words, this individual works for cash, reports no income, and makes no social security contributions. Would you report such a person to the IRS? Why or why not?

Decision Making

4. Your community recently incorporated as a city. Now you must fund your own school system. Which of the taxes listed below would you consider the best funding source? Explain why you think your choice is superior to each of the others.

   • City wage tax
   • Property tax
   • Sales tax

SUGGESTED ACTIVITY

For one week list all the taxes paid by you and your family. Include taxes on all purchases you make—food, clothing, transportation (fuel and/or use of toll bridges or highways), entertainment, and utilities (telephone, gas, electricity, and water). Then answer the following questions:

• What was the total amount paid?
• Do you think this is a fair amount given the services you receive? Explain.
• Do you think you and your family are overtaxed? Would it change your opinion to know that in most European countries a gallon of gasoline that costs you $1–$2 sells for $4–$5, mostly because of much higher excise taxes?

Social Security Services

OBJECTIVES

After studying this chapter and doing the activities, you will be able to:

- explain the basic idea of the social security program;
- list four major social security benefit programs;
- describe the Medicare health insurance program;
- describe unemployment insurance and worker's compensation; and
- explain how changes in financing will help pay social security's growing expenses.

TERMS TO KNOW

work credits
disabled worker
survivor benefits
retirement benefits
Medicare
unemployment
 insurance
worker's compensation

*F*or many years American families of several generations lived to-gether. This allowed younger family members to take care of older family members and healthy members to take care of those who were sick. As America changed from an agricultural to an industrial society, many family members left home to work in the cities. Family and friends were separated. When someone became too old or ill to work, there was no one nearby to help.

The Great Depression of the 1930s made matters worse. Many people came to believe that the government should do something to help the needy. In 1935 Congress passed the Social Security Act. This act outlined a national social security plan that would provide money to those who were temporarily out of work, unable to work, and retired from work.

Today, after almost 60 years, the social security system is supporting millions of people. In this chapter you will learn how the system works and what benefits are available.

1 *How the Social Security Program Works*

In Chapter 5 you learned about having a social security card. You probably already have this card that shows your social security number. If you don't, you should apply now at the social security office in your area.

Your social security number is very important. It helps link you with the social security program. The social security program sets aside funds for people who are retired, disabled, or temporarily unemployed.

The basic idea of the social security program is simple. During their working years, people make social security payments to the government. When they can no longer work, they receive benefits based on these payments, the number of years they have worked, and other factors.

Receiving Your Social Security Number

Receiving your social security number is the first step in becoming part of the social security program. Your social security number is your identification number within the program.

Social security payments are made through your employer. The Social Security Administration uses your social security number to keep track of how much money you pay into the program. They also use this number to keep track of where and how much you work in order to determine your social security benefits. That is why you need a social security number before you apply for a job. In fact, you may need to list this number on your job application.

Your social security number is used for other identification purposes as well. Banks and other financial institutions will use it to report the interest you've earned on savings accounts. The IRS identifies all people by their social security numbers. In this way they avoid confusing two people who have the same name. The military service also uses social security numbers as identification numbers.

When you apply for a social security number, you will receive two cards. Carry one of these cards in your billfold. Place the other one in a safe place, like a safety deposit box at the bank. If you know your number, you can replace a lost card by going to the local social security office. If you change your name (through marriage, for example), ask for a card with your new name but with the same number.

If you ever find out that your number is incorrect on your check stub or on any other form, get in touch with a social security office promptly. Someone there will help you correct that record. It's

Not so long ago, people got their social security cards when they got their first jobs. Now tax laws require that parents filing federal income tax returns list social security numbers for their dependent children aged two or older. How many card holders are shown here?

Social security taxes are usually withheld from paychecks by employers. How much has been withheld from this person's paycheck for social security contributions? How do you know?

important to take care of this so that you are properly credited for your work and your payments. Of course, you will also want to notify your employer.

Making Contributions

As stated earlier, social security payments are made through your employer. You may recall from Chapter 22 that your employer deducts taxes from your paychecks. The taxes deducted under the word *FICA* on your paycheck are your contributions to the social security program. Your employer will pay an equal amount.

If you are self-employed, you pay about twice as much as the employee rate. These payments are made with other taxes which are paid to the government four times a year.

As long as you have earnings covered by the social security law, you will continue to make payments. You will make these payments regardless of your age, even if you are receiving social security benefits.

Nine out of every ten workers participate in the social security program. Chances are you will, too, if you aren't already.

Receiving Benefits

After you have begun to work and are making payments into the social security program, you will become eligible to receive social security benefits under certain conditions. The law that establishes the social security program is very precise about who is eligible for benefits and who is not. This law also clearly states how much in benefits a person may receive.

The amount of a benefit depends primarily on the number of work credits you have. **Work credits** are measurements of how much time you have worked. For each 3 months of work you receive one quarter of credit. Four quarters, or 12 months, represents a full work credit.

Having enough work credit, though, means only that you qualify for minimum benefits. It doesn't determine the full amount of your benefit. This amount will usually depend on your average earnings covered by social security.

The type of benefit involved also affects the amount of benefit. You will learn more about this in the next lesson.

✓ CHECKING UP

1. What is the basic idea of the social security program?
2. Why is it important to have a social security number?
3. Name three factors that determine how much in social security benefits a person is likely to receive.

2 *Types of Benefits*

Chances are that when you think about social security you think mostly about older people and retirement. That's not the whole story, though. Several different kinds of benefits are paid by the social security system. Young people, as well as older people, receive these benefits.

Disability Benefits

One type of social security benefit is paid for disability. Disability is the physical or mental condition that prevents someone from working. A worker who has a disability is called a disabled worker.

Social security laws are very exact about who is and who is not a disabled worker. A **disabled worker** is one who will be (or has been) unable to work because of a mental or physical condition for at least 12 months. Someone who is expected to die as a result of such a condition is also considered to be a disabled worker.

Several factors determine the amount of the benefits a disabled worker receives. Age and work credits are the two most important factors (see Figure 23-1). The type of disability involved can also be a factor. You should contact social security for the most recent disability requirements.

Disability benefits can be very important to workers and their families. These benefits may be the family's only source of income while the wage earner is disabled.

Survivor Benefits

Another very important part of social security is the plan for survivor benefits. **Survivor benefits** are payments made to the family of a worker who has died. These payments can be very important to the family of a parent who has died unexpectedly.

In 1990 more than 10.7 million people received monthly social security checks as the survivors of deceased workers. Included among these people were the unmarried children of many deceased workers and people who became disabled before reaching age 22. Others receiving benefits were widows and widowers, divorced wives, grandchildren, and the parents of deceased workers. Certain guidelines determine the eligibility and the amounts of the benefits received by each person.

Work Credits for Disability

The years of work credit needed for disability checks depends on your age when you become disabled.

- **Before 24**—You need credit for $1\frac{1}{2}$ years of work in the 3-year period ending when your disability starts.

- **24 through 31**—You need credit for having worked half the time between 21 and the time you become disabled.

- **31 and older**—You need the amount of credit shown in the following chart.

Born after 1929, become disabled at age	Years of work credit you need
31 through 42	5
44	$5\frac{1}{2}$
46	6
48	$6\frac{1}{2}$
50	7
52	$7\frac{1}{2}$
53	$7\frac{3}{4}$
54	8
55	$8\frac{1}{4}$
56	$8\frac{1}{2}$
58	9
60	$9\frac{1}{2}$
62 or older	10

Figure 23-1 Disability benefits depend on when a worker becomes disabled and the number of years he or she has worked. Does a 27-year-old who has worked five years have enough work credits for disability benefits? a 46-year-old who has worked the same number of years?

Retirement Benefits

One of the most important features of the Social Security Act is the plan that regulates retirement benefits. **Retirement benefits** are payments made to workers after they retire from their jobs.

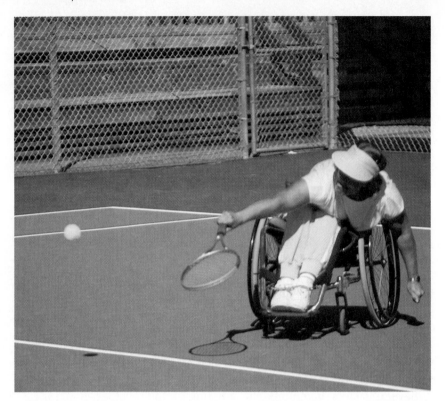

Not all people who are physically disabled would be considered disabled workers. What kind of work could this individual perform despite his being confined to a wheelchair?

To receive full retirement benefits a worker must have worked for a minimum of ten years. The ten years may be worked over a long period of time, and they need not be consecutive. Workers can move from one job to another without losing their work credits.

Case Study *1*

A 29-year-old father of two small children, both under 5, was killed in an accident in 1990. He had maximum earnings covered by social security each year. As a result, his widow and children received almost $1,232 per month in social security checks. This was about $14,784 per year at 1990 benefit rates. By the time the oldest child reaches 18, this family probably will have received at least $200,000. It's likely they will get higher monthly checks in future years. This is because the social security law provides for automatic benefit increases as living costs rise.

Most people do not count on social security alone to take care of all their financial needs. The retirement plan is not set up to provide all the money needed after retirement. Since most people will need another income, they save money during their working years. They may also receive benefits from their employers' retirement plans. Still others may do part-time work to supplement their social security benefits.

There have been changes in the retirement benefits and the eligibility for those benefits in recent years. The age and number of dependents, as well as years worked and average yearly earnings, are part of the formula that calculates the monthly benefit. In the 1990s payments have increased as a result of cost-of-living adjustments. However, it is still difficult, especially for low-income earners, to live on social security payments alone.

The number of work credits needed to retire have increased as well. In 1981 a worker needed 7½ work credits to retire at age 62. Today a worker needs 10 work credits to do the same.

Retiring at 62 has been considered early retirement. This means a worker who chooses to retire then will receive reduced benefits because he or she will be receiving benefits for a longer period of time. A worker who chooses to retire at age 65 will receive full payment.

This, too, is changing. After the year 2000, the age to receive full payments will gradually increase. The retirement age then will be 67. Reduced payments will still be available at a younger age.

SITUATION
SOLUTION

Taking Early Retirement

Your father is almost 62 and is thinking about taking early retirement. He is tired of his job and feels he will be an ineffective worker if he continues. He also feels, however, that the family would benefit from the income if he continued working until age 65. He wants to discuss it with all of you before making a decision.

1. You believe your parents really need the income from his job. What would you say to encourage your father to stick with his job a little longer?

2. Are there other options your father could take? What alternatives would you suggest to him?

3. This situation makes you think about your own situation. What plans would you make for your own retirement?

Case Study **2**

Last March Jo Oliver told her friend Marie, "I've worked for the LaForte Company for 38 years. In June, I'll be 62 years old. I'm going to retire. I don't have any children to help me, but I'll have my company retirement and social security. Even if I had children and grandchildren, I wouldn't want to move in with them."

"I see your point," Marie responded, "but if benefits start before age 65, your checks will be smaller. You'd better find out about that."

At the social security office, Jo was told that Marie was correct. If she retired at 62, her payments would be less. This was because she'd be getting benefits for a longer time. The earlier she retired, the smaller her benefit checks would be.

Jo was given an estimate of the amount of each social security payment. She also found out at the LaForte personnel office how much her retirement checks would be. Jo looked over her expenses for the past year. She realized that after retirement she would spend less on transportation, lunches, and clothing. By saving on these expenses, she was sure she could manage. After all, she would have company retirement, social security, and a small income from money saved over the past 38 years.

Health Insurance Benefits

Many older people living on low incomes can't afford the medical care they need. Private companies do offer medical insurance for older citizens, but this insurance is expensive. Many people can't pay for it.

To solve this problem, in 1965 Congress added a plan for hospital and medical insurance to social security. The insurance program was called **Medicare.**

Medicare was originally planned for people 65 and over. Since then it has been extended to include more people who need assistance. For example, almost all people needing special treatments or kidney transplants are covered by Medicare. Disabled workers under 65 who have received disability payments for 24 consecutive months

may also be covered under Medicare. Providing health care payments for those over 65, however, is still the major function of Medicare.

The Medicare program covers a percentage of a person's hospital expenses. It also pays part of the cost of doctor bills and other medical services.

Unemployment Benefits

Although not part of the social security system, unemployment insurance was created by the Social Security Act and is a type of social insurance. **Unemployment insurance** pays benefits to workers who have lost their jobs. These payments help families get through the difficult times when there is no regular paycheck coming in.

Strive for Success

Champion of the Elderly

"Ageism," he once said, "is as odious as racism and sexism." For all of his public life, Claude Pepper fought against the stereotype of the elderly as "toothless, sexless, humorless, witless, and constipated."

Pepper was born in 1900, the eldest of four children in a poverty-ridden section of Alabama. He was a true son of the South—both his grandfathers had served in the Confederate Army during the Civil War.

Pepper got his B.A. from the University of Alabama. Later, he worked his way through Harvard Law School by waiting on tables. Despite the extra work, when he graduated, he was one of the top six in his class.

Pepper started his career in politics in the state of Florida when he was elected to the state House of Representatives at the beginning of the Great Depression. Almost immediately, he started working to relieve the burdens of the elderly—by championing a bill to waive fishing license fees for those over 65. Pepper also defended the rights of others. When the Florida House of Representatives made a motion to censure Mrs. Herbert Hoover for inviting a black to the White House for tea, Pepper voted against the motion. His colleagues and his constituents were outraged. He was not reelected.

Pepper's political career was far from finished, however. He became Senator Pepper in 1936, a "fighting liberal" as President Franklin Roosevelt called him. Pepper's first speech to the Senate was in defense of Roosevelt's New Deal and its sweeping social reforms. The speech was called "one of the greatest of its kind ever heard in the Senate."

Political views go in and out of fashion, and politicians are known for moving with the current trends. Pepper, however, never changed. As a result, he was the one to go out of fashion. In 1950, he lost his seat in the Senate after a particularly vicious campaign run by his opponent. When a new Congressional district was created in Miami in 1962, however, Pepper was back in Congress, this time serving in the House of Representatives.

As years went on, Pepper became something of a folk hero among older Americans. He was always in the forefront of the battle to raise social security benefits. He spearheaded the movement to end mandatory retirement. He fought for long-term care for the elderly, supported national health insurance and government-sponsored medical research, and helped establish the National Institutes of Health.

In 1977 he became chairman of the House Select Committee on Aging. Although the Committee was short-lived, it helped give more federal aid to the elderly, saw improvements in health and nutrition programs, and sponsored the establishment of the National Institute for Arthritis. "When government lends a hand," Pepper once said, "the possibilities can be limitless."

When asked, Pepper said he planned to retire in the year 2000 but that he might change his mind when the time came. He didn't make it. The Senator who could terrorize his colleagues by mobilizing millions of older citizens died in 1989, at the age of 88.

State governments manage the payment of unemployment insurance. The employers are taxed at a certain rate, creating a fund that is used to make the payments. Although employers pay for the biggest part of unemployment, some states also put money into the fund.

Young workers are more likely than older workers to be unemployed. When factories and businesses are forced to lay off workers, the people with the least seniority are usually the first to lose their jobs. As a young member in the labor force, you should know something about your state's unemployment laws.

Each state has its own regulations about who is and is not qualified to receive unemployment benefits. Some fairly common requirements are listed below. Workers must

- become unemployed through no fault of their own,
- register at a public employment office to get a job,
- be willing to take a job similar to the one lost,
- make claims for benefits, and
- have made a certain amount of money or worked a certain length of time.

If you need to find out whether or not you are entitled to unemployment benefits, go to your local employment office. The address is in the telephone book under the name of your state.

You usually may *not* draw unemployment benefits if you

- are unemployed as a result of a labor dispute,
- quit your job without cause,
- are discharged for misconduct,
- refuse to apply for or take a suitable job,
- misrepresent facts or make fraudulent claims, or
- are discharged after conviction of theft.

The amount of earnings and the length of employment are used to calculate the amount of benefits you may receive. The formula used varies from state to state. Generally the benefits received are equal to one-half your weekly salary. In a number of states, your benefits are based on your earnings during a prior 12-month period. Unemployed workers cannot receive benefits indefinitely. In many states, 39 weeks is the maximum length of time for receiving benefits.

Worker's Compensation

Another social insurance program is known as worker's compensation. **Worker's compensation** is an insurance program that makes payments to workers injured on the job and to the survivors of these workers. Worker's compensation pays medical bills, pensions, and other benefits. In addition to paying for injuries, some job-related diseases, such as black lung disease, also qualify workers for payments.

As with unemployment insurance, worker's compensation programs are administered by the states. Every state has its own program. The laws governing worker's compensation vary considerably from one state to another. There are also some federal compensation programs.

Employers pay into the funds that are used to make payments in worker's compensation programs. Employers are taxed at a given rate, depending on the requirements of state law.

If you are injured on the job, report the injury to your employer or supervisor immediately. This is necessary for your physical well-being and required if you are going to make a worker's compensation claim.

✓ CHECKING UP

1. Name four major social security benefit programs.
2. What is Medicare?
3. Describe the two social insurance programs that are not part of social security.

3 The Future of Social Security

The social security program has been changed several times since it first began in 1935. Each time more workers have been included in the program. Also, population studies show that many people are living longer. This means that more people qualify for benefits and that people receive benefits for a longer period of time. The percentage of pay that goes toward social security contributions has increased, but cost-of-living adjustments have meant higher payments for those receiving benefits. The question is often asked, "Who will pay for social security as it continues to grow and becomes more expensive?"

Federal legislators have made several changes in the way social security is funded in order to keep up with its increasing expenses. Over the years, workers have been paying a higher percentage of social security taxes on more of their earnings.

In 1978 the FICA tax rate was 6.05 percent. This meant that workers paid 6.05 percent of their earnings into the social security program. In 1985 the rate increased to 7.05 percent. In 1990 it rose to 7.65 percent. The tax rate for the self-employed was raised from 13.02 percent in 1989 to 15.30 in 1990. These rates will continue to rise as cost-of-living adjustments are made for inflation.

Today's elderly are healthier and wealthier than ever. In recognition of this fact, do you think their social security benefits should be frozen or even taxed? Why or why not?

MAKE A DECISION

You have recently graduated from high school and have gone into business for yourself. Your local bank gave you a loan to buy a truck, and you are now pulling trailers loaded with fruit for a local company. The social security tax for a self-employed worker is 15.3 percent. The tax makes it very difficult for you. One member of the U.S. Senate wants to reduce the FICA rate for self-employed workers. The lower rates may result in lower benefits for disabled and retired workers. What's your decision—will you write the senator in support of lowering the FICA tax rate, or will you write the senator to leave the FICA tax rate as it is? Give the reasons for your decision.

The wage base for social security payments has also risen. This base is the maximum amount of earnings on which social security taxes are paid. In 1978 the wage base was $17,700. In 1985 it was $39,600; in 1989, $48,000; and in 1990, $50,400.

Changes have also been made in the way benefits are paid for Medicare. Before 1983, hospitals were paid based on the reasonable cost of patient care. Medicare payments were more flexible. Since 1983, however, benefits have been paid based on predetermined, or fixed, rates—a certain amount for a certain treatment. This has controlled the amount spent on Medicare.

✓ CHECKING UP

1. Why has social security become more expensive?
2. Have FICA tax rates been increasing or decreasing?
3. What three changes have been made to help pay for social security's growing expenses?

Review Your Learning

CHAPTER SUMMARY

Congress passed the Social Security Act in 1935. This act established a plan of social insurance that provides money to certain workers or their survivors through disability benefits, survivor benefits, and retirement benefits. The social security program also helps elderly people and others pay medical expenses through Medicare. Other social insurance programs such as unemployment benefits and worker's compensation provide additional assistance to workers.

Before you begin working, your social security number links you to the social security system. You will need this number even to apply for a job.

While you are working, you will pay a percentage of your earnings to the social security system. Your employer will pay an equal amount to be reserved for you when you retire or if you become disabled. If you should die, your family will receive monthly benefits. Your work credits, average earnings, and the type of benefit involved affect the amount of benefit for which you are entitled.

The social security program has changed many times in order to continue to pay benefits. The FICA tax rate has increased, the wage base has increased, and Medicare payments are now preset. Because social security has been changing, you will need to contact the Social Security Administration to get the most recent information.

TERMS TO KNOW

On a separate sheet of paper, write one or two paragraphs that describe the social security program. Use each of the terms below:

work credits
disabled worker
survivor benefits
retirement benefits
Medicare
unemployment insurance
worker's compensation

STUDY QUESTIONS

1. Why was social security needed less by people who lived many years ago than by people today?
2. What other organizations use social security numbers as identification numbers?
3. How do workers make contributions to the social security program?
4. What factors affect disability benefits?
5. How can social security help a child whose deceased parent was part of the social security program?
6. Until the year 2000, at what age can a person retire with full benefits? After the year 2000, how will this change?
7. Name two groups of people who are eligible for Medicare payments.
8. List five conditions under which workers usually cannot draw unemployment benefits.
9. What two things have been changed to increase the amount of money being paid into the social security program? Describe the nature of the changes that have been made.

CRITICAL THINKING

1. Three months ago you began working at the Stereo Lab. You are paid twice a month. You noticed on your last paycheck they have printed your social security number incorrectly. You look over all of your pay stubs since you began working and discover they have all been printed incorrectly. How do you correct this problem? Why is it important that you correct it?

2. You have been unable to work at your job as a cashier since you hurt your wrist two months ago helping a customer lift a 20-pound turkey. Which benefit(s) would you apply for? Defend your choice(s).
3. Describe how the combination of an increase in the wage base and an increase in the FICA tax rate can affect the funding of social security.

DISCUSSION STARTERS

1. If there were no social security program, how would people prepare for retirement?
2. What would be the advantages and disadvantages of making the social security program voluntary?
3. Since social security payments provide only part of the money needed for retirement, what other retirement plans should most families have?
4. Some social security recipients receive more in benefits than they ever contributed to the program. Is this fair to other recipients? Why or why not?

BUILDING BASIC SKILLS

Math

1. You are a self-employed contractor and made $60,000 last year. Using 1990 FICA tax rates, how much should you pay into social security for the year?

Communication

2. You want to check on your social security contributions and plan to call the social security office. Write out what you plan to ask about the contributions you have made. Remember, you will need your social security number and work record when asking for information.

Citizenship

3. On your way home from school you find a brown envelope on the street. Inside is what looks like a social security check. However, the payee's name and address are unreadable because the envelope has been run over many times. What would you do with the check and why?

SUGGESTED ACTIVITIES

1. Write a short report on the social insurance programs of another country.
2. Visit or contact the social security office nearest you to request literature about the social security program. Select one of the brochures most interesting to you. Prepare a two minute summary of your findings and present it to the class.
3. If you do not have a social security card, go to your local social security office and apply for one.

Your Changing Role

OBJECTIVES
After studying this chapter and doing the activities, you will be able to:

- estimate the expenses involved in moving;
- create a checklist to compare new places to live;
- discuss the causes and effects of stress;
- list ways to cope with stress; and
- find out how to register to vote in your area.

TERMS TO KNOW
security deposit
utilities
tenant
lease
subletting
stress

*W*hen you get a full-time job and start earning your own money, you will become more and more responsible for your own actions. Many young people look forward to this exciting time of independence and freedom. Others are very much afraid of the new responsibilities. These young people have doubts about their ability to handle the problems they will need to face.

No book can tell you how to make the countless decisions you must make from day to day. You must live your life as you choose. This chapter, however, will acquaint you with some of the responsibilities you will be facing soon. In this way you can be better prepared for the decisions you will be making soon. Living on your own, coping with stress, and being a good citizen are just some of these new responsibilities. Knowing what may lie ahead is the first step in dealing with your changing role.

1 *Your Own Home*

Almost everyone eventually moves away from their childhood home to start a life of their own. Some people leave home even before they finish high school, while others may not move out until they are in their late twenties or early thirties. Sooner or later, however, most of us do set out on our own.

When you get your first full-time job, you may have the choice of staying at home or moving into your own place. If this is the case, you might want to consider the advantages of living at home, at least for a short period of time while you are working. For example, it is less expensive to live at home than to rent or buy your own place. You could probably save more money if you lived at home. Also, you might find living by yourself lonely at times if you are used to the companionship of brothers, sisters, and parents. Another advantage might be the help with household chores from family members. After a hard day at work, doing the cooking, cleaning, or laundry can be difficult.

The main advantage of living on your own is the opportunity to be in charge of your own life. You will have the freedom and the responsibility to make your own choices.

Moving out on your own is a change in your life that you shouldn't take lightly. You must consider what is most important to you and make your decision accordingly.

Planning Your Move

Before you begin looking for a place of your own, you must answer many questions. Where will you live? How much can you afford to pay? In what type of place—apartment, house, or mobile home—will you be most comfortable? What furniture will you need? Will you live alone, or would you prefer a roommate?

The most important issue is how much you can afford to spend to live on your own. There are many expenses you may not have considered that are connected with moving.

Once you have determined what you can afford, you must look at how you want to live. This leads directly to another important issue—whether or not to live by yourself. We will look at these issues in this section.

New Expenses   There are many expenses associated with moving and living on your own of which you may not be aware. The most obvious expense is, of course, rent.

Houses, apartments, mobile homes, and condominiums are available in a wide range of prices. To determine how much you can afford, you will need to figure out how much of your income you want to spend for rent (or a house payment if you decide to buy). Many experts recommend that the cost of your housing be no more than about 25 percent of your monthly gross income.

You will also have several initial expenses when you move into your own place. For example, you'll

There are advantages and disadvantages to living on your own. Where laundry is concerned, what might be the advantages? the disadvantages?

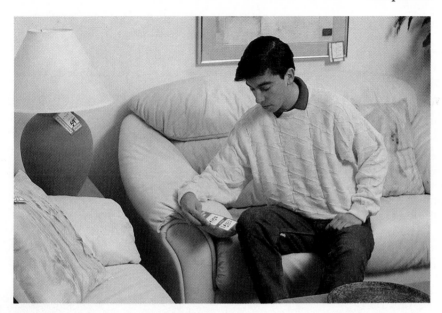

Living on your own means taking care of your own needs. Some of those needs can be very expensive. Could you afford to buy all the furniture you will need? How could you keep these costs down and still live comfortably?

probably have to pay one or two months' rent in advance as a security deposit. A **security deposit** is money that a landlord holds as a guarantee against damages. If you don't do any damage, you get the money back when you move out.

You will also have to pay hook-up charges for utilities. **Utilities** are services such as electricity, gas, and water. In addition to the necessary utilities, you will probably want telephone and, perhaps, cable television service. Not only must you budget for the initial hook-up charges, but you must also be sure you can afford the monthly payments for these utilities. Sometimes rent will include certain utilities.

Some other expenses you must plan for are housewares, such as sheets, towels, pots and pans, dishes, glasses, and silverware. There will also be all sorts of inexpensive things—can openers, cooking utensils, shower curtains, wastebaskets—that can add up. You may need to do your laundry at a laundromat, which can cost $2 to wash and dry each load of laundry. New furniture can be very expensive. (Even used furniture can cost a great deal of money.) In addition, you may want to consider buying renter's insurance.

The most important thing you can do is plan. Go back to Chapter 17 and follow the guidelines there for budgeting your money. Talk to your parents or friends who are on their own to make sure you are considering every expense.

You must know what you can afford *before* you move out. Three or four months after you've

bought furniture and paid utility hook-up costs is not the time to find out you can't afford to pay your rent.

Roommates   There are many reasons to live with a roommate. The principal one, however, is economic—it's cheaper to share. Utility expenses, rent, and food costs can be cut in half if you have a roommate. Thousands of people all across the country share apartments and houses with friends and acquaintances so that they can live in places they could not otherwise afford.

Another advantage to having a roommate is companionship. Also, many people feel more comfortable and secure if they don't live alone. Be careful, however, not to assume your roommate will be your best friend and constant companion. That can add complications to a roommate situation.

While many roommate experiences go well, many friendships have ended because of conflicts that arise between roommates. Before you take an apartment with a friend, ask yourself the following questions:

- Will a roommate prevent me from doing the things I want to do?
- How will I get along with this person? Will I want to spend a good deal of time with this person? Will this person interfere with my activities with other people?
- Will this person be willing to share the expenses?

- Will this person be willing to share household chores?
- What will happen if we can't get along or my roommate loses his or her job and has to move out? Will I be able to afford all the expenses until I get another roommate?

You must answer these questions before you decide to share an apartment. Whether or not your roommate experience is pleasant and satisfying depends on how you choose your roommate.

Another word of caution—be careful about whom you choose for a roommate, especially if you don't know the person well. Don't feel embarrassed about asking questions. You can save yourself much uneasiness if you know for sure that the person's life-style matches your own.

MAKE A DECISION

You've found an apartment that is perfect, but the rent is too much for one person. You know someone who is looking for a roommate, but you think this person might be hard to get along with. You'd really rather live alone, but to do that you would have to take a place not nearly as nice as the one you want. What's your decision—nice apartment with a roommate or a less-than-nice apartment and living alone? Give the reasons for your decision.

Finding the Best Place

After analyzing your financial situation and making a decision about a roommate, you are ready to begin looking for a place to live. This is a consumer activity much like any other. You will want to follow all the suggestions you learned in Chapter 16 for wise, responsible buying.

Where do you begin looking? Probably the best place to start is by asking family members, friends, and co-workers. One of these people might have a place to rent or know of a place that is especially nice for the money.

The most common way to find a place is to read the rentals section of the classified ads in your local newspapers. These ads are frequently divided into two groups—furnished and unfurnished. Look at Figure 24-1. This will give a good idea of the way apartments are listed in a newspaper.

Case Study 1

Joanne and Anna were friends all through high school. They graduated a year ago and started working full time. They lived at home for nearly a year and then decided to rent an apartment together. Neither could afford to live alone, but together they thought they could pay expenses and have money left over.

Joanne and Anna looked at apartments for several weeks and finally decided on an unfurnished one. The rent was much less than that for furnished apartments. Joanne agreed to buy some used furniture, and Anna paid a bigger share of the rent. By the third month in their apartment, Joanne had furnished the place beautifully.

A week later, Anna took a job in another city and moved. Joanne couldn't afford to pay the rent herself, so she moved back with her family. She stored her furniture in her grandparents' attic. She's still making payments on some of the items.

Unless you have already made a decision about wanting either a furnished or unfurnished apartment, you may want to compare the values. If the rent is quite a bit less for unfurnished apartments, buying some furniture may save you money. Think about what furniture you will need. Perhaps your family or a close friend can lend you some of the pieces you need. In many cases a refrigerator and a stove are included even with unfurnished apartments.

If you have no luck finding a place you can afford through the classifieds, check the Yellow Pages of the telephone book. There you will find listings for real-estate agencies. These agencies may have places to rent that aren't advertised. A real-estate agency often charges a fee for renting a place. Find out who—you or the owner—must pay the fee.

In most cases you will find several possible places listed in the newspaper. When you start looking at these places, you may find yourself becoming confused, forgetting which place had which features. They will all start to run together in your mind after you have looked at several.

JACKSON PARK
2BR/1BA. $335-$365. 306-8196

JEFFERSON AREA   1BR/1BA DPLX, 2 prvt entrance. Utils paid by owner. 217-4399

KENMONT   1BR. On busline, quiet. $250 + deposit. 789-4401 after 5 p.m.

KENMONT   5 min from SU. 2BR, dishwasher, storage. Top shape. $385/mo. 785-9843

KENMONT   2BR-$385, 1BR-$295. 789-3229

LINNETT   Hampton Ridge. 1 BRs from $399, 2 BRs from $459. 448-7321

LINNETT   Large 2BR/1&2BA. Move-in bonus. From $440. 448-7804

MAJOR POINTE   2BR/2BA. Special savings, 2 floorplans. 415-0110

NIGHLAND   Ponce de Leon area. 1BR/1BA, full kit., terrace. Electricity, water paid. $360. 584-6374

PEACHTREE INDUSTRIAL
1BR/1BA, spacious, W/D furn. Ask about our special move-in bonus! 417-9882

ROSWELL   2BR/2BA. Some utils pd. $550. 692-8114, lv. mesg.

ROSWELL   Furn'd rm. Share laundry, kit, LR, & utils. $70/wk + $70 deposit.   Call 687-8912 eves.

ROSWELL   2BR/2BA, new bldg. $495/mo w/washer-dryer, $450/mo w/o washer-dryer. Special discount on 1st mo. 299-9979

ROSWELL   Nr Northridge.   2BR/2½ BA twnhse, LR w/fplc, DR, storage plus. $500/mo + utils. 299-6547

ROSWELL   2BR/2½ BA luxury apt. W/D included, grnhse. 397-0048

SANDY SPRINGS   Exclusive area off of Columns Dr. 2BR apartment. Call 889-7504

SANDY SPRINGS
4BR/2BA. $750/mo. 721-3641

TENNESAW   1,2,&3BR apts. Corporate & furnished, W/D included. 404-8115

TOLIVER-STUDIO or 1BR, new 1 story bldg. Fully furn'd, kids/pets ok. $119/wk. 904-7781

URBANA   1BR/1BA. Bright, new, completely furn'd. All utils paid. $500/mo. 355-6417

VERBENA PARK   1BR CONDO for rent by owner at Petri Twrs. Furn'd, great view. All utils paid. $650/mo. 313-5568.

VERBENA PARK   2BR/1BA. Furn'd, prvt, conven. $450. 313-9876

ZOLAR 1BR/1BA, new units. Nicely furn'd. Utils paid, 6 mo. lease. Now accepting applications. 317-6223

Figure 24–1   This is a section from the classified ads of a local newspaper. Notice all the different abbreviations used to describe apartments. What do you think each of the following stands for: 2BR/2BA, LR w/fplc, and W/D furn?

Using a checklist to compare specific features will help you decide which place you like best. You can rate each place according to the points on your list. The following features are ones you will probably want to look at.

Inside Areas   You will spend a great deal of time in the place you choose. Be sure you would feel comfortable there. Think about what it would be like to live in each place. Consider the following points.

- *Condition of hall and steps.* Are the halls and steps in good condition? Will you be able to safely use them even when your arms are loaded with groceries? Does it look as though someone cleans regularly?
- *Fire escape.* Are there at least two ways to get out of the building?
- *Cleanliness.* Will you have to do a great deal of cleaning before you move in? Does it look as though the present or former occupants took care of the apartment?

- *Room arrangement.* Do you like the floor plan? If you have a roommate, will your sleeping arrangements give each of you enough privacy?
- *Storage.* Will there be enough room to store everything? How many closets are there? Is there enough cabinet space in the kitchen?
- *Condition of kitchen fixtures.* Do all furnished appliances work? Do cabinet doors and drawers work smoothly?
- *Condition of bathroom fixtures.* Is there a shower, a bath, or both? Does all of the plumbing work properly? Was there plenty of pressure and hot water when you tried the faucets?
- *Condition of windows, screens, and locks.* Is there any broken glass? Do the windows close easily? Do they lock? Do they look as if they would be tight in the winter? Are there screens for the summer? Are there any holes in them?

The appearance of the public areas of an apartment building can say many things about the building, the people who live there, and the neighborhood. What does this lobby tell you?

- *Condition of doors.* How many and what kinds of locks are on the doors?

- *Laundry facilities.* If there are machines, do they work? Are they located conveniently, or will you have to go to a laundromat?

Outside Areas   Many people look only at the inside of an apartment and forget to check the outside. Take time to look around the outside of the building. Drive around the neighborhood to get a feel for what it's like. Compare the outside areas of the apartments on the following points.

- *Location and neighborhood.* Do you like the area? Would you feel comfortable living there? Is there enough privacy? What is the condition of the surrounding buildings?

- *Grounds around the building.* Is there a yard? Will you need to mow the grass? Are the grounds free of litter and trash?

- *Exterior quality of the building.* Is the building in good condition? Will you have to get the owner to make repairs?

- *Noise and air pollution.* Is there a great deal of traffic noise? Is the air clean? Do there seem to be many animals in the area?

- *Parking facilities.* If you have a car, where can you park it? Will this cost extra?

- *Locked mailbox.* A locked box provides safety. Will you have one available?

- *Safety precautions.* Is the outside area safe to walk through, even at night?

- *Transportation.* If you don't have a car, you'll probably need public transportation. How close is the nearest bus stop or train, trolley, or subway station?

- *Recreation.* What sort of recreational facilities are available nearby? Does the apartment complex have a pool, tennis court, or recreation room?

Rental Terms   You will find that landlords use a wide variety of charging procedures for their apartments. Some include utilities in the rent; some don't. Some require a deposit and lease; some don't. To get the most economical apartment, you must carefully compare the various terms.

- *Rent and due date.* Consider the amount you must pay for what you are getting. Is the place worth this amount? When is the rent due? It may be convenient if it is due a few days after you get paid.

- *Security deposit.* How much is the security deposit? Does the owner have an inventory of all items in the apartment and their condition (Figure 24-2)? How soon do you get your money back if nothing is damaged?

- *Availability.* When will the apartment be available? To avoid having empty apartments, landlords advertise vacancies before the apartments are actually vacant. Make sure you know when you can move in.

- *Utility charges.* Sometimes the owner will pay for such utilities as water, garbage collection, heating, and lighting. Because landlords do this in so many different ways, you must be very careful in your comparisons. A $400 unit with utilities paid may be less expensive than a $300 unit without.
- *Painting and repairs.* These are usually taken care of by the owner. Sometimes the owner will charge less rent if you agree to do some painting or repair work.
- *Pets.* Are you allowed to have pets? Some landlords allow pets, others don't. Make sure the landlord knows you will want to

have a pet if that is the case. If there is no written agreement, the owner may forget he or she gave permission for pets.

Working with a Landlord

When you are looking for a place to rent, you may have to sell yourself as if you were applying for a job. This is especially true if you want to live in some of the more desirable places. The landlord or apartment manager may have certain expectations of a tenant. (A **tenant** is a person who rents an apartment or house.) They may desire renters with no children or people from a given occupational group. When looking for an apartment, it is a good practice to dress as if you were interviewing for a job.

Apartment Inspection Checklist					
Area	**Condition**	**Area**	**Condition**	**Area**	**Condition**
Entrance		**Kitchen**		**Bedroom**	
Door		Doors		Doors	
Light		Walls		Walls	
Doorbell		Windows		Windows	
Living Room		Ceiling		Floor/carpet	
Doors		Floor		Light fixtures	
Walls		Cabinets		Closet	
Windows		Counter		Furnishings	
Ceiling		Stove			
Floor/carpet		Oven			
Light fixtures		Refrigerator			
Closet		Furnishings			
Furnishings				**Heating/Air Cond.**	
		Bathroom		**Other**	
		Doors			
		Wall/tile			
		Medicine chest			
		Tub and shower			
		Sink			
		Toilet			

_____ Date   Owner/Manager _____

Figure 24-2 An apartment manager will often furnish an inspection checklist like the one shown here, which you will both sign. If you are not given such a list, you should prepare one of your own. Why is this a good idea?

This new tenant wants to establish a good working relationship with the apartment manager, who represents the landlord. Do you think he's succeeding? Why do you think the effort is important?

However, don't let a landlord intimidate you. Remember, he or she has something to sell, and you may be interested in buying. Also, don't let a landlord discriminate against you for illegal reasons, such as race or religious beliefs. Prospective renters do have rights.

Most landlords will want to learn about your ability to pay the rent and your credit record. You will be asked to complete an application form. Be sure the information you give is accurate and complete.

When you find the house or apartment you'd like to rent, you will need to work with the landlord to achieve mutual respect and understanding. You probably will be asked to sign a lease. Also, you should know your rights and responsibilities—and your landlord's.

Leases   A **lease,** also known as a rental agreement, is a contract between a landlord and a renter that states the responsibilities of both parties. Most leases are binding for one year, although you may be able to negotiate the length of the lease. Some landlords require a lease, others do not. Once you

sign a lease you are obligated to pay the rent for the specified time whether you live in the apartment or not. If you're not sure how long you will need the apartment, a more expensive apartment that doesn't require a lease may be more economical than a less expensive one that does.

As you learned in Chapter 21, you should not sign any contract until you have read it. You should make sure you understand all the terms of the lease. The lease should address the following issues:

- What is the length of time for the lease?
- Can the landlord raise the rent during the period of the lease?
- Is there a late fee if the rent is late? When is the rent considered late?
- How much notice must be given before moving?
- How much is the security deposit? Under what conditions will it be returned? When will it be returned?
- Under what conditions may the owner enter during the tenant's absence?
- May the apartment be sublet and, if so, under what conditions? **Subletting** is the process whereby the original renter rents the apartment to a second renter, usually with the landlord's approval. If you think you may want to move before the lease is over, whether or not you are allowed to sublet the apartment is an important question.
- Under what conditions may the landlord evict the tenant (force the tenant to move out)? Most states have laws regarding the conditions and procedures for eviction.

When signing a lease, take your time reading it, and don't be pressured into signing something you're not sure of. You and the landlord need to understand each other fully.

Tenant's Rights and Responsibilities   As a tenant, you will have rights and responsibilities. When you rent an apartment or other dwelling, you can expect it to be reasonably clean and safe. You can also expect the landlord to perform maintenance and repairs within a reasonable amount of time. For example, if your heater stops working in the middle of a very cold night, you can expect the landlord to have it fixed the next day.

As a tenant, you are expected to take care of the apartment as if it were your own personal property. Any damage other than usual wear is your responsibility to pay for. You are also responsible for paying the rent on time and following the agreement stated in the lease.

Landlord's Rights and Responsibilities
The landlord also has certain rights and responsibilities. The landlord may make certain changes in and around the apartment that were not otherwise mentioned in the lease. This may include the assignment of parking spaces or the scheduling of apartment complex sports activities, such as the use of tennis courts, swimming pool, and game room. The landlord must keep the property in good condition and provide a private, quiet, and safe environment.

SITUATION
SOLUTION

More than Usual Wear?

Your company has been renting space in a small office building for three years. Now business is expanding, and you've decided to move to larger quarters in a better part of town. You've given the building's owner 30 days' notice, as specified in your lease.

On moving day the owner informs you that your deposit will not be returned because the carpets are stained and the walls have holes where your people have hung pictures, bulletin boards, and other items. You consider the holes usual wear, and the carpet was stained when you moved in.

1. The manager offers to give back your deposit if you fill the holes, paint the walls, and have the carpet cleaned. Would you agree? Why or why not?

2. You offer to fill the holes but no more. What documentation might you have to show that painting the walls is not your responsibility and that the carpet was stained before you moved in?

3. What would you say in a letter to the manager threatening to go to small-claims court?

Organizing Your Living Space

Many people find it is easier to move if they organize their new living space in advance. Where will you put the couch? Which bedroom will be

yours? Where will you store certain things? These are questions many people like to answer before they move into a new home.

One way to do this is by drawing the floor plan to scale on graph paper. The scale may be one foot of floor space equals one inch of graph paper. By measuring your furniture, you can figure out where most pieces will fit. It's easier to make changes on paper than to rearrange a room full of furniture.

When planning your new home, keep in mind how different areas will be used. For example, you will probably need a quiet, well-lit place to study, pay bills, write letters, and so on. Some people might put this area in the living room. However, others might prefer using a corner of their bedroom for more privacy. If you're lucky, you might have an entire room for such a purpose. In any case, keeping these things in mind before setting up the furniture will decrease the chances of having to move it later.

In many apartments storage can be a problem. This may be something else to plan before you move. If you think creatively, you may have more room for storage than you think. Chests, trunks, baskets, and boxes can store many items and still be attractive. Discount and department stores also sell a wide variety of storage items, such as boxes designed to fit under your bed and wrapped-wire shelves that hang inside a door. Look into these methods of storage.

You may also want to plan a decorating scheme before you move. Depending on the kind of place you choose to live, your new home may or may not be furnished with carpeting, drapes or blinds, and kitchen appliances of a certain color. You may be allowed to paint or wallpaper walls, and you may choose to paint your furniture. You may have the talent to sew or build pieces that will make your new home more comfortable. There are many books and magazines with decorating ideas. Look through them, get an idea of what you like best, find out what you are allowed to do to your new place, and decorate accordingly.

Moving

If you make your decisions and plan carefully, the day will finally come when you are to move into your own place. As with everything else, moving will go much easier if you plan it carefully.

The young woman has rented an apartment in an older building. The kitchen has very little storage space. What could she do to make more available?

A poorly planned move can result in wasted time, damaged furniture, and a poor start to independent living.

In most cases the best method for moving depends on how much furniture you have. It will also depend on how far you will be moving and how much you can afford to spend.

If you will be moving large, heavy furniture to a second-floor apartment, you may want to hire a professional mover. This is the most expensive option. If you will be moving only dishes, bedding, clothing, and small furnishings, you can probably handle the move yourself. The in-between alternative is to rent a van or truck and ask your friends to help.

If you decide you need a professional mover to move your furniture, you'll need to sign a contract. The contract should detail the exact charge and the mover's responsibility for damage. You will save money by packing dishes and clothing yourself since the mover will charge extra for packing.

There are several things you should take care of before you move. If your new place needs cleaning,

do it before you move in. You will be able to do a much better and faster job of cleaning while the apartment is empty.

You will also want to make sure that your utilities are hooked up before you move in. Call the gas, electric, water, and phone companies a week or two prior to moving in. You may need to be present when the utilities are hooked up.

Another thing you can do ahead of time is report your new address to the post office. Filling out a change-of-address card before you move will help prevent lost or delayed mail.

✓ CHECKING UP

1. What are some of the new expenses you will have to pay when you move out on your own?
2. List some of the rental terms to compare when looking at new places to live.
3. Describe some of the issues addressed in a lease.

2 Stress

The time when you first move out on your own will probably be an exciting, fun time in your life. There may be a new job, new friends, and new experiences. You will probably be busy and happy, especially if you have followed the career decision-making and planning guidelines you have learned in this book.

You will discover that with freedom and independence come responsibilities and problems. No longer will someone else take care of the things that need to be taken care of from day to day. No longer will someone else be making the difficult decisions about your financial situation and your career. You will be responsible from now on.

Along with increased responsibility, decision making, and work comes stress. **Stress** is physical, emotional, or mental strain. It is the hardship that your mind and body feel as a result of hard physical and mental work.

Effects of Stress

Some stress is good for you. For example, you may regularly cause your body stress while performing some physical activity, such as tennis or jogging. This stress helps keep your body in good physical condition. In the same way, a certain amount of problem solving is a good mental activity.

The most troublesome kind of stress is emotional stress, which is often caused by frustration. People who are constantly frustrated often become physically or mentally ill from stress. If these people do not reach some of their goals and end the frustration, they risk serious health problems.

Emotional stress affects different people in different ways. Some people get ulcers. Some develop severe headaches. Others appear to age faster than normal. Stress can generally weaken your body and make you more susceptible to many diseases. It can also cause you to lose your self-confidence.

Causes of Stress

As you get older, the possible causes of stress increase. You may need to support a family. There may be pressure to become successful in your career. If you are like many people, you will also have to deal with the added pressure of managing a household while working outside the home. All of these factors will contribute to the stress you feel.

Among the main causes of stress are the inability to reach personal goals and problems in human relations. These causes are described below. Although discussed separately, these causes are often related.

Inability to Reach Personal Goals   If you can't do something that you want very much to do, you become frustrated. Almost everyone must deal with some frustration every day. Getting stuck in a traffic jam, not being able to find something you've misplaced, or failure to solve a problem in the time you thought it would take are just a few examples. These small, minor frustrations, which are usually beyond your control, can add up to a great deal of stress.

What are the most common reasons for not reaching your goals? In many cases it's a lack of ability resulting from too little aptitude or training.

Work you can't do well or don't like is extremely stressful. When you consider how much time you will spend doing your job, you can see how this kind of stress can add up.

Many times you can't do what you want because you don't have enough money. Sometimes you simply don't have enough time.

Regardless of the reason for your inability to reach a personal goal, it is frustrating. This frustration leads to stress.

Human Relationships   Much of the stress that people experience is caused by their relationships with other people. You will find this especially true in the world of work where you can rarely choose the people you work with. Even if you practice all the rules you learned earlier for getting along with and being effective with people, you will encounter some difficulties.

Disagreements are almost unavoidable. Even the most open-minded, accommodating people run into conflicts with others. You may even have serious arguments with friends and members of your family. Unless you care little about other people, these personal conflicts will cause a great deal of stress.

A specific cause of stress in human relations is intimidation. Intimidation is the use of fear to force someone to do something. You probably know one or two people who try to get their way by threatening others with physical harm or some other sort of injury. This kind of intimidation causes a great deal of stress for the person being intimidated. You will probably encounter people on the job who try to use intimidation to get their way.

Grief is another common cause of stress in human relationships. Grief is unavoidable. If you lose someone close to you, you can't help but feel sad and lonely. These feelings are very stressful.

Coping with Stress

Everyone is exposed to stress—it can't be avoided. To protect your physical and mental health, you must learn how to cope with, or handle, a certain amount of stress. Here are some ways to cope with stress.

Exercise Regularly   Vigorous physical activity helps you work off stress. Exercise actually changes your body chemistry. These changes relieve the bad effects of emotional stress. If you seem overwhelmed with stress, ask yourself if you are getting enough exercise each day.

Talk Out Problems   You will usually feel better if you can talk about your problems with a trusted friend or family member. This is an excellent way to handle stress. This method is often overlooked by people who feel they need to sort things out on their own.

Eat Well and Get Enough Sleep   Bad eating habits can cause many types of health problems. Eating too much junk food can increase the bad effects of stress.

Sleep is important, too. Almost everyone needs seven or eight hours of sleep per night. People who don't get enough sleep are more likely to suffer from stress. If you are having trouble sleeping, see a doctor.

Help Someone   Doing things with and for others can improve your general attitude. Helping others also gets your mind off your own problems for a while. Later, your problems may not seem so big.

Learn to Compromise   No one is right all the time. Sometimes, even when you want your way, it is better to give in. Consider just how important it is that you have your own way. Ask yourself, "Wouldn't it be better to compromise and relieve the stress?"

Be careful, however, not to compromise too easily. Some people are so afraid of conflict that they always give in to other people. Never getting your own way is frustrating. This can lead to stress, too.

Don't Self-Medicate   There are many drugs available, both legally and illegally. You may be tempted to use drugs to relieve stress. Don't do this unless your doctor prescribes them for you. The body gets used to the drugs, and soon they are no longer effective. This can lead to taking larger, more dangerous doses.

Taking two different kinds of drugs at the same time can be especially dangerous. They can work together to create an effect greater than those of the

The responsibilities of being out on your own will probably subject you to stress you've never experienced before. How will you cope? What stress management technique is illustrated here?

Strive for Success

Winning Against Addiction

We often dream of fairy tale endings, the happy-ever-afters when the princess kisses the frog-prince and is carried off to his magic castle. However, the dream can become a nightmare when the story involves drug or alcohol addiction.

A fairy tale should have started for former First Lady Betty Ford when her husband, Gerald Ford, was elected to Congress. People in political office have it all—money, power, prestige—or so it appears to many of us. However, they and their families face the constant stress of living in the spotlight. They must be perfect, must never make a mistake.

As the pressure of her husband's position grew for Ford, her social drinking turned into alcohol dependence. When she started taking medication for a pinched nerve, she found that pills and alcohol could take her to a "fuzzy place" where everything was all right.

Things were far from all right for her family, however. Her husband, embarrassed, made constant excuses for her. Their children were afraid to bring friends home, afraid Ford would be drunk. Her youngest child, Susan, didn't know her mother was ill. She thought Ford was crazy. She didn't want a crazy mother.

Things came to a head in the late 1970s after the Fords had left the White House. Ford was increasingly incoherent. She shuffled around the house and rarely got dressed before noon. She fell and broke several ribs. Finally, Susan, afraid her mother would die, sought help from a physician. He arranged an "intervention." Ford's entire family and close friends participated in the process, which allowed them to confront her with her problem in an honest, caring atmosphere.

At first Ford didn't want to hear what they were saying. She wasn't an alcoholic, she thought. She just had a few drinks. She couldn't be addicted to pills. They were all prescribed by doctors. When her daughter-in-law, Gayle, said she wanted her children to know a normal, healthy grandmother, Ford suddenly realized she might not live to see any grandchildren at all.

The doctor made a list of all the pills she was taking and added up the dosages for her. At that

moment, said Ford, "you have to be a dummy not to realize you're in trouble." She agreed to accept treatment.

Detoxification and therapy followed. Ford admitted she was "not a model patient." She was a former First Lady, used to being treated as someone special. She had nothing in common with the people in her therapy group. However, when a young woman in the group refused to acknowledge her drinking problem, Ford decided to face hers. She found the courage to speak up and say, "I'm Betty. I'm an alcoholic."

In 1979 when she had been free of pills and alcohol for about a year, she was approached by a friend at the Eisenhower Medical Center in Palm Springs, California. He suggested they join forces and start a drug and alcohol rehabilitation center there. The center was named for Betty Ford.

Ford was responsible for raising much of the money to fund the center and remains active in the organization. Her recovery, her return to life, has convinced her family that nothing is impossible.

Case Study 2

Don was having a very successful career selling insurance. He just seemed to have a knack for persuading people they should buy more life insurance.

After three years of successful sales, Don was promoted. He was made assistant manager in charge of hiring and training new salespeople.

Don found that teaching and motivating other people to sell life insurance was much more difficult than selling it himself. He was a better salesperson than he was recruiter and motivator. He didn't have as much natural ability for the management responsibilities as he did for the sales job.

Don worried that he couldn't handle the added responsibility. He became irritable and jumpy, even on his days away from the job. He began to have frequent fights with his wife. He had to let his frustration out somehow, and she became the target.

Finally, Don began to consider giving up his management position. He thought he would go back to his sales job even though this would be a step backward. It was a difficult decision, but Don knew he and his family would be much happier.

MAKE A DECISION

You've noticed that you've been very irritable lately. Just the slightest problem or inconvenience seems to make you angry. You think the pressure at work is getting to you, and you'd like to talk to a professional who knows about stress and how to cope with it. You're not really sick, so it seems foolish to see a doctor. Maybe you should just try to deal with the problem yourself. What's your decision—seek help or handle the problem yourself? Give the reasons for your decision.

Getting angry over little things—passing remarks, minor mishaps, or short delays—is often a symptom of stress. If the young man shown here were your best friend and you were on the receiving end of his anger, how might you defuse the situation?

separate drugs. For example, some people drink alcohol, which is a drug, while taking another drug. This practice has often led to the deaths of those who have tried it.

Stress Signals There are some signals that indicate stress is becoming too much for you to handle. An important part of coping with stress is recognizing these signals. They include the following:

- Trouble concentrating on one thing at a time
- Getting angry over little things
- Inability to relax
- Loss of interest in recreation
- Getting tired very easily

If several of these descriptions apply to you, try to relieve the stress yourself. If this doesn't work, ask for help. You might first try talking with a trusted family member. If professional help is needed, a teacher or minister might be able to refer you to someone who is qualified.

✓ CHECKING UP

1. How does emotional stress affect people?
2. What are two of the main causes of stress?
3. List some of the ways of handling stress.

3 *Being a Good Citizen*

As a full-time worker you will begin to take on the responsibilities of citizenship. These include respecting the rights of others, being informed and involved, and voting.

Respecting the Rights of Others

To respect the rights of others, you must know what their rights are. One way to determine this is to think about your rights. For example, if you work the night shift, you will want to sleep at a time when many people are getting up. You have the right to a certain amount of peace and quiet when you need to sleep. Therefore, others also have that same right, and you should respect that right.

Respecting the rights of others helps us to get along because it means being considerate and thoughtful. If you think about the effects of an action on others before you act, you are more likely to act wisely. This kind of thoughtfulness helps people understand one another better and creates better relationships.

Being Informed and Involved

To be a good citizen you must be informed and involved. Members of a community, whether it is local, statewide, or nationwide, are responsible for the operation and maintenance of our most prized public institutions. Institutions such as schools, churches, and all levels of government are run by the citizens of that community. To participate in the operation of these institutions, you will need to know what is going on and how things are done.

There are many ways to be informed. You can read newspapers, magazines, and books. You can watch television and listen to radio programs. Becoming an active member of an organization is an excellent way to become informed. For example, by joining a group concerned with the outdoors and the environment, you will learn about recycling efforts in your community.

Being an active member of an organization is also an excellent way to become involved. As an active member you can help to choose how the organization will be run. You will become part of the decision-making process. You will also be able to help the people and causes you believe have the greatest need.

Being involved also means writing letters to government officials. This will let them know how to represent you on a certain issue. Another way to be involved and communicate with your government representatives is by voting.

Voting

Voting is the very heart of our democratic system of government. It is the primary responsibility of every citizen because a democracy is a participatory form of government. Voting is part of that participation.

By voting we elect government officials who are supposed to represent our best interests. They should make decisions based on the needs and wishes of the people they represent. If they don't, we can replace them in the next election.

By voting we show how we feel about certain issues. We can vote for or against an issue. This also has the effect of telling our government officials how we want them to vote on that issue.

It is important to vote based on an informed decision, however. You will want your vote to reflect accurately how you feel about things. If you are not properly informed, you could vote for someone or something with which you disagree.

Before you can vote, you will need to register. To do so, contact your county registrar's office. You can find the telephone number under the name of your county in the telephone book. When you call the registrar's office, they will tell you where to go to register, when to register, and what documents you may need to register.

To be a good citizen you must be informed, involved, and vote. There is too much at stake in the way we live to let others make all the decisions. You can't be informed about and involved with every issue and candidate. If you choose the issues that are most important to you, however, you are on your way to becoming a good citizen.

✓ CHECKING UP

1. What are some ways of being an informed and involved citizen?
2. Why is it important to vote?
3. Whom should you contact to find out about voting in your area?

24 *Review Your Learning*

CHAPTER SUMMARY

When you leave school and start your first full-time job, you will take on many new responsibilities. You may want to move into an apartment, house or other place of your own. Before you move, you must consider the additional expenses involved with living on your own.

To find a new place to live, you will want to inspect and compare each place to find the one that best meets your needs. You can do this by making a checklist so you can remember which apartment had which features.

When living on your own you will need to learn to work with a landlord. You will be asked to sign a lease, which is a contract that addresses many issues involved with the renting of an apartment or house. You must also know your rights and responsibilities as well as your landlord's.

With the new responsibilities you will be assuming, you will also be under more pressure and stress than ever before. You should be aware of the causes and effects of stress, and you should learn how to cope with it.

As a full-time worker you will be expected to take on more of the responsibilities of citizenship. To be a good citizen, you need to respect the rights of others, be informed and involved in community affairs, and vote to express your views on certain issues.

TERMS TO KNOW

On a separate sheet of paper, write a paragraph using all of the following terms:

security deposit
utilities
tenant
lease
subletting
stress

STUDY QUESTIONS

1. What are three advantages of living at home?
2. What is the one major advantage of moving out on your own?
3. What percent of your income do experts recommend that you spend for rent?
4. What are two advantages of having a roommate?
5. What is the most common way to find places to rent?
6. What are the rights and responsibilities of a landlord?
7. How can storage be increased and improved in a small apartment?
8. What are three things you should do before moving into an apartment?
9. How does regular exercise help you cope with stress?
10. List the five signals of stress.
11. What are the major responsibilities of being a good citizen?

CRITICAL THINKING

1. You have a job just a few miles from home with a very good starting salary. Your parents would like you to continue living at home. However, a friend who is also working would like you to share an apartment. What factors will you consider before making a choice?
2. What is the cartoon on page 409 saying about the rights and responsibilities of roommates? As part of your answer, include an agreement in paragraph or list form specifying what you think roommates have a right to expect from each other. Consider your statement/list an addition to a lease—in other words, something that must be

carefully read and signed before any joint living arrangement can become a fact.

3. You have just taken a job in a city hundreds of miles from your home. You enjoy the job very much, but you miss your family and friends. Lately you've been feeling very anxious and irritated. What is happening to you? What can you do to feel better?

4. You have a favorite aunt who is blind. She belongs to an organization that speaks out on behalf of the blind. They write letters to state and national leaders and provide information to the blind about laws that may affect them. How would joining an organization such as this demonstrate good citizenship?

DISCUSSION STARTERS

1. What would be most difficult about going from being a full-time student to being a full-time worker?

2. What do you look forward to most about becoming a full-time worker?

3. If you had a well-paid job close to home, would you prefer to live at home or in your own place? Why?

4. Do you think it's a good idea to share an apartment with a roommate? Why or why not?

5. Have you ever experienced stress? If so, what do you think caused it? What did you do to cope with it?

6. Name some organizations that benefit society. Do you belong to any of them? Why or why not?

BUILDING BASIC SKILLS

Math

1. You've recently taken a job that pays $1,300 per month. You are thinking about getting an apartment that would cost $400 per month to rent. Is this apartment too expensive for you? How do you know?

Communication

2. The parking in your apartment complex is unorganized. Many times when you come home in the evening, there are no vacant parking places. You have mentioned the problem to the manager, but no action has been taken. Write a petition to circulate among the tenants that asks the manager to hold a meeting to discuss the parking problem.

Citizenship

3. You are a bookkeeper for a small business and live in a downtown apartment. A number of retired people live in the building, and many of them need help preparing their income taxes. What can you do to help?

SUGGESTED ACTIVITIES

1. Make a list of all the items you would need if you were to move into an unfurnished apartment. Assume the apartment has a stove and a refrigerator. Next to each item write its cost based on your research of several places from which you could buy it. What is the total cost of these items? Report your findings to the class.

2. Read the rentals section of the classified ads in your local newspaper. Compare the prices of apartments based on location and features listed. Then write a brief report summarizing your findings.

The Workplace in the Year 2000

If you were entering the work force in the 19th century, you might expect to work 12 to 16 hours per day, six to seven days a week, under conditions that might be difficult or uncomfortable—and sometimes even hazardous. There would be no laws governing wages, hours, employee health, or safety.

Today, however, workers have a right to expect clean, comfortable, safe workplaces and fair wages. Many companies offer health and vacation benefits, pension plans, flexible hours, day care, and programs for further education.

As society changes further, the workplace will change to keep pace with it. By the year 2000 you may work under conditions that your counterparts in the 20th century could never have imagined. Let's take a look at how your work day might go in the new world of the 21st century.

You leave for work early in the morning—your company's flextime program allows you to start at 6 a.m. Although you work better in the morning, the schedule also means you get off work early enough to pick up your daughter and son from school when they get out at three. Your wife's job starts later, so she drops the children off on her way to work.

Your wife works ten hours a day, four days a week. On her free day, she attends classes at the local community college. The extra training should give her the competitive edge she needs to get a promotion she wants.

You are not the only one in your house to get up before the sun. Your mother gets up to go to work with you. She suffered a slight stroke a

couple of years ago, and you are uncomfortable leaving her home alone. Fortunately, your company—AI International, Inc.—is one of the growing number of firms that recognize modern, two-income families must often care for aging parents as well as for their children. AI provides a family care center where older people can get together with others their own age or work with small children. In case of an emergency, there is always medical help at hand. Your mother is in the middle of a cutthroat bridge tournament with others at the center. When she is not playing cards, she reads to some of the children or plays games with them. She wouldn't miss a day at "work," and you work better not having to worry about her.

You stop at a park-and-ride lot on your way to pick up Nobu and Anna. The three of you trade driving responsibilities, and the lot is centrally located for all of you. AI encourages its employees to ride-share by giving them a small bonus for each day they carpool or use vanpools.

When you pull into the parking lot, lights are on all over the building. AI specializes in the rapidly expanding field of artificial intelligence. The firm designs and manufactures software and hardware to support their systems. Because AI has clients and suppliers worldwide, the company has found it more cost effective to have employees work 24 hours a day. Round-the-clock operation reduces office space parking and equipment requirements. It also allows employees to take advantage of lower phone rates at off-peak hours. Because AI depends heavily on computer networks, fax machines, and old-fashioned conversation to get its business done, this adds up to substantial savings.

When you reach your desk and flip on your computer, you can't suppress a little thrill of pride. Although you are in the marketing, and not the product, division, you helped design this particular piece of hardware.

AI encourages employees to make suggestions about policies, procedures, and products. If the idea is good and it's used, the company pays a bonus. For your suggestion about the computer, you received $1,500.

In your fax box is a message sent during the night from your colleague Dale, who is in Nairobi setting up a system for a university research department. To answer her questions, you access the company's computerized clipping service to see copies of recent articles that affect your field. (AI also subscribes to several information services that provide the full text of newspapers, periodicals, and an encyclopedia.) Once you have the information Dale needs, you send her copies with your computer's PC-fax function.

Another message in your computer mail is from your boss, Elizabeth, who wants to meet with you at 11 a.m. to discuss a proposal you and three co-workers have made. There is also a memo about CPR classes and a notice posted by someone interested in starting a singing group.

Just before 8 a.m., Connie, who has the work space next to yours, comes in. A talented graphic designer, she is also a single mother. She tells you about her son who is hatching a secret with your mother downstairs in the family care center.

Barbara, another designer, arrives in time to hear the end of the story. At 53, former attorney Barbara has been practicing her second career for only six years. She prefers to work part-time because her husband is disabled. In the afternoon her time-share partner, Marvin, comes in and takes over her board.

Marv, 72, has been a successful commercial artist all his life. Bored with retirement, he came to AI four years ago, knowing that the company was aggressive about hiring older workers. Marv works only in the afternoons. In the mornings he seriously pursues a second retirement career as a wildlife artist.

About 10 a.m. you get a call from Diego, a copywriter who lives about 150 miles from the AI offices. Diego works for the company full time at home, as do about a fifth of AI's employees. Diego is enthusiastic about the arrangement because he can stay at home with his young daughter while his wife works at a job she enjoys at a company near their home.

Diego has questions about a piece he is writing for a new advertising campaign. You pull up the copy he has sent to your computer, and the two of you hammer out the problems.

A few minutes before 11, you head for Elizabeth's office. Connie comes with you, bringing her portfolio. Ted and Chris are already there.

Next to Chris is a cart loaded with equipment prototypes she hopes will revolutionize AI's way of building computer systems. Chris built her first computer in high school. She perfected her skills at a local vocational school before coming to AI.

Ted, from the research department, has figured out how parts for the new systems can be made recyclable. Connie has come up with a sensational industrial advertising campaign for the new line. You have figured out how much money and personnel the project will take and how soon the new product line will begin to show a profit.

You're nervous but well prepared, and the presentation goes smoothly. You don't know it yet, but in a few weeks the company will establish a new product division—with you and your team in charge. The MBA you earned by taking evening classes broadcast on television will have paid off. It will also have paid off for AI, which reimbursed you for your education. The firm will now have a new, and potentially very profitable, division. You will now have new challenges, expanding opportunities, and a very bright future. Welcome to the world of work in the year 2000!

Glossary

A

ability   A skill that has already been developed. (p. 23)

acclamation   In parliamentary procedure, a method of voting to approve a motion without a ballot. (p. 264)

annual percentage rate (APR)   The percentage cost of credit on a yearly basis; used to compare credit costs regardless of the amount borrowed or how many payments must be made. (p. 329)

apprentice   Someone who learns how to do a certain job through hands-on experience under the guidance of a skilled worker. (p. 64)

aptitude   A knack, or potential, for learning certain skills. (p. 23)

area   The number of squares of a certain measure that a surface covers. (p. 194)

assertive   Having the ability to stand up for your rights, beliefs, and ideas. (p. 143)

attitude   Your way of looking at the world and the people in it. (p. 101)

audiovisuals   All the things you watch and listen to, such as films, slide presentations, tape cassettes, and videotapes. (p. 51)

B

bail   Money deposited with the court so that an accused person can be freed from jail until trial; forfeited if the person fails to appear. (p. 359)

bait and switch   Form of consumer fraud in which a bargain is advertised to lure customers into a store, whereupon salespeople try to interest them in a more expensive item. (p. 282)

balance   The amount of money in an account. (p. 310)

bank statement   A record of bank account activity during the previous month. (p. 316)

body language   Things people say through their physical actions. (p. 136)

boot   To load an operating system into a computer; usually done by placing the disk in the disk drive. (p. 220)

budget   The plan you use to manage your money. (p. 293)

C

CAD   Computer assisted design; programs that make it possible to design in three dimensions at a computer terminal. (p. 221)

calorie   A measure of the energy that food supplies. (p. 148)

CAM   Computer assisted manufacturing; programs that allow CAD designs to be output directly to electronic robots that perform the actual manufacture of items. (p. 222)

canceled checks   Checks that have been cashed and processed by the bank on which they were drawn. (p. 310)

capital   Anything other than land that is used to produce more wealth; includes machines, buildings, and money. (p. 229)

cardiopulmonary resuscitation (CPR)   First aid technique that not only helps a victim breathe but also provides artificial circulation. (p. 160)

career   The work a person does over a period of years. (p. 5)

career consultation   Talking with someone who has worked in a particular career for many years, with the express purpose of obtaining information about that career. (p. 52)

career interest area   Category of jobs that are similar in terms of the interests they involve. (p. 32)

cash value   The amount of money a life insurance policyholder can take by either borrowing against or cashing in his or her policy. (p. 346)

certificate of deposit (CD)   A piece of paper that says a bank will pay back your money, plus interest, on a certain day. (p. 308)

charge account   The privilege of being able to buy on credit. (p. 324)

circumference   The perimeter of a circle. (p. 195)

collateral   Something of value that you own and promise to give up if you can't make credit payments; usually required by banks as security that you will repay a loan. (p. 327)

commission   A payment that is a percentage of the total amount sold by a salesperson. (p. 107)

communication   The process of exchanging information; how we transmit thoughts and ideas from one person to another. (p. 166)

competent parties   People who are responsible for their actions. (p. 354)

compounding   The banking practice of paying interest on interest. (p. 305)

consideration   Whatever one party to a contract gives the other in return for the promise to do something. (p. 355)

consumer   Someone who consumes, or buys and uses goods and services. (p. 227)

consumer fraud   The practice of tricking or cheating consumers. (p. 281)

Consumer Product Safety Commission (CPSC) Government agency that determines and enforces safety standards for consumer products. (p. 289)

contingency basis   Fee arrangement under which an attorney is paid only if he or she wins the case. (p. 360)

contract   A legal agreement between two or more people. (p. 353)

cooperative programs   Vocational work experience programs featuring cooperation between schools and employers (employers pay students at least minimum wage, and schools grant credit for time spent on the job). (p. 53)

corporation   A business owned by a number of people who buy stock in the firm, elect a board of directors, and share the profits. (p. 248)

countersign   To sign a contract in support of someone else. (p. 354)

credit   A method of buying in which a business trusts you to pay later for a good or service they give you today. (p. 323)

credit bureau   An agency that keeps track of how people pay their bills. (p. 331)

credit card   Plastic card embossed with your name and account number that allows you to use a certain amount of credit. (p. 323)

credit rating   An estimate of how likely a person is to pay his or her bills on time. (p. 331)

D

data   Facts, such as numbers, words, and symbols. (p. 21)

database   A collection of stored, computerized information. (p. 212)

decimal number   A fraction or mixed number whose denominator is a multiple of ten. (p. 191)

deductible   The amount of a loss an insurance policyholder must pay. (p. 336)

deduction   A personal expense that can be subtracted from income before figuring tax. (p. 375)

deficit   A shortage. (p. 233)

deflation   An economic condition in which prices in general fall. (p. 299)

delegating   Giving jobs and responsibilities to others. (p. 129)

dependent   A person who is supported by a taxpayer. (p. 375)

depression   Common form of mental illness marked by symptoms ranging from mild and persistent feelings of sadness to intense, suicidal despair. (p. 151)

difference   The result of subtracting one number from another. (p. 187)

disabled worker   For social security purposes, a worker who will be (or has been) unable to work for at least 12 months because of a mental or physical condition. (p. 385)

discrimination   Treating someone unfairly because of prejudice based on factors such as race, religion, gender, age, or disability. (p. 109)

disk drive   Computer device that receives and operates a disk. (p. 218)

disposable income   Money you have left after paying income and other taxes. (p. 370)

down payment   A certain percentage of a product's total price (usually 10-20 percent) paid at the time of purchase. (p. 324)

E

economic system   Method by which a society produces and distributes goods and services to the people who need and want them. (p. 227)

electronic fund transfer (EFT)   Computer procedure that allows you to deposit or withdraw money from an automatic teller machine (ATM). (p. 318)

empathize   To see someone else's point of view and sympathize with their situation. (p. 138)

endorse   To write your name on the back of a check. (p. 313)

entrepreneurs   Producers who start new businesses. (p. 229)

enunciation   Speaking each syllable clearly and separately. (p. 170)

Environmental Protection Agency (EPA)   Federal agency charged with protecting the environment. (p. 159)

esteem   Your worth or value as seen by others. (p. 10)

exemption   A set amount of money that is not taxed. (p. 375)

extemporaneous   Spontaneous and unprepared. (p. 260)

F

face value   The amount of protection stated in an insurance policy. (p. 346)

Federal Reserve   Government agency responsible for controlling our nation's money supply. (p. 237)

Federal Trade Commission (FTC)   Government agency that administers laws ensuring fair trade (specifically, those relating to competition, unfair or deceptive sales practices, warranties, labeling, and advertising). (p. 286)

feedback   The receiver's response to the sender's message. (p. 171)

felony   A serious crime punishable by a large fine, a prison term, or even death. (p. 357)

finance charge   Interest based on the unpaid portion of the amount owed each month. (p. 328)

financial responsibility Responsibility where money is concerned. (p. 296)

floppy disks Magnetic media in the form of flat disks encased in paper or plastic; also called diskettes. (p. 219)

Food and Drug Administration (FDA) Federal agency that regulates the production and sale of food and drugs. (p. 286)

franchise The legal right to sell a company's goods and services in a particular area. (p. 243)

free enterprise Economic system in which people have the right to make their own economic decisions. (p. 227)

fringe benefits Extras provided by many employers, including such things as paid vacations, health and life insurance, bonuses, and retirement plans. (p. 48)

G

Gross National Product (GNP) The value of all the goods and services a nation produces in one year. (p. 232)

H

hardware The components making up a computer system. (p. 217)

health maintenance organization (HMO) An alternative form of health insurance; members use special medical facilities and pay for health care services in advance by making monthly payments. (p. 345)

Heimlich maneuver First aid technique used to help victims of choking; employs abdominal thrusts to force air out of the lungs and clear the windpipe. (p. 161)

I

identity The personal quality or activity by which you are best known. (p. 7)

income statement A document that clearly shows how much a business has earned or lost; also called a profit and loss statement. (p. 253)

income tax return A formal statement of a person's income and taxes. (p. 374)

inflation An economic condition in which prices rise sharply. (p. 237)

inflection Use of the voice to alter the meaning of a spoken message. (p. 170)

initiative Doing what needs to be done without being told to do it. (p. 103)

installment plan A form of credit in which you agree to make regular payments on a good while using it. (p. 324)

insurance A financial precaution against injury, loss, or damage; insureds pay a relatively small amount of money at regular intervals to guarantee that they will receive a large sum should they ever need it. (p. 336)

interest Money that banks pay their depositors for the privilege of investing their money. (p. 305)

interests The things that you enjoy doing the most. (p. 20)

Internal Revenue Service (IRS) The federal agency responsible for collecting taxes. (p. 365)

interview A formal meeting between an employer and a job applicant. (p. 93)

inventory 1. The total amount of goods in stock, or available at any given time. 2. To make a list of items you have. (p. 252)

J

jargon Words or phrases that have meaning only within a particular career field. (p. 175)

job The collection of tasks or duties that a person does to earn a living. (p. 5)

job lead Information about a possible job opening. (p. 77)

L

layoff notice A statement from your employer that your period of employment is over, usually temporarily. (p. 113)

lease A contract between a landlord and a renter that states the responsibilities of both. (p. 400)

liability Responsibility; a form of insurance coverage that pays the expenses of those who suffer injury, loss, or damage for which you are responsible. (p. 339)

life-style The way we live, including where we live, the kind of food we eat, the way we spend our free time, and what we do to support ourselves. (p. 5)

liquid assets Assets that can easily be turned into cash. (p. 299)

M

marketing The process of getting goods and services to the consumers who want them. (p. 230)

Medicare A social security insurance program that provides health care payments to those over 65. (p. 387)

merit raises Bonuses for especially outstanding work. (p. 119)

micros Microcomputers; small computers that can be easily carried in the trunk of a car or placed on a desk. (p. 215)

misdemeanor A less serious crime punishable by a small fine, a short jail term, probation, or community service. (p. 357)

modem A special piece of computer equipment that connects a computer to a telephone line. (p. 212)

motion A formal proposal for action. (p. 266)

N

net profit The amount of money remaining after all expenses have been paid from a business's revenues. (p. 253)

nonaccredited Not officially approved. (p. 283)

O

Occupational Safety and Health Administration (OSHA) Federal agency created to determine safety and health standards for workplaces. (p. 158)

operating expenses All the expenses that must be paid to keep a business going. (p. 253)

overdrawn Describes an account from which an amount in excess of the balance has been withdrawn. (p. 315)

P

parliamentary procedure A democratic method of conducting meetings. (p. 263)

partnership A business owned by two or more persons who share both the profits and the risks. (p. 246)

party Legal term for a person who enters into a contract. (p. 352)

peer pressure The influence people in your group have on you. (p. 276)

percent Number as compared to some standard or base divided into 100 parts. (p. 199)

perimeter The distance around a shape, such as a rectangle or square. (p. 194)

perseverance Finishing what you start. (p. 121)

personal career profile Document that allows you to arrange side-by-side what you have learned about yourself and what you have learned about your career choices. (p. 58)

personal effectiveness The ability to make things happen your way. (p. 133)

personal income Income people receive from all sources, including wages, interest on savings, and profits from a business. (p. 370)

personality The combination of all the attitudes, interests, values, behaviors, and characteristics that make you the person you are, different from every other person on earth. (p. 26)

physical limitation The inability to do certain physical tasks. (p. 156)

planning goals All the steps you must take to get from where you are now to where you want to be. (p. 61)

point of order In parliamentary procedure, a statement made by a member to question a ruling by the Chair or to enforce the regular rules. (p. 267)

policy A contract between a person buying insurance and the insurance company that sells it. (p. 336)

preferred provider organization (PPO) An alternative form of health insurance under which specific doctors and hospitals agree to provide health care for groups of employees at reduced rates. (p. 345)

premium The amount of money a policyholder agrees to pay an insurance company at regular intervals for his or her coverage. (p. 336)

previewing Reading only those parts of a document that outline or summarize its contents. (p. 180)

product The answer to a multiplication problem. (p. 188)

profession A career that requires specialized training and a long period of academic preparation. (p. 66)

profit The amount of money taken in by a business that is more than what was spent. (p. 229)

profit ratio Percentage computed by dividing net profit by total revenue; used by owners and financial analysts to measure the health of a business. (p. 253)

progressive tax Tax whose rate goes up as the amount taxed rises. (p. 370)

promotion Advancement to a higher-level job. (p. 121)

pronunciation The way a word sounds. (p. 170)

Q

quorum   In parliamentary procedure, the minimum number of members that must be present at a meeting for the group to conduct official business. (p. 265)

quotient   The answer to a division problem. (p. 189)

R

references   People who will speak on your behalf, who will tell a prospective employer that you would be a good employee. (p. 83)

resume   A brief, written summary of personal information, education, skills, work experience, activities, and interests. (p. 89)

retirement benefits   Payments made to workers after they retire from their jobs. (p. 385)

S

salary   A fixed amount of pay for a certain period of time, usually a year or a month. (p. 107)

second   In parliamentary procedure, a statement made to show approval of a motion made by another member of the group. (p. 264)

security deposit   Money that a landlord holds as a guarantee against damages. (p. 395)

sedentary   Requiring a great deal of sitting. (p. 148)

self-concept   The way you see yourself; your feelings about your own worth and value. (p. 26)

self-realization   Reaching all the important goals in your life. (p. 10)

seniority   The privileged status that results from continuous service with one company. (p. 121)

severance pay   A check equal to one, two, or several weeks' pay given to you when you are laid off. (p. 113)

skimming   Reading through something very quickly, picking out the key points. (p. 181)

software   Computer programs; instructions that tell a computer how to do a certain task or group of related tasks. (p. 220)

sole proprietorship   A business completely owned by one person who keeps all the profits and has total responsibility for payment of all debts. (p. 245)

standard English   The formal style of writing and speaking you have learned in school. (p. 82)

stress   Physical, emotional, or mental strain. (p. 403)

subletting   The process whereby an original tenant rents an apartment to a second tenant, usually with the landlord's approval. (p. 400)

sum   The total of numbers added. (p. 186)

supervisor   Someone in charge of other workers. (p. 125)

survivor benefits   Payments made to the family of a worker who has died. (p. 385)

T

table   In parliamentary procedure, to postpone making a decision on an issue under discussion. (p. 267)

tact   Saying and doing things in a way that will not offend others. (p. 134)

taxes   The payments people must make to maintain their government and provide government services. (p. 364)

tenant   A person who rents an apartment or house. (p. 399)

termination notice A statement from your employer that you have been dismissed from your job because of unsatisfactory performance. (p. 111)

trade An occupation that requires manual or mechanical skill. (p. 64)

tuition The cost of attending a school. (p. 66)

U

unemployment compensation Money given to people who have recently become unemployed and who are both able to work and actively seeking jobs. (p. 113)

unemployment insurance Form of insurance that pays benefits to workers who have lost their jobs. (p. 387)

utilities Services such as electricity, gas, and water. (p. 395)

V

values The ideas, relationships, and other things that are important to you. (p. 19)

vocation The work that a person does to earn a living. (p. 65)

volume Measure of the space inside various shapes. (p. 197)

W

wages Pay received for hourly work. (p. 106)

warranty A guarantee of a product's quality; usually contains the manufacturer's promise to repair or replace an item that fails as a result of defective parts, materials, or workmanship. (p. 289)

work Any productive activity that results in something useful. (p. 5)

work credits Measurements of how much time you have worked. (p. 384)

work environment Working conditions, such as the sounds, smells, sights, and temperature surrounding the worker; also includes the physical demands placed on the worker. (p. 45)

worker's compensation An insurance program that makes medical, pension, and other payments to workers injured on the job and to the survivors of these workers. (p. 389)

Index

Index

Index

Index

D

Index

Index

E

Index

Index

Index

Index

Index

Index

Index

Index

Index

Cover Photography by Walter Hodges/Westlight

Photography

441